Seventh Edition

THE EVOLUTION OF AMERICAN URBAN SOCIETY

Howard P. Chudacoff
Brown University

Judith E. Smith
University of Massachusetts, Boston

Peter C. Baldwin
University of Connecticut, Storrs

Prentice Hall
Boston   Columbus   Indianapolis   New York   San Francisco
Upper Saddle River   Amsterdam   Cape Town   Dubai   London   Madrid   Milan
Munich   Paris   Montreal   Toronto   Delhi   Mexico City   Sao Paulo   Sydney
Hong Kong   Seoul   Singapore   Taipei   Tokyo

Editorial Director: Leah Jewell
Acquisitions Editor: Charlyce Jones Owen
Editorial Assistant: Maureen Diana
Director of Marketing: Brandy Dawson
Project Manager: Holly Shufeldt
Senior Art Director: Jayne Conte
Cover Designer: Bruce Kenselaar
Manager, Visual Research: Beth Brenzel
Manager, Rights and Permissions: Zina Arabia
Image Permission Coordinator: Nancy Seise

Manager, Cover Visual Research & Permissions:
 Karen Sanatar
Cover Photo: Museum of the City of New York
Full-Service Project Management: Chitra Ganesan
Composition: GGS Higher Education Resources,
 A division of PreMedia Global, Inc.
Printer/Binder: R.R. Donnelley & Sons
Cover Printer: R.R. Donnelley & Sons
Text Font: 10/12 Minion

Credits and acknowledgments borrowed from other sources and reproduced, with permission, in this
textbook appear on pages 282–3.

Library of Congress Cataloging-in-Publication Data
Chudacoff, Howard P.
  The evolution of American urban society / Howard P. Chudacoff, Judith E. Smith,
Peter C. Baldwin.—7th ed.
    p. cm.
  Includes bibliographical references and index.
  ISBN-13: 978-0-13-601571-0
  ISBN-10: 0-13-601571-9
  1. Cities and towns—United States—History. 2. Urbanization—United States. 3. United
States—Social conditions. I. Smith, Judith E., 1948— II. Baldwin, Peter C., 1962— III. Title.
  HT123.C49 2009
  307.760973—dc22

                                                          2009030095

Prentice Hall
is an imprint of

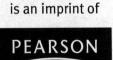

www.pearsonhighered.com

ISBN 10:   0-13-601571-9
ISBN 13: 978-0-13-601571-0

CONTENTS

PREFACE

This edition of *The Evolution of American Urban Society* includes several new features. Foremost among them is the addition of a third coauthor, Peter Baldwin of the University of Connecticut, an urban historian who has written on public urban space, and on nighttime in the city. In the past five years, much has changed on the national and urban landscape, and this book has tried to explore the significance of these changes. As in all previous editions the bibliography has been updated to reflect new scholarship on all periods of American urbanization. Also as in previous editions, the authors have made concerted effort to make each chapter readable for specialists and nonspecialists alike. Some chapters have been reorganized as well as updated, while Chapter 10, on the most recent developments in urban and suburban history, has been considerably revised.

NEW TO THIS EDITION

Much of the book's new material focuses on issues of transportation, the environment, immigration, institution-building, gender, and race and ethnicity. In the final chapter, there is new and expanded coverage of deindustrialization, globalization, the most recent immigration, crime, gentrification, and suburban sprawl. All of these developments have had consequences, seen and unforeseen, and many of these consequences have explanations rooted in history. The urban crisis of the mid-1970s in retrospect can now be understood as reflective of a transitional period in race relations, economics, suburbanization, and other trends, and the analysis in Chapter 9 reflects those developments. As well, suburbs, which now have become the most common residential and commercial experiences of Americans, receive increased attention, including the social and economic diversities that over the past third of a century have come to characterize suburbia. This book is now as much an analysis of the evolution of American suburban society as it is of American urban society. Finally, the effects of the economic crisis that began to unfold in 2008 are now just beginning to be analyzed, and the serious challenges these effects pose to both urban and suburban residents and their institutions are introduced in the last chapter.

CHAPTER-BY-CHAPTER CHANGES

Chapter 1 Expanded coverage of Cahokia.

Chapter 2 More detailed examination of the transportation revolution. Increased focus on the rise of Chicago. Expanded coverage of the U.S. acquisition of the Southwest and the growth of San Francisco.

Chapter 3 Coverage of antebellum Irish and German immigration. Additional discussion of the Chinese in San Francisco in the 1850s and 1860s.

Chapter 4 Expanded section on home ownership.

Chapter 5 Focus of the chapter is now the post–Civil War period and there is additional material on Catholic institution-building.

Chapter 9 An expanded section on the process of racial transition (and the accompanying racial conflict) coverage of Mobile during World War II, and the Young Lords in the 1960s.

Chapter 10 Covers major trends since 1975, including the changing economies of central cities, new immigration, suburban sprawl and the effects of the recent disasters in New York and New Orleans.

CHAPTER 1

Urban America in the Colonial Age, 1500–1776

URBAN BEGINNINGS

When the conquistador Hernán Cortés rode into the Aztec capital of Tenochtitlán in 1519, he was astonished to find an enormous city surpassing anything he had seen in Spain. Some 200,000 people lived in Tenochtitlán at the time Cortés arrived with his band of 400 men to meet the Aztec emperor. The white city of stone and lime-plastered adobe stood on an island in a shimmering lake, linked to the shore by causeways. Its temple pyramids rose as high as cathedrals, the palaces of its nobility rivaled those of Spanish aristocrats, and its broad avenues were swept each day by a crew of a thousand men—unlike the winding, manure-choked streets of Europe. Stone-edged canals laced through the city, navigated by canoes that carried produce from the hinterland and barges hauling away waste. The marketplace at Tlatelolco, wrote Cortés, was twice as big as that at Salamanca, the Spanish city where he had attended the university. It had "arcades all around, where more than sixty thousand people come each day to buy and sell, and where every kind of merchandise produced in these lands is found."[1]

The Spaniards appreciated cities almost as much as they appreciated gold. Tenochtitlán was destroyed by Cortés in 1521, in a war in which he overthrew the Aztecs with the help of thousands of Indian allies, a smallpox epidemic, and amazing luck. Yet the conquerors had been so impressed by the city's magnificence that they established their own capital, Mexico City, on its ruins. Spanish conquerors followed this same practice through the 1500s as they overran much of the New World and destroyed its powerful Indian empires. They built Lima, Cartagena, and Bogotá on the sites of ruined cities, sometimes literally on the older foundations.

No city north of Mexico matched the size or wealth of those created by the Aztec and Inca empires. Yet on a smaller scale, native peoples in what is now the United States had also built permanent settlements long before Europeans arrived.

Indians in the Mississippi Valley built a settlement known as Cahokia, a sprawling complex of earthen mounds and buildings of wood and thatch near what is now East St. Louis. At the core of the city was a ceremonial temple mound, a grand plaza, and possibly the homes of the ruling elite, all encompassed by a stockade fence. There is evidence of markets, clusters of housing, specialization of crafts, mortuaries, and huge ritual feasts in the late summer. At its peak around 1100 A.D., Cahokia's population is now believed to have reached as high as 15,000.[2] Its trade network extended throughout much of the Mississippi Basin and beyond. Archaeologists have uncovered artifacts made of copper from Lake Superior, lead from southern Missouri, and sea shells from the Atlantic and the Gulf of Mexico. Cahokia was abandoned by 1400 for reasons that remain unclear. The Spanish explorer Hernando de Soto reported seeing other towns during his exploration of the lower Mississippi Valley from 1540 to 1542, but these too had vanished by the time Europeans settled the region in the early 1700s, perhaps because of the smallpox epidemics that decimated native populations upon European contact.

In the same years in which de Soto was exploring the Mississippi valley, Spanish explorers in the Southwest encountered settlements of stone and adobe, each housing hundreds or a few thousand people. The initial reports suggested that among these might be the mythical "Seven Golden Cities of Antilla," but further exploration proved disappointing. There were at least 134 Native American towns in New Mexico and eastern Arizona in the late 1500s, called *pueblos* by the Spanish. Among those that have survived to the present day is Acoma Pueblo (now called Sky City, New Mexico), which occupies a strong defensive position atop a mesa. The oldest continuously inhabited town in the United States, Acoma dates back perhaps as

The Native American City of Cahokia. This photograph is based on a reconstruction of Cahokia printed by Valerie Waldorf. At the center of community life was the large earthen temple that rose to a height of one hundred feet. Cahokia artisans mass-produced knives, salt, and stone hoe blades for local consumption and export. Note the outlying farms surrounding the more densely settled areas. Cahokia was a crossroads of trade and water travel in the heartland of North America.

far as the twelfth century A.D. Numerous Indian villages were scattered throughout eastern North America, but these were typically small and impermanent.

The Spanish soldiers who conquered the Aztecs had declared their intent to serve God and their King, and also to get rich—not necessarily in that order. Similar motives could be found among the other Europeans who colonized what is now the United States. A vast continent of untapped riches seemed to beckon the Spanish, French, Dutch, and English, but before they could plunge into the wilderness, they needed cities that could serve as beachheads for conquest, ports for transatlantic shipping, and centers for administration. If there were no cities already existing, they would have to build new ones from scratch.

Spaniards committed to securing territory and Christianizing Indians established outposts in Florida and New Mexico. St. Augustine, the first permanent European city in what is now the United States, was founded in 1565. It was intended to defend the Spanish claim to the region and prevent Florida from being used as a base for attacks on Spanish shipping. In New Mexico, the Spanish conquered the pueblos in the 1590s and began converting the inhabitants to Christianity. Franciscan friars established Santa Fe in 1610 amid the native settlements, close enough for conversion efforts but not so close as to heighten conflict over land use. The conversion effort did not go smoothly, particularly once the governor began trying to crack down on "witchcraft" by imprisoning and executing medicine men in the 1670s. One medicine man, Popé, united the people of many pueblos in 1680 to drive out the Spanish. The Spanish were able to retake Santa Fe in 1693, but they never fully controlled all the New Mexican pueblos.

Spanish colonizers were committed to founding cities because the Spanish system of government consisted of city-states and because Spaniards identified not with a kingdom or a province but with a city. Cities served a critical function as local symbols of political authority. The boundaries of a Spanish city extended into the hinterlands until they ran into the sphere of influence of another Spanish city. Until the late eighteenth century, St. Augustine represented in a corporate fashion all Spanish interests east of Santa Fe. The Spanish also developed a formal system of town planning that they applied to their colonies in both North and South America. This was the Laws of the Indies, proclaimed by Phillip II in 1573, that synthesized earlier practices of settlement, some from Roman times. The Laws specified uniform requirements for town location, street layout, and land use, and they shaped urban beginnings in Florida and the American Southwest. Early maps of St. Augustine, San Antonio, and San Diego show how the Laws influenced a common design of rectangular blocks, straight streets, and right-angle intersections grouped around a large, central plaza.

Spanish colonization intended to distinguish among types of settlements: *pueblos* (towns) were to be centers of commerce and colonization; *misiones* (missions) were established to promote religious conversion, and *presidios* (forts) were military outposts. But such distinctions often faded once actual settlement occurred. For example, San Antonio was originally established at the headwaters of a river on the site of an Indian village. Called Yanaguana by the Indians, it was rechristened in 1691 as San Antonio. A band of seventy-two soldiers, settlers, and monks settled in San Antonio in 1718, and a quarrel between the chief military leader and the

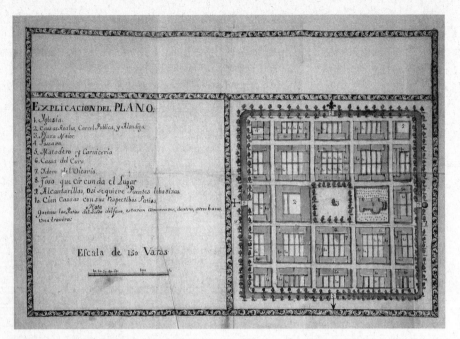

Plan of San Antonio, Texas.   Spanish colonists built this town according to a 1573 ordinance that specified a layout that situated the church and government buildings around a central plaza. Countless settlements, especially in the American West, followed the same design.

missionary priest led to separate settlements of a presidio and the mission, later famous as the Alamo. Presidios were established at San Diego in 1769, San Francisco in 1776, Los Angeles in 1781, and Santa Barbara in 1782, but soon house and farm buildings sprang up beyond the presidio walls, and the military communities looked indistinguishable from the civil settlements of the pueblos.

In contrast to the Spanish, the first French explorers came not as colonizers but as individual traders. Needing centers for the exchange of goods, they founded commercial ports along the waterways of colonial North America's perimeters. In the north and west, they built Quebec, Montreal, and Detroit, towns of varied design that usually conformed to the area's topography. These places acted as staging points for fur traders and missionaries who combed the Great Lakes and Mississippi River regions in the early 1700s. In 1718, Jean-Baptiste Le Moyne, sieur de Bienville, founded New Orleans near the mouth of the Mississippi, on a site previously used by Choctaw tribes, as the staging area for a project to expand the Bourbon Empire by creating a colony based on slave-produced tobacco. By 1721, the population of New Orleans was half slave, and by 1731, slaves were four times as numerous as white settlers or French soldiers. In 1763, at the conclusion of the European colonial conflict known as the Seven Years' War, New Orleans was ceded to the Spanish. Designed as a large-walled settlement with square blocks and an open field on the waterfront, New Orleans developed into an important commercial crossroads later in the century when settlers spilled across the Appalachian Mountains toward the western river valleys. Also in 1763, French merchants from New Orleans established the upriver trading post of St. Louis. The two cities maintained their French culture under Spanish rule, and even after passing to the United States in 1803.

Dutch colonizers, like the Spanish, brought elaborate urban plans with them. Colonists from the Dutch West India Company arrived on Manhattan Island in 1624 and 1625 with intentions to build a trading center called New Amsterdam, complete with a twenty-five-foot-wide main street and a central marketplace. In a faint echo of old Amsterdam, the city eventually boasted a muddy little canal along part of what is now Broad Street. The Dutch West India Company was a chief international supplier of slaves, and not surprisingly, slaveholding was extensive in New Amsterdam. Although the Dutch used New Amsterdam mainly as a fur trading center and made little effort to develop its harbor, the town soon would become one of the continent's great seaports.

These projects set important precedents for future American cities, but the English colonies along the North Atlantic coast were more numerous and ultimately more influential in shaping American urban life. It was especially in the several settlements along or near the Massachusetts coast that the urban frontier began. At first, these towns combined Puritan notions of social and religious harmony with the village orientation of peasant society. The town of Boston, however, recast the mold. According to the founder John Winthrop, the colony of Massachusetts Bay was to be "as a Citty upon a Hill," a place that bound people together in worship. But when, in 1630, the settlers relocated from Charlestown across the Charles River to Boston in order to take advantage of the better harbor there, they began a process that was to obliterate Winthrop's vision. Boston was to become more than an agrarian-based town; it swelled into a commercial and administrative hub, a worldly city with a large, diverse population.

Several other cities sprouted up along the Atlantic coast in subsequent decades, all sustained like Boston by trade. In 1639, a group of religious dissenters

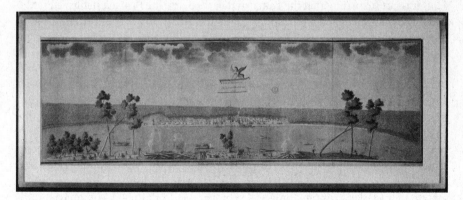

New Orleans, 1726. This French watercolor shows an infant port town carved out of the forest along what subsequently became known as the Mississippi River. For the French settlers as well as the English, waterborne commerce was vital to urban survival.

founded Newport, Rhode Island, ostensibly as a haven for the persecuted. The site they chose had the best harbor in southern New England, and it was this geographic advantage rather than religious tolerance that assured the town's future. When the British captured New Amsterdam from the Dutch in 1664, they inherited the finest natural port in North America. They preserved the city's commercial functions and made it the capital of New York colony. In 1680, proprietors of Carolina colony moved their chief settlement from a marshy location to a peninsula jutting out between the Ashley and Cooper rivers in order to utilize its harbor and more healthful environs. The settlement, named Charles Town (later Charleston), soon became the largest and wealthiest town in the southern colonies. And in 1682, William Penn chose the site for Philadelphia one hundred miles up the Delaware River where it was joined by the Schuylkill. This was to be not only the capital of Pennsylvania colony and the most extensive experiment in city building that the colonies had yet witnessed, but also a place intended as "the most considerable for merchandize, trade, and fishery in these parts."

There were and would be others—Providence, Albany, New Haven, Baltimore, Williamsburg, Norfolk, Savannah—but throughout the British colonial period, the five cities of Boston, Newport, New York, Philadelphia, and Charleston were the largest and most powerful. Although their origins spanned a half century, these cities resembled each other in several important ways. Most fundamentally, all were ports. As the major depots for immigration, they were continually receiving new arrivals from Europe. Their economic life focused on the waterfront and, by extension, on the port cities across the Atlantic Ocean. As links in the mercantilist system, the colonial ports collected and dispatched raw materials such as grain, rice, fish, furs, and lumber that were needed by England, and they received the manufactured wares of British merchants for American consumption. Thus most lines of commerce initially extended from individual cities to the mother country rather than among the colonies themselves. In addition, all five cities had planned beginnings, and all were products of the same civilization. All except Newport originated in intent and leadership in London and Amsterdam, both centers of societies that judged cities to be essential. Thus it is not surprising that the Dutch and particularly the British established settlements that assumed characteristics of genuinely urban places: the concentration of people, resources, and ideas. These cities represented for their colonizers the transfer of civilization—meaning an urban environment and the activities associated with it—from the Old to the New World.

The major colonial cities grew rapidly, as the population figures in the following table reveal. True, none could compare with even the secondary commercial centers of Western Europe, such as Lyons, which had reached forty-five thousand in the 1530s, or Norwich, which had grown to nineteen thousand by the 1570s. American port towns were small because they served regional populations that were still themselves small and because the risks of trade, the lack of agricultural hinterlands, and the low level of credit available to seaport entrepreneurs limited opportunities for growth of a market economy on a scale comparable to European commercial capitals. Still, this surge of urban population satisfied the British Crown's objectives of centralization for the sake of control.

Population by Year

	1690	1742	1775
Boston	7,000	16,382	16,000
Philadelphia	4,000	13,000	24,000
New York	3,900	11,000	25,000
Newport	2,600	6,200	11,000
Charleston	1,100	6,800	12,000

But the growth and economic opportunities of these cities also prompted activities that eventually threatened the colonial system. It was not long before colonial towns bred merchants and tradesmen who began to look to the interior settlements in search of markets for locally produced as well as imported goods. Consequently, each city began to cultivate its own commercial hinterland, an activity that turned the colonial ports into small commercial powers themselves and enabled them to expand their economies beyond English goals of simple self-support. Just as the mercantile relationship to England drained the colonies of raw materials and what little silver currency circulated, the cities began to draw products and coin from the countryside. As early as the 1640s, Boston traders expanded commercial ties westward and southward to Springfield, Hartford, and along Long Island Sound. By the eve of the Revolution, inland trade had become an important concern to all of urban America. In Rhode Island, for example, a Providence merchant, Welcome Arnold, shipped processed lime—a necessity for the production of mortar and plaster—not only to Boston, New York, Philadelphia, and Baltimore but also to smaller settlements in the New England interior. Arnold added retail consumer goods to his inland lime traffic, and he helped attach a broad hinterland to Providence that choked off any potential expansion by Newport, helping Providence to surpass Newport's size and become New England's second city by 1800.

The importance of commerce partly explains why most major British colonial cities were located in the North. With the exceptions of Charleston, Savannah and Norfolk, the South lacked the deep, safe harbors that benefited northern ports. But unlike the North, the South had many rivers that were navigable far inland. Ports were therefore less important in the South because trading ships did not have to stop at the coast to transfer cargoes to wagons and smaller boats that could travel into the interior. Also, the Southern economy tended to be less dependent on trade than that of the North. Southern plantations produced much of their own food and clothing, and more of the region's wealth was invested in labor—that is, in ownership of slaves—than in commerce and industry. Finally, because a large proportion of Southern residents were slaves and indentured servants rather than wage laborers, there were relatively fewer people in the South with expendable incomes for commercial exchange.

Environmental factors gave the northern ports both advantages and disadvantages. Because Philadelphia was located on the Delaware River and thereby had a freshwater rather than saltwater harbor, boats could dock there for long periods

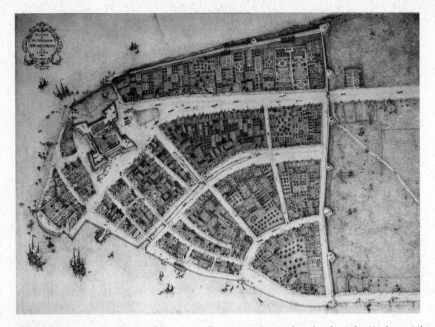

Colonial New Amsterdam.   This extraordinary map is a redrawing by John Wolcott Adams and N. Phelps Stokes of the Castello Plan of New Amsterdam, first drawn in 1660. The street leading out from the fort and into the undeveloped area is Broadway. The road along the fortification separating the settled area from the unsettled land is Wall Street.

without suffering damage from sea worms (barnacles) that lived in salt water and ate away at wooden bottoms. But the river also froze for several months in winter, stopping navigation. New York, with easy access to the ocean, had a harbor that never froze and was deep enough to accommodate the largest ships. Though barnacles endangered boats in New York harbor, its location near Long Island gave it protection from hurricanes and other storms that threatened the Atlantic Coast. Boston, another saltwater port, was protected from severe ocean storms by Cape Cod. Charleston, by contrast, was more vulnerable. In September of 1752, for example, a vicious hurricane blew all vessels in the harbor ashore, washed away all wharves and warehouses, destroyed 500 homes, and killed over 100 people.

Size and commercial activity, combined with benign neglect on the part of England, also forced colonial cities into the expansion of self-government. Most towns were created by charters granted by the king or the provincial government. These charters defined the form and scope of local administration. Gradually, every colonial city except Charleston assumed self-management of local affairs, acquiring power either by piecemeal grant or by charter revision. Philadelphia, and (after 1664) New York, resembled English municipal boroughs administered by a mayor and council. As in English cities, their local governments reflected their particular commercial quality. Voting was the privilege of those who had skills or property, and the vast majority of local officials were chosen from merchants and artisans. In Philadelphia, many officers served for life, and in New York City the same officials were generally reelected year after year. Local ordinances were concerned with regulating and promoting trade. Most laws concerned such issues as limiting entry into certain skilled crafts, establishing standard weights and measures, fixing prices for locally produced goods, and controlling the quality of those goods. In New York and Philadelphia, the municipal corporation fixed a just price for bread and set the fees that carters could charge. Most city revenues were derived from license fees and rental of market stalls.

In contrast, the affairs of Boston and Newport were attended to in town meetings, an institution that resembled the assemblies of rural England yet also grew out of Puritan congregationalism. Several times a year all male residents (freemen) of the town met to conduct local business—to elect officials, pass laws, levy taxes, and settle disputes. Town meetings were thus symbols of order as well as agencies of government. However, like New York and Philadelphia, the governmental power in Boston and Newport rested in the hands of a few men. Town meetings took place only a few times a year. In between, selectmen—chosen as executive officials—assumed governmental duties. Their power over appointments, judicial decisions, and administration often diminished the democratic initiative of the town meeting. The same men, usually those of high standing in both marketplace and church, tended to monopolize councils of selectmen. Traditions of deference meant that a community's wealthiest and most well-established men stood for election and were regularly returned to office. Political parties were considered dangerous, and municipal elections were not seen as forums for expressing differing political ideologies. Nor was political representation understood as expressing competing social, residential, or economic interests. Elections were a traditional means of confirming existing patterns of social order.

Throughout the colonial era the government of Charleston remained in the hands of the provincial assembly that appointed commissioners to manage the city's affairs. Assemblymen and commissioners often did not live in Charleston, and they represented interests that were seldom sympathetic to the city's welfare. The particular form of urban rule in Charleston burdened the city with the least responsive government of the five ports.

Similar hierarchies were also the rule in non-British cities. During the French years in New Orleans, the city was governed by the superior council, the sole administrative and judicial body in the colony, run by a handful of planters appointed by the Crown. During Spanish sovereignty, the superior council was replaced by a Spanish council, *cabildo,* composed of the governor, six perpetual *regidors,* two judges, an attorney general, and a clerk. In reality, however, Spanish New Orleans was run by military officers and courts backed by a garrison of Spanish-speaking white or mestizo troops from Cuba. In Spanish Santa Fe in the seventeenth and eighteenth centuries, residents elected a four-member *cabildo,* which had responsibility for advising the Spanish-appointed governor and electing a magistrate, a bailiff, and a notary.

PROBLEMS OF GROWTH

The urban settlements of the British colonies did not seem much like cities in the early 1700s. Cattle grazed behind crudely built houses, and hogs wallowed in muddy streets. Urban dwellers of different classes, ethnic backgrounds, and occupations lived crowded together along streets near the harbor and wharves. No one could remain anonymous in a place whose boundaries extended no more than a mile in any direction. Currency was scarce, so people often bought things by bartering with something they had grown or made. The church provided the principal social community beyond family and work lives; there were few newspapers, theaters, or other diversions. News traveled by word of mouth rather than printed words, and people's behavior was shaped by a combination of superstition and religious belief.

Yet, from their inception, local governments felt the pressures of urban growth. Many of the physical and social problems that vex modern urban society haunted every colonial city. Although the colonials lacked practical experience and technological tools to solve these problems, each town improvised, adjusted, and borrowed methods of response from Europe and from each other. Initially, individual citizens took steps to remove inconveniences, but quite early they combined and made collective efforts, often surrendering private initiative to government directive.

Urban organization requires efficient transportation and communication, so it is not surprising that town governments devoted much effort to determining where, how, and when new streets should be constructed. In every city—even Philadelphia, where gridiron street patterns had been established prior to settlement—individuals laid out new roadways where they were needed. As a result, narrow streets wound chaotically through some districts. Government intervened in the 1700s, and construction of new streets became accepted as a function of public policy, even though such roads were merely open stretches cleared of obstructions. In New York City, officials expected private citizens to assume the cost of laying out roads as well as filling in swamps, digging wells, erecting bridges, dredging harbors, and building wharves. The city's control of public property made it possible for the municipality to impose these responsibilities on individuals.

Altering the environment for the laying of streets, however, involved more than locating a route, removing stumps and rocks, and, occasionally, paving with gravel and cobblestones. Mud and stagnant water impeded traffic and threatened health, making drainage a pressing concern. Boston was most successful in meeting this problem: after 1713 the city began grading streets so that they slanted from the middle to side gutters. By the 1760s, other cities had initiated drainage projects. Cities dealt with related problems as well. The governments of Boston, New York, and Newport fined builders who erected structures in paths of traffic. Several towns constructed bridges over streams and marshes.

Once streets, gutters, and bridges were built, the difficulties were far from over, for as colonial cities grew, so did their traffic. Streets served as play areas for children and foraging grounds for hogs, dogs, and cattle. By the mid-seventeenth century, congestion and accidents had become common street nuisances. To protect pedestrians and playing children, several towns levied fines for riding too fast and for failure to keep horses and other draft animals under tight rein.

The best streets were those of Boston and Newport, whose governments could levy taxes for highway improvements. Other cities' efforts to grade and pave their streets depended on private means or other sources of funds, such as fines, license fees, or lotteries. After the Spanish gained control of New Orleans, the *cabildo* raised revenue for levee repairs by an anchorage tax on every vessel. Where projects were elaborate, as in Boston, full-time laborers were hired at public expense. Most cities, however, followed the English custom of requiring each householder to devote a certain number of days each year to labor on public works or hire a substitute. Slaves did most of the public work in Charleston, and in Boston each free African American was forced to work on the roads eight days a year instead of doing watch duty, from which blacks were prohibited.

Fire was one of the most feared hazards of urban life. Blazes could spread quickly through the closely packed wooden buildings of colonial American cities. Lacking firefighting technology, local authorities could take only precautionary measures, such as regulating storage of combustibles like gunpowder and establishing the first American building codes that included prohibitions on reed and straw roofing and on wood and plaster chimneys. Authorities also attempted to prevent fires by limiting places in which brush or rubbish could be burned and banning construction of wooden buildings in the center of town (brick structures were preferred). In 1649, Boston adopted the English curfew, requiring all house fires to be covered or extinguished between 9 P.M. and 4:30 A.M. Nearly all American towns adopted the European tradition of community responsibility for extinguishing fires. Each city contained at least one volunteer fire company composed of private citizens.

Unfortunately, towns usually did not react to such urban dangers as fires until after a disaster had occurred. This was to be a recurring pattern in American urban history. Destructive or disruptive events usually provoked some reform, but then

Firefighting Scene. Fire posed a serious danger to colonial cities, and putting one out was no easy task. Firefighting forces consisted of volunteers, and firefighting equipment was primitive, consisting of ladders, hoses, and buckets of water passed along a line (bucket brigade).

concern would dwindle to apathy until another disaster struck and galvanized a new spurt of action. After the first of several major conflagrations struck Boston in 1653, public alarm prompted creation of the colonies' first urban fire code. The measure required every householder to keep a ladder to facilitate fire fighting. The town also bought ladders and hooks, and officials assumed the authority to order the leveling of any burning structure. Few other precautions were taken until 1676, when another conflagration threatened Boston. After it was extinguished, the town bought a fire engine from England and appointed a supervisor and twelve assistants to operate it. Even these measures were not enough, for in 1679 one of the worst fires in American history swept Boston, ravaging most of its commercial section. This disaster forced officials to organize the city into districts for more efficient fire control. Other towns acted similarly to meet the threat of fire, but Boston's destructive fires resulted in regulations and equipment that ranked among the most advanced in the world.

Law enforcement posed another problem to the young cities. Seamen and transient laborers attracted to the ports by the promise of jobs threatened the orderly world of family and communal governance. There was as yet no professional police force. Instead, American cities copied the European system of daytime constables with full arrest powers, and night watchmen appointed to patrol the streets. Though few in number, the night watchmen served as the eyes of the sleeping public; they would walk through the city questioning suspicious people, suppressing public disturbances, and watching for signs of more serious trouble. If they saw a fire or a crime in progress, they would raise a "hue and cry" to summon help from the surrounding neighborhood. New York attempted in the 1600s to rely on a citizens' watch, paying the drafted watchmen in beaverskins and firewood. Finding it difficult to make people serve their turns, New York, like other cities, relied on a paid watch for most of the eighteenth century. Cities paid so little that the dangerous, thankless work attracted mainly laborers and poor artisans who also held day jobs, and those with few other employment options, such as old men. The watchmen were notoriously unmotivated and sleepy. In some cities each watchman was expected to ring a bell as he made his rounds or to "proclaim the season of the weather and the hour of the Night." Though this noise warned burglars to hide and interfered with people's sleep, it had the advantage of forcing the watchman to stay awake. Watchmen were held in such low esteem that they were the frequent target of pranks.

Notions of public health in the colonial era were even more primitive than those of fire and police protection. Colonial Americans followed the European practice of tossing their refuse into the street. Their streets quickly became cluttered with human and animal waste, ashes, bones, and shells. Wandering hogs grew fat from feeding on the rubbish. Cities hired laborers or arranged with private contractors to remove garbage and manure from the streets. People at the time thought that the foul smells from decaying waste and stagnant water were the direct causes of sickness; the germ theory had not yet been established. Nevertheless, attempts to eliminate malodorous vapors also succeeded in removing some of the breeding grounds of disease. Most cities eventually passed measures that regulated the location and depth of privies and graves, and confined tanneries and slaughterhouses to the edge of town. Such measures were enacted with little, if any, objection to the use of governmental authority.

Town dwellers feared epidemics as much as fires and found them just as difficult to stop. The seaport cities were vulnerable to epidemics brought in by infected seamen, vermin, and insects. Smallpox was the most frequent and dreaded danger. Boston and Charleston suffered smallpox epidemics that killed hundreds at a time. But as with fire, misfortune helped to create progressive policy, for by the 1760s, Americans were beginning to accept inoculation as the best preventive measure. Cities combated the spread of fevers by requiring inspections of entering ships and refusing landing to those on which sickness was found. By the early 1700s, most cities had followed Boston's lead in establishing quarantine regulations. Despite these efforts, cities continued to suffer devastating outbreaks of yellow fever and cholera in the nineteenth century.

Another problem of urban growth was the large number of indigent residents, whose care became a major responsibility of each city. Poverty is not a problem peculiar to cities, but it can be particularly visible in a densely populated urban setting. In the early years of settlement, the incidence of poverty was low, especially relative to English towns. Generally, widows, orphans, and people with disabilities, impoverished by circumstances beyond their control, were the ones who required assistance. Colonists accepted the seventeenth-century English notion of public responsibility for the support of dependent classes. Poor relief accounted for much of local government expenditures. People in need remained with their families or in the homes of neighbors and were provided with clothes, firewood, and bread.

As towns grew, their involvement with unpredictable market forces brought increasing economic uncertainty—good times and bad times, high and low wages, periodic unemployment. The burden of providing manpower and resources for the European wars of 1689 to 1697, 1702 to 1713, and 1739 to 1747, and the inflation caused by emergency issuance of paper money, hurt a growing part of the urban population. In Boston, Newport, and other ports, many households were headed by women because of the deaths or disappearance of husbands in dangerous maritime jobs. Poverty was not just a condition suffered by the aged, widowed, and crippled. A broad range of lower-class people felt its effects whenever jobs grew scarce, prices rose, or war called away the main breadwinners. Boston, New York, and Philadelphia built almshouses in the 1730s in an attempt to reduce the cost of caring for the growing number of poor citizens by sheltering them under one roof. Some cities required the willing poor to support themselves by picking vegetables, weaving cloth, and making shoes. Almshouses also housed sick poor who could not work and the "Vagrant & Idle Persons" who would not work and were classed as criminals. Some cities stigmatized those on relief by requiring them to wear or carry badges designating their status as paupers. Another form of relief consisted of assigning (binding out) the needy to private businesses in a form of indentured servitude.

Many cities tried to minimize pauperism—as well as the money spent on the poor—by restricting immigration. Philadelphia, New York, and nearly all the New England towns had provisions requiring the registration, bonding, or inspection of all newcomers. Those who had no friends or relatives to vouch for them or who lacked visible means of support were ordered away. As the cities grew in size, however, so did the need for laborers and the opportunity for anonymity. By the early 1700s, the restrictions were breaking down, and many places were openly encouraging immigration.

Aid from private agencies increasingly supplemented public relief efforts. In the eighteenth century, organizations such as the Scots Charitable Society in Boston and New York, the Carpenters' Company in Philadelphia, and the Fellowship Society in Charleston, as well as churches and wealthy individuals, made substantial contributions for the alleviation of poverty. Still, as time passed, the numbers of urban poor grew ever larger. The proportion of a city's population assisted by public or private money at any one time is difficult to discern. But it seems that for every relief recipient several more lived at the subsistence level and received no aid and that poverty plagued American cities from the very beginning.

Attempts by colonial cities to solve their problems highlight an intertwining of private interest and public welfare. On the one hand, problems were common to all cities. They were predicaments of urban life, of many people living close together, and they required community regulation of formerly private activities. In a rural society, where a family built its house, dug its well, and threw away its trash seldom affected other humans. But in cities, these activities could become threats to other people's health and safety, and thereby necessitated surrender of individual rights to public control. Many problems of health, fire, water, and communications were insoluble at the time, and colonial city dwellers simply tried collectively to minimize them and then to adjust as technological and scientific developments offered solutions. Social problems such as disorder and poverty remained baffling. Nevertheless, a kind of public unity plus the inheritance of a European tradition of public endeavor enabled colonial cities to address their problems and to set precedents for future urban generations.

THE SOCIAL MOSAIC

Between 1690 and 1740, the small colonial seaports grew into commercial centers that rivaled British provincial ports such as Hull, Bristol, and Glasgow. Like their counterparts abroad, the American towns not only experienced similar problems but also developed similar social mosaics that set them apart from the surrounding countryside. Racial, cultural, and socioeconomic diversity jumbled urban society. Restrictions on immigration seldom worked; varied peoples quickly diluted the English composition of most cities. By the early 1700s, Africans and African Americans were almost as numerous as whites in Charleston, and there were substantial numbers of slaves in cities all the way up the coast to Boston. Scotch-Irish and Germans constituted important segments of the populations of Philadelphia and New York, where they met the growing need for laborers. The cities also housed more institutions for the entertainment, edification, and refreshment of their residents than did rural areas. The increasing population provided cities with human and economic resources for the creation of educational facilities and the dissemination of information from the outside world.

Most colonists migrated or descended from European society, where a distinct hierarchy of status prevailed, and they accepted the existence of social differences in America as being divinely sanctioned. Thus a Boston merchant asserted in 1700 that God "hath Ordained different degrees and orders of men, some to be High and Honourable, some to be Low and Despicable, some to be Monarchs, Kings, Princes, and Governours, Masters and Commanders, others to be subjects, and to be com-manded." From the beginning, an ordered social structure crystallized in colonial America, but it operated differently in the cities than in the country. In cities the mar-ket economy offered opportunity to accumulate wealth. But it also created growing inequalities between those whose extensive resources allowed them to take risks and make profits and those whose modest resources made them more vulnerable to eco-nomic fluctuation. Though everyone lived close together in the compact cities, social distances increasingly separated rich from poor, employers from workers.

Colonial urban society consisted of four socioeconomic groups, distinguished by male occupation and wealth. In the top rank were affluent merchants and in-vestors, plus an occasional clergyman or government official. They generally were men who had become wealthy from overseas and inland commerce or had accumu-lated enough capital to use in lucrative moneylending or land-rental businesses. Merchants often did more than buy and sell goods. In a time when banks, law offices, and construction companies were rare, merchants used their money and influence to assume the role of banker, legal arbitrator, and land developer. As historian Gary Nash has argued, those who controlled mercantile endeavors gained a disproportion-ate share of economic power in colonial cities through their impact on shipbuilding, credit, real estate, and the flow of marketable goods.[3]

White males in the top status group controlled most of the local wealth (which consisted primarily of property) and filled the high positions in local government. As time passed, they procured proportionately more of the wealth than those in lower ranks. According to data compiled by Nash, in 1687 the wealthiest 10 percent of Boston's population controlled 46 percent of the taxable wealth; by 1771, the top 10 percent owned 63 percent. In Philadelphia, over a comparable period, the richest 10 percent of the population increased their holdings from 46 to 72 percent of that city's taxable wealth.[4] In Boston and Philadelphia, as well as in other cities, this upper order was not a closed aristocracy. Its membership was large and diverse, including men who had risen from a lower rank as well as those who had advantages of birth and position. Throughout the colonial period, wealth, more than birth, was the prin-cipal criterion for admission to this upper group.

Wives of wealthy merchants led lives that were very different from rural women. Wealthy urban women had the benefit of a pool of less-wealthy female workers who could be hired as servants. Supervision of domestic labor was an in-volved and time-consuming activity. But because wives could send servants to buy and prepare food and could hire seamstresses to create clothing, they had time to write letters and diaries and to engage in rounds of social visiting. In cities, because goods were available for purchase, household production decreased as wealth and privilege rose. Once urban women were able to buy items such as tea, milk, butter, candles, linens, coats, and gowns, the seventeenth-century mode of housewifery symbolized by the spinning wheel became increasingly a badge of lower status.

Beneath the merchants and their allies was a large, diverse, fluctuating population of craftsmen, retailers, minor jobbers, and innkeepers who constituted the "middling" rank. Among the craftsmen and retailers were coopers, who provided barrels and kegs that were essential for shipping and storage; carpenters and woodworkers, who provided housing and furnishings; food dealers; metalsmiths; and printers. These individuals carried on local manufacturing and merchandising in the preindustrial city, running the shops that predominated in every town. Often they were aided by an apprentice, indentured servant, or wife. Individual shopkeepers and craftsmen generally lived and worked in the same house.

Within most of the crafts a wide range of wealth and status existed, reflecting the hierarchy within each craft from apprentice to journeyman to master craftsman. The range of wealth was thus related not only to age but also to the possibilities within each craft. Artisans working with precious metals were more likely to earn a comfortable living than were cobblers, and house carpenters were more likely to become property owners than were tailors and weavers. Artisans strived to earn a "competency," enough money to live in relative comfort, and in every city the average craftsman or shopkeeper usually owned enough property to vote, sometimes even holding a minor office. Shopkeepers' and artisans' wives probably did not have to spin or weave cloth, but occasionally they assisted in businesses and acted in place of their husbands in case of absence or death. They had responsibility for food preparation, which often included cultivating a garden and raising poultry. Daughters and wives also sewed extensively to keep their families clothed.

Economic expansion and the opportunity to rise in importance by acquiring wealth attuned colonial city dwellers to bourgeois standards. But such conditions also made "middling" classes vulnerable to economic dislocation: their position on the social scale rose and fell over time, depending on economic developments. The early years of urban growth offered lucrative opportunities for small-scale investors and entrepreneurs. As the cities grew, however, so did the size and specialization of their economic operations. By 1750 or so, larger businesses were squeezing small investors out of high-return areas such as commercial shipping. Between 1687 and 1771 the proportion of taxable wealth owned by Boston's and Philadelphia's middle classes declined while the percentage owned by the upper segments rose. Evidence indicates that economic opportunities of the urban middle class in most cities shrank until westward expansion and the dawn of industrialization in the early 1800s opened new avenues for advancement.

The third economic group consisted of a growing number of free unskilled laborers, mariners, and some artisans. These people owned little or no property. Many were transients, earning a living on the docks and at sea or moving from town to town in search of work. They loaded, unloaded, and served as crew on cargo ships that sailed between the seaports, Europe, and the West Indies. Other laborers dug wells, graded streets, and hauled goods. Their wives and daughters took in washing, kept boarders, spun cloth, and served as seamstresses and housekeepers for middle- and upper-class families. Many working-class families lived in crowded two- or three-room cottages at a bare level of subsistence, but in labor-scarce cities some could command high wages and acquire property. Geographic mobility and chances for improvement precluded the development of a permanent urban proletariat. The entrance to most crafts remained open, and local restrictions on newcomers failed to prevent working-class families from migrating. Still, cities housed much higher proportions of poor and propertyless people than did rural areas. By the close of the colonial period, the poor constituted between 20 and 30 percent of many a city's population—though the percentage was smaller in Southern towns, where large numbers of slaves reduced the proportion of white laborers. The fortunes of the free urban working classes were especially sensitive to economic fluctuations. If the local economy was expanding, they could subsist and even improve their lot. But when economic uncertainty and decline brought sacrifice and deprivation to the middle and upper classes, the working classes struggled for survival.

The fourth broad social category comprised indentured servants, free blacks, and slaves. Most indentured servants were immigrants who had traded four to seven years of labor for passage across the Atlantic. On arrival, they were sold at the docks to the highest bidder. They became, as one of them wrote, "Voluntary Slaves, who are the least to be pitied." By the 1730s, German and Scotch-Irish provided the majority of bound white laborers and were most numerous in Philadelphia. There they worked in households, ropewalks, shipyards, bakeries, and liveries; by the mid-1740s, they constituted more than one-fifth of the city's white male work force.

A rising standard of living and moderate mobility up the social scale were possible for about four-fifths of colonial city dwellers—a sizable majority—but the remainder, consisting of Africans, African Americans, and Indians, both slave and free, formed a permanent, inescapable lower class. In the Southwest the availability of exploitable Indian labor near the mission at San Gabriel was a main attraction prompting northern Mexican colonists to found the city of Los Angeles. Indian slaves could be found in the Eastern ports as well, though by 1715, the difficulties of dealing with Indian slaves prompted Massachusetts, Rhode Island, and Connecticut to pass laws forbidding importations from Charleston, the center of the Yamasee Indian slave trade.

African slaves were the most common form of bound labor everywhere. In 1690, about one in nine Boston households included at least one slave, and in 1698, more than one-third of New York households had slaves. Although the Quakers who dominated Philadelphia later repudiated slavery, other early settlers freely bought and sold slaves. After 1714, sizable numbers of slaves were imported into all northern port towns. By 1750, about one-fifth of all Boston families owned slaves. By 1746, an estimated one-half of New York households owned slaves.

Slaves in colonial cities did much of the heavy manual work and provided most of the domestic service. Slave ownership was almost universal among the urban elite; costumed slave coachmen and livery grooms were a common way of visibly displaying wealth. Newspaper advertisements in New York City for skilled male slaves suggest that some members of the artisan class prospered sufficiently to substitute bondsmen for apprentices. In all the ports, male slaves worked as seamen and in the ropewalks, shipyards, and sail manufactories. The importance of these slaves to the commercial growth of cities increased during the eighteenth century.

Northern slavery differed from slavery in the Chesapeake Bay area and low-country South. For one thing, northern slavery was disproportionately urban. During the eighteenth century, between one-fifth and one-fourth of the slaves in New York colony lived in New York City, one-third of the slaves in New Hampshire and Massachusetts lived in Portsmouth and Boston, and nearly half of Rhode Island's slave population lived in Newport. Crowded urban housing conditions forced slaves into back rooms, lofts, and makeshift alley shacks. Under these circumstances few masters held more than one or two slaves, and masters discouraged their slaves from establishing families. As a result there were more male than female slaves in the cities, especially in the early years, and slave women had fewer children than did white women. As historian Ira Berlin has argued, "The inability or unwillingness of urban masters to support large households of slaves put a severe strain on slave family life, but it also encouraged masters to allow their slaves to live out, hire their own time, and thereby gain a measure of independence and freedom."[5]

In the cities, slaves tended to live and work near whites. This proximity gave slaves firsthand knowledge of their masters' world, as well as familiarity with the circumstances of working-class whites, with whom they interacted in taverns and at fairs. This knowledge of white culture in combination with the job opportunities provided by the complex Northern economy, the close ties between master and slave, and the social life of city streets helped urban slaves to make better lives for themselves. In the eighteenth century some urban slaves informally enjoyed the rights to hold property of their own, visit friends, live with their families, or hire out their own time, prerogatives that did not exist on plantations.

The cosmopolitan nature of the cities also sped the transformation of African to African American. In the early years of Northern urban slavery, most slaves did not arrive directly from Africa but came through the West Indies or the mainland South. This seasoning in slavery had worked to destroy ties to African tribal culture but had also prepared slaves to turn urban opportunities to their own advantage. Between 1732 and 1754, slaves were imported into the cities directly from Africa. As Berlin has written, "Newly arrived Africans reawakened urban slaves to their African past by providing direct knowledge of West African society."[6] The result was the construction of separate communities, where blacks could find friendships, marriage partners, and other kinds of association based on racial commonalities. Northern slaves designated their churches "African" and called themselves "Sons of Africa." They displayed their new knowledge of African culture most clearly in the celebration of Negro Election Day, a West African ritual festival of role reversal celebrated commonly in New England and middle-colony towns in the mid-eighteenth century. Celebrations took different forms in different communities, but everywhere a day of merrymaking that drew in slaves from the surrounding countryside culminated in the selection of kings, governors, and judges. While the "governors" settled minor disputes, slaves dressed in their masters' clothing and rode their masters' horses. Negro Election Day ritualized a momentary release from bondage and also endorsed leadership within the African-American community. (Whites, confident of their control over the institution of slavery, supported Election Day, even sometimes joining in the festivities themselves.) In these interstices of urban life, slaves developed strong and cohesive African-American traditions that would sustain future urban black communities.

In Southern cities like New Orleans, where Africans and African Americans outnumbered whites, the possibility of free blacks made whites nervous. Although a master very occasionally freed a slave, most slave owners abided by the laws discouraging emancipation. A rare exception occurred in 1729, when the governor, concerned about threats from Natchez Indians allied with the French, freed two dozen slaves in exchange for their leading a bloody attack on a nearby Indian village. These freed slaves served as a regular company to fight with whites against the Natchez and Chickasaw in the 1730s. In 1751, however, the Louisiana superior council passed police regulations tightening the racial regime, prescribing regulations for the day-to-day governance of all blacks, not just slaves, by all whites.

After 1769, Spanish policy in New Orleans expanded opportunities for slaves to buy their freedom. The Spanish hoped that these opportunities, along with the ever-increasing regulations on the lives of all blacks, would actually strengthen white control by dividing the slave majority. They expected that the chance for liberation would give a stake in the system to a small but growing number of slaves who saved money they made from gardening, working at trades, hunting, or nursing the sick. Taking advantage of this policy by industriously buying their freedom and often their homes as well, free blacks expanded their community in New Orleans slowly at first but at an increasing rate that would alarm French planters by the 1790s.

Slaves constituted more than half of the population of southern port cities like Charleston and Savannah through the eighteenth century. Slaves did most of the heavy work of transporting and processing plantation staples such as rice and indigo; they also loaded and unloaded the ships that docked at the wharves, and they did the cooking, cleaning, and other tasks in urban households. Slave artisans played a large role in urban life, employed by master craftsmen in every variety of work: as shipwrights, coopers, and ropemakers along the waterfront, and in the higher trades as silversmiths and cabinetmakers. In addition, slave women controlled much of the marketing in the low-country ports, mediating between slave-grown produce from the countryside and urban consumption.

Mobile, often skilled, and occasionally literate, southern urban slaves understood the white world and, like their counterparts in northern cities, used their knowledge to enlarge their independence. They hired out their own time, earned wages, kept market stalls and shops, lived apart from their masters, and rented houses of their own. Some female slaves gained special positions as a result of sexual relations with white masters, and the small free mulatto population of Charleston was the product of such relationships. An increasingly independent African-American culture flourished in the small communities below the bluff in Savannah and along Charleston's Neck. The outnumbered slaveholders in those cities grew concerned, and imposed rigid restrictions on blacks' activities and on their efforts to build communal institutions. By the early 1700s most towns—North and South—had passed ordinances limiting the liberties of all nonwhites, slave and free. These included curfews, regulations of movement on city streets, and prohibitions on certain purchases.

Actual slave insurrections in New York City in 1712 and at the Stono River in South Carolina (twenty miles from Charleston) in 1739, and rumors of slave conspiracy in New York City in 1741 inspired whites to react with terror and execution, exposing the violent coercion that lay just beneath the surface of white paternalism. After the 1712 revolt, thirteen slaves died on the gallows; one starved to death in chains; three were burned at the stake; one was broken on the wheel; and six committed suicide. Mounted whites who stopped rebels marching southward from Stono to

Florida killed several slaves and set their heads on mileposts along the road. In New York in 1741, vengeful whites sentenced eighteen slaves and fourteen whites to be tortured and hanged; condemned thirteen slaves to burn to death at the stake; and deported another seventy to the West Indies.

White married women, like slaves, were viewed as dependents whose status derived from their place within the household. Commonly accepted norms of paternal power, female submission, and mutual obligation dictated the nature of relations between wife and husband, just as they ordered those between man and God, slave and master, child and parent. The nuclear family was the central focus of colonial society, even more than in England, because migration had severed individuals and families from wider kin connections. As dependents, women generally were assumed to be incapable of expressing political or religious opinions. An adult woman's authority was based on her role as mistress of the household. Under her husband's supervision she directed the household's daily affairs, and should fate or circumstance prevent her husband from fulfilling his role as household head, the wife could appropriately stand in his place without changing the patriarchal order of society. Over time, however, colonials passed statutes that allowed women some limited powers to run businesses when a husband was absent. The laws did not endorse women's economic independence; rather they were a means of preventing women whose men were dead or absent from relying on public relief. Nevertheless these laws facilitated women's economic activity, and they implicitly allowed a married woman to have a separate estate.

Unmarried women had somewhat broader independence, though that status often included greater poverty. In cities such as Philadelphia, single and widowed women comprised up to 20 percent of the adult female population, and in Boston 13 percent of the city's residents were widows. In both the seventeenth and eighteenth centuries, some working widows managed trades inherited from their husbands, at least until their sons could replace them, and were therefore found in every type of occupation—including morticians, blacksmiths, and, among Quakers, ministers. Most employed women worked at trades connected to household production and in ventures such as midwifery and laundering, which catered to female clients. But also, unmarried women operated commercial establishments. In Philadelphia, women ran an estimated half of the city's retail establishments and one-fourth of the taverns. In Baltimore, 8 percent of the city's households were headed by women in 1796; two-thirds of them were widows and the rest were unmarried. Although their number included publishers, mill owners, and speculators, positions they inherited when they became widows, most of Baltimore's working women, like those elsewhere, entered trades related to domestic work: seamstresses, laundresses, soap and candle makers, and lacemakers. As shop proprietresses, they dealt in china, groceries, pastries, dry goods, and millinery. They also ran schools, inns, boardinghouses, and taverns. In every city, whether self-employed or working for others, women earned less than unskilled white men or hired-out male slaves, barely eking out a living for themselves and, if they had families, their children.

Ironically, by the late eighteenth century when colonial men were striving for independence from England, unmarried women were losing much of the economic independence they once had held. Whereas previously, property ownership had qualified women for limited political participation such as signing petitions and making speeches, by 1750 local politics had become masculinized. Moreover, women's access to poverty relief diminished. Previously, women, who dominated the poverty relief rolls everywhere, had received "outdoor relief"—food, clothing, and fuel to be used at home. But as almshouses began to replace outdoor relief, poor relief focused more on rehabilitating men into productive laborers, and the needs of poor women, especially unmarried women, were frequently disregarded. Thus a new gender politics adversely affected colonial urban women.

The developing market economy in cities and the resultant economic specialization heightened distinctions between the world of men in the marketplace and the world of women in the home. Historian Mary Beth Norton has found that by the time of the Revolution, urban women's knowledge of family property was limited to the furnishings of the houses in which they lived, unless they were widows or had worked outside the home, while rural women's household tasks sometimes gave them access to information about family property in fields and livestock.[7] Men's knowledge of household accounts and household purchases was similarly limited. Norton's findings suggest that men and women did indeed inhabit different worlds and that the distinctive qualities of urban life sharpened the boundaries separating men's and women's daily lives. In wealthy families in the North and South, use of servants for cooking and cleaning reoriented women's domestic activities to child rearing, and the importance

Inside a Colonial Tavern.   Taverns, inns, and grog shops served as centers of male sociability, business, and politics in virtually every colonial city. This trade card, a form of advertisement by a Philadelphia tobacconist, shows the link between pipe smoking and drinking in a tavern.

Source: The Library Company of Philadelphia.

of women's maternal responsibilities began to be recognized. In the North, the special concerns of Quakers and Puritans with children's spiritual upbringing had the same effect of emphasizing the maternal role of women.

During the initial period of growth of American towns, religion pervaded every aspect of life. Whether in the Puritan North, the Anglican South, or the more divided middle colonies, the clergy were held in high esteem and exerted power over family life, education, and government. Religion defined and enforced social discipline and even influenced economic relations. As time passed, two developments peculiar to urban growth threatened the supremacy of organized religion in the colonial cities. First, population growth and diversity spurred the multiplication of rival sects, which broke down religious unity. Baptists, Presbyterians, and Anglicans contested Quaker preeminence in Philadelphia and Congregational hegemony in New England cities. Particularly in New England, Puritan ministers could no longer command communal deference, because many families imitated the British aristocracy and joined the Church of England. The evangelical revivals known as the Great Awakening of the 1730s and 1740s had special force in the cities, where crowds massed by the thousands to hear the charismatic George Whitefield and other preachers assault traditional sources of authority and permanently shatter the monopolistic hold of the educated clergy on religious discourse. Second, cosmopolitanism and economic opportunity provided townspeople with tempting alternatives to church attendance. Secular activities and amusements increasingly lured some people away from worship, provoking Puritan minister Cotton Mather to lament with characteristic alarm that "the peculiar Spirit and Error of the Time [is] Indifference to Religion." Although church membership grew in nearly every city, it rose slowly, and as a result the gap between a town's total population and its total church membership continually widened.

Family and church had the primary responsibility for education in colonial America, but supplementary schooling was fairly widespread in the cities, where most educational and cultural opportunities were concentrated. Following the lead of Boston, many cities supported some type of public school by 1720, and they all could boast several private schools for the wealthy as well as religious and charity schools for the poor. Even Indians and African Americans could obtain education, however limited, from English missionary groups such as the Anglican-based Society for the Propagation of the Gospel in Foreign Parts. At the same time, scores of bookstores appeared in the larger cities, and the colonial bookseller became instrumental in the spread of literary culture. Cities, notably Boston and Philadelphia, also pioneered the establishment of public libraries.

Printing presses sprouted up in the largest cities to serve the increasingly literate population. By 1700, printers in Boston, Philadelphia, and New York were producing books and pamphlets of secular and religious prose and poetry. These printers also supplied almanacs and newspapers, vital to urban life. In the eighteenth-century seaports the printing and distribution of political pamphlets, minutes of legislative proceedings and assembly votes, instructions to representatives, and special election pamphlets had the effect of broadening politics, giving all literate colonists access to discussion of controversial issues previously within the reach of only the political elite. Townspeople could hear news read aloud and discussed at taverns, at the town market, at the public slaughtering pen, and at other public places. And because the cities were the sites of almost all of the museums, scientific associations, concerts, and theaters, they dominated science and the arts. Plays and dance exhibitions were increasingly popular in New York and Charleston; and writers from all colonial cities contributed scientific papers to the Philosophical Transactions of the Royal Society.

A far more inclusive urban institution was the tavern. By the early 1700s, taverns and groggeries drew men of all classes to drink, eat, talk, and hear news of the day. These public houses served more than mere social functions; they were centers for discussion of politics, transaction of business, distribution of broadsides and pamphlets, and delivery of mail from visiting ships. As the number of taverns multiplied and as members of various social groups began seeking out people of their own sort, some establishments acquired a reputation for catering to one class or another, but most still drew a wide range of people. Of course the services provided were for males only; it was highly improper for a respectable woman to be seen tipping a cup of grog. The informality and heavy drinking in the taverns made them natural locations for disorder and vice. In response to rising complaints, most towns adopted the English policy of licensing establishments. This did not diminish the number of public houses—by the 1720s, there were more than a hundred licensed taverns in Boston, and in the peak year of 1752, New York authorities issued 334 licenses—but it did give governments more control. Coffeehouses and inns also served as important centers for social, political, and commercial activity. They also became places where city dwellers discussed the grievances that led to the American Revolution.

CITIES IN THE AMERICAN REVOLUTION

Relations between the colonies and the mother country were relatively calm for over a century, but British control was quietly undermined by the growing political and economic autonomy of the North American seaports. First, in order to meet immediate problems of local organization and services, the colonial towns had developed their own governments. These institutions exercised considerable authority over local ordinances, taxes, and finances because the Crown and Parliament either were uninterested in devoting attention to every detail of colony management or were unable to do so. This situation was particularly true in Boston, where the town meeting influenced so many local matters. By 1750, every one of the dozen or so other major colonial towns also had achieved some degree of governmental independence, and they jealously protected it.

Second, colonial merchants had managed to coexist with the restrictive Navigation Acts by arranging with sympathetic customs collectors to pay only a fraction of the required duties or by evading the law altogether and engaging in illicit trade. Thus much of the trading community acquired and expected profits outside of the mercantilist system. Such profits were not always assured, though. When British creditors demanded payments before American merchants were able to comply, or when local or foreign customers were unable to pay on time for goods delivered, a credit crunch staggered commerce. Such instances, however, prompted Americans to search even more avidly for new markets, outside the British colonies as well as inside. Third and perhaps most important, many colonial townspeople came to view their self-government and commercial independence as the most natural and just system for them, and any interference with it as illegal and tyrannical.

The Peace of Paris, which ended the French and Indian (Seven Years') War in 1763, signaled a new era during which new British policies agitated these forces and converted them into the sparks of American independence. At the end of the war Great Britain faced the tasks of organizing a newly enlarged empire abroad and relieving economic pressure at home caused by soaring costs of colonial defense and administration. Thus, in 1764, Parliament, under the leadership of George Grenville, passed the Molasses Act, attempting for the first time to collect meaningful revenue in America. This measure clamped down on smuggling and provided for stricter enforcement of import duties on molasses. The Stamp Act followed in 1765, the first direct internal tax ever levied on the colonies. It required revenue stamps, costing from a halfpenny to upwards of twenty shillings, to be attached to all newspapers, almanacs, broadsides, pamphlets, advertisements, licenses, bonds, leases, and other legal documents and commercial papers. These acts hit cities the hardest, affecting merchants, lawyers, and printers directly and artisans, shopkeepers, and laborers indirectly. Repeal of the Stamp Act in 1766 did not lighten the burden, for in 1767 Parliament passed the Townshend Acts, adding import duties to glass, lead, paper, paint, and tea.

It is not surprising, then, that cities provided the arenas for much of the resistance to new British policies. The earliest and most organized activity came from merchants. For them the Peace of Paris brought not only restrictive taxes but also the demise of wartime prosperity, which had been derived largely from trade with England's enemies. The merchants' first reaction was to try to recapture evaporating profits by encouraging more inter- and intracolonial trade. In April 1764, some Boston merchants organized the Society for Encouraging Trade and Commerce Within the Province of Massachusetts Bay, and in the following months New York and Philadelphia merchants formed similar associations. That year, several prominent New Yorkers revived the Society for the Promotion of Arts, Agriculture and Economy (which had existed briefly forty years earlier) to encourage more local manufacturing and ostensibly offset the Navigation Acts and the high prices of imported goods. Leaders of other cities followed this example. None of the efforts worked. They failed to change not only Parliament's policies but also the skewed balance of trade that drained the colonies of hard money, the only medium accepted by royal tax collectors and London creditors. Therefore, in 1765, merchants, particularly in the northern cities, adopted new tactics—boycotts and the nonimportation of British goods. They also formed associations to petition Parliament and the Crown for relief, to enforce nonimportation agreements, and to communicate with other colonies. It was this community of interests, activated in the 1760s but dating back to the seventeenth century, that coordinated resistance against the British and tied the first knots of American union.

Early protest activities included few notions of American independence. Merchants wished mainly to revive conditions that had existed before 1763 and that had brought prosperity to traders in every city except Boston. To be sure, the merchant community was not unified. Some merchants, such as Thomas Hutchinson and his brother-in-law Andrew Oliver, were deeply enmeshed in British mercantile trading networks and obligated by profitable royal connections to support parliamentary policies. Men like Hutchinson and Oliver lived a lifestyle modeled on that of the British aristocracy and favored more, rather than less, British presence in America. Other merchants, however, had won wealth and status from smuggling as well as legitimate trade, without any help from the mother country, and cared little about the English social hierarchy. As their protests to economic restrictions mounted, they became increasingly antimonarchical and resentful that royal officials and restrictions blocked their exercise of political power. Still, until the 1770s, most merchants were concerned far more with profits than with independence.

While debate among the merchants was beginning to undermine the previously unquestioned consensus concerning the prerogatives of British government, conflict among merchants and artisans continued over who should rule at home. English norms of deferential politics had been challenged in periodic upheavals of divisive political partisanship. In Boston, as early as 1689 a thousand townspeople resisted the usurpation of local prerogatives by Sir Edmund Andros, pouring into the streets, forming militia units, and surrounding the Town House. A committee of safety, consisting primarily of merchants and clergymen, assumed control and imprisoned Andros. This unusual mobilization of ordinary people prompted demands for a broadened suffrage and left in its wake continued questioning of the proper relationship between rulers and the ruled.

Similarly in the late 1600s, tensions between elite and plebeian segments of New York's population surfaced during the few years in which Jacob Leisler, a militia officer of German origin, established an interim government amidst the power vacuum created by the Protestant revolt going on in England. Shortly after they assumed power, the Leislerians freed imprisoned debtors. Then they called for the election of justices of the peace and militia officers and petitioned the Crown for a charter "in the like manner and with the same or more privileges as Boston," clearly aiming for a more participatory system. Leislerian mobs went so far as to attack the property of some of New York's wealthiest merchants. But when a newly appointed royal governor arrived in March 1691, Leisler surrendered the government. He was tried and found guilty of treason by an all-English jury, but the ethnic and class tensions that surfaced during his reign persisted. Also, in Philadelphia between 1684 and 1689 a religious schism split the Quaker community and expressed not only religiously inspired but also widely felt political and economic grievances.

Political and economic questions continued to divide the urban community through the eighteenth century. How much paper money should be issued, and would it be redeemed to benefit wealthy creditors or poor debtors? How best might Boston intervene in the provision of foodstuffs: to ensure a profit for provisioners or to make food available to citydwellers at the lowest costs? In New York, could the Morris faction of merchants successfully challenge the political hold of Governor Cosby? In Philadelphia, could Penn's proprietary party be dislodged from power? Even in a city like St. Augustine, where loyalty to the British seemed widespread and there were no organized groups of opposition, dissent within the governing elite opened questions about who should govern the city. A group of dissenters led by Chief Justice William Drayton challenged the authority of the British-appointed governor by calling for an elected house of assembly. The governor saw the opposition as fomented by revolutionary fervor, considering Drayton's principles as resembling "the seditions and rebellions in the other colonies." These issues aroused communities and transformed the character of urban politics from hierarchy and deference to contentiousness and participation.

The factional mobilization around these issues, the heightening of partisanship through the distribution of inflammatory political broadsides, pamphlets, and newspaper articles, the fluctuations between prosperity and hard times, war-inflated prices, and scarce money prompted artisans, shopkeepers, and small merchants to organize as political actors. These groups encountered the additional challenge of upper-class resistance to their economic and political ambitions. Nevertheless most craftsmen qualified for the franchise, and used their leverage at the polls to gain positions in local government and civic organizations. In Philadelphia, artisans filled half or more of local offices by the 1770s, and in Charleston in 1769, artisans assumed one-third of the positions on a committee to enforce a boycott against the Townshend Acts. Merchants and artisans could on occasion put aside their differences to cooperate on boycotts and nonimportation. In the end, both groups sought to advance their own interests, and increasingly their objectives were the same—relief from British oppression.

The grievances of the propertyless classes also intensified in the two decades before the Revolution, but these groups could not vote, and none held office in colonial cities. High prices and severe unemployment in the 1760s threatened calamity for those who already lived at or near the subsistence level. Jobs were even scarcer in cities where British troops were stationed, such as New York and later Boston, because many soldiers bolstered their meager pay by underbidding local laborers and artisans for employment. Moreover, the British navy continued to forcibly impress— or arbitrarily draft—American seamen and laborers for service on British ships, angering and frightening whole communities. Historian Jesse Lemisch has estimated that on one night in 1757 a force of three thousand British soldiers operating in New York impressed some eight hundred men, about one-fourth of the city's adult male population.[8] Several hundred men were subsequently released, but the scope of the raid reveals the impact that mass impressment could have on a city.

Even without the vote the lower classes had a powerful way to express their political voice. When the rich would not act to relieve suffering in a period of economic decline, common people felt justified in taking collective action through rallies, petitions, club activity, and physical attack. In Boston there was a tradition of crowd action when working-class people felt that ideals of community well-being were being sacrificed to entrepreneurial greed. They had rioted to punish an unscrupulous grain merchant during bread shortages in the 1710s, and had destroyed a public market in 1727 to protect small retailers from unfair competition. The lower classes used the same kinds of protest against what were viewed as unjust British interventions in American affairs and in doing so established themselves as a distinct political entity. A crowd battled against impressment by British naval officers for three days in Boston in 1747, attacking naval officers and their press gangs. Another crowd battled British soldiers in New York's Liberty Hill riot in 1770. In many circumstances the crowds acted with the tacit approval of men of higher position. But the inclusiveness of the

New Hampshire Stamp Master in Effigy.   This woodcut, produced fifty years later, shows a crowd parading the effigy of the New Hampshire stamp distributor through the streets of Portsmouth in 1765. The crowd carries a coffin to symbolize the death of the Stamp Act.

Source: The Metropolitan Museum of Art, Bequest of Charles Allen Munn, 1924. (24.90.1566a).

crowd, drawing women, children, servants, and black people into insurrectionary activity, and its empowering of otherwise dispossessed people always contained the threat of wider social revolt.

Cities moved dangerously close to social upheaval during the Stamp Act crisis of 1765. Boston crowds went beyond their goal of intimidating the stamp distributor by burning and beheading his effigy, attacking his house, and forcing him to promise not to fulfill the duties of his office. Nine days later the crowd attacked the homes of several customs officials and then settled some old scores with Lieutenant Governor Thomas Hutchinson by demolishing his elaborately built house. In New York City, crowds pushed merchants beyond the boycott and nonimportation strategy into openly defying Parliament by continuing commerce without any stamps. In Charleston, an organized crowd forced the resignation of the South Carolina stamp distributor. By November 1, 1765, when the Stamp Act was to go into effect, not a single stamp distributor in the colonies was willing to carry out the duties of his office, due in large part to crowd activities in colonial ports. In most cities the merchant gentry held the revolutionary initiative as the impending armed struggle with the British drew near, but crowd activism, an enduring legacy of eighteenth-century urban life, was having increasing effect.

Resistance was particularly strong in Boston, which had been facing economic troubles long before the 1760s. Once the dominant seaport in British North America, Boston by the mid-1700s was losing both trade and population. Philadelphia and New York undercut its dominance of transatlantic commerce, while nearby towns such as Providence, Portland, Salem, Gloucester, and Lynn encroached on its trade with the

New England interior. Amid increasing demands for poor relief and heavy expenses for municipal improvements, Boston's public commitment to social welfare became a liability; taxes soared. The city now seemed less attractive than its rivals. Alone among American cities, it saw its population decline from 16,382 in 1743 to 15,631 in 1760.

The mass protests that began with the Stamp Act crisis receded in the other colonial seaports after the Townshend Acts were repealed in 1768, but not in Boston. There, the harassment of customs officials by the Sons of Liberty provoked the British into sending two regiments of troops. The presence of redcoats only deepened anxiety on both sides, and tensions burst on the night of March 5, 1770, when a line of soldiers fired into a jeering crowd in front of the customshouse, killing five and injuring six. Radicals such as Sam Adams were quick to capitalize on the "Boston Massacre," spreading word of all the gory details (and some extras) throughout the colony and down the Atlantic Coast. Although not the first clash between troops and colonists, the Boston Massacre deepened anger in Boston and raised fears in other cities that they would be the next victim of British brutality.

Boston became the center of resistance three years later in a confrontation over the Tea Act, in which Parliament granted a virtual monopoly of the American tea trade to the British East India Company. When the first three ships carrying newly taxed tea arrived at Boston Harbor in December 1773, Sam Adams and his associates summoned a mass meeting. Five thousand people attended, nearly one-third of the city's population and the largest mass assembly in the city's history. As the meeting adjourned on the night of December 16, a number of men wearing Indian costumes boarded the ships and dumped their tea into the bay, in an exuberant burst of defiance known as the Boston Tea Party. The harsh British reaction helped turn colonial resistance into rebellion. Parliament closed the Boston port and tried to bolster imperial authority in a series of four "coercive" acts; these limited town meetings and elections in all of Massachusetts, reasserted British prerogative to quarter troops in the colony's towns, removed the ability of the towns to try British officials accused of crimes in America, and organized a provincial government in Quebec without a representative legislature.

Only the Port Act punished Boston directly. But the Coercive Acts all struck at the most cherished aspects of American urban life—commerce and self-government. Bostonians now faced certain ruin of the remainder of their maritime trade, the core of their economy. Moreover, their town meetings and local elections had been reduced to meaningless exercises. All their attempts at reform and redress had failed, and their desperation deepened. It was not difficult for Sam Adams to spread the fear that if the British could tether the freedoms of Massachusetts and Boston, they could do the same to other colonies and cities. When Adams and the Committee of Correspondence sent an appeal to Philadelphia and New York asking all Americans to join a boycott of trade with Great Britain, New York merchants responded by organizing the Continental Congress, which ultimately conceived American independence and nurtured American union. When British redcoats marched to Lexington and Concord in the spring of 1775 to arrest Adams and other radicals, it was clear that cities had played a major role in the timing of and justification for the American Revolution.

Once the Revolution began, and American men went to war, women in cities were critical to its success. They were central to the boycotts of imported products and later to the production of household manufactures. Their operation of businesses in their husbands' absence allowed cities to keep functioning during wartime. Women took part in revolutionary crowds and in New York countered wartime price inflation by forcing storekeepers to charge just prices. These activities did not expand the boundaries of women's sphere but rather took place in the areas where household and community interests overlapped and at a historical moment when household and community life were politicized. Neither interest in politics nor patriotic contribution enabled women to become full citizens, but the revolutionary years were shaped by women's as well as men's activities.

African Americans in cities did as much as they could to use revolutionary rhetoric and circumstances to challenge slavery. Slaves in Portsmouth, New Hampshire, pleaded with the legislature there that "the name of slave may not more be heard in a land gloriously contending for the sweets of freedom." Their efforts contributed to the northern states' gradual abolition of slavery in new state constitutions and laws written after 1776. Many other slaves declared their own personal independence during the war by fleeing their masters and taking refuge behind British lines or joining the Black Pioneers to fight on the British side. British-occupied New York City attracted nearly 4,000 escaped slaves, mostly from the Hudson Valley and northern New Jersey. Some were recaptured at the end of the war; several hundred others moved to Nova Scotia.

The predicaments of cities did not alone cause the American Revolution; the final break with England resulted from the merging of several forces. Yet cities were deeply involved in the major events not only because they bore the weight of British policy but also because they possessed the facilities and human resources to implement resistance and then rebellion. Their meetinghouses provided forums for debate and protest, their printing shops spread news and propaganda, and their taverns and coffeehouses furnished workshops where logistics were planned.

The separation of the thirteen colonies from Great Britain mirrored a process that had been developing in the American cities for nearly one hundred years. Residents of each town ultimately cast off traditional notions of deference and replaced them with politics more contentious and more participatory, and these lay at the heart of new revolutionary understandings of representation. Urban citizens had developed a sense of community and an allegiance to a particular place where older visions of commonwealth mingled with newer visions of individual enrichment. Motivated by familiar ideals of public interest and newly developed conceptions of self-interest, merchants and mechanics could urge resistance to new British taxes and ultimately to the British Empire itself. In the process of freeing themselves, urban dwellers found that they had new thoughts of freedom, the perfectibility of humanity, and the desire to shape their own futures. By the 1770s, common interests and grievances, aided by increased intercolonial communication, had spread these concepts of community, individualism, and personal agency beyond particular cities to encompass all the colonies. Thus cities, with their experience of collectivism, opportunity, and diversity, not only kindled but fed the flames of American independence.

Bibliography

Studies of colonial urban growth and government include Sylvia D. Fries, *The Urban Ideal in Colonial America* (1977); and Jon C. Teaford, *The Municipal Revolution in America: Origins of Modern Urban Government, 1650–1825* (1975). On Spanish colonial towns, see Dora P. Crouch, Daniel J. Garr, and Axel I. Mundigo, *Spanish City Planning in North America* (1982); Kathleen Deagan, *Spanish St. Augustine: The Archeology of a Colonial Creole Community* (1983); and Jean Parker Waterbury, ed., *The Oldest City: St. Augustine, Saga of Survival* (1983).

The cities of Boston, New York, and Philadelphia have received particular attention from colonial historians. Gary B. Nash's richly detailed study of the development of popular political consciousness in the century preceding the American Revolution focuses on these cities: *The Urban Crucible: Social Change, Political Consciousness, and the Origins of the American Revolution* (1979). See also Joyce Goodfriend, *Before the Melting Pot: Society and Culture in Colonial New York City, 1664–1730* (1991); Hendrik Hartog, *Public Property and Private Power: The Corporation of the City of New York in American Law, 1730–1870* (1983); Cathy Matson, *Merchants and Empire: Trading in Colonial New York* (1997); and Simon P. Newman, *Embodied History: The Lives of the Poor in Early Philadelphia* (2003).

On urban slavery in this period, see Ira Berlin, *Many Thousands Gone: The First Two Centuries of Slavery in North America* (1998); Philip Morgan, *Slave Counterpoint: Black Culture in Eighteenth Century Chesapeake and Lowcountry* (1998); Thelma Foote, *Black and White Manhattan: Race Relations and Collective Identity in Colonial Society, 1626–1783* (2004); Kimberly S. Hanger, *Bounded Places, Bounded Lives: Free Black Society in Colonial New Orleans, 1769–1803* (1997); Graham Russell Hodges, *Root & Branch: African Americans in New York and East Jersey, 1613–1863* (1999); Leslie M. Harris, *In the Shadow of Slavery: African Americans in New York City, 1626–1863* (2002); and Jill Lepore, *New York Burning: Liberty, Slavery and Conspiracy in Eighteenth-Century Manhattan* (2005).

The situation of women in colonial urban America is discussed in Kathleen Brown, *Good Wives, Nasty Wenches, and Anxious Patriarchs: Gender, Race, and Power in Colonial Virginia* (1996); Mary Beth Norton, *Founding Mothers and Fathers: Gendered Power and the Forming of American Society* (1996); Norton, *Liberty's Daughters: The Revolutionary Experience of American Women, 1750–1800* (1980); and Karin Wulf, *Not All Wives: Women of Colonial Philadelphia* (2000).

Works elaborating the roles of city inhabitants and economies in the Revolutionary years include Edward Countryman, *A People in Revolution: The American Revolution and Political Society in New York, 1760–1790* (1981); Thomas M. Doerflinger, *A Vigorous Spirit of Enterprise: Merchants and Economic Development in Revolutionary Philadelphia* (1986); Sylvia Frey, *Water from the Rock: Black Resistance in a Revolutionary Age* (1991); Paul Gilje, *The Road to Mobocracy: Popular Disorder in New York City, 1763–1834* (1987); Paul Gilje, *Liberty on the Waterfront: American Maritime Culture in the Age of Revolution* (2004); Charles G. Steffen, *The Mechanics of Baltimore: Workers and Politics in the Age of Revolution, 1763–1812* (1984); and Peter Thompson, *Rum Punch and Revolution: Taverngoing and Public Life in Eighteenth Century Philadelphia* (1999).

Notes

1. Jonathan Kandell, *La Capital: The Biography of Mexico City* (New York: Henry Holt, 1988), 112.

2. William R. Iseminger, "Culture and Environment in the American Bottom: The Rise and Fall of Cahokia Mounds," in Andrew Hurley, ed., *Common Fields: An Environmental History of St. Louis* (St. Louis: Missouri Historical Society Press, 1997), 49.

3. Gary B. Nash, *The Urban Crucible: Social Change, Political Consciousness, and the Origins of the American Revolution* (Cambridge, Mass.: Harvard University Press, 1979), 18.

4. Ibid., 395.

5. Ira Berlin, "Time, Space, and the Evolution of Afro-American Society on British Mainland North America," *American Historical Review* 85 (February 1980), 48.

6. Ibid., 53.

7. Mary Beth Norton, "Eighteenth-Century Women in Peace and War: The Case of the Loyalists," *William and Mary Quarterly,* 3d ser., 33 (July 1976), 386–409.

8. Jesse Lemisch, "Jack Tar in the Streets: Merchant Seamen in the Politics of Revolutionary America," *William and Mary Quarterly* 25 (July 1968), 371–407.

CHAPTER 2

Urban Expansion in the New Nation, 1776–1860

The new nation that emerged from the American Revolution still clung to the Atlantic rim, facing Europe. All of the original thirteen states fronted on tidewater, and so did all of the five largest cities: Philadelphia, New York, Boston, Charleston, and Baltimore. (Newport, one of the five largest in the colonial era, never regained its importance after the damaging British occupation during the war.) Yet the territory of the United States now stretched back beyond the Appalachian Mountains into the thinly populated interior of the continent. As ambitious settlers poured westward into the Ohio and Mississippi River valleys, they turned frontier settlements into major urban centers and created new cities virtually overnight. The pace of urban growth quickened in the nineteenth century, as the Atlantic ports and western cities boomed, and as a new constellation of industrial towns appeared throughout the Northern states. Cincinnati, Chicago, and Buffalo, all founded after American Independence, ranked among the nation's ten largest cities in 1860. As the territory of the United States expanded, cities founded by the French and Spanish were added to the young country's urban network, from New Orleans to St. Louis to San Francisco. Only five American cities could boast ten thousand or more inhabitants at the time of the first federal census in 1790; that number had risen to twenty-three by 1830, and it reached nearly one hundred by 1860. The number of people living in urban places swelled from two hundred thousand in 1790 to 6.2 million in 1860, approximately one-fifth of the total national population. By drawing population across the continent and by guiding the national economy, cities steered the course of national development.

CITIES IN THE NEW REPUBLIC

The first years of independence were difficult ones for the new republic and particularly its Atlantic ports, even after the war ended in 1783. Although free of the restrictions imposed by the British mercantile system, merchants found themselves deprived of the economic advantages and protection they once had taken for granted. The middle and lower classes faced shortages of housing and consumer goods, accompanied by rises in prices, unemployment, and rents. Between 1785 and 1787 a severe economic depression deepened distress among all classes. Because hard money and precious metals remained as scarce as before the Revolution, states issued paper money to serve as currency. Lack of uniform standards of this paper money tangled commercial exchange. In addition, uncertainty over the worth of money in circulation sparked conflicts between capitalists, who wanted a limited supply of stable currency, and debtors, who wanted more paper money that would reduce the cost of their debts. These tensions often involved geographic divisions, pitting commercial interests from urban and densely populated eastern regions against cash-poor farmers from the western frontier. The fiercest struggle occurred in 1786–87, when a band of two thousand debtor farmers from western Massachusetts, led by former Revolutionary War captain Daniel Shays, threatened a federal arsenal and blocked the state from seizing property for nonpayment of taxes. The farmers dispersed only after merchants from eastern Massachusetts hired a militia to hunt them down.

The Tontine Coffee House.   This painting, from around 1797, illustrates the importance of commerce to early American cities. The Tontine Coffee House, shown here at the corner of Wall and Water Streets in New York, served as the location of the Stock Exchange and several insurance offices. In the background on the right are the masts of ships in the harbor, showing the vitality of waterborne trade and its proximity to the city's commercial nerve center.

Shays' Rebellion strengthened the hands of citizens who were eager to replace the Articles of Confederation with a stronger form of central government. Urban merchants involved in overseas trade were the first to agitate for a central government that would facilitate commerce and create economic stability, and this group played a leading role in the creation and adoption of the Constitution. Though only 5 percent of all Americans lived in cities, twenty of fifty-five delegates to the Constitutional Convention in Philadelphia in May 1787 were city dwellers, and another twenty, mostly lawyers and merchants, had extensive urban contacts. The delegates wrote a new Constitution that protected mercantile interests by granting Congress powers to tax, to borrow and coin money, and to regulate commerce. States were prohibited from levying their own tariffs or issuing their own currency.

When the Constitution was sent to state ratifying conventions, city interests lined up on the side of adoption. Not just merchants but also artisan organizations and the press came out in support of delegates to these conventions who favored a stronger national government. Out of a hundred or more urban newspapers printed in the 1780s, only a dozen opposed the Constitution. Cities, towns, and their tributary regions in

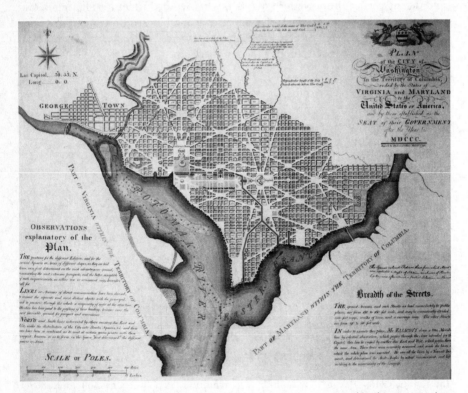

L'Enfant's Plan of Washington, D.C.   Most of this plan was incorporated in the construction of the capital. Note the importance of wide, diagonal avenues on the gridiron layout. Although a few new towns copied this plan, most developers in the nineteenth century preferred a strict gridiron street system because it was easier to construct and made lot sizes more uniform.

every state voted for delegates who supported the Constitution, while areas dominated by small farms chose delegates who opposed it. New Hampshire's coastal and river towns, commercially linked to Boston, helped swing the state in favor of ratification, and New Hampshire became the ninth and deciding state to accept the Constitution.

The port cities grew rapidly in the 1790s and early 1800s. No longer inhibited by the British Navigation Acts, American-owned ships soon took over 90 percent of the trans-Atlantic trade with Europe. Philadelphia—the largest city in 1790 if one includes its adjacent neighborhoods of Northern Liberties and Southwark—doubled its population by 1810 but was surpassed by the even more rapid growth of New York. Baltimore more than tripled in size as it became an outlet for the wheat and other products of the Susquehanna valley. Prosperity came to a sudden halt in 1807. The British, locked in a long-running conflict with Napoleon Bonaparte's France, tried to block American trade with Europe. British navy vessels stopped American merchant ships on the high seas and "impressed" many American sailors into the British navy. Under the leadership of President Thomas Jefferson, the United States government tried to retaliate with a trade embargo that banned any American ship from sailing to any foreign port. This embargo hurt the United States far more than it hurt the British, plunging the seaports into an economic depression. Over a thousand men in New York City alone were imprisoned for debt in 1809, many of them ordinary workingmen owing less than a week's wages.[1] The United States modified the embargo in 1809 to apply only to trade with Britain and France, but the underlying problem of British interference persisted. Matters only worsened during the War of 1812. British ships blockaded the Atlantic coast, and British soldiers burned Washington, the new capital city, in August of 1814. The war was deeply unpopular in New England, where talk of secession began to spread. But the grumblers were silenced in early 1815 by news that the war had ended in a compromise. Thereafter, a new commercial treaty allowed free trade to resume with Britain.

REVOLUTIONS IN TRANSPORTATION AND THE ECONOMY

Some of the smaller New England ports, such as Salem, Massachusetts, were devastated by the long interruption of trade, but most American cities resumed their growth after 1815, in part because a "market revolution" was transforming their rural hinterlands. Farmers who had been relatively self-sufficient now began to turn their attention to what could be sold for profit. At least in the North, farmers began to concentrate on just one or two cash crops that could be sold at nearby market towns or carried to distant ports.

Farmers' ability to profit from long distance trade was greatly enhanced by early nineteenth century improvements in transportation. Before 1800, it had been prohibitively expensive to transport bulky farm products long distances, except for cattle and pigs that could be herded to market. Roads were extremely primitive, so commercial agriculture thrived mostly near navigable rivers. Elsewhere, farmers grew crops mainly for their own use or for barter with their neighbors. They also sold small amounts of homemade whiskey, maple sugar, potash or salt pork; this modest cash income allowed them to pay their taxes, buy necessary tools, and have a bit left over for luxuries like tea or window glass.

Wagon travel grew easier with the opening of thousands of miles of improved roads in the early 1800s. This road building, along with other economic advances, was made possible by a major change in the structure of American commerce. The Revolution had loosened traditional restraints on incorporation, allowing the formation of many limited-liability corporations such as banks, insurance companies, and manufacturing concerns—plus turnpike companies. In the 1790s, a private company launched the turnpike boom by creating the Philadelphia-Lancaster Turnpike, a 60 mile toll road of graded, crushed stone, with stone bridges over the streams. Imitators sprang up throughout densely settled parts of the country. Most turnpike companies focused their efforts on short routes radiating from the major port cities, but many cruder, long-distance toll roads were also constructed throughout the Northeastern states. In New York State alone, privately operated turnpike companies had completed 4,000 miles of toll roads by 1820.[2] The federal government undertook the most ambitious of the road projects: a "National Road" from Maryland across the mountains to Ohio, completed in 1818. The road became an important route for westward migration, and was subsequently extended into Illinois.

The smoothest, fastest, and cheapest method of transportation was still by water. Water travel became much more efficient once inventors discovered that steam engines could make boats run upstream against the current. The first commercially successful steamboat, Robert Fulton's *North River Boat,* was launched in 1807. The ugly, smoky craft was capable of churning its way up the Hudson River from New York to Albany at average speeds of over 4 mph. By the end of 1812, Fulton was running six steamboats on the Hudson; he and his partners were making efforts to expand their operation to the Ohio River.

The Ohio and its tributaries formed the main transportation system of the quickly developing states west of the mountains: Ohio and Kentucky, soon to be followed by Indiana and Illinois. Transportation through the mountains was so difficult and costly in the early years of the United States that western settlers preferred a different trade route to the sea. Flatboats—often little more than rafts laden with flour, corn, pork, and tobacco—rode the current down the Ohio to the Mississippi, and then south to New Orleans, the Spanish-owned seaport near the Gulf of Mexico. President Jefferson, taking office in 1801, regarded the Spanish control of New Orleans as a grave danger to the development of the west and the unity of the United States. "There is on the globe one single spot, the possessor of which is our natural and habitual enemy. It is New Orleans, through which the produce of three-eighths of our territory must pass," he wrote.[3] Spain could at any time put a halt to the trade, as it had for three years in the 1780s and again briefly in 1802. Learning that Spain was in the process of ceding Louisiana back to France, Jefferson sent Robert Livington and James Monroe to France to try to buy New Orleans. To their surprise, Napoleon offered in 1803 to sell not only the city but all of Louisiana Territory, the entire western half of the Mississippi Valley. They took it for the bargain price of $15 million. Doubling the territory of the United States, for only 3 cents an acre, it was the biggest real estate deal in history.

New Orleans occupied a miserable site, a soggy island in a swamp. Its inhabitants had to endure mosquitoes, malaria, and hurricanes. Above all, there was the danger that the Mississippi could break out of its banks and flood the city—or worse, cut a new path to the Gulf that would leave New Orleans an isolated outpost in the muck. Wretched though it was, the site was still the best one available for a major seaport near the mouth of the Mississippi. Below New Orleans, most of the land was little more than a storm-swept salt marsh. So, as many American observers had predicted, the city's control of western trade promised to make it rival New York and Philadelphia as the dominant North American port. The steamboat helped tremendously. By 1830, a thousand steamboats travelled the Mississippi River system, their huge paddlewheels pushing them north to St. Louis or northeast up the Ohio toward Pittsburgh. With only about 10,000 inhabitants at the time of the Louisiana Purchase, New Orleans grew to over 100,000 by 1840, the fastest growth of any major city in those years. Its levee along the Mississippi, wrote one observer in 1845, "is crowded with vessels of all sizes, but more especially ships, from every part of the world—with hundreds of immense floating castles and palaces, called steamboats, and barges and flat boats innumerable. . . As the depot of the west, and the half-way house of foreign trade, it is almost impossible to anticipate its future magnitude."[4]

Upstream, the Ohio River valley towns of Louisville, Cincinnati, and Pittsburgh had already established themselves as what the historian Richard Wade has called an urban frontier.[5] Founded in the 1700s as military and commercial outposts, they had prospered after 1800 by supplying the new settlers who came in search of inexpensive farmland, and by processing the goods the farmers produced.

Cincinnati from across the Ohio River, ca. 1855.   One of the pioneer towns of the West, Cincinnati, like its East Coast predecessors, depended on water transportation for its commercial lifeblood. The towns of Covington and Newport, Kentucky, are depicted in the foreground of this lithograph.

Enthusiasts called Cincinnati the "Queen City of the West." Detractors preferred "Porkopolis," because of the innumerable hogs slaughtered by its meatpacking companies. By 1860, the three great cities of the Mississippi River system—New Orleans, Cincinnati, and St. Louis—each boasted more than 160,000 people.

But by then the supremacy of river travel had been challenged by two other transportation improvements: canals and railroads. Together, these redirected much of the western trade back to the East Coast, and particularly to New York. Canals came first, allowing water travel along an intricate web of routes not served by navigable rivers. The most important of these was the Erie Canal, an astonishing project by the state government of New York to link the Atlantic Ocean to the Great Lakes. The route of the Erie Canal ran west from the Hudson River at Albany, through the gap made by the Mohawk River in the Appalachian mountain range, across the low hills and marshlands south of Lake Ontario, to reach Lake Erie at Buffalo. New York City Mayor Dewitt Clinton had advocated the canal as a great benefit to the entire state and a way to make his city "the great depot and warehouse of the western world."[6] Construction began on "Clinton's Ditch" on July 4, 1817, just three days after Clinton was elected governor of the state. The 363-mile canal, the longest in the western world at the time, was dug mostly by men wielding picks, shovels and plows—assisted by horse-powered machinery and here and there some blasting powder. Stone aqueducts carried the canal across rivers; locks lifted it up the sides of hills.

The canal was so narrow and shallow that it could only be used by mule-drawn barges instead of steamboats. Still, it proved an enormous success upon its completion in 1825. Shipping costs from Lake Erie to New York dropped by more than 90 percent, and within a few years the canal carried more freight than reached New Orleans by the Mississippi. Tolls soon paid off the expense of construction. Villages along the canal route grew into cities that supplied the needs of the settlers flocking into upstate New York, served the travelers along the canal, and milled the grain from the region's new farms. "Every thing in this bustling place appeared to be in motion," wrote a visitor to Rochester in 1827. "The very streets seemed to be starting up of their own accord, ready-made, and looking as fresh and new, as if they had been turned out of the workmen's hands but an hour before—or that a great boxful of new houses had been sent by steam from New York, and tumbled out on the half-cleared land."[7] By 1860, Rochester and Albany were among the 20 largest cities in the United States. The biggest winner was New York City, which extended its trade empire not just through the Empire State, but into the Great Lakes system.

Like the Philadelphia-Lancaster turnpike, the Erie Canal spawned many imitators throughout the Northeast and Midwest. Two thousand miles of canals were built during the 1830s, including a ridiculously expensive Main Line from Philadelphia to Pittsburgh, which required 174 locks and a portage train to pull canal boats over the crest of the Appalachian mountain range. Like the Main Line, most of the canals created during the canal boom lost money for the states that built them. Still, they succeeded in reducing shipping costs and stimulating the growth of the cities at their termini.

Linked to the system of manmade canals, Lakes Erie, Huron, and Michigan formed a superior inland water route. From the end of the Erie Canal at Buffalo, large sailing vessels and steamships carried settlers out to the farming districts of the Old Northwest, and returned with wheat and corn to fill the lakefront warehouses. Two other growing ports on Lake Erie, Cleveland and Toledo, were served by canals reaching south through the countryside to the Ohio River. Detroit and Milwaukee farther along the lake route joined the ranks of America's big cities by 1860, as did Chicago, which emerged as the biggest of all the lake ports.

Thanks to the Erie Canal and the lakes, Chicago was accessible by water from New York City despite its location deep in the interior of the continent. Moreover, Chicago was separated from the Mississippi River system by only a few miles and a low, almost imperceptible ridge that had often been portaged by fur traders with canoes. In the early 1830s, as Illinois began planning a canal across the muddy portage to link Lake Michigan to the Illinois River, New York investors saw another chance for profits.

Though Chicago was just a fur-trading post in a marsh, real estate speculators began paying high prices for lots inhabitable only by ducks and muskrats. A choice lot that sold for one hundred dollars in 1832 brought three thousand dollars by 1834 and fifteen thousand dollars the following year. "I never saw a busier place than Chicago was at the time of our arrival," wrote one visitor in 1836. "The streets were crowded with land speculators, hurrying from one sale to another . . . it seemed as if some prevalent mania infected the whole people." Similar land booms were underway in promising locations throughout the United States as entrepreneurs plotted out new towns and then sold the land for hefty profits to other eager speculators who hoped the property would appreciate even more. Yet for every urban venture that succeeded, several did not. Many an optimistic urban speculator from the East came west holding a deed, only to find his property located in a mosquito-infested swamp.

That was the case in Chicago too, but there the hype became reality. During the construction of the Illinois and Michigan Canal from 1836 to 1848, builders put up a small, shabbily constructed city that profited by selling land, outfitting new settlers, and trading with farmers. The completed canal gave Chicago a big advantage over other lakeshore towns, drawing to it the trade from throughout northern Illinois. Further, investors anticipating the city's future importance had begun creating an even more important piece of infrastructure: a web of railroad tracks radiating from the city. Railroads had a number of advantages over canals: they were cheaper to build, they could run through areas with somewhat rougher terrain, and they didn't freeze in the winter. Merchants and local officials in the 1830s, 1840s, and 1850s hastened to build rail systems to capture the interior trade and speed it to their cities. By the end of the 1850s, more than 30,000 miles of track had been laid in the United States, mostly in the North. Telegraph lines ran along many of these tracks. Telegraphs quickened the pace at which business was done; no longer did merchants and manufacturers have to depend on ships and stagecoaches to bring them news about markets.

Chicago's emergence as the Midwest's railroad hub would eventually help make it the largest city of the region. Investors in the rival city of St. Louis were slower to build railroads. There at the heart of the great Midwestern water network, on the west bank of the Mississippi between its junctions with the Ohio and the Missouri rivers, St. Louis merchants were confident that their city would forever dominate the commerce of the Midwest. But by the 1850s, farmers in new western areas found it more convenient to send their grain and livestock to market by rail or canal. The lines ran to Chicago, where the flour was milled and the cattle slaughtered before being sent eastward to New York. As early as 1851, New Orleans editor J. D. DeBow complained that northern canals and railroads had "rolled back the mighty tide of the Mississippi and its ten thousand tributary streams until its mouth, practically and commercially, is more at New York and Boston than at New Orleans."

BOOSTERISM

As the experience of Chicago suggests, nineteenth-century urbanization was intensely competitive. Many people believed that their city had to keep growing to prevent economic stagnation and to stay ahead of rival cities. Increased immigration, markets, and transportation connections fed upon one another to produce a multiplier effect, a spiraling process that spun off greater and greater profits.

Entrepreneurs who invested in a city's real estate hitched their fortunes to that city's quick development; the faster their city grew, the faster they got rich. The frenzied speculation that surrounded urban development at this time encouraged the growth of "boosterism," the optimistic promotion of a city in grandiose language. It was this spirit that prompted a St. Louis booster to predict that "we have but commenced to tell the wonders of a city destined in the future to equal London in its population, Athens in its philosophy, art, and culture, Rome in its hotels, cathedrals, and grandeur, and to be the central commercial metropolis of a continent." If enough people believed such rhetoric, and put their money into that city, the predictions might actually come true. It was more than a matter of persuading a few wealthy investors. The growth of a city depended on amenities that were often beyond the capacity of private capital, so many projects had to be financed with state and local funds, thus linking the public interest and private profit. Urban promoters attempted to create a loyalty to place that personified cities to their residents. A railroad or canal claimed to serve not only the interests of residents of Baltimore, Philadelphia, or Chicago but also Baltimore, Philadelphia, and Chicago as entities themselves.

Boosterism sometimes had negative effects. In San Diego, boosterism entailed an effort to separate the Anglo community residentially and commercially from the old Mexican pueblo. Beginning in the 1850s, Richard Henry Dana, author of the popular travel narrative, *Two Years Before the Mast*, led San Diego's Anglo merchants in a campaign to promote a "New San Diego" by attracting Anglo settlers and investors and building new hotels and a wharf. Within a few years the town had taken on an Anglo character and the original Mexican settlers had been pushed aside. Elsewhere, the premium on rapid growth contributed to unplanned urban expansion. Buildings were poorly constructed and prone to catastrophic fires; water systems were inadequate. Railroads were built hastily with little concern for safety. Booster rhetoric could be used by con artists interested more in getting rich quick than in city building.

But boosters also helped to create institutions that were public resources as well as personal monuments. William B. Ogden's investments in land and railroads in

Chicago made him a multimillionaire and helped simultaneously expand Chicago from a village when he arrived in 1835 to a metropolis of half a million people when he died in 1877. Dr. Daniel B. Drake, whose writing brought fame to Cincinnati, planned and invested in canals and railroads there. Ogden and Drake participated in most public enterprises undertaken by their respective cities—bridges, sewers, parks, hospitals, libraries, and medical colleges.

A lack of successful boosterism almost doomed the nation's new capital, Washington, D.C. As directed by Congress, President George Washington in 1791 selected the site for the city along the Potomac River next to Georgetown and appointed Pierre Charles L'Enfant, a French engineer and architect who had fought in the Revolutionary War, to prepare a design. L'Enfant envisioned a grand metropolis with broad avenues, public squares, fountains, and statues. When the impetuous L'Enfant balked at selling public land quickly to raise money for the project, Washington fired him. Meanwhile, real estate sales foundered, the syndicate responsible for sales went bankrupt, and the city acquired a reputation as a bad investment. Though the federal government moved there from Philadelphia in 1800, Washington grew slowly, hampered by unfinished buildings and muddy streets. Nevertheless, in 1900 a bill passed by Congress provided for completion of much of L'Enfant's plan, including a grandiose mall between the Capitol and the Potomac River.

The South experienced much slower urban growth, except for around its periphery. The cities of Baltimore, Charleston, Savannah, Mobile, New Orleans, Memphis, St. Louis, and Louisville encircled the South by 1840, each joined to its hinterlands by commercial connections stretching along the South's abundant navigable waterways. Southern urban economies revolved around the cultivation, marketing, and processing of a staple crop for its eventual delivery to a northern port. The dependence of southern merchants on New York City in particular for marketing, shipping, and credit inhibited the growth of parallel facilities in southern cities and drained capital from the region, thus limiting the extent of southern urbanization.

Towns in the Far West and Southwest experienced a series of important changes between 1820 and 1860. Three centuries of Spanish rule came to an end in 1821, when Mexico achieved its independence. In northeastern Mexico, English-speaking immigrants launched a successful rebellion in 1835–36 that created the independent Republic of Texas, admitted to the American union in 1845 as a state with its capital in the new town of Austin. The United States acquired an even larger chunk of territory at the end of its 1846–48 war with Mexico, including all or part of the current states of California, Nevada, New Mexico, Arizona, Utah, and Colorado.

Just days before the end of the Mexican-American War in 1848, gold was discovered northeast of San Francisco in the foothills of the Sierra Nevadas. The news, which reached the East Coast that summer, inspired tens of thousands of young men to seek their fortunes in the gold fields: Americans, Mexicans, Chinese, Australians, South Americans, and Europeans. Nearly 40,000 people arrived in San Francisco in 1849, overwhelmingly men bound for the gold fields; people kept coming at an average rate of about 30,000 a year for the next 20 years. Businessmen in San Francisco and other California towns were among the biggest beneficiaries of the Gold Rush. Grocers sold food, clothing and other necessities at inflated prices to the eager new arrivals. With housing desperately scarce, and hundreds of ships abandoned in port by gold-crazed sailors, clever entrepreneurs established floating hotels. At the time gold was discovered, only about a thousand people lived in the village of Yerba Buena, as San Francisco was called then. Four years later, San Francisco was a city of 35,000 people; by 1860 it was home to 57,000.

BEGINNINGS OF URBAN INDUSTRIALISM

The commercialization of the countryside and growth of manufacturing in the cities proceeded in tandem. Farmers who raised cash crops needed to buy everyday necessities from urban craftsmen who manufactured shoes, cloth, furniture, wagons, and farm tools. Increased demand for such goods paved the way for changes in the organization of production. In the eighteenth century, master craftsmen and journeymen had produced goods directly for individual customers; thus a shoemaker made and sold shoes in the same room. In the nineteenth century, shoemakers began producing for a broader, more impersonal market. The business of selling shoes was separated from the process of making shoes, and the method of making shoes was subdivided into many steps, each requiring less skill than the formerly integrated process. Even before the development of mechanization and factories, control over production fell from shoemakers to merchant capitalists who had the cash and credit resources to purchase raw materials, organize large-scale production, market the finished product, and await delayed payment. Similar developments among metalworkers, tailors, hatters, clothiers, and boat builders diluted traditional skills, expanded the size of the work group, and enabled merchant capitalists to control profits and the work process.

Before the 1840s, most manufacturing in American cities was confined to two types of products: (1) consumer items, such as refined sugar, rum, and leather goods that merchants could exchange for raw materials like grain and cotton; and (2) commerce-serving items, such as ships, sails, paper, and barrels. However, along some New England rivers and streams, mechanized textile mills were beginning to establish genuine factory organization as early as the 1790s, and communities were emerging around them. Many of the mill towns in Connecticut, Massachusetts, and Rhode Island never grew beyond a few hundred people, most of them landless agrarians or families who split their time between millwork and farming. A few much larger mill towns developed, among them Lowell, Chicopee, and Holyoke, Massachusetts, each of which was financed by a group of investors called the Boston Associates. Lowell was the most famous of these. It was created in the 1820s as a model industrial community with supervised boarding houses for the workers, primarily young women from the New England countryside.

The factory system transformed work routines wherever it took hold. Use of mechanized devices instead of hand tools made ownership of the means of production almost impossible for wage earners, because only the wealthy could afford to invest in costly machines, especially those run by water or steam power. The use of machines to break down production into simple repetitive tasks meant that most workers no longer needed as full a range of craft skills or had responsibility for the quality of the item produced. The pace of machines regimented the workday in a way artisans had never experienced. Called to work by a bell, prohibited from talking to other workers, producing at the speed of the machines, and disciplined by foremen, factory workers could not slip off to go fishing, share a round of ale, or compete in foot races, as artisans' control over their workday had accustomed them to do.

Still, in many cities the factory system coexisted with traditional small-scale manufacture, because swelling urban populations continued to need the products and services of many crafts. Historian Bruce Laurie has identified five different types of production coexisting in antebellum Philadelphia: factories powered by steam or water, not-yet-mechanized central shops employing twenty-five or more workers, small sweatshops employing six to twenty-five workers, small neighborhood artisan shops where fewer than six toiled, and individual outworkers who did piecework in their homes. As evidence of fast economic growth, in 1850, nearly two-thirds of Philadelphia retailers had entered their business since 1845. In some places, particularly northeastern mill towns, an industrial working class constituted a large proportion of the population. But in larger, more diverse cities the occupational distribution retained a varied character.

Early manufacturers in the Northeast, particularly textile manufacturers, had built their factories near quickly moving rivers and waterfalls in order to harness the

An Early Factory.   This factory in Waltham, Massachusetts, built by early textile manufacturer Francis Cabot Lowell, unified production under one roof. Using power-driven looms and machinery, such a building served as a prototype for textile mills built in other sites.

water power. That is why they were willing to go to the expense of building new cities such as Lowell. The increasing use of coal-fired steam engines after 1840 made it easier for manufacturers of all sorts to locate in cities that already had potential workers and necessary infrastructure: railroads and canals to bring in the raw materials and to carry the finished goods to distant markets. Blessed with abundant coal, and good transportation, the Midwest began to become an important manufacturing region.

SOCIETAL EFFECTS OF ECONOMIC CHANGE

Changes associated with the market revolution extended into intimate corners of daily life. Until the expansion of the market economy and the emergence of industrialization, most urban wage earners—apprentices and journeymen—lived with their employers and shared their private lives. Now the hallmark of the employer's home was its separation from production and its private social life. Apprentices were no longer thought to be members of the master's family; rather, they were considered trainees in a business that was now conducted outside the household. Masters and journeymen viewed themselves more as employers and employees. Their interests were more distinct and conflicting than before, and they formed new class-conscious organizations to protect those interests.

The increasing wealth of American cities concentrated more than ever in the hands of the rich. In Boston, where 5 percent of the population had owned 44 percent of all taxable property in 1771, the richest 4 percent owned 59 percent of the wealth in 1833 and 64 percent by 1848. In New York, the upper 4 percent owned 49 percent of the wealth in 1828 and 66 percent in 1845. Similar concentrations of wealth could be found in Philadelphia, Brooklyn, Baltimore, St. Louis, and New Orleans. Every city had families with lofty fortunes who had maintained or increased the wealth accumulated by their forebears. Housed in mansions, transported in private carriages, clothed in the finest fabrics, fed the choicest delicacies, waited on by servants, entertained in exclusive clubs, the wealthiest urban residents could remove themselves from contact with the new urban masses. The middle and lower classes could advance by acquiring property or by moving into shopowner or skilled occupations. But such attainments were precarious. National economic panics and depressions, which occurred almost regularly—1819, 1837, 1857—and the growing scale of businesses stifled the chances of many a small investor. Thus even though upward occupational mobility seems to have remained fairly stable in places such as Boston and Philadelphia between 1830 and 1860, downward mobility increased.

Pressures of city life weighed heavily at the lowest end of the social spectrum. Wages rose slightly between 1820 and 1860 but remained meager in relation to prices. Daily pay for unskilled workers rose from eighty or ninety cents a day in the 1840s to slightly over a dollar a day in 1860. Factory workers earned even less. Spinners in textile mills, for example, received on average only $2.73 a week in 1842; by 1860 they were drawing only $2.85. Meanwhile prices for food, housing, and clothing rose more than 10 percent, offsetting wage increases. Some skilled workers, such as blacksmiths, machinists, and carpenters, earned $12 a week or more, but painters and wheelwrights received much less. Male factory workers could earn a dollar a day, but female factory workers, many of whom toiled fourteen or more hours a day, made barely $1 or $1.50 a week.

Few working-class families could manage on one income. According to the *New York Tribune*, the minimum budget for a family of five in 1851 came to $10.37 per week. This figure included $3 for rent, $2 for clothing, $1.40 for meat (two pounds a day at 10 cents a pound), 50 cents for a half-bushel of potatoes, 14 cents for milk, and 62.5 cents for one-eighth barrel of flour. The only nonessential item included was 12 cents for newspapers. When asked if such a budget was too high, its compiler replied, "Where is the money to pay for the amusements, for ice-creams . . . to pay the doctor or apothecary, to pay for pew rent in the church, to purchase books or musical instruments?" No wonder then, that thousands of families depended on women and children to supplement the earnings of the household head. Peddling, scavenging, theft, and prostitution joined casual laboring, sewing, and domestic employment as the means by which women and children helped their families make ends meet.

Much that was written about the American city in these years in novels, stories, and sketches portrayed it as a font of evil and wickedness. Intellectuals such as Ralph Waldo Emerson scorned the materialism and artificiality of urban life, and Nathaniel Hawthorne half seriously proposed that "all towns should be made capable of purification by fire, or of decay, within each half century." But popular nonfiction accounts of city life looked beyond sensationalism to attempt a comprehensive description of the new urban society. Their central revelation was the increasing wealth and pretentiousness of the very rich and simultaneous desperation of the very poor. It was not urbanization per se but the unequal distribution of wealth and income that accounted for the disintegration of community; in New York City the geographic distance was minimal, but the economic divisions were enormous from Broadway's opulence and Wall Street's financial might to Five Points, the locus and symbol for the squalor and misery of the very poor.

The polarization between rich and poor was perhaps the most dramatic aspect of urban class structure, but the emergence of a middle class as a self-conscious group was equally important. The development of far-flung markets and the increasing complexity of business enterprises created a need for salesmen, clerks, and managers—men who were neither manual workers nor controllers of capital. Engaged in "commercial pursuits," they were what we would now call white-collar workers, as opposed to the blue-collar workers in "mechanical trades." Men in middle-class jobs viewed themselves as distinct from production workers and often worked in separate spaces.

Given the era's economic instability, Americans could fall out of the middle class as rapidly as they rose into it. Nevertheless, the urban middle class developed its own recognizable styles of consumption, thought, and behavior. Collectively, these made up the elusive quality of "respectability," which was as important as the work process in defining middle-class status. A respectable middle-class home displayed certain consumer goods: carpeting, pianos, books, and magazines. Middle-class men and women dressed differently from working-class people. They learned different manners, often with the help of etiquette manuals. They espoused values that they thought set them apart: hard work and upwardly mobile striving for men; moral guardianship and sentimental nurturance for women; self-restraint for both. They also responded strongly to the evangelical religious renewal known as the Second Great Awakening, joined new voluntary associations, and supported codes of morality such as temperance, which they attempted to popularize among or impose upon the working classes.

The most distinguishing characteristic of the urban middle class was its family life. Home came to be defined by its isolation from the public world. In sharp contrast to the past, the home was supposed to be free from the intrusions of paid labor, commerce, and employees (except domestic servants). Paid work became tied to the routine of a clearly defined working day outside the home. It was what men did while women stayed behind to cook, clean, and care for the children. In reality, family incomes were so uncertain that women sometimes had to keep boarders, sew or open schools in their homes to make ends meet. Nevertheless, the idealization of the home as spiritual refuge imbued household work and child care with new significance. Middle-class men and women increasingly perceived the home as an institution shaped by maternal love rather than paternal authority.[8] The home was considered a bastion of feminine virtues—piety, morality, affection, and self-sacrifice—qualities absent from the public world ruled by male values of competition and aggressiveness. Although middle-class affluence depended on the man's income, respectability depended on women's domesticity and sexual restraint. The smaller size of the urban middle-class family was a critical factor by which respectable people distinguished themselves from farmers, workers, and immigrants. Fewer children allowed families more resources to invest in education and allowed mothers to devote more time to instilling values that would enable their children to maintain a middle-class position.

Evangelical Protestantism bolstered the ideology of women's sphere. Christian virtues of humility, piety, and charity coincided with new descriptions of female moral character. Although many men were converted in the evangelical revivals that swept the urbanizing Northeast and moved westward along the trail of settlement, women comprised the majority of converts and the bulk of congregations thereafter. By 1814, for example, women outnumbered men in religious societies of bustling Utica, New York, and the most zealous activists of the early revivals there were wives and daughters of men with white-collar occupations. Forming voluntary associations with evangelical goals extended the realm of domesticity beyond the household. Middle-class women were excluded from business and politics, but, imbued with a positive sense of their responsibilities as women and supported by ministers, they created a community of their peers and an associational life that claimed space for women in between the poles of domesticity and male-dominated public life.

The ideology of a separate women's sphere coexisted with exceptions to it. By midcentury, 10 percent of adult women, most of them in cities, worked for pay. Single women's alleged superior moral qualities made them prime candidates to fill teaching jobs, which were increasing with the spread of common schools. By 1860, in heavily urbanized Massachusetts, almost four-fifths of the teaching force was female, and one out of five women had taught at some point in their lives. For those largely unmarried women who produced textiles, clothing, and shoes in factories, constituting one-fourth of all laborers in manufacturing, the experience of living outside the family and earning wages appears to have altered their future domestic lives. They married at later ages than their mothers, wed men who were more their equal in age, had fewer children, and settled disproportionately in cities rather than the countryside. The crowds of poor women in cities, competing for miserably paid garment piecework or peddling food or utensils for pennies on street corners to feed their families, were excluded by definition from the culture of domesticity.

PROBLEMS OF GROWTH

Economic and population growth strained established forms of urban government. Colonial municipalities had customarily regulated the operation of food markets, the price of labor, and the cost of essential commodities. What had once seemed necessary to protect the community now appeared in the early nineteenth century to be an improper interference with commerce. Price regulations gradually collapsed, and municipally controlled markets disappeared. Local businessmen campaigned for new city charters that would let the city's government raise enough money through taxes and borrowing to pay for improvements in support of trade. Despite some public opposition, most cities' charters were revised between 1820 and 1860 to let local governments finance better water supplies, harbor improvements, canals, and railroad connections. Cities cleared away obstacles to economic development projects by invoking the legal doctrines of eminent domain (the taking of private property for public use) and police power (government's prerogative to protect public health and safety). Attention to economic development deemed beneficial to the community replaced the old common-law emphasis on the sanctity of individual property and the need to keep one person's use of property from injuring another.

Newer cities of the Ohio Valley and Great Lakes regions consciously emulated the older seaports. Charters of western towns intentionally included the same regulatory and taxing powers as those in the East. The government of Lexington, Kentucky, sent a leading citizen to Philadelphia to inspect the street lighting system, and Pittsburgh sent a delegation to Philadelphia, Baltimore, and New York on the same mission. The city council of Cincinnati ordered its board of health to consult officials in Boston, New York, Philadelphia, and Baltimore for recommendations on construction of a sewer system.

One threatening aspect of urban growth between 1830 and 1860 was the rise of what historian Roger Lane has termed "murderous disorder:" rioting, brawling, and homicide.[9] Unlike the eighteenth-century crowd actions that had been directed mainly against property, the antebellum riots were more likely to be aimed at specific groups of victims and more likely to hurt or kill. The causes of the antebellum riots are discussed in the next chapter, but regardless of how they started they resulted in the deaths of nearly a thousand people. Young white men—typically unmarried, and usually unemployed or underemployed—were the most likely group to hurl bricks and wield clubs in street brawls. They were also largely responsible for the murders that plagued city streets. Though murders in cities were greatly outnumbered by murders in the rural South, where customs of racial violence and defending one's honor made for a perilous mix, city folk were beginning to kill each other to a frightening extent. Lane found that in Philadelphia 90 percent of the homicide indictments named poor or working-class white males, whom he identified as part of a rough bachelor subculture organized around the pastimes of drinking and fighting. Although nearly one-fourth of the city's murders took place inside homes, nearly 40 percent occurred on the streets and another 10 percent in saloons.[10]

Violent crime was most common in poorer neighborhoods, where both criminals and victims were part of the lower classes. Yet property owners throughout the city were worried by an increase in burglary and arson, brought on, they feared, by troubling new conditions of urban life: the new mix of urban population, widening disparities of income, and decline of older patterns of household and neighborhood authority. Law enforcement agencies of constables, sheriffs, and night watchmen were incapable of suppressing either the riots or the crime. In St. Louis in the 1850s, only fifty daytime constables policed a population of one hundred thousand. Boosters were concerned that a reputation for lawlessness would hurt their city's attractiveness for commercial investment.

By midcentury, a sense that crime and disorder were on the increase prompted cities to establish full-time, uniformed police forces. Most cities until that point had still relied on the colonial system of daytime constables with full arrest powers, and poorly paid night watchmen with limited authority. The night watchmen were often older men or part-time workers with day jobs. They were given little respect, and were prone to dozing off or drinking on the job. The police reforms of the 1830s, 1840s, and 1850s created a single force of full-time policemen to patrol the city day and night (most were on night duty, when crime was thought to be most serious). The new policemen were paid better and were outfitted with uniforms or at least badges to make them plainly visible. Residents of these cities soon discovered, however, that creating a police force failed to solve old problems of law enforcement and even raised new ones. First, there seemed never to be enough policemen to do the job. Between 1845 and 1855, New York City's population grew from 250,000 to 630,000, while its police force was increased only from 800 to less than 1,200. Because there were too few officers to patrol an entire city, police protection was concentrated in commercial and affluent residential districts and was minimal in crowded, working-class neighborhoods. As a result, crime rates tended to rise in poorer districts; such neighborhoods were labeled as criminal by definition and their residents dismissed as "dangerous classes."

In addition, law enforcement could become embroiled in political conflict. Often, a police force was responsible to the political party in office who hired them and funded their salaries. In an attempt to lift police appointments in New York City out of party politics, the New York General Assembly in 1857 created a state-controlled metropolitan police force. Mayor Fernando Wood resisted this imposition of state power over his regime and refused to disband the local police, with the result that the city temporarily was patrolled by two competing police forces. The U.S. Court of Appeals forced Wood to back down, and the metropolitan force remained in operation until the 1870s, even though it failed to improve law enforcement. Yet the New York example sparked the subsequent creation of state-controlled municipal police in more than a dozen large cities, including Baltimore, San Francisco, Detroit, and New Orleans.

More important, the police as agents of law enforcement were buffeted between conflicting urban groups who held different notions of what the law was and

Boston Policeman.   Patrolling city streets without a uniform, early police officers had to battle not only criminals but also citizens' distrust of military-like authority. Not until the 1850s did residents of big cities give in and allow policemen to wear uniforms and carry arms.

Source: The Beauties of Street Sprinkling, NYC, by Thomas Worth, 1856, watercolor on paper, 12 1/4 × 16 5/8". Collection of the New York Historical Society, 1924.151.

how it should be enforced. Some citizens, for example, demanded strict enforcement of vice and temperance laws. Yet police action in these areas could antagonize other citizens who saw no harm in a little gambling, or who enjoyed their beer and whiskey. Roger Lane has pointed out that "depending on the political winds of the moment, [police] were alternately supposed to enforce or ignore a whole host of laws against drinking, gambling, and whoring that were widely unpopular in their own class and neighborhoods; there was more money in ignorance than in outrage. They could count on no automatic respect for The Law in cities full of clashing values and peoples."[11]

Fire departments were reorganized during this period for similar reasons. Volunteer fire companies had proven inadequate to the task of protecting the buildings, wharves, factories, and homes of the growing cities. The volunteers were often artisans who could leave their work to chase a fire and who enjoyed a battle with competing fire companies for access to water as much as the excitement of battling the fires. By the 1860s, most cities had replaced hand pumps with steam engines and disbanded volunteer fire companies. In their place, cities hired full-time firefighters on alert in specially constructed fire stations.

With or without the professional reorganization of firefighting, communities were not really safe from fire until they had efficient access to ample water. At an early date, fear of fire and disease induced urban officials to think more seriously about providing water for their citizens. In the 1790s, yellow fever ravaged the Northeast—particularly Philadelphia—convincing civic leaders that cleanliness was the only way to prevent or minimize disease. This need for sanitation meant more liberal use of water. Most urbanites had drawn their water from public or private wells, but the springs that fed these wells could not supply tens of thousands of people, and they were often polluted with seepage from privies and graves. Attention focused on nearby rivers and streams as sources of larger, purer water supplies. Who should undertake projects to tap these sources, the municipality or private corporations?

Under pressures resulting from the yellow fever epidemics, Philadelphia constructed the country's first major public waterworks. In 1798, the Philadelphia City Council hired engineer and architect Benjamin Latrobe. He devised a system to pump water from the Schuylkill River to a high-ground reservoir called Centre Square, from where it could be pumped through wooden pipes to various parts of the city. Although it operated at a loss—largely because people could not readily accept the idea of paying for water and because the steam pumps often broke down—the Centre Square waterworks won national admiration. The system eventually accustomed Philadelphians to consider water as a public utility. When the city outgrew the system, it constructed a larger waterworks in 1811, raising water from the Schuylkill to reservoirs atop Fairmount Hill and distributing it through iron pipes.

Philadelphia's public water company was the exception in these early years. Other cities purchased water from private companies, whose quality of service ranged from adequate in Baltimore to intolerable in New York. Few private corporations were willing to commit huge amounts of capital to the construction and maintenance of an elaborate water system. They were particularly reluctant to extend service to low-income districts that would furnish little revenue. City leaders, looking to the example set by Philadelphia, eventually began to press for public waterworks. In 1835, New York voters solidly approved a project to bring water to the city through an aqueduct from the Croton River. In 1845, an act passed by the Massachusetts General Assembly enabled Boston to construct its own water system. In 1857, Baltimore purchased its private waterworks and began constructing an additional reservoir. In factory towns, industrialists pressured city officials to protect their property with municipal water systems. By 1860, the country's sixteen largest cities had reasonably efficient water systems, only four of which were still privately owned.

Abundance of water and higher standards of public health encouraged new habits of consumption. Private households, especially among the wealthy, had more accessible water for personal use in bathtubs, wash basins, and "water closets," the primitive forerunners of flush toilets. Industries used increasing amounts of water for steam, cooling, and cleaning. The growing demand for water soon threatened to surpass the capacity of the waterworks, but running water remained unavailable in the homes of the poor.

Professional police, fire, and water services relieved some problems of commercial cities, but poverty, delinquency, mental illness, disease, and moral decay defied easy solutions. Colonial practices of warning out debtors, fining and whipping criminals, and placing paupers and orphans with relatives and other townspeople were unfeasible in the nineteenth century. Cities grew too large for officials to keep track of all newcomers, and old forms of punishment and relief failed to stem increasing crime, sin, and poverty. Moreover, constant population migration churned the social structures of all cities, increasing anonymity and aggravating fears of anarchy and social breakdown.

To combat overcrowding, unemployment, and poverty, middle-class reformers created remedies that were shaped by their own gender, class, and ethnic prejudices. A characteristic response of antebellum reformers was to try to convert those whom they identified as poor and depraved, infuse them with Christian morality, and establish institutions that would inculcate values of diligence, order, and restraint. Housed together, away from their families and the temptations of city life, the poor could be rehabilitated in a controlled environment. Between 1820 and 1840, scores of communities opened almshouses and workhouses for the poor. These institutions won support as much because they removed the poor from the streets and were more economical than outdoor assistance as for their reforming functions. Nevertheless they signaled a new approach to welfare policy.

Penitentiaries, asylums, and houses of correction were constructed to serve the same functions for the criminal, the insane, and the delinquent that almshouses served for the poor—removing "deviants" from the city's temptations and restoring mental health and lawful behavior by exposure to a regimented institutional life. With the goal of returning inmates to an idealized pre-urban social harmony, the institutions were located in rural settings, although the values of moderation, punctuality, and obedience that the institutions represented were more suited to life in the present than the past. Moreover, as David Rothman has shown, the ideal of confining deviants and dependents in order to reform them could easily harden into the objective of incarcerating these groups simply to isolate them from the rest of society.[12]

Almshouses, penitentiaries, and asylums could neither house nor reform all the poor, however. A more inclusive institution was needed to destroy the cycle of poverty, a process, according to some reformers, whereby succeeding generations of the same families failed to escape indigence and became perpetually dependent upon public support. Beginning in the 1820s, urban leaders rallied behind state-supported free education as the instrument that would break the chain of destitution while restoring social order in the same fashion as other institutional reform.

Among the most influential advocates of taxpayer-supported public education were Horace Mann, a Boston lawyer, Henry Barnard, a leading citizen of Hartford, and Calvin Stowe, professor of biblical literature at Cincinnati's Lane Theological Seminary. Schooling, they claimed, would instill virtue and patriotism in the lower classes and lift them from poverty into hardworking respectability. It would assimilate immigrants and teach all children to withstand temptations. As cities grew and social conflict became more threatening, the public education movement gained momentum. In the 1820s and 1830s, the most insistent voices for expanding public education were those of urban politicians, humanitarians, and educators who campaigned for school reform as insurance against social upheaval. Boston established free elementary schools in 1818, New York followed in 1832, and Philadelphia in 1836.

By the 1850s, the majority of cities and states in the North and the West had some system of publicly funded education. Uniformly designed school buildings proliferated in diverse urban neighborhoods. Moreover, school organization had become more uniform. Pupils were placed in grades according to age and ability, procedures for advancement from grade to grade were standardized, decisions about curriculum and textbooks were centralized, and teachers were required to meet certain professional qualifications. Control was more firmly consolidated in the hands of city and state bureaucracies.

Public schooling in diverse communities was now shaped by the political, economic, and cultural agendas of native Protestant leaders, who intended schools to train students in punctuality, obedience, honesty, and persistence. McGuffey's series of readers, which after 1836 became the basic reading textbooks, taught schoolchildren to accept their position in the class hierarchy and strive for respectability rather than the trappings of wealth. The content of public education expressed values antagonistic to the cultures of Catholic, African-American, rural, southern, immigrant, and working-class peoples, the very groups who favored local community control of schools in opposition to the reformers' vision of centralized, homogenized education. When Catholics in New York City lost a challenge to the Protestant monopoly of public education in that city, the Roman Catholic church decided to establish its own school system, a costly program that took decades to complete. After Los Angeles was incorporated as a city in 1850, its Hispanic mayor, Antonio Franco Coronel, and the city council, the majority of whom were Mexican, supported the establishment of bilingual public schools. When the school board failed to find teachers who could teach in both English and Spanish, the first school opened with only English permitted for instruction, alienating many would-be attendees.

Reformers succeeded in winning public support for enormous expenditures on education because politics in antebellum cities called for a literate, informed electorate; because disorder and diversity in cities made bureaucratic standardization appealing; and because commercial expansion created demand for well-trained workers and managers. Despite its triumphs, however, the reach of public schooling was still limited. In many cities, population increased faster than schools could be built. As immigration accelerated in the 1840s, illiteracy rose instead of declined. More and more children were squeezed into existing classrooms. In 1850, Boston schools provided only one teacher for every fifty-five students. At the same time, school reformers, attempting to bring all children into schools, contended with officials and taxpayers determined to hold down costs and with working-class and immigrant families who resisted educators' intervention into their children's upbringing.

In the 1850s, the criticism of immigrant and working-class families implicit in calls for asylums and public schools became more explicit in a new reform strategy. The reformers active in the New York Children's Aid Society and the Association for Improving the Condition of the Poor initiated an ambitious campaign to eradicate poverty by clearing children and women from the streets and transforming working-class family life. The new ways in which the middle class perceived the work ethic and ideology of domesticity made traditional working-class street life, particularly the visible activities of children, seem especially dangerous. Middle-class reformers were generally insensitive to working-class families' needs for incomes that women and children could earn in factories and street trades and thus believed that the enclosed, privatized, protected home and that the clearly differentiated roles for men, women, and children needed to be emphasized and protected.

From reformers' perspective, the active engagement of women and children in public wage work and social life rather than sheltered in a safe, moral home environment became in itself evidence of parental neglect, family disintegration, and the root cause of poverty. According to reformers, working-class households that sent women and children to find casual labor in the streets were not doing their civic duty. Some reformers viewed children on the streets as orphaned or abandoned, although in many cases they were neither. To "save" such children, New York reformer Charles Loring Brace established the Children's Aid Society (CAS) in 1853 to remove children from troubled households, shipping boys off to farm labor in the countryside and teaching girls sewing, cooking, and housecleaning as preparation for a life of domesticity as wives or servants. Although the CAS solutions did not alleviate urban poverty, its attempts to control the streets and shape family life raised antagonisms among the poor that would remain long after the reform societies abandoned their mission.

By the eve of the Civil War, America's cities had undergone immense changes. Though the United States was far from an urbanized nation by 1860, the preceding three decades had witnessed the fastest rate of urbanization this country would ever experience. The number of urban residents grew by 64 percent between 1830 and 1840; 92 percent between 1840 and 1850; and 75 percent between 1850 and 1860. By 1860, twenty-two cities had more than forty thousand inhabitants (see Table 2–1). The "market revolution" had stimulated Americans' participation in trade. The new turnpikes, steamboats, canals, and railroads had made transportation cheaper and faster, further stimulating commerce. The development of the hinterlands and the new urban residents helped increase the size and number of domestic markets. Although most American cities still based their economies largely on trade, the increasing use of steam engines was allowing them to become centers of mechanized industry. A new era in urban life had begun.

TABLE 2–1 Populations of Major Cities, 1830–60

	1830	1840	1850	1860
New York	202,589	312,700	515,500	813,600
Philadelphia	161,271	220,400	340,000	565,529
Brooklyn	15,396	36,230	96,838	266,660
Baltimore	80,620	102,300	169,600	212,418
Boston	61,392	93,380	136,880	177,840
New Orleans	46,082	102,190	116,375	168,675
Cincinnati	24,831	46,338	115,435	161,044
St. Louis	5,852	14,470	77,860	160,773
Chicago		4,470	29,963	109,260
Buffalo	8,653	18,213	42,260	81,130
Newark	10,953	17,290	38,890	71,940
Louisville	10,340	21,210	43,194	68,033
Albany	24,209	33,721	50,763	62,367
Washington	18,826	23,364	40,001	61,122
San Francisco			34,776*	56,802
Providence	16,833	23,171	41,573	50,666
Pittsburgh	15,369	21,115	46,601	49,221
Rochester	9,207	20,191	36,403	48,204
Detroit	2,222	9,102	21,019	45,619
Milwaukee		1,712	20,061	45,246
Cleveland	1,076	6,071	17,034	43,417
Charleston	30,289	29,261	42,985	40,522
Total urban population	1,127,000	1,845,000	3,544,000	6,217,000
Percentage of U.S. population that was urban	8.8	10.8	15.3	19.8
Percentage of increase in urban population		63.7	92.1	75.4

Sources: U.S. censuses of 1850 and 1860; The figure given here comes from the 1852 California census.

Bibliography

The growth of new cities between 1780 and 1860 is examined by Jeffrey S. Adler, *Yankee Merchants and the Making of the Urban West: The Rise and Fall of Antebellum St. Louis* (1991); William Cronon, *Nature's Metropolis: Chicago and the Great West* (1991); Diane Shaw, *City Building on the Eastern Frontier: Sorting the New Nineteenth-Century City* (2004); Richard C. Wade, *The Urban Frontier: The Rise of Western Cities, 1790–1830* (1959).

Among the many works on economic change in this era are David R. Meyer, *The Roots of American Industrialization* (2003); and Charles Sellers, *The Market Revolution: Jacksonian America, 1815–1846* (1991). For a recent overview of social change during this period, see Christopher Clark, *Social Change in America: From the Revolution Through the Civil War* (2006).

The development of city services has received attention in Susan Craddock, *City of Plagues: Disease, Poverty, and Deviance in San Francisco* (2002); Robin Einhorn, *Property Rules: Political Economy in Chicago, 1833–1872* (1991); Joanne Abel Goldman, *Building New York's Sewers: Developing Mechanisms of Urban Management* (1997); Amy S. Greenberg, *Cause for Alarm: The Volunteer Fire Department in the Nineteenth-Century City* (1998); David Johnson, *Policing the Urban Underworld: The Impact of Crime on the Development of the American Police, 1800–1887* (1979); Carl F. Kaestle, *The Evolution of an Urban School System: New York City, 1750–1850* (1973); Gerard T. Koeppel, *Water for Gotham: A History* (2000); Roger Lane, *Policing the City: Boston, 1822–1885* (1967); Roger Lane, *Murder in America: A History* (1997); Alan I. Marcus, *Plague of Strangers: Social Groups and the Origins of City Services in Cincinnati, 1819–1870* (1991); Martin V. Melosi, *The Sanitary City: Urban Infrastructure in America from Colonial Times to the Present* (2000); Joel A. Tarr, *The Search for the Ultimate Sink: Urban Pollution in Historical Perspective* (1996); and Mark Tebeau, *Eating Smoke: Fire in Urban America, 1800–1950* (2003).

For the impact of economic change on the community, see Tyler Anbinder, *Five Points: The 19th-Century New York City Neighborhood that Invented Tap Dance, Stole Elections, and Became the World's Most Notorious Slum* (2001); Thomas Bender, *Toward an Urban Vision: Ideas and Institutions in Nineteenth-Century America* (1975); Paul Boyer, *Urban Masses and Moral Order in America, 1820–1920* (1978); Donald L. Miller, *City of the Century: The Epic of Chicago and the Making of America* (1996); and Sam Bass Warner, Jr., *The Private City: Philadelphia in Three Periods of Growth* (1968).

Works on early nineteenth-century social structure include Elizabeth Blackmar, *Manhattan for Rent, 1785–1850* (1989); Stuart M. Blumin, *The Emergence of the Middle Class: Social Experience in the American City, 1760–1900* (1989); Alan Dawley, *Class and Community: The Industrial Revolution in Lynn* (1977); Paul Johnson, *A Shopkeeper's Millennium: Society and Revivals in Rochester, New York, 1815–1837* (1978); Mary P. Ryan, *The Cradle of the Middle Class: The Family in Oneida County, New York, 1790–1865* (1981); Billy Smith, *The "Lower Sort": Philadelphia's Laboring People, 1750–1800* (1990); Richard Stott, *Workers in the Metropolis: Class, Ethnicity, and Youth in Antebellum New York City* (1990); Stephan Thernstrom, *Poverty and Progress: Social Mobility in a Nineteenth Century City* (1964); and Sean Wilentz, *Chants Democratic: New York City and the Rise of the American Working Class, 1780–1850* (1984).

On women in antebellum towns and cities, see Suzanne Lebsock, *The Free Women of Petersburg: Status and Culture in a Southern Town, 1784–1860* (1984); Mary P. Ryan, *Women in Public: Between Banners and Ballots, 1825–1880* (1990); Christine Stansell, *City of Women: Sex and Class in New York, 1789–1860* (1986); and Lisa C. Tolbert, *Constructing Townscapes: Space and Society in Antebellum Tennessee* (1999). For other works on women and reform, see Bruce Dorsey, *Reforming Men and Women: Gender in the Antebellum City* (2002); Lori D. Ginzberg, *Women and the Work of Benevolence: Morality, Politics, and Class in the Nineteenth-Century United States* (1990); Nancy Hewitt, *Women's Activism and Social Change: Rochester, New York, 1822–1872* (1984); Teresa Anne Murphy, *Ten Hours' Labor: Religion, Reform, and Gender in Early New England* (1992).

Notes

1. Charles Sellers, *The Market Revolution: Jacksonian America, 1815–1846* (New York: Oxford University Press, 1991), 25.
2. Ibid., 15, 41.
3. D.W. Meinig, *The Shaping of America: A Geographical Perspective on 500 Years of History, Volume 2, Continental America, 1800–1867* (New Haven: Yale University Press, 1993), 10.
4. Benjamin Moore Norman, *Norman's New Orleans and Environs* (1845; repr., Baton Rouge: Louisiana State University Press, 1976) 81–82.
5. Richard C. Wade, *The Urban Frontier: The Rise of Western Cities, 1790–1830* (Cambridge, Mass.: Harvard University Press, 1959).
6. Peter L. Bernstein, *Wedding of the Waters: The Erie Canal and the Making of a Great Nation* (New York: W.W. Norton, 2005), 178.
7. Captain Basil Hall, *Travels in North America, in the Years 1827 and 1828, Vol. 1*, 3rd ed. (Edinburgh: Robert Cadell, 1830), 160.
8. Christine Stansell, *City of Women: Sex and Class in New York, 1789–1860* (New York: Knopf, 1986).
9. Roger Lane, *Murder in America: A History* (Columbus, Ohio: Ohio State University Press, 1997), 92.
10. Ibid., 122–26.
11. Ibid., 107–8.
12. David J. Rothman, *The Discovery of the Asylum: Social Order and Disorder in the New Republic* (Boston: Little, Brown, 1971).

CHAPTER 3

Life in the Walking City, 1820–1865

THE WALKING CITY

Until the 1850s, almost all American cities could be characterized by their compactness. Located near harbors or river junctions, they focused their activities on the waterfront. Here warehouses, mercantile offices, and small manufacturing establishments were located because access to water transportation was of principal importance. Public buildings, churches, hotels, and shops clustered nearby. Homes of prominent families often were interspersed among these structures or, as in Cincinnati, Providence, and St. Louis, sat on a hill overlooking the port. Around these cores and in the valleys between hills were the residential areas of craftsmen, storekeepers, and laborers. The two- and three-story structures in these districts contained shops and workshops on the lower floors and residential quarters in back or above. Businesses needing water supplies—mills, tanneries, slaughterhouses, breweries—grouped along nearby streams. As the nineteenth century progressed, some heavy industry, particularly base metals, grew in the outskirts near railroad connections. Most business establishments, however, remained dispersed throughout the settled areas of town.

Wagons, carriages, horses, and pedestrians jammed the central streets. Neither public officers nor mechanical signals regulated the speed and direction of traffic. People seldom observed any custom of keeping to one side of the street or the other; right of way at intersections went to the boldest or most reckless. Cobblestones or gravel paved only a fraction of urban thoroughfares; most retained their original dirt surfaces, which nature and traffic turned into choking dust or clogging mud. Though animal-drawn vehicles were common on the streets of the early American city, the vast majority of people walked to their destinations, and it was this form of transportation that determined a city's size and shape. Until the 1850s, the settled areas of even the largest cities, such as New York, Boston, and Philadelphia, rarely extended beyond two miles from the city center—the average distance a person can walk in half an hour. Thus historians have labeled this early urban configuration the "walking city" because of its size and major mode of conveyance. No policies or legislation limited the area of any city; it was simply more convenient for people to locate businesses and residences on available sites that had access by foot to most work, shopping, and social activities.

The compact geography of cities had several important features. First, land use was mixed; commercial, storage, residential, and industrial buildings mingled together. There were few distinct districts; even waterfront property had various uses. Business districts became more defined as cities grew, but residences and small factories remained interspersed with stores, banks, and offices.

Second, city dwellers were relatively integrated. Short distances separated poor from rich, immigrant from native, African American from white—a proximity that may have sparked some of the conflicts over turf discussed in Chapter 2. Factory owners often built their residences next to their factories, within sight of workingmen's homes, and common laborers lived along alleyways inside blocks where the more well-to-do resided. Slaves in southern cities such as Charleston and New Orleans inhabited compounds behind their masters' houses. Row housing, the characteristic urban style in early nineteenth-century cities, accentuated the appearance of homogeneity, making inequalities of wealth less visible. Moreover, people lived not only nearby one another but also near, or at, their places of work. Those who worked away from their residences walked to and from their jobs. As time passed and populations increased, enclaves did form. In Boston, newly arrived Irish filled the North End and neighborhood along the wharves. In Philadelphia, African Americans

Hazards of Street Cleaning.   Early nineteenth-century city streets became littered with debris and animal droppings, so that one of the earliest urban services was street cleaning. But as this drawing depicts, the service could be hazardous, as pedestrians who got into the way of spraying mechanisms could find themselves unwitting targets.

clustered in the southern wards. Residential districts of free blacks and living-out slaves grew on or outside the edges of Charleston and Richmond. Still, however, the relatively small areas of all cities left all groups of people physically close together.

Political leadership reflected circumstances of the integrated community. City councils were usually elected to represent the city as a whole rather than from distinct districts. Early nineteenth-century urban governments were composed of members of the city's social and economical elite—bankers, merchants, lawyers. Rarely were those in the lower three-quarters of the social order elected. Without distinctive geographic enclaves that corresponded to social class, the capacity of the working classes to develop and effectively express a clear political view was limited.

Just as the necessity of walking kept cities from growing too far outward, technological limits kept it from growing upward. Before the introduction of passenger elevators and iron structural support in the 1850s, buildings rose no more than a few stories in height. The skyscraper, with its steel frame and electric elevators, did not appear until the 1880s. Until then the built environment developed primarily when new structures covered remaining empty property within the walking city or when developers reclaimed land by leveling hills, draining marshes, or filling in coves and bays. As cities filled up and vacant lots disappeared, land values soared, especially in comparison with construction costs. In Chicago, for example, total valuation for land within a one-mile radius of the central business district increased from $810,000 in 1842 to $50,750,000 in 1856, a 6,000 percent gain.

Meanwhile, many cities were practically bursting at their seams. It has been common for Americans to consider urban crowding a consequence of industrialization and mass immigration during the late nineteenth and early twentieth centuries. Yet at no time in the country's history were total urban densities as high as they were in the mid-nineteenth century. An almost annual excess of new arrivals over those departing doubled and tripled populations of most established cities between 1840 and 1850. Crowding in settled areas swelled. By 1850, there were 135.6 persons per acre in New York, 82.7 in Boston, 80.0 in Philadelphia, and 68.4 in Pittsburgh. In many cities at midcentury an average of two families occupied every dwelling, a much larger figure than in similar-sized European towns or even in fast-growing industrial cities of England. Inner-city wards in most large American cities would become even more densely packed in the latter half of the century, but because urban areas were smaller at midcentury, crowding spread to a larger proportion of their districts.

In the 1820s and 1830s, ferries and bridges opened up new areas for development. Smaller towns adjacent to and often dependent on a major city had existed since colonial days, but now many more neighboring regions became accessible. Areas of new settlement included the Jersey shore across the Hudson River from Manhattan; Roxbury, Cambridge, and Charlestown near Boston; and land across the Schuylkill River at Philadelphia, across the Allegheny and Monongahela at Pittsburgh, the Cuyahoga at Cleveland, and the New Buffalo Creek at Buffalo. Populations in these suburban places doubled and tripled in a single decade. Regular steamboat ferry service between Brooklyn and New York City began in 1814, and by 1860, various East River ferries carried 33 million passengers per year. On the eve of the Civil War, Brooklyn contained more people than Boston and was the third most populous city in the country.

Many newly developed areas had their own economies and retained political independence, preferring only to purchase services such as water and gas from the nearby city. Settlements such as Boston's first suburbs were involved in a fringe economy that flourished between 1815 and 1840, housing those who raised and processed goods for city use, linking urban and rural economies by supplying milk and produce, and creating industries producing such urban necessities as bricks and glass. At the same time, the peripheral settlements gave big-city merchants opportunities to sell goods to new markets. Between 1845 and 1860, Boston's suburbs gained more than ten thousand commuters. These suburbanites would reshape the peripheral communities as domestic retreats for some of the wealthiest families to escape the crowded walking city, and to build homes, schools, and churches in more attractive surroundings.

SOCIAL COMPLEXITY AND CONTESTED TERRAIN

Migration, population increase, and economic change brought sweeping social changes to the walking city. Perhaps the most striking feature of the early nineteenth century was the diversity of peoples and fragmentation of earlier communal institutions that had at least partially bridged social divisions. Now, a greater complexity arose as new groups competed for jobs, housing, political inclusion and social recognition.

A free black community of institutional complexity was a particularly new feature of urban life. Before the Revolution, only a tiny fraction of the nation's African-American population had been free, consisting mainly of those who were either the product of mixed racial unions or former slaves who were too old to undertake productive work for their masters. But after the Revolution, a considerable number of slaves obtained freedom, in the North through statewide emancipation, and in the South through individual manumissions or successful illegal flight from bondage. Free African Americans moved to cities in large numbers, making cities centers of free African-American life. While the total free black population of Virginia more than doubled between 1790 and 1810, that of Richmond increased fourfold and that of Norfolk increased tenfold. By 1820, the nation's largest free African-American community lived in Baltimore, but Boston, New York, Philadelphia, Cincinnati, Charleston, New Orleans, and Mobile also had sizable free black populations. In New York City, the free black population swelled to 7,470 by 1810, as the city attracted freed slaves from the countryside and mulattoes fleeing Saint-Domingue after the successful slave-led Haitian Revolution. After 1810, slaves who were freed by the Gradual Manumission Act increased New York City's free African-American population even further.

Ex-slaves were drawn to cities because of opportunities for employment and because the concentration of free African Americans offered a greater chance to find an acceptable marriage partner, establish a family, and participate in activities of African churches, schools, fraternal societies, and benevolent organizations. In northern seaports, most free African-American men worked as laborers or mariners, but a few managed to work as artisans, particularly in trades identified with servile or

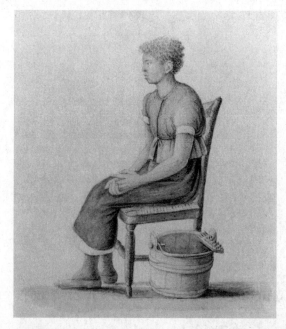

African-American Scrubwoman. In spite of their improved status over southern plantation slaves, urban slaves and free blacks normally held the lowest occupations. Domestic work was the most common form of job done by urban black women.

Source: Costume of a Scrubwoman, by Baroness Hyde de Neuville, watercolor and graphite on paper, $7^1/_2 \times 6^1/_2$", accession number 1953.251. Collection of the New York Historical Society.

dirty labor like barbering and butchering. In New York City, freed slaves were more than twice as likely to possess a skill than in Philadelphia, because white New York artisans had relied heavily on slave labor throughout the eighteenth century and because many of the city's mulatto émigrés from the South had skilled trades. A few freedmen were able to serve the urban black community as small proprietors, ministers, and teachers. In Charleston, free African-American men constituted 16 percent of the city's skilled male workforce and 11 percent of the unskilled male laboring population. In Richmond and Lynchburg, Virginia, free African-American men comprised nearly 30 percent of the unskilled male workforce.

In most cities, however, the majority of the free African-American population were women, who faced a much narrower range of occupational possibilities, working primarily as domestic servants, laundresses, produce sellers, and prostitutes. A few kept small shops and ran boardinghouses. In some places, such as Petersburg, Virginia, a few free black women worked as nurses, midwives, storekeepers, and bakers, and free women managed to accumulate half the property owned by African Americans in the city.

Although most free African Americans remained poor and propertyless, a group of black leaders emerged in Boston, Philadelphia, Baltimore, Richmond,

Mrs. Juliann Jane Tillman, Preacher.   Free African Americans in northern cities were able to form their own institutions and assume leadership positions within them. This lithograph depicts a female preacher in a Philadelphia African Methodist Episcopal Church in 1844.

Savannah, and Charleston. Wealthier and better educated than their rural counterparts, urban African-American leaders petitioned Congress and state legislatures to abolish slavery and grant full political rights to black citizens. They also established community institutions where African Americans could pray and educate their children. By 1800, African-American communities from Boston to Savannah supported their own churches, and in 1816, leading African-American churchmen from various parts of these regions joined to form the first independent black denomination, the African Methodist Episcopal Church.

From the beginning, African Americans gave their churches, schools, mutual assistance associations, and fraternal organizations names with African references, to signify their own group identity and to distinguish themselves from white society. In Philadelphia, the Angola Beneficial Society was established in 1808, the Africa Insurance Company in 1809, the Sons of Africa in 1810, and the African Female and Male Benevolent Societies in the following years. By the 1820s in Philadelphia, African Americans had created an institutional life that was richer and more stable than that of the lower-income whites with whom they shared neighborhoods. In a mixed uptown area in New York City, where small craft shops bordered on larger factories, a group of free blacks of modest means who had been able to purchase cheap house lots in the 1820s supported two black Methodist churches and a racially mixed Episcopal church, as well as a "Colored School," by the 1850s. In Boston, the African

Society, founded in 1797, established the African School in 1798 and the African Meeting House in 1805. Although slaves living in white households were scattered throughout a city, free African Americans moved away from prior masters to cluster in particular neighborhoods, nearby African churches and schools. In New York City, many African Americans occupied the most inexpensive cellar housing. Urban African-American self-expression and sociability could flourish in dance halls and neighborhoods where African Americans were concentrated.

As the free African-American urban population grew, so too did social conflict as white people used legislation to limit blacks' economic opportunities and to restrict their rights to vote and testify in court. But the dense network of urban black institutions and a rich community life made it more possible in cities than in the countryside for free African Americans to try to protect themselves and even sometimes to confront racism. This network provided a base for protest, supporting struggling black newspapers and sending delegates to black conventions to attack slavery and agitate for civil rights. Free blacks, particularly in cities, would play an active role during the Civil War and Reconstruction by asserting notions of black citizenship to include suffrage and by demanding that they themselves define the meaning of freedom.

Free blacks, however, remained a minority of the African American population in the South, even in most cities. In the antebellum years, slaves were an indispensable part of the workforce in southern cities. In Charleston, Richmond, and Lynchburg, slaves constituted from 50 to 60 percent of all workingmen; in Mobile, Baton Rouge, and Nashville, they constituted 25 to 35 percent of the adult male workforce. Nearly all slaves did manual labor of some sort, ranging from domestic duties to artisan trades and industrial labor. Throughout the urban South, white merchants, professionals, factory owners, and some governments remained the largest employers of slave labor, and for the most part, these employers required unskilled rather than skilled laborers.

By the 1850s, slave "hiring out," whereby masters rented slaves to other employers, was commonplace and profitable to both masters and slaves. It provided slave owners, particularly widowed women, a steady income, and it gave slaves experience with wage labor and the marketplace, a possibility of accumulating cash, and an added measure of control over their lives. Because their work required them to travel on city streets, urban slaves enjoyed greater mobility and cultural autonomy than did their rural counterparts. Bondsmen on plantations lived in the slave quarters and saw only their masters' families and occasionally slaves from a nearby plantation. City slaves partook of a wider world. They had access (even when it was illegal) to food, drink, entertainment, and the common sociability of urban life. They sometimes ran their own churches, and they often sneaked away to talk and drink with fellow slaves, free African Americans, and even working-class whites in back-alley groceries and grogshops scattered throughout every southern city. Preferring to avoid costs of housing their slaves, some masters gave their bondsmen permission to live out as well as work away. When slaves lived out, they often resided in rented rooms on the fringes of town where free blacks and poor whites also lived.

An underlying contradiction characterized urban slavery. The institution of slavery requires absolute control of bondsmen by masters, but it was impossible for urban slaveholders to supervise their slaves every minute—particularly slaves who hired out. In the fringe neighborhoods, a fugitive from a plantation might hide and purchase forged freedom papers. A Richmond newspaper complained in 1860 that "not only free Negroes but low white people can be found who will secret a slave from his master." Cities responded to this challenge with stringent restrictions on the activities of all black people, slave and free. These codes, enforced with increasing vigor after 1830, resulted in formal segregation—the exclusion of black people from most public accommodations. A variety of laws required people of color to have licenses for certain occupations and barred them from others, forbade them to assemble without a license, and prohibited them from being taught to read and write and from testifying in court against white people.

In addition, white employers reacted by hiring more unskilled white laborers and by selling slaves to the plantations. As a result, between 1830 and 1860, the number of slaves in the workforces of southern cities decreased relative to the numbers of immigrant laborers. In 1840, the total slave population of the ten largest southern cities was 67,755; in 1860, it was 68,013. Meanwhile, the total white population of the same cities rose from 233,000 to 690,000. Only in Richmond, where slave manpower was essential to iron and tobacco processing, did a large proportion of slaves still persist in 1860. In New Orleans, on the other hand, the number of slaves dropped from 23,000 in 1840 to 13,000 in 1860.

IMMIGRANTS

American cities since the beginning had been populated by immigrants. Immigrants from Britain continued to flow into American cities after Independence, and were joined in the 1830s, 1840s, and 1850s by a strong surge from Ireland and Germany. Many Europeans who had worked as tenant farmers found themselves displaced in the nineteenth century when landlords turned their lands toward more efficient commercial agriculture. Small landholders found it difficult to provide enough property for all their children, forcing younger sons to look elsewhere for work. Competition from machine-made goods threatened the livelihoods of craftsmen. In addition to these pressures, rural people in Ireland, Germany, and other parts of Europe suffered a severe blow from the mid-nineteenth-century potato blight. The Irish had grown especially dependent on potatoes, a crop that produced high yields from tiny plots of land. The potato blight that struck Ireland in 1845–1847 destroyed the food supply for countless families and hastened a rural exodus already created by landlords' mass evictions of tenants. During the Great Famine of the late 1840s and early 1850s, 1.7 million Irish fled to the United States, while others escaped to England, Scotland, and Canada. Many of those arriving in America were so poor that they had little choice but to remain in the port where they landed and to take whatever work they could find.

By the 1850s, more than half the residents of Boston and New York City were foreign born, and in Philadelphia 30 percent of household heads were born in Europe. Major concentrations of Irish immigrants could be found in New York, Boston, Philadelphia, and San Francisco, and strong German communities emerged in Cincinnati, Louisville, St. Louis, and Milwaukee. Southern cities in this era also received newcomers from abroad. By 1860, 40 percent of New Orleans's population was foreign born. Immigrant workers, mostly from Ireland and Germany, constituted more than half of Charleston's and Mobile's free adult workingmen's populations, and between 40 and 50 percent of free adult workingmen in Richmond, Nashville, and Baton Rouge.

Immigration had important effects on the economic life, housing and culture of cities. By driving down the price of labor, immigrants encouraged the growth of urban industry. Desperately poor arrivals from Ireland packed into the cheapest housing available. Landlords converted cramped attics and damp basements into apartments, and squeezed new buildings into rear lots. Immigrants brought with them new dialects, dress, social institutions, and culinary and drinking habits (wine and beer now competed with traditional American rum and whiskey). One of the most consequential of the new features was religion. Between 1840 and 1890, 7.5 million Irish and German immigrants arrived in America; of these, 5.5 million were Catholics who

Election Day in Philadelphia, 1816. Viewing the consumption of alcoholic drink destructive to the family and the home, this temperance society offered a pledge, here taken by a husband and wife, certifying that the couple was banishing "demon rum" from their household.

transformed the United States from a Protestant to a Protestant-Catholic nation. By 1870, 40 percent of all churchgoers in the country were Catholics. Irish and German Catholics formed their own parochial schools so that their children would not have to endure discrimination in the public schools.

In Northern cities, the huge new populations of European immigrants dwarfed the established communities of African Americans. Blacks made up a shrinking share of the urban population despite their steady increase in numbers. African Americans had constituted over 10 percent of the population in New York City in 1810; by 1860, they represented only 1.5 percent of all New Yorkers. In Philadelphia, more than 12 percent of the population was black in 1830; by 1860, that proportion had dropped to less than 4 percent. The black share of urban population would not return to early-nineteenth century levels in Philadelphia until the 1920s, and not until the 1940s in New York and Boston. (New Orleans, as always, was a distinct case; African Americans there made up 63 percent of the population in 1810 and 14 percent in 1860. New Orleans was a white-majority city from 1840 until the 1970s).[1]

New arrivals from Ireland were often unfamiliar with American racial prejudices. Being as poor as many African Americans, they initially were willing to work with them, socialize with them, live with them, and even intermarry. Some native-born Americans expressed equal contempt toward the Irish and the "smoked Irish" (blacks). Irish immigrants soon learned that in order to reap the benefits of a white skin in a racist society, they had to insist that they were superior to African Americans and entitled to better treatment. By the 1850s, Irish were forcing blacks out of many jobs by refusing to work alongside them. "Every hour sees us elbowed out of some employment to make room for some newly arrived emigrant from the Emerald Isle," complained the black abolitionist Frederick Douglass in 1853.[2]

Though they were often favored over African Americans, Irish immigrants remained the targets of hostility. Employers placed discriminatory job advertisements in newspapers, openly declaring that they did not want Irish or Catholic applicants. Tense competition for jobs and housing, combined with bigotry, led to the outbreak of bloody clashes. In 1834, Protestants burned and sacked an Ursuline convent near Boston. In 1844, Protestants and Irish Catholics fought in Philadelphia, and thirteen were killed; a mob destroyed an Irish neighborhood in Lawrence, Massachusetts, in 1854. Churches were burned in other cities. Germans, many of whom were also Catholic, were the targets of violence too. In 1855, twenty died in a battle between Germans and nativists in Louisville. Anti-Catholic nativists charged that Catholics' allegiance to the Pope make them unsuited for American citizenship. Nativists formed a secret society called the "Order of the Star Spangled Banner," ran candidates for office, and helped create a national political party, the American Party, in 1854. Nativist political goals included restrictions on citizenship and the passage of temperance laws aimed at suppressing German and Irish traditions of socializing in taverns. Nativists in Chicago attempted in 1855 to impose prohibitively high license fees on taverns, and force them to close on Sunday—workers' only day of leisure. The conflict exploded into a "lager beer riot," in which police opened fire on a German protest march.

Older non-English cultures persisted in American cities founded by the Dutch, French, and Spanish. The Dutch language continued to be heard in the streets, homes, and churches of New York well into the nineteenth century. French-speakers in New Orleans held themselves aloof from the English-speaking Americans who flooded into their city in the early 1800s. The expanding city was divided between a "French Quarter" and an "American Quarter," separated by a street with a broad median called the "neutral zone." Spanish and French traditions of carnival were celebrated in New Orleans, Mobile, and St. Augustine. Maskers, Harlequins, and Punchinellos paraded the streets with guitars, violins, and other instruments in the days before Lent. In St. Augustine, maskers on St. John's Eve marked the summer solstice with ritualized gender inversion, with paraders dressing up as highborn persons of the opposite sex. By the 1830s and 1840s, New Orleans revelers were throwing flour and pieces of brick as well as candies, cake, apples, and oranges to people along the parade route, and newspapers appealing to middle-class standards of civility were dismissing Mardi Gras celebrations as "vulgar and tasteless."

San Francisco had an unusually diverse population, with men drawn there from around the world during the Gold Rush. During the 1850s, a surge of gold-seeking Chinese immigrants crossed the Pacific to California, which they called "Jinshan," or "Gold Mountain." Some 20,000 arrived in 1852 alone. They were initially welcomed, and participated like other immigrant groups in civic events—"one of the most worthy classes of our newly adopted citizens," the governor called them in 1852. But by then the white miners in the gold fields had begun asking the state to protect them from competition by Chinese miners, or even to exclude them from California altogether. The state imposed a tax on "foreign" miners that encouraged many of the Chinese to leave the gold fields, which were becoming depleted anyway; some returned home, and others moved to towns and cities. During the 1860s, the Chinese population of San Francisco rose from 2,719 to 12,022. Chinese workers found jobs in woolen mills, shoe factories, cigar factories, and laundries.

ROOTLESS MEN AND WOMEN

Crowds of transient white men and women looking for work were also a new sight in early nineteenth-century American cities. In manufacturing cities like Lowell and Lynn, farm sons and daughters worked in new textile mills and shoemaking workshops. In commercial boom towns like Rochester, New York, predominantly male migrants were drawn from the countryside to work on canals and railroads. By the 1820s and 1830s, a rising percentage of the urban population were propertyless wage earners. Many were new unskilled laborers and factory hands, unaccustomed to the particular patterns of impersonal employment or the discipline of manufacturing work.

As working-class neighborhoods became distinct from middle-class areas, separate patterns of sociability heightened the sense of distance between classes. Unmarried employed men and women living outside of family households occupied rooms and lodging houses and participated in a working-class youth subculture that included new kinds of entertainment and relationships. As historian Christine Stansell has described New York City's Bowery, "At the end of the working day and on Saturday night, the dance halls, oyster houses, and the famed Bowery Theatre, built in 1827, came alive with workingwomen, journeymen, and laborers looking for marital prospects, sexual encounters, and general good times."[3] Variety shows offered skits, comedy, singing, and dancing; and theaters featured melodrama, burlesque, and blackface minstrelsy.

As unmarried men and women left the constraints of communities where they were known, they exchanged the haven of family and friends for the temptations and dangers of the city, including its vices and crimes. The lurid side of urban life was highlighted in 1836 when the reading public was transfixed by reports surrounding the shocking murder of Helen Jewett, a New England woman who had moved to New York City and become a highly paid prostitute. Evidence for the murder pointed to a young clerk, Richard Robinson, who had been one of Jewett's steadiest customers and ardent lovers. When Robinson was acquitted after a dramatic trial, his fellow bachelor clerks cheered him, but the incident prompted observers to fret over the vulnerability of unattached young people in the impersonal city.

URBAN POLITICS

This diversification of urban population occurred within the context of broadened suffrage for male citizens, circumstances that reshaped political life. After the Revolution, open competition for office increased, and the turnover of legislative representatives accelerated. Still, until the 1820s, and later in some states, property restrictions continued to disenfranchise many men. Even among those granted the ballot, political interest and electoral turnout usually remained low. Many citizens appeared to have retreated from the extraordinary political demands of the revolutionary period, instead deferring once again to the political leadership of the community's most distinguished men.

After 1820, the gradual abandonment of restrictions on white male suffrage in state after state coincided with a reemergence of citizen interest in politics, including at the local level. But citizens, fearing loss of local control over economic decisions, were deeply divided on the direction the economy ought to take and the role government should play. Commercial transformation and ethnic, religious, and class tensions helped to spark a process by which community factions were institutionalized in the form of political parties with socioeconomic identities. Entrepreneurs, usually Whigs, relished the possibilities of using government to tie localities to new markets and to expand commercial facilities such as docks, warehouses, and transportation. The rise of workingmen's parties, either separate workers' organizations or affiliations of the Democratic Party, in urban areas seemed to spring from a similar set of questions and unease about the direction of commercial capitalism. First Federalists and Republicans, then Whigs and Democrats created formal organizations at the town level. As early as 1810, political sectarianism was a durable feature of local politics, although especially in older settled towns, politics sometimes returned to a search for consensual, nonpartisan solutions to community questions.

The growth of local parties meant that political leadership by the community's social and economic chieftains was sometimes challenged by a new breed of professional politicians who assiduously courted newly enfranchised workingmen. Men from low-income groups were still rarely elected to city councils; elections at large provided a structure for those dominant in the community's social and economic life to dominate in its formal political life as well. But political competition often set members of the business elite against each other, and the increasing numbers of working-class voters could sometimes check the ability of elites to exercise political influence commensurate with their economic and social power.

Urban politics often reflected new urban diversity. No issue was as politically divisive in early nineteenth-century cities as temperance. Drinking had previously been assumed to be an inevitable aspect of an artisans' working day. According to historian Paul Johnson, "liquor was embedded in the patterns of irregular work and easy sociability sustained by the household economy," and public drinking traditions persisted in the interstices of the expanding commercial economy where these older economic forms persisted.[4] But in the minds of employers, new standards of discipline within large workshops and factories required abstinence from alcohol. Indeed, in Massachusetts the manufacturers who were most technologically innovative were also those who most enthusiastically supported temperance. For the new middle classes, sobriety became the key to economic efficiency, individual success, happy homes, and quiet streets. The baser passions, including drunkenness, were considered inimical to the new, more private home life, under the guidance of pious housewives. Factory owners were among the first to banish liquor from their workshops and from their own homes, and as they did so, nonuse or use of whiskey marked the dividing line between middle-class respectability and working-class sociability. Drinking became a means of resistance and a common prerogative of an autonomous working-class social life, even before Irish and German immigrants brought distinctive ethnic drinking traditions to American cities.

The first temperance reformers were wealthy Federalists, whose organizations hoped to encourage drinkers to imitate their betters in abstaining from alcohol. In the 1820s, the success of evangelical revivals inspired formation of middle-class temperance organizations that were as hostile to wealthy drinkers as to the poor, denouncing liquor retailers as trafficking in vice. In Rochester, hotel proprietors and tavern keepers whose livelihoods depended on working-class drinking reacted by letting their church memberships lapse. But those manufacturers, merchants, lawyers, shopkeepers, master artisans, and skilled journeymen whose lives were changed for the better by the commercial revolution became enthusiastic supporters of the revivals and temperance. Progressing from tactics of moral suasion and conversion to firings, boycotts, and political campaigns to outlaw drink, the evangelical reformers by the 1830s converted thousands to new ideas about temperance and respectability.

It was not until the 1840s, after severe economic collapse following the Panic of 1837, that a genuine working-class temperance movement, the Washington Society, arose. In Cincinnati, the Washingtonians drew men who had formerly resisted temperance into an altogether different style of temperance organization than those organized by evangelical Protestants. Noisily public and male-oriented rather than under the moral guardianship of women, Washingtonian societies recruited in streets and grogshops, gathered together supporters in picnics and parades rather than in prayer meetings, and dramatized alcohol's depths of degradation rather than the righteous fruits of abstinence. In Philadelphia in the 1840s, waves of revivalism

The Astor Place Riot.   On May 11, 1849, a serious riot and challenge to police authority occurred outside New York City's Astor Place Opera House when supporters of the popular American actor, Edwin Forrest stormed the theater where Forrest's rival British actor William Macready was performing. The violence, in which twenty-two people died and more than 150 were injured, reflected class and nationalistic conflict as well as the highly emotional following that entertainment "stars" collected.

Source: Collection of the New York Historical Society, 73259.

sparked a working-class temperance movement, attracting master craftsmen, journeymen, shopkeepers, and the most ambitious unskilled laborers to its membership.

In all cities a decision to abstain from alcohol was the key symbol of a new morality and a commitment to self-improvement. But in the 1840s, native-born evangelical workingmen measured their own sobriety and discipline against the unreconstructed drinking habits of laborers from expanding Irish and German immigrant neighborhoods. While the Whig party drew churchgoing merchants, professionals, and master workmen into a campaign for coercive temperance, nonevangelical Protestants, immigrant Catholic workingmen, and the petty retailers who served them found refuge in the antitemperance, anti-coercion stand of the Democratic Party. Native-born enthusiasm for temperance translated into passionate anti-Catholicism, sharply splitting the working class along ethnic lines and turning neighborhoods into battlegrounds. Incidents like the destruction of Irish weavers' looms and houses by native-born weavers in Philadelphia's Kensington in 1844, the fierce fighting between Philadelphia native-born and Irish fire companies in the 1830s and 1840s, the riot that ensued from a collision between a native-born fire company and an Irish funeral procession on Boston's Broad Street in 1837, and other anti-Catholic and anti-Irish riots in Baltimore, St. Louis, and Louisville that occurred in this period need to be understood in this context.

Abolition vied with temperance as an incendiary issue lying beneath the surface of political debate, fought out largely in extralegal battles in the 1830s. The political rhetoric of many northern workingmen increasingly featured claims to citizenship as free white men who stressed their distance from slavery as well as from free African Americans. Meanwhile, however, the campaign against slavery intensified. Between 1834 and 1835, the abolitionist organization, the American Anti-Slavery Society, became dramatically more visible. The number of local societies increased, and their constituency of women and free black people defied conventional notions of the exclusion of these groups from political participation. Using new penny postage and steam printing technology, abolitionists increased their distribution of antislavery propaganda, sending out millions of antislavery tracts, newspapers, children's readers, even medals, emblems, bandannas, and chocolate wrappers. But in local communities, "gentlemen of property and standing"—prominent lawyers, bankers, merchants, doctors, and political leaders of both the Democratic and Whig parties—acted to defend the status quo by mobilizing disruption of antislavery conventions, attacks on abolitionist leaders, and destruction of abolitionist meeting places and printing presses. In Utica in 1835, a Democrat congressman led a crowd that drove the New York Anti-Slavery Society out of town. Abolitionist leader William Lloyd Garrison was nearly lynched by a crowd of respectable Bostonians in 1835, and abolitionist Elijah Lovejoy was killed while trying to defend a printing press from a crowd of prominent citizens in Alton, Illinois, in 1837. In 1834, leading New Yorkers cheered a crowd of butcher boys and day laborers who smashed and burned the home of Lewis Tappan, a prominent and wealthy local supporter of antislavery.

In other incidents, crowds turned on free African-American communities. Here, rioters were often white workingmen who expressed their economic and social grievances through racial violence. In the summer of 1835, in Washington, D.C., an angry crowd of striking ship carpenters searched the homes of free African-Americans for abolitionist literature, destroyed a black-owned restaurant, and burned or stoned other free black businesses, schools, churches, and homes. The mobs of mechanics and artisans who terrorized free African-American communities in Cincinnati, Providence, and New York City in the 1830s and 1840s were not directly competing with blacks for jobs but were fighting for urban turf, especially in neighborhoods that bordered African-American neighborhoods.

Other confrontations too explosive to be calmed through established political channels took place on the streets of antebellum cities. When the Pennsylvania state legislature gave permission in 1839 for a railroad to extend track down the main street of Philadelphia's Kensington section, residents voiced fears that burning coal embers and fast-moving trains would endanger their shops, homes, and children. When petitions to the legislature proved futile, and railroad workmen began to tear up the street to build the railroad tracks, residents used the upturned paving stones as weapons to wage war on the proposed railroad. Two years of sporadic street battles and noisy public demonstrations finally resulted in the state legislature's acceding to neighborhood demands and revoking the railroad's right of way. Similarly, the limits of political action and legal recourse were tested in Baltimore in 1835, where citizens rioted when trustees and secret partners of the failed Bank of Maryland used various legal tricks for over a year to avoid settlement of the bank's affairs. The kinds of concerns that drew crowds into the streets could not be redressed through the ballot. The extraordinary pressures of diverse populations, new experience with heightened social and economic inequality, and fierce competition between groups contending for political power left the social and political terrain of antebellum cities deeply scarred and divided.

CITIES AND THE CIVIL WAR

The Civil War, like all wars, had a disruptive effect on American cities. Unlike the Revolution, when cities were relatively united in their support for independence from England, the Civil War provoked fierce conflicts within many cities. The issues of slavery and secession stirred local political debates, and the war itself pumped life into outfitting and manufacturing centers, particularly in the North. But the conflict also sparked social and economic conflicts that had been gathering long before the war began.

A characterization of a dichotomy between an urban-industrial North and a rural-plantation South before the war would exaggerate actual conditions. The North was still largely rural and only partially industrialized in the antebellum years; the economies of northern cities from Boston to Chicago remained guided by commercial functions. The South was neither nonurban nor antiurban. Southern cities such as Louisville, New Orleans, Memphis, Mobile, and Savannah resembled northern counterparts in their commercial functions and social complexity. Southern businesspeople did, however, depend on northern capital and markets. New York City especially influenced southern affairs. By the 1850s, New York merchants bought and shipped much of the South's cotton and tobacco, and they imported many of the goods demanded by southern consumers. Investments from New York bankers helped finance the Southern urban economy. In various Northern cities, businesspeople valued southern customers and worked to keep them satisfied.

Although southerners expressed resentment over northern merchants' alleged high prices and profits, urban dwellers of both regions generally took conciliatory positions toward each other, even as the debates that would ultimately provoke war heated up. In this regard, they differed considerably from rural dwellers in each region who were more easily drawn to the extreme positions of the sectional conflict. Commenting on political divisions in its region in 1860, the *New Orleans Delta* noted that "three-fourths of the planters are of one party, and an equal proportion of merchants are the opposite." And the *New York Herald* similarly observed, "While merchants in the [southern] cities desire peace and Union, the planters desire protection in the Union, or independence under their own self reliance out of it."

The balloting in the presidential election of 1860 revealed a moderate stance of cities in contrast to the radicalism of rural districts in both South and North. Generally, urban dwellers from both sections favored either the Democrat party candidate, Senator Stephen A. Douglas of Illinois, or the Constitutional Union Party candidate,

Senator John Bell of Tennessee, both of whom represented compromise, if not concili-
ation, in the sectional dispute over the extension of slavery. Meanwhile, Southern rural
voters strongly backed John C. Breckinridge of Kentucky, who had bolted from the
Democratic Party to run on a proslavery platform, and Northern rural voters favored
Abraham Lincoln, the Republican Party candidate, who spoke out against slavery and
for preservation of the Union. There were some notable exceptions to this pattern.
A few Northern cities, such as Pittsburgh and Chicago, strong centers of the fledgling
Republican Party, backed Lincoln. In the South, leaders in Charleston and Savannah
backed Breckinridge and secession in hopes of finding in a separate Southern confederacy independence from New York and the economic health they had lost to competition from Mobile and New Orleans. But generally, the votes cast by urban dwellers in
the election implied a preference for moderation.

The war itself had varying effects on cities. In some, such as Philadelphia,
relative unity prevailed. Industries there prospered by providing war matériel, and
workers' wage increases enabled them to keep pace with inflation. Philadelphia residents responded relatively calmly to federal government quotas requiring that the
city furnish a certain number of recruits for the Union Army, and a strong police
force deterred potential social upheaval. Other Northern cities experienced turmoil,

Richmond After the Civil War.   Southern cities suffered extensive damage from Union
troops during the Civil War. Richmond, Virginia, the Confederate capital, was particularly
hard hit, along with those cities, such as Atlanta, that were burned by General William
T. Sherman's destructive sweep through the South near the end of the war.

particularly New York. Once Southern states began seceding after Lincoln's election, Democratic Mayor Fernando Wood proposed that New York City should become an independent, neutral nation that could trade with both sides. The idea went nowhere, but the war remained a divisive issue in New York. For four days in July 1863, a bloody riot raged in the streets in opposition to the military draft. By the time order was restored, more than 100 people were dead, making it one of the bloodiest urban uprisings in U.S. history. It had several causes: labor unrest, an unfair draft law, class and ethnic tensions, and growing violence of street gangs. It was also a race riot, involving attacks on African Americans and wealthy Republicans by white laborers, many of them Irish immigrants, who feared that antislavery Republicans would encourage freed blacks to come North to fill the jobs vacated by men who had been drafted into the Union Army.

The crises of the Civil War fell particularly heavily on Southern cities. Preparing for and carrying out the military effort speeded Southern urbanization. For example, the establishment and expansion of the Confederate government's bureaucracy helped to triple the population of Richmond. But the Union Army's blockade of Southern ports, the breakdown of the Southern transportation system as a result of military activity, and wartime inflation exacerbated patterns of urban hardship, especially food shortages, which in some places reached starvation levels. In 1863, food riots broke out in cities across the South, including Atlanta and Richmond. In the latter city, crowds, mostly composed of women, broke into bakeries in search of bread. By the end of the war, both Atlanta and Richmond lay in smoldering ruins, victims of the Union Army's invasions.

The war also had profound effect on Midwestern cities, where urban expansion not only influenced the war's outcome but also hastened the rearrangement of trade routes. Before the war began in 1861, Chicago's growing rail network had already allowed it to cut into St. Louis's commercial hinterland. An increasing share of the Midwest's trade headed east by rail through Chicago rather than south by the Mississippi River through St. Louis. When hostilities broke out, the Union Army closed the lower Mississippi River to commercial traffic and imposed strict surveillance over all goods shipped out of St. Louis, even those headed northward. These conditions paralyzed St. Louis' business and redirected commerce to Chicago. By the time St. Louis recovered after the war, Chicago had surpassed it to become the principal commercial metropolis of the nation's heartland.

Bibliography

For a discussion of the form of early urban and suburban communities, see Henry Binford, *The First Suburbs: Residential Communities on the Boston Periphery, 1815–1860* (1985); Kenneth T. Jackson, *Crabgrass Frontier: The Suburbanization of the United States* (1985); and Sam Bass Warner, Jr., *The Urban Wilderness: A History of the American City* (1972).

On African Americans in cities before the Civil War, see Leonard P. Curry, *The Free Black in Urban America: The Shadow of a Dream* (1986); Leroy Graham, *Baltimore: The Nineteenth Century Black Capital* (1982); Arnold R. Hirsch and Joseph Logsden, eds., *Creole New Orleans: Race and Americanization* (1992); James Oliver Horton and

Lois E. Horton, *In Hope of Liberty: Culture, Community and Protest Among Northern Blacks, 1700–1860* (1997); Gary B. Nash, *Forging Freedom: The Formation of Philadelphia's Black Community, 1720–1840* (1988); John Wood Sweet, *Bodies Politic: Negotiating Race in the American North, 1730–1830* (2002); and Shane White, *Somewhat More Independent: The End of Slavery in New York City, 1770–1810* (1991).

On antebellum immigrants, see Kathleen Neils Conzen, *Immigrant Milwaukee: 1836–1860* (1976); Hasia Diner, *Erin's Daughters in America: Irish Immigrant Women in the Nineteenth Century* (1983); Jay P. Dolan, *The Immigrant Church: New York's Irish and German Catholics, 1815–1865* (1975); David Gerber, *The Making of American Pluralism: Buffalo, New York, 1825–1860* (1989); and Oscar Handlin, *Boston's Immigrants: A Study in Acculturation*, rev. ed. (1959).

On disorder and social reform in Jacksonian cities, see Jeffrey S. Adler, "Streetwalkers, Degraded Outcasts, and Good-for-Nothing Huzzies: Women and the Dangerous Class in Antebellum St. Louis," *Journal of Social History* 25 (Summer 1992), 373–55; Jed Dannenbaum, *Drink and Disorder: Temperance Reform in Cincinnati from the Washingtonian Revival to the WCTU* (1984); Michael Feldberg, *The Turbulent Era: Riot and Disorder in Jacksonian America* (1980); Feldberg, *The Philadelphia Riots of 1844: A Study of Ethnic Conflict* (1975); Timothy J. Gilfoyle, *City of Eros: New York City, Prostitution, and the Commercialization of Sex, 1820–1920* (1992); Paul Gilje, *The Road to Mobocracy: Popular Disorder in New York City, 1763–1834* (1987); Robert C. Harpel, *Temperance and Prohibition in Massachusetts, 1813–1852* (1982); and Jama Lazarow, *Religion and the Working Class in Antebellum America* (1995).

For works linking the development of egalitarian democracy and racialized white consciousness, see David R. Roediger, *The Wages of Whiteness: Race and Making of the American Working Class* (1991); and Alexander Saxton, *The Rise and Fall of the White Republic: Class Politics and Mass Culture in Nineteenth Century America* (1990).

Political and cultural uses of public space are discussed in Susan G. Davis, *Parades and Power: Street Theater in Nineteenth-Century Philadelphia* (1986); David Henkin, *City Reading: Written Words and Public Spaces in Antebellum New York* (1998); Mary Ryan, *Civic Wars: Democracy and Public Life in the American City During the Nineteenth Century* (1997); and David Waldstreicher, *In the Midst of Perpetual Fetes: The Making of American Nationalism, 1776–1820* (1997).

For works on cities and the Civil War, see Iver Bernstein, *The New York City Draft Riots: Their Significance for American Society and Politics in the Age of the Civil War* (1990); J. Matthew Gallman, *Mastering Wartime: A Social History of Philadelphia During the Civil War* (1990); and Ernest A. McKay, *The Civil War in New York City* (1990).

Notes

1. Campbell Gibson and Kay Jung, "Historical Census Statistics on Population Totals by Race, 1790 to 1990, and by Hispanic Origin, 1970 to 1990, for Large Cities and Other Urban Places in the United States," Population Division Working Paper no. 76, U.S. Census Bureau, Feb. 2005 (http://www.census.gov/population/www/documentation/twps0076/twps0076.html).
2. Quoted in Noel Ignatiev, *How the Irish Became White* (New York: Routledge, 1995), 111.
3. Christine Stansell, *City of Women: The Female Laboring Poor in New York City, 1790–1860* (New York: Knopf, 1986), 89.
4. Paul Johnson, *A Shopkeeper's Millenium: Society and Revivals in Rochester, New York, 1815–1837* (New York: Hill and Wang, 1978), 56–57.

CHAPTER 4

Industrialization and the Changing Shape of the City, 1865–1920

The building of railroads and canals, the increased use of waterpower and steam engines, and the introduction of the factory system in the North laid the foundation for the explosive urban industrial growth of the late nineteenth and early twentieth centuries. During the half century after the Civil War, transcontinental railroads created a much larger national market for goods and services, and new technology radically altered production, business, employment, and living styles. The giant industrial centers that developed during this period—notably Chicago, Pittsburgh and Detroit— were shockingly different from anything the nation had ever seen. Previously, small factories were clustered along rivers or scattered among the mix of houses and businesses that characterized the walking city. Small towns and cities dominated by industry, such as Lowell, Massachusetts, had nestled in otherwise rural valleys; mill workers could enjoy Sunday strolls into the surrounding countryside. But now, vast industrial complexes began to dominate much of the urban landscape, and the city sprawled out for miles. Travelers approaching an industrial metropolis by rail could see the ominous cloud of smoke on the horizon long before the first buildings came into view. Horrified observers suggested that there was nothing natural or of human scale about such places. A visitor to Pittsburgh in the 1880s compared it to Hell:

> "By all means make your first approach to Pittsburg in the night time, and you will behold a spectacle which has not a parallel on this continent. . . . Around the city's edge, and on the sides of the hills which encircle it like a gloomy amphitheatre . . . fiery lights stream forth, looking angrily and fiercely up toward the heavens, while over all these settles a heavy pall of smoke. It is as though one had reached the outer edge of the infernal regions, and saw before him the great furnace of Pandemonium with all the lids lifted."[1]

The Industrialized New South.   In the closing decades of the nineteenth century, southern cities became the sites for important industrial development. One of the principal industries was steel making, and Birmingham, Alabama, became the southern center for the manufacture of this vital product.

But millions of people made their homes in industrial cities and found ways to make them manageable, even pleasant. The very fact that cities drew huge numbers of newcomers hints at their appeal. People found the city not to be a dehumanizing industrial terror, but a place with an understandable structure, where a transit system linked residential neighborhoods to workplaces and commercial districts. They enjoyed urban attractions unavailable in the countryside or even in older walking cities: new public parks where they could relax amid natural scenery; brightly-lit downtowns where department stores displayed a tempting array of consumer goods; libraries, theaters, dance halls, and brothels to suit every taste for amusement. People with a bit of money—middle-class and even some working-class people—could afford to live in homes with yards and still travel into the denser parts of town on the streetcar. Industrialization and mass transportation together helped create a new urban form distinct from the old walking city, and a way of life radically different from that of the countryside.

THE QUICKENING PACE OF INDUSTRIALIZATION

All western cities and most eastern ones were founded on a speculative and commercial base. Their commercial functions—attracting and distributing raw materials, wholesaling and retailing goods and services—remained integral to their industrial development and their economic viability because they created capital for investment and generated a multiplier effect of spiraling growth. In the century's closing decades, manufacturing provided the major impetus to urban growth, but still no city could exist without its commerce.

Railroads were essential to both commercial and industrial growth. In the South, an expansion of the region's previously underdeveloped railroad system fostered wider commercial and industrial possibilities in cities such as Memphis and Nashville, and the development of a more complex industrial base in cities such as Atlanta and Birmingham. Southern boosters of industrialization envisioned a "New South," with textile factories, steel mills, and tobacco and lumber processing plants. The vision of the New South proponents did not fully materialize; the fruits of industrialization flowed disproportionately to northern investors, and low wages barely provided subsistence to southern families dependent on factory work. Tensions related to the expansion of the factory system, the racial segregation of factory employment, and the new economic and social power of industrialists would only increase in years to come.

Four transcontinental railroads pushed westward to the Pacific in the 1860s and 1870s, triggering urban growth along their routes. The railroads helped to complete the national urban network whose framework was laid in the first half of the century. Between 1860 and 1910, the number of cities with populations over 100,000 swelled from 9 to 50; the number with 25,000 to 100,000 grew from 26 to 178; and those with 10,000 to 25,000 increased from 58 to 369. A list of prominent new cities boosted by the railroads contains nearly the entire urban West: Albuquerque, Butte, Cheyenne, Dallas, El Paso, Fort Worth, Kansas City, Los Angeles, Minneapolis, Oklahoma City, Omaha, Portland, Reno, St. Paul, Salt Lake City, San Antonio, San Diego, San Francisco, Santa Fe, Seattle, Spokane, and Tacoma.

These western cities assumed particular regional characteristics. Desert cities like Albuquerque, El Paso, Phoenix, and Tucson stagnated until the coming of the railroad transformed them into focal points for surrounding farms, ranches, and mines. Extension of the railroad to Albuquerque created two towns: a boomtown of saloons and gambling halls that grew up around the railroad and the original part of Albuquerque, which became known as Old Town. The coming of four railroad connections to El Paso dramatically expanded its population from less than one thousand to more than ten thousand from 1880 to 1890. Once a sleepy village by the Rio Grande, El Paso soon boasted such urban amenities as gas lighting, electricity, telephones, streetcars, fire companies, police, churches, and schools. In places like Los Angeles, San Diego, and Santa Barbara the dramatic growth of the Anglo population began a process that shifted the local economy, lowering the status of Chicanos, residentially segregating them in barrios, and reconstituting them as an unskilled and semiskilled working class.

Most of the towns that railroads helped boost to cities had been centers of commerce before any track had been laid. Omaha, for example, was an important outfitting center for settlers crossing the Missouri River, and Seattle served as a lumber port and intermediary transfer point between San Francisco and northwestern Canada. These places became obvious locations for terminals once the railroads began construction, and the iron horse turned them into boom towns. Competition for railroad connections amplified the urban imperialism that was so characteristic of American economic expansion. Omahans subscribed money to build a railroad bridge across the Missouri River; leaders of Kansas City offered railroads generous subsidies and land grants; and citizens of Seattle laid their own stretch of track—all to lure railroads to their front doors. Cities, therefore, built railroads as much as railroads built cities.

Meanwhile, other technological changes were enabling new methods of industrial production. During the 1860s, French and American inventors developed methods of mass-producing high-quality steel, thereby providing the basic staple of industry. Over the next generation technicians harnessed electrical energy to power huge machines or to light streets and buildings. At the same time, the refinement of petroleum, the production of high explosives, and the creation of alloys such as aluminum opened new possibilities for manufacturing. Inspired by these successes, would-be inventors deluged the U.S. Patent Office with ideas, academic institutions expanded programs for training scientists and engineers, and large businesses established their own laboratories. The demands for capital made by expanding industry encouraged widespread adoption of corporate organization with limited stockholder liability for company debts and bureaucratic management of operations. Increased scales of production, use of more power machinery, and adoption of interchangeable parts as a means of standardizing products paved the way for assembly-line manufacturing. Industrial growth needed unskilled workers to run the machines, skilled repairmen to fix breakdowns, foremen to oversee the workers, and clerks and managers to staff the offices. These developments created employment opportunities that attracted immigrants to America and prompted migration from one place to another inside the country's borders (see Chapter 5).

As places that centralized resources, labor, transportation, and communications, cities became the chief arenas of industrial growth. By the end of the nineteenth century, urban factories were responsible for nine-tenths of America's industrial output. The types of industrial cities responsible for this production were quite varied. Some utilized unskilled immigrant labor and new techniques of production to furnish

Northern Industry. This photograph depicts silk warping and skein winding to spools at the Royal Weaving Company in Pawtucket, Rhode Island, about 1910. Machines and female operatives extend almost endlessly into the background, showing how an economy of scale permeated the textile industry.

goods for mass consumption. Thus the shoe industry became prominent in Rochester and Philadelphia, the clothing industry in New York, and textile manufacture in Lawrence, Lowell, and Fall River. Other cities processed products of their agricultural hinterlands: flour in Minneapolis; cottonseed oil in Memphis; meat in Omaha; beer in Milwaukee. Others grew by extracting and utilizing other nearby resources: minerals in Denver; fish and lumber in Portland and Seattle; coal and iron in Cleveland, Pittsburgh, and Birmingham; oil in Dallas, Houston, Los Angeles, and Oklahoma City. And various cities specialized in products for the modern age: Detroit's automobiles, Akron's tires, and Dayton's cash registers.

Much of this production came at an environmental cost. Railroads and most factories were fueled from the burning of soft, bituminous coal that caused choking pollution. Skies over cities such as Pittsburgh and St. Louis were darkened by smoke that coated clothing, furniture, and statues with inky dust. Sometimes the ground-level smog was so dense that the streetlights were lit during the daytime. By 1900, doctors reported a link between coal smoke and respiratory diseases such as bronchitis and pneumonia. Chicago and a few other cities passed antismoke legislation and hired smoke inspectors, but courts often declared such laws unconstitutional. San Francisco burned natural gas as a fuel, which was cleaner, and New York City tried to ban use of bituminous coal, but most cities could do little, especially since electric plants, as well as factories, burned coal to produce energy. Pittsburgh had a tantalizing few years of relatively clean skies from 1884 to 1892, thanks to natural gas, but then coal smog returned when the gas supply was exhausted.

Urbanization and industrialization were not the same process. Cities had grown long before modern manufacturing was possible, and factories could and did develop outside of urban areas. But after the Civil War, the twin forces of urbanization and industrialization fed upon each other. Together they sparked unprecedented economic change and freed the United States from reliance on European products and capital. Imports and foreign investments still flowed into the country, but, increasingly, cities and their factories transformed the United States from an agricultural, debtor nation into a manufacturing and financial power.

THE GROWTH OF MASS TRANSIT

Before the emergence of mass transportation, only the wealthy could enjoy the habit of riding passenger vehicles through city streets. Keeping a horse and carriage was prohibitively expensive for most city people, and few could afford to hire a hackney (an early horse-drawn taxi) except on special occasions. Other than cartmen and farmers driving wagons into town, ordinary people walked everywhere. The introduction of new forms of urban transportation in the mid-nineteenth century let a much broader range of people take up the habit of riding, and thus it enabled the urban area to expand outward beyond "walking distance." The ensuing effects on urban geography were profound.

The earliest form of mass transportation was an ungainly vehicle that appeared incapable of launching revolutionary changes of any sort. This was the omnibus, a large, horse-drawn coach that carried passengers on a fixed route for a fixed price. It combined the functions of two traditional types of public transportation: the hackney, which carried urban passengers wherever they wished; and the stagecoach, which operated over long-distance routes at scheduled times. The idea originated in France and first appeared in the United States in 1827 when Abraham Brower ran a stagecoach up and down Broadway in downtown Manhattan, picking up and discharging passengers at their request for a fee of one shilling (twelve and a half cents) per ride. The scheme spread quickly as other entrepreneurs adopted it. By 1833, some eighty omnibuses operated on the streets of New York, and by the middle of the decade similar transportation companies had appeared in Boston, Philadelphia, New Orleans, Washington, D.C., and Brooklyn.

Most omnibuses were owned by individuals whose main objective was to make as much money as they could rather than provide a public service. Thus they ran their vehicles only on streets that promised the most riders. Almost all stretched their routes between two important centers of activity, usually a wharf, railroad depot, or suburb at one end and a focal point of the business district at the other. By midcentury the omnibus had become essential for travel in many cities. New York City alone granted licenses to 108 omnibuses in 1837, 260 in 1847, and 683 in 1853. One observer claimed that one coach coming from each direction crossed a particular intersection on lower Broadway every fifteen seconds. In busy areas coach traffic clogged thoroughfares and endangered human safety. Despite efforts by municipalities to force omnibus companies to operate more responsibly, citizens complained that drivers intentionally ran down pedestrians and private carriages. The situation for passengers was not much better. An omnibus drawn by two horses normally seated twelve people, but drivers would not hesitate to pack several more riders inside. The seats were usually hard benches, uncomfortable to sit on as the omnibuses jolted and bounced along cobbled streets. There was never enough ventilation in summer and always too much in winter. Such inconvenience did not discourage people from riding, however. An 1853 New York guidebook advertised that some 120,000 passengers rode the city's omnibuses daily.

Those riders were mainly from the middle and upper classes. Fares on most omnibus lines ranged from six to twelve and a half cents per ride, outside the price range of ordinary workers at a time when many received only a dollar or two a day. Still, the omnibus made wheeled transportation available to more people than did hackneys and carriages, and it carried riders on a reasonably predictable schedule. It facilitated intracity communications in an age when economic specialization was making such communications increasingly necessary. Probably most important, the omnibus created true commuters—enabling the affluent to escape the crowded walking city and live in outlying regions.

The commuter railroad, even more than the omnibus, was a convenience for the wealthy. Short-distance commuter service began almost as an afterthought on steam railroads intended to carry freight and passengers over long distances. By midcentury nearly all trains leaving Boston made stops within fifteen miles of the city, and railroads based in New York and Philadelphia ran several trains daily to and from nearby towns. Over the next decade such service spread into the Midwest. A person living outside the city could now take the train into town and then ride an omnibus to his or her ultimate destination. A one-way train ticket cost fifteen to twenty-five cents, far too high for most working people. But, like the omnibus, the commuter railroad opened outlying areas for settlement. In 1854, for example, the Chicago and Milwaukee Railroad (later renamed the Chicago and Northwestern) built a depot in Evanston, Illinois, and helped populate that Chicago suburb. By 1859, forty trains ran daily between Philadelphia and nearby Germantown, and almost all their passengers were commuters.

The New York and Harlem Railroad pioneered the next major development in urban mass transportation when, in 1832, it combined technologies of the omnibus and the railroad. By running horse-drawn coaches over rails instead of cobblestones, the company could offer faster, smoother rides and enable the horses to pull larger, heavier cars. Over the next two years the New York and Harlem laid four miles of track in Manhattan and began operating the first street railway. By 1860, street-railway (or "horse railway") companies were operating in at least eight other major cities, and there were 142 miles of track in New York and 155 in Philadelphia. The cars held two or three times as many passengers as omnibuses and could travel faster, while utilizing the same number of horses. In addition, because horsecars moved on rails only down the middle of the street, they interfered less with other traffic than did omnibuses.

Mass transit now followed completely fixed routes and predictable schedules. This certainty, combined with the emphasis on punctuality produced by industrialization, encouraged people to live more regimented lives: daily routines came to be dictated by transit schedules and working hours. The successive improvements in transportation technology made urban travel faster, more comfortable, more reliable and—above all—cheaper.

The years in which transit became more affordable coincided with the renegotiation of racial boundaries. After the Civil War, streetcars were increasingly vital as a means of getting to and from employment in a city that had exceeded its walking boundaries, and they were symbolically important as a kind of contested public space. In several cities, African Americans campaigned for open access to streetcars. In New Orleans, African Americans rejected the all-black "star" cars the streetcar companies offered them in the 1860s, arguing that exclusion from "white" cars was inconvenient, a reminder of slavery, a public insult, and a mark of racial inferiority. They expressed their opposition by petitioning government officials, by boarding white cars and refusing to leave, and on occasion by stopping white cars and beating up the drivers. They were encouraged in their struggle by news of successful campaigns to integrate streetcars in San Francisco, Mobile, and Philadelphia. The widow of an African-American sergeant in the Union army was successful in her lawsuit to integrate streetcars in New York City in 1864.

When southern cities established Jim Crow laws that formally segregated African Americans at the end of the nineteenth century, protests over streetcar discrimination continued. In 1904, African Americans in Vicksburg, Jackson, and Natchez, Mississippi, launched a boycott of streetcars to protest a new law requiring segregated trolleys. Between 1900 and 1906, African Americans in twenty-five cities from former Confederate states engaged in various direct action campaigns against streetcar segregation. Although these campaigns were only intermittently successful, the demand for access to public transportation would continue to resurface whenever political and social change opened up new potential for success.

As transit companies expanded, the issue of control became more pressing. Early omnibuses had evoked few public regulations. Local governments established little more than licensing taxes, vehicle inspection, and speeding restrictions. But the laying of track and capitalization of horse-railway companies complicated relations between mass-transit companies and public authority. Incorporation of a company required a charter from the state, and construction of tracks on city streets necessitated permission from the local government. Beginning in the 1850s, such permission was usually obtained in the form of a franchise that enabled a company to operate over a specific route for a limited, though renewable period. Most early franchises granted monopolistic or semimonopolistic privileges, often for terms of fifty to one hundred years. Although contracts generally set maximum fares, usually five cents, the privilege of an exclusive franchise, plus almost certain population growth—and therefore increasing numbers of passengers—assured high profits.

With several street-railway and omnibus companies contesting for such grants, mass transportation inevitably became involved in local politics. Besides mass transit, utilities such as street lighting and water were provided by private companies that also sought franchises. Some local officials were so intent upon securing these services for their community that they paid little heed to the consequences of generous franchises. In their anxiety, they gave transit and utilities companies long-term, exclusive contracts that included low tax rates on their property and revenues, no responsibility to repair torn-up streets, and other advantages. Often, they provided these favors in return for bribes, kickbacks, and illegal stock transfers.

Perhaps the most important breakthrough in urban mass transportation occurred in the last quarter of the nineteenth century when innovators applied mechanical power to vehicles, beginning with the cable car. Cleaner and faster than horses, the cable car was introduced in San Francisco by Andrew Hallidie in 1873. Hallidie, a wire manufacturer, had witnessed English miners hauling coal cars along large cables, and he decided to try the idea on San Francisco's steep hills, where horsecars could not operate. His system utilized a continuously moving, underground wire rope driven by a steam engine, somewhat like the chair-lift cables at modern ski resorts. Each cable car ran along a track and moved by means of a clamp that extended through a slot in the pavement and attached to the cable. Brakes, similar to those on horsecars, could halt the vehicle after the operator released the grip from the cable.

Although the cable car has persisted as a historic relic in San Francisco, its widest use was in Chicago. Here cable car lines spread rapidly in the 1880s, particularly to the city's South Side, and by 1894 Chicago had 86 miles of cable track and 1,500 grip and trailer cars. Initial costs of construction and equipment were very high, but cable cars were more economical to operate than horsecars, mainly because horses required higher maintenance costs. Cable cars had their drawbacks, however. A break in the cable halted all traffic, the intricate mechanical equipment suffered frequent breakdowns, and operating a car required considerable skill. Nevertheless cable lines existed for varying periods of time in Washington, D.C., Baltimore,

Philadelphia, New York, Providence, Cleveland, St. Louis, Kansas City, Omaha, Denver, Oakland, and Seattle.

The cable car era lasted less than two decades. By the beginning of the twentieth century, electric trolleys had almost completely replaced horse railways and cable cars as the major mode of urban transportation. Since the 1830s, inventors in Europe and America had been experimenting with electricity to power vehicles, but it was not until 1886 that a major breakthrough occurred that revolutionized urban mass transit. The previous year James Gaboury, a leading promoter of mass transit in the South, had hired Charles J. Van Doeple, a Belgian engineer, to construct an electric railway in Montgomery, Alabama. Service began in the spring of 1886. The vehicles resembled those pulled by horses but contained a motor on the front platform. A chain running from the motor to the wheels powered the vehicle, and a cable from an overhead wire to the motor transmitted electrical energy. During the same time a young electrician, Frank Sprague, built a similar system in Richmond, Virginia. Its vehicles received electricity from a cable attached to a wheeled device that ran along the overhead wires. This device was called a troller due to the manner in which it was pulled, and a corruption of the word produced "trolley," the term used for electric streetcars. In 1888, Sprague demonstrated that his cars could conquer the steep grades of Richmond and that electrical generators could provide enough power to operate several cars concentrated on a short stretch of track.

During the 1880s and 1890s, nearly every large American city granted franchises to trolley companies. In 1890, when the federal government first surveyed the nation's street railways, it found 5,700 miles of track for vehicles operated by animal power, 500 miles of track for cable cars, and 1,260 miles of electrified track. By 1902, the total of electrified track had swelled to 22,000 miles, while that of horse railways had dwindled to 250 miles.

At the turn of the century, companies in some of the largest, most congested cities raised part of their track onto stilts, giving vehicles unrestricted right of way and freeing them from the interference of pedestrians and animal-powered vehicles. These were the electric elevated railways—the els—and they became prominent in New York, Chicago, Boston, Philadelphia, Brooklyn, and Kansas City. Although New York had had a successful steam-powered elevated since the 1870s, the noise, dirt, and danger to traffic below made other cities unwilling to risk an el. Thus it appeared in only a few places, even after Frank Sprague designed a mechanism that enabled els to be electrified.

Subways were a much more expensive way to separate mass transportation from street traffic, and they developed in only a few of the largest cities. The subway originated in London in the 1860s when coal-burning locomotives began pulling mass-transit cars through tunnels beneath the city. Promoters presented the idea to American cities, particularly New York, but fears of smoke and tunnel cave-ins, plus heavy opposition from street-railway companies, thwarted construction. Electrification removed some of the objections, and in Boston Henry M. Whitney, who had consolidated most of the city's transit lines under his ownership, obtained permission to construct a subway one and two-thirds miles in length underneath Tremont Street. In 1897, its first year of operation, the service handled more than fifty million passengers,

Trolley Cars in Chicago Suburb. Trolley lines pulled residential areas outward from the city center to the periphery, giving women and men of the middle class new forms of commuting transportation and, as this photograph of suburban Chicago shows, a means to avoid muddy streets.

running as many as four hundred cars in each direction at peak periods and still reducing travel time through the downtown area. This success revived interest in building subways in New York, and in 1904 that city's first subway opened. The extraordinary costs of subway construction limited expansion, however. With the exception of a combined el-subway that appeared in Philadelphia in 1908, no additional underground projects occurred until the 1930s, when one began in Chicago.

At first omnibus and street-railway companies made huge profits from a population anxious to cut down travel time—or at least to travel farther in the same amount of time. There were other beneficiaries too. Land values along streetcar lines soared, and real estate developers scrambled to buy up property on projected routes. The screeching wheels and unnerving vibration of els eventually drove the wealthy classes away, but land adjacent to elevated track remained lucrative for tenement and commercial investment. Because elevateds, subways, and street railways required heavy outlays of capital, mass transportation in many cities quickly became the domain of just one or two large-scale operations. Colorful personalities such as Henry M. Whitney of Boston and Charles Tyson Yerkes of Chicago deftly and ruthlessly established citywide systems and huge personal fortunes.

Systems such as those of Whitney and Yerkes brought several benefits to their riders. The increased scale of operations enabled companies to preserve the five-cent fare, and the constant quest for new riders pushed track into new districts. The merger of several lines produced free transfers from one route to another, enabling passengers to travel farther for a single fare. Yet the powerful companies that controlled mass transportation found it difficult to balance profit-making with public service. The limits of a five-cent fare—whether self-imposed or legislated by government—forced companies to seek higher revenues by increasing their ridership, a difficult goal to accomplish. There was a limit to how many more passengers could be crammed into each trolley car, but adding cars was expensive. Extending track into new districts was also costly, and the increase in ridership was uncertain. If companies restricted operations to densely settled areas, they faced public charges of inadequate and discriminatory service.

Transit companies often cited financial problems as an excuse for failure to improve service. Moreover, when reform-minded citizens sought to regulate public transportation, they were frustrated by the corrupt alliance between transit interests and local politicians. Indignation at this unsavory collusion prompted reformers to seek municipal ownership of mass transit. New York in the early 1890s and Chicago in 1907 established municipal authorities to build or buy public transit systems. As scores of companies went bankrupt during and after World War I, public ownership became the only way that many cities could sustain mass transit. By then, private automobiles were beginning to replace streetcars as the major mode of transportation, but the omnibus and its descendants had made a lasting imprint on urban life.

THE GEOGRAPHY OF THE STREETCAR CITY

Mass transit transformed the shape of the city, stimulating both outward sprawl and greater specialization of land use. Sidney George Fisher, an affluent resident of suburban Philadelphia, observed in 1859 that streetcars "offer great facilities in traversing the city, now grown so large that the distances are very considerable from place to place." The street railways made it so convenient for people to commute to and from the outskirts of Philadelphia that Fisher predicted they would "spread the city over a vast space, with all the advantages of compactness and advantages, moreover, of pure air, gardens and rural pleasures. Before long . . . cities will be mere collections of shops, warehouses, factories and places of business."[2]

Horse railways did indeed spread people into outlying areas—as did omnibuses, commuter trains, and electric trolleys. Boston's outskirts in 1850 lay scarcely two miles from the old business district; by 1900 the developed area extended ten miles. But outward expansion proceeded unevenly. In St. Louis, for example, mass transit stretched the built-up area far to the northwest, but land to the southwest remained underdeveloped because it lacked transit service. The cost of building and maintaining a streetcar line was far greater than the cost of running an omnibus, so transit owners built track only where it appeared settlement would be most dense. When builders constructed housing within walking distance of the tracks, the result was a city that stretched fingers of settlement into the countryside while vacant land was still abundant in neighborhoods without good streetcar service. Further, new urban and suburban neighborhoods developed as patchworks of housing interspersed with vacant lots—the products of individual enterprise by numerous small investors. Land speculators laid out far more lots than could be readily used. Real estate developers in the Chicago region created 800,000 residential lots between 1890 and

1920—lots that could have housed five to six million people in the unlikely event that they were all used.

The unplanned sprawl of the streetcar city looked messy, but it was not random. By 1925, the sociologist Ernest Burgess claimed to see a new urban structure: concentric rings of development, each with its own character. Around the rim of the city was a thinly settled zone occupied by wealthy commuters. Inside that was a belt of single-family residences, also relatively affluent. Next was a denser zone of "workingmen's homes," followed by a ring of slums inhabited by recent immigrants and the poor. This ring of slums was a "zone in transition," gradually being converted to industrial uses. At the core was a belt of factories and transportation facilities surrounding a central business district. According to Burgess, this was not a static model: as land values rose near the center of a growing city, dense development spread outward and converted the successive rings to more profitable use. Burgess acknowledged that this model of urban space was an oversimplification even in Chicago, the city where it made the most sense. The concentric rings were distorted or fragmented by sectors of dense development radiating outward along streetcar lines, by clusters of dense tenement housing around outlying factories, and by natural features such as rivers and lakes. Nonetheless, the general pattern was evident in many cities.

Prior to the development of mass transit, only the wealthiest merchants and professionals, who could afford leisurely trips to town in their own horse-drawn carriages or on expensive commuter railroad lines, had been able to buy a "box in the country," as Bostonian Harrison Gray Otis described his house in nearby Watertown. But after 1870, horsecars and trolleys opened up new residential areas that offered the opportunity for people with middle-class occupations and income to escape the central city's unappealing qualities. They could afford homes (if not to build or buy, then to rent) as well as the fares to commute to and from work every day. So they moved into the rings of residential areas that were forming outside the old urban cores.

Here they could fulfill a dream of a pastoral private life in a single-family dwelling, secure in an economically homogeneous community. When suburban builders advertised through brochures and newspapers, they promised an escape from the problems of poor health, social unrest, and immorality associated with urban life. A private dwelling in a safe residential neighborhood would protect especially women and children from the city's dangers. Greenery and fresh air supposedly would invigorate spirits deadened by urban drabness, and porches and yards would facilitate social contacts—while maintaining the boundaries of family privacy—to substitute for the uncontrollable sociability of urban streets. Promoters tried to identify their projects with the more exclusive picturesque retreats for the wealthy, but they were aiming for a different market. Subdivisions of small- or moderate-sized lots, near transit lines, were intended to attract families of salesmen, schoolteachers, clerks, and carpenters.

Suburban builders promised a combination of urban comfort and rustic simplicity, made possible by technological innovation. Availability of land, improvements in building techniques, and mass production of building materials enabled construction of houses with larger and more rooms than in homes of earlier eras. In the eighteenth century, only the wealthy could afford houses with three or more bedrooms and separate living and dining areas. By the 1880s, however, such facilities were possible for

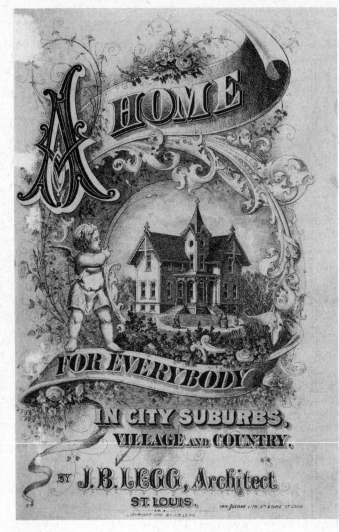

The Suburban Dream.   This illustrated title page from an architecture book published in 1876 suggests the pastoral and romantic qualities of the suburban ideal.

a much larger segment of the urban population. The specialization of space inside the home, with formal social space, kitchen work space, and private upstairs bedrooms, paralleled the specialization of urban space the suburbs themselves helped to create. Initially, the suburban residential ideal had been promoted by men, with women apparently more reluctant, more interested in the social conveniences of urban living and more confident that they could remake the city along the lines of the domestic ideal. By the eve of World War I, both men and women of the native-born middle and upper classes felt less confident of their ability to shape city life in the face of the cultural challenge from immigrant and nonwhite urban residents. And for different reasons,

The Suburban Reality. Houses with balloon frame construction, shown in process on the far right of the photo, could be built quickly and efficiently, enabling suburban settlements, such as this neighborhood near Chicago, to sprout up almost overnight. Note how close the houses were to each other.

each felt more invested in a companionate ideal of marriage and family life, reflected in the increasing number of suburban houses in which sexually segregated parlors and libraries were replaced by multipurpose living rooms.

City outskirts became places of detached houses, private yards, and tree-lined streets, but suburban development was not uniform. Commuter railroads enabled the growth of suburban villages in which affluent residents could conveniently walk to the train station for a ride into the city. The Chicago suburb Riverside, designed by Olmsted and Vaux, and Chestnut Hill, near Philadelphia, were luxurious communities inhabited by wealthy suburbanites. Site plans of affluent suburbs, featuring curving paths and English garden landscaping, differed dramatically from the gridiron plots that facilitated subdivision of less expensive suburbs. Chicago's Ravenswood and Normal Park, Boston's Roxbury and Dorchester, much of New York's Queens, and Milwaukee's Humboldt and Wauwatosa offered inexpensive lots to families of more modest means.

By the late nineteenth century, residential districts of single-family cottage homes—modest wooden structures of two to six rooms—were multiplying within and around growing cities, especially in the Midwest. Carpenters in the first half of the century had incrementally simplified older construction techniques to speed the completion of housing. Instead of heavy timber frames with intricately crafted mortis and tenon joints, which were common in eighteenth-century New England, late nineteenth-century houses typically had lightweight "balloon frames" of standardized machine-cut lumber held together with nails. They were heated with mass-produced iron stoves instead of the central stone fireplaces of the past. Houses could now be built quickly and cheaply, with less need for skilled carpentry. By 1880, factory-produced doors, windows, and moldings further simplified the process. Cottages, the characteristic housing of working-class residential districts of the Midwest, were inexpensive not just because of these construction techniques but also because they were designed to fit into small, narrow lots. The low cost enabled many people of modest means to own their own homes. In some instances, a two-story cottage provided living space for two families, one on each floor, but most were occupied by a single family.

Homeownership rates varied from city to city. About one family in four owned their own homes in Chicago and Philadelphia in 1900, while more than one in three did so in Detroit and Cleveland. Immigrant families were particularly likely to own their own homes, even though they tended to be less affluent than native-born Americans. In Milwaukee, more than 60 percent of immigrant families were home-owners in 1900, compared to less than 40 percent of native-born Americans.[3] Chicago's leading developer, Samuel Eberly Gross, actively targeted working-class immigrants by distributing promotional brochures in different languages, and offering band concerts and picnics to lure prospective buyers to his developments. A real estate syndicate in nearby West Hammond, Illinois, sold exclusively to Polish immigrants, some of whom took in boarders to help make ends meet. Both Gross and the West Hammond syndicate sold homes on an "easy payment system" that allowed people to buy without having to pay the full price at the time of purchase.

As development extended beyond the city limits, some cities annexed the new suburban areas as a way of holding on to the tax base and spreading the cost of city services. In 1854, Philadelphia's annexation of Philadelphia County allowed the city to expand from 2 to 130 square miles. In 1889, Chicago annexed 133 square miles of suburban territory, including the communities of Lakeview, Hyde Park, Woodlawn, South Chicago, and Pullman; residents of the suburban districts voted to join the city in order to get better water and police and fire protection. In 1898, New York City grew from 44 to 299 square miles with the consolidation of Manhattan, Brooklyn, Queens, Staten Island, and the Bronx. Los Angeles, a city largely composed of discrete suburban developments, expanded from six thousand people in 1870 to nearly one hundred thousand by 1887, adding new residents in sixty new communities outside the former city boundaries. Early Boston suburbanites agreed to annexation in exchange for the provision of services, and the annexation of streetcar suburbs Roxbury, West Roxbury, and Dorchester added 20 square miles to the city. But Brookline's refusal to be annexed in 1873 marked the beginning of a trend of suburban insistence on political independence, sparking a more antagonistic relationship between central cities and suburbs.

Improved rail and streetcar service contributed to the emergence of large industrial districts. Contrary to what Burgess's model of concentric rings predicted, these were often at some distance from the city's core, even beyond the city limits. Chicago's meatpacking companies at the close of the Civil War consolidated their operations at Union Stockyards on what was then the edge of the city, where they had convenient access to major rail lines. Dense working-class neighborhoods such as Back-of-the-Yards soon developed nearby to house the workers; streetcars allowed others to travel from greater distances. More distant industrial areas developed in the Chicago region in the 1880s, 1890s, and 1900s. Some, such as Pullman, were in territory annexed by the city, while others including Cicero, Hammond, and Gary remained independent municipalities. Similar patterns could be seen in many industrial cities. One common feature was the continuous strip of industry found along

A Typical City Traffic Jam.   This jumble of people, animals, and vehicles on a Philadelphia street in 1897 combines nearly all early forms of urban transport: pedestrians, horse-drawn wagons and carriages, and an electric trolley car.

riverfronts and especially rail lines. Some of these districts stretched for miles and spawned distant industrial suburbs, as in the Monongahela Valley south of Pittsburgh. Outlying industrial areas were quickly surrounded by tenements and row houses for the industrial workers, such as the eastern edge of Birmingham, Alabama, where steelworkers' housing clustered around the mills.

Secondary business districts emerged in the late nineteenth century in outlying neighborhoods. This was another aspect of urban development that did not fit neatly into Burgess's diagram. So many people traveled on mass-transit lines from the city periphery that grocers, pharmacists, and saloonkeepers set up business near convenient transfer points, such as at streetcar intersections and elevated railway stations. Eventually the small shops were joined by chain stores, banks, and theaters that had branched out from the main business district. The secondary business districts developed into important centers for neighborhood life.

Nearly half the urban population could not afford to move to the new outer neighborhoods. Families whose breadwinners earned only a dollar or two a day, and whose children worked in mills and sweatshops to help feed their brothers and sisters, had to remain in cramped apartments near the center of the city. Many could not even spare the nickels for streetcar fare, let alone pay for a house. Eventually (often within the span of one generation) some lower-income families did escape the inner districts of tightly-packed tenement houses, but at a price. Able to afford only modest payments for mortgages and rents, newcomers often had to double up in dwellings originally built to house one family. Families that left the slums undoubtedly improved their own living conditions to some extent, but they brought with

A Secondary Business Center.   The intersection of Milwaukee Avenue and Chicago Avenue in Chicago became one of many nodes of retail activity that grew around crossroads of important arteries and streetcar routes.

them the consequences of intensive land use—more people per acre, more traffic, more garbage, and more noise.

While mass transit fueled growth on the urban periphery, it also altered the center of the city. What had once been the entire walking city now became the zone of work, crammed with offices, stores, and warehouses. Frequently, commercial buildings replaced the remaining residential structures, creating districts exclusively devoted to business. More than ever before, downtowns contained an extraordinary concentration of economic and cultural functions. Downtown acquired a clear image: a place where tall buildings of stores and offices formed canyon walls surrounding streets clogged with human and vehicular traffic.

Retailing was transformed by the appearance of department stores. In New York, A. T. Stewart's magnificent Marble Palace, opened in 1846, was the prototype of grand downtown department stores to come, such as Macy's, Bloomingdale's, and Lord and Taylor in New York, Wanamaker's in Philadelphia, Marshall Field's and Carson Pirie Scott in Chicago, Jordan Marsh and Filene's in Boston, Rich's in Atlanta, Hutzler's in Baltimore, Bullock's in Los Angeles, and I. Magnin in San Francisco. The department store's function was to display the abundance of mass production, its magnificence shining through large plate-glass windows, bestowing its aura on the surrounding sidewalks. Another feature of the emerging downtown was the way in which it was shaped by ideas about gender. Department stores sought to attract wealthy women customers by making downtown safe for the "lady" potentially endangered by the social and sexual mixing that seemed to be integral to downtown life. To counteract the threat, department stores such as Macy's offered ladies' lunchrooms and ladies' parlors. Big-city hotels also demarcated women's space, offering

Skyscrapers dwarfing NYC's older buildings. The 792-feet high Woolworth Building on the left, completed in 1913, was one of New York City's earliest skyscrapers and, along with other tall buildings helped to define the new downtown. This photograph captures the old and the new, as the skyscrapers dwarf the city's old post office and City Hall in the center.

ladies' parlors and drawing rooms. Libraries began to provide ladies' reading rooms, and even some post offices offered a ladies' window. By contrast, the banks, brokerage firms, and insurance companies, that serviced the concentration of capital, were downtown landmarks that were more clearly demarcated as male, increasingly likely to be housed in new multistory office buildings that shaped the city skyline.

Thus, in pushing city borders outward and creating separate social and economic districts, mass transit was simultaneously a centripetal and centrifugal force.

Consumerism in the Modern City.   This busy Chicago street corner in the 1890s shows throngs of shoppers outside the famous Marshall Fields department store, an emporium of consumer goods now available to the public.

On the one hand, most of the city's important economic activities remained centralized within the old core, and commuters streamed inward each day on the trolleys and els to work and to shop. On the other hand, the streetcars launched the people who could afford it into the periphery, and the people drew businesses that began small-scale operations in the outskirts.

THE GEOGRAPHY OF LEISURE: PARKS AND COMMERCIAL AMUSEMENTS

As the open countryside receded farther and farther from the city's core, people felt a greater need for parks. Historical precedents for parks included both formal hunting preserves and ornamental squares, and unimproved town greens used for grazing, militia practice, public assembly, and festivals. The antebellum forerunners of parks were the rural cemeteries, such as Mount Auburn Cemetery (1831) in Cambridge, Massachusetts, and Laurel Hill Cemetery (1836) in Philadelphia, designed to inculcate morality by exposing the living to the contemplation of a constructed rural landscape.

The most important development in the American urban park campaign occurred in New York City. The New York state legislature in the 1850s used its eminent domain power to take possession of more than eight hundred acres for the construction of Central Park in Manhattan. Leading bankers and merchants campaigned for a park to demonstrate the city's claims to grand cosmopolitanism. Uptown landowners saw the creation of the park as a means to enhance real estate values by clearing out the vast plot of land, which according to the historians Roy Rosenzweig and Elizabeth Blackmar was the site of "a jumble of small craft shops, large factories, tiny garden patches, two-hundred-acre farms, plank shanties, country estates, and institutional homes for the poor, criminal, and insane."[4] Evicting the area's residents, 90 percent of whom were African Americans and immigrants, and clearing the land would allow both the creation of a park and the redevelopment of the surrounding area as an elite neighborhood. Public figures, such as landscape architect Andrew Jackson Downing and poet William Cullen Bryant, advocated that the park would have an uplifting effect on the city. As Downing wrote in 1848, "[Parks] will be better preachers of temperance than temperance societies, better refiners of national manners than dancing schools, and better promoters of general good-feeling than any lectures on the philosophy of happiness." A state-appointed commission sponsored a competition to determine the best design for the park. They awarded the prize to a young landscaper and journalist, Frederick Law Olmsted, destined to become one of the most influential figures in American urban and landscape design.

As superintendent of the Central Park project, Olmsted tried to bring what he believed to be the blessings of rural beauty to city dwellers. Olmsted thought that quiet contemplation of park scenery would calm "the rough element of the city" and "divert men from unwholesome, vicious, destructive methods and habits of seeking recreation." The planners also hoped that if women accompanied men to the parks, they might be able to add their domestic influence to softening the rough manners of men. Olmsted and his associate Calvert Vaux provided separate park facilities for quiet contemplation of beauty and for active recreation. First, they included a series of carefully designed vistas, some rough in terrain, others more formal. They also built sunken roadways to conceal city traffic and planted trees strategically to screen out abutting buildings. Second, they inserted special facilities to meet different needs for human action. They laid 114 miles of pipe to feed and drain ponds for boating and skating, provided trails for riding and hiking, and designed a mall for social gatherings and concerts.

As the park opened for use between 1858 and 1860, its promoters deemed it an instant success, partly because wealthy and middle-class New Yorkers were the primary users of its drives and pathways. By 1879, Olmsted boasted that "no one who has closely observed the conduct of the people who visit Central Park can doubt that it exercises a distinctly harmonizing and refining influence upon the most unfortunate and lawless classes of the city—an influence favorable to courtesy, self-control, and temperance." Rosenzweig and Blackmar's research suggests that working-class New Yorkers were infrequent users of the park in the early years, their access restricted by long hours of work, low wages, relatively high costs of public transportation, and the park's distance from the downtown neighborhoods where they lived. In 1870, a new city charter shifted control of the park from a state appointed board of commissioners to politically connected municipal officials. Though maintenance of the park now suffered, over time the new commissioners lessened restrictions, such as

Swan Pond in Central Park. New York City's Central Park, opened in 1863, provided city dwellers with space for leisure. The park's Swan Pond enabled park-goers to shut out the bustle of the city and promenade and boat in peaceful repose.

prohibitions against walking on the grass and against Sunday activities, thereby allowing a broader range of the city's residents to enjoy the park. Olmsted remained as superintendent until 1878 and constantly studied the use and misuse of the park in order to preserve his vision of its purpose.

Central Park inspired similar projects throughout urban America, many of them undertaken by Olmsted and Vaux or by their influential contemporary H. W. S. Cleveland. In eastern cities, where space was at a premium, park planners sometimes tried to exclude what they called the "boisterous fun and rough sports" of the working classes. Their parks were designed for individuals or small groups to quietly contemplate nature, not for a rowdy, collective style of play. The clash between conflicting definitions of a park's purpose—the upper-class definition with its emphasis on culture and refinement, and a lower-class definition emphasizing fun and games—characterized the history of park evolution in many communities. Several cities built multiple parks with varying functions. Boston park design consisted of an "emerald necklace" of interconnected parks and roadways, a multipart green corridor stretching out to the city's suburban reaches. Chicago and Kansas City also built metropolitan park systems; Chicago's ultimately covered almost sixty thousand acres. Some large parks contained ponds, pavilions, and picnic areas, and were located at excursion distance from the built-up parts of their cities, often at the end of a trolley line. Everywhere the establishment of recreational parks signified new specialization of urban space.

Commercial amusements demonstrated a similar pattern of specialization in the second half of the nineteenth century. Amusements in the walking city had been part of an informal public life with little class segregation, but this was changing by 1850. As the middle and upper classes became preoccupied with ideals of restraint and decorum, "good" women were increasingly insulated from a rowdy public life. Men could still pursue informal pleasures in the semipublic milieu of the saloon or dance hall, but these were clearly separate from the institutions of respectable society. As well, early nineteenth-century theaters had produced a variety of performances in a single evening, so that there would be something for everyone; mixed audiences might view drama, circus, opera, and dance on the same bill. In New York's Park Theatre, each class had its own section of seats, but all attended; mechanics in the pit, upper classes and women in the boxes, and prostitutes, lower-class men, and blacks in the gallery. After 1850, theaters were increasingly differentiated by class and function, and the legitimate theater and concert hall, appropriate for women and the genteel upper classes, distinguished themselves from popular performances of minstrelsy, variety, and burlesque. These popular entertainments were often located in the saloon, a lower-class and male preserve that offered liquor, sports talk, boxing, politics, and sometimes dancing and singing.

The spread of gas lighting in the mid-nineteenth century, and the widespread use of electric power after 1880, added to the allure of nightlife in the downtowns of major cities. Streetlights flooded the shadows, making going out seem safer as well as more exciting. The lower fares on electric trolleys helped downtown thrive as a central shopping and entertainment district, easily accessible from outlying residential areas. Between 1900 and 1930, the expanding number of white-collar workers with more free time and discretionary income were the most avid consumers of an ever increasing number of popular theaters, vaudeville variety shows, dance halls, ballrooms, cabarets, and, eventually, motion pictures. These entertainments attempted to guarantee their respectability in order to attract a broad range of the public, including women and family audiences. One means of protecting their respectability was the use of formal and informal means to exclude people of color. Racist representations of black culture continued to be a staple of popular entertainment, but even after talented black performers became featured attractions, African-American audiences could gain access to commercial amusement only in all-black venues or, occasionally, on separate days or in designated balconies.

The clear delineation of vice zones also stood as a hallmark of the new spatial specialization. In New York City, prostitution became more visible after 1820 as it moved from the docks to be more closely linked with the commercialized leisure in saloons, theaters, dance halls, hotels, and cheap lodging houses. Prostitution accompanied the city's explosive growth in the antebellum years, probably related to the rise in migration, the increasing misery of women as commercialization undermined skilled work, and the growth of transience in general. After 1850, prostitution in New York City was more clearly confined to "red-light" vice districts. In St. Louis, in the 1850s, the police tried to control brothels by raiding them when they became too connected with other criminal activity such as theft, if they became too publicly disruptive, or if they broke rules of social and sexual order by publicly displaying interracial sex. Red-light areas became more clearly demarcated when legal authorities used vagrancy laws to arrest streetwalkers (women working more informally or part-time as prostitutes), enabling madams to consolidate prostitution in brothels. The segregation of well-known red-light districts such as New York's Tenderloin, San Francisco's Barbary Coast, Chicago's Levee district, and New Orleans's Storyville, separated rough from respectable neighborhoods.

Of course, men of all classes continued to have access to red-light districts, and there were many small entrepreneurs and local political bosses with economic and political interests in resisting the "morals reformers." Existing outside the boundaries of polite society, these areas also constituted a meeting ground where racial borders were often crossed. In many cases they provided the only possible public interracial venue, given that interracial mixing was by definition antithetical to norms of public respectability. Vice districts in New Orleans, Memphis, and Kansas City as well as other cities of the South and Southwest provided the performance spaces for development of blues, jazz, and "hillbilly" music. These popular musical styles reflected the results of many cultural exchanges between white and black migrant musicians, railroad workers, coal miners, and sharecroppers, with additional traces of local and regional Italian, Polish, and Latin musical traditions.

POPULATION MOBILITY

Besides physical expansion and the specialization of land use, a third consequence of mass transportation was its effect on population mobility. The new urban sprawl reinforced the migratory tendency that had always marked American life. The numbers of people moving from one home to another throughout the nineteenth century and into the twentieth clearly reveal that residential mobility has been one of the most dynamic and pervasive features of American history. There are three kinds of population movement that affect cities: in-migration, out-migration, and intraurban migration. The first two are part of the process to be discussed in the next chapter. The third type,

A Product of Geographical Mobility.   Budding towns such as Helena, Montana, photographed here in 1870, sprouted all over the West as migrants sought their fortunes in urban as well as rural communities. Here a street of crude shops greets an arriving wagon train of settlers.

change of residence within the same city, was (and is) one of the most constant characteristics of city life. It affected practically every family, every neighborhood. It made the ideal of a stable community a fantasy, and it became an available means for those who sought a path to higher socioeconomic status.

Today analysts note with wonder that each year one in five Americans changes residence. Yet residential mobility was just as frequent a century ago as it is today, if not more frequent. A study of Omaha, Nebraska, at the end of the nineteenth century and the beginning of the twentieth revealed that less than 25 percent of the city's young and middle-aged family heads lived in one place for as long as five years; only 3 percent failed to move in twenty years. Not every group shifted with the same frequency: the foreign-born moved less often than the native-born, and white-collar workers moved less often than blue-collar workers.[5] However, differences between groups were slight; more important was the entire population's remarkable impermanence. May 1 was the usual moving day in New York and Chicago in the late nineteenth century. Each year on that day, overloaded wagons carried furniture through the streets, exposing valued possessions to the elements and to the inspection of nosy neighbors; many people devoted considerable effort and expense only to end up in an apartment similar to the one they left.

Certainly some of those who skipped from one home to another within a city never improved their condition; they were fleeing high rents or were seeking new quarters because their old residences were to be torn down. So they moved to a house or tenement down the street or around the corner. Yet it appears that many more people *did* better themselves by changing residence. In Boston, Atlanta, Omaha, and numerous other cities, thousands of families followed the streetcar lines into newer neighborhoods, where housing was roomier and yards were greener. A common residential pattern involved a series of moves, usually radiating outward from the central city toward the periphery or suburbs. The frequency of movement often frustrated reformers who sought to order society by creating stable communities. "I want to arouse neighborhood interest and neighborhood pride," pleaded housing reformer Jacob Riis in 1901, "to link the neighborhood to one spot that will hold them [sic] long enough to take root and stop them from moving. Something of the kind must be done or we perish."

Such a goal disregarded the dynamics of urban life. Quests for more space, more convenience, and better facilities uprooted families and overturned neighborhoods. In the half century after the Civil War these urges were as strong as before the war. Only, now new forces of urban growth and opportunity—outward sprawl, real estate booms, and mass-transit construction—spread people in many new directions.

Bibliography

On the development and daily life of industrial cities, see Herbert Gutman, *Work, Culture, and Society in Industrializing America: Essays in American Working-Class and Social History* (1976); S.J. Kleinberg, *The Shadow of the Mills: Working Class Families in Pittsburgh, 1870–1907* (1991); Steven J. Ross, *Workers on the Edge: Work, Leisure, and Politics in Industrializing Cincinnati* (1985); and Olivier Zunz, *The Changing Face of Inequality: Urbanization, Industrial Development, and Immigrants in Detroit, 1880–1920* (1982).

Pertinent works on Chicago include Robin F. Bachin, *Building the South Side: Urban Space and Civic Culture in Chicago, 1890–1919* (2004); Perry R. Duis, *Challenging Chicago: Coping with Everyday Life, 1837–1920* (1998); Robert Lewis, *Chicago Made: Factory Networks in the Industrial Metropolis* (2008); Carl Smith, *Urban Disorder and the Shape of Belief: The Great Chicago Fire, the Haymarket Bomb, and the Model Town at Pullman* (1995); and Karen Sawislak, *Smoldering City: Chicagoans and the Great Fire, 1871–1874* (1995).

On southern cities, see Eric Arneson, *Waterfront Workers of New Orleans: Race, Class, and Politics, 1863–1923* (1991); Don Doyle, *New Men, New Cities, New South: Atlanta, Nashville, Charleston, and Mobile, 1860–1910* (1990); David Goldfield, *Cotton Fields and Skyscrapers: Southern City and Region, 1607–1980* (1982); and Thomas W. Hanchett, *Sorting Out the New South City: Race, Class, and Urban Development in Charlotte, 1875–1975* (1998); David Fort Godshalk, *Veiled Visions: The 1906 Atlanta Race Riot and the Reshaping of American Race Relations* (2005).

On the Southwest, see Philip J. Ethington, *The Public City: The Political Construction of Urban Life in San Francisco, 1850–1900* (1994); Rosales Francisco and Barry J. Kaplan, eds., *Houston: A Twentieth-Century Urban Frontier* (1983); William Issel and Robert W. Cherny, *San Francisco, 1865–1932: Politics, Power, and Urban Development* (1986); and Bradford Luckingham, *The Urban Southwest: A Profile History of Albuquerque, El Paso, Phoenix, and Tucson* (1982).

Studies of the development and consequences of mass transportation include Charles W. Cheape, *Moving the Masses: Urban Public Transit in New York, Boston, and Philadelphia, 1880–1912* (1980); John Henry Hepp IV, *The Middle-Class City: Transforming Space and Time in Philadelphia, 1876–1926* (2003); Clifton Hood, *722 Miles: The Building of the Subways and How They Transformed New York* (1993). See also Clay McShane and Joel A. Tarr, *The Horse in the City: Living Machines in the Nineteenth Century* (2007); and John B. Stilgoe, *Metropolitan Corridor: Railroads and the American Scene* (1985).

Works on the suburbanization process include Michael H. Ebner, *Creating Chicago's North Shore: A Suburban History* (1988); Robert Fishman, *Bourgeois Utopias: The Rise and Fall of Suburbia* (1987); Kenneth T. Jackson, *Crabgrass Frontier: The Suburbanization of the United States* (1985); Ann Durkin Keating, *Building Chicago: Suburban Developers and the Creation of a Divided Metropolis* (1988); Margaret Marsh, *Suburban Lives* (1990); John Stilgoe, *Borderland: Origins of the American Suburb, 1820–1939* (1988); Jon C. Teaford, *City and Suburb: The Political Fragmentation of Metropolitan America, 1850–1970* (1979); and Sam Bass Warner, Jr., *Streetcar Suburbs: The Process of Growth in Boston, 1870–1900* (1962).

On the importance of gender in structuring urban space, see Peter C. Baldwin, *Domesticating the Street: The Transformation of Public Space in Hartford, 1850–1930* (1999); Sarah Deutsch, *Women and the City: Gender, Power, and Space in Boston, 1870–1940* (2000); Mary P. Ryan, *Women in Public* (1990); and Sharon E. Wood, *The Freedom of the Streets: Work, Citizenship, and Sexuality in a Gilded Age City* (2005).

On housing, see Joseph C. Bigott, *From Cottage to Bungalow: Houses and the Working Class in Metropolitan Chicago, 1869–1929* (2001); Margaret Garb, *City of American Dreams: A History of Home Ownership and Housing Reform in Chicago, 1871–1919* (2005); David P. Handlin, *The American Home: Architecture and Society, 1815–1915* (1979); and Gwendolyn Wright, *Building the Dream: A Social History of Housing in America* (1983).

On downtowns, see Gunther Barth, *City People: The Rise of Modern City Culture in Nineteenth-Century America* (1980); and Robert Fogelson, *Downtown: Its Rise and Fall, 1880–1950* (2001). On parks, see Galen Cranz, *The Politics of Park Design: A History of Urban Parks in America* (1982); Mona Domosh, *Invented Cities: The Creation of Landscape in*

Nineteenth-Century New York and Boston (1996); Roy Rozenzweig, *Eight Hours for What We Will: Workers and Leisure in an Industrial City, 1880–1920* (1983); Roy Rosenzweig and Elizabeth Blackmar, *The Park and the People: A History of Central Park* (1992); and Cynthia Zaitzevsky, *Frederick Law Olmsted and the Boston Park System* (1982).

On popular amusements, see Robert C. Allen, *Horrible Prettiness: Burlesque and American Culture* (1991); Howard Chudacoff, *The Age of the Bachelor: Creating an American Subculture* (1999); Francis G. Couvares, *The Remaking of Pittsburgh: Class and Culture in an Industrializing City, 1877–1919* (1984); Perry Duis, *The Saloon: Public Drinking in Chicago and Boston, 1880–1920* (1983); Katrina Hazzard-Gordon, *Lookin': The Rise of Social Dance Formulation in African-American Culture* (1990); Randy D. McBee, *Dance Hall Days: Intimacy and Leisure among Working Class Immigrants in the United States* (2000); David Nasaw, *Going Out: The Rise and Fall of Public Amusements* (1993); Kathy Peiss, *Cheap Amusements: Working Girls and Leisure in Turn-of-the-Century New York* (1986); Madelon Powers, *Faces Along the Bar: Love and Order in the Workingmen's Saloon, 1870–1920* (1998); Steven Riess, *City Games: The Evolution of American Urban Society and the Rise of Sports* (1990); and Robert W. Snyder, *The Voice of the City: Vaudeville and Popular Culture in New York* (1989).

On lighting, see David E. Nye, *Electrifying America: Social Meanings of a New Technology, 1880–1940* (1990); Harold L. Platt, *The Electric City: Energy and the Growth of the Chicago Area, 1880–1930* (1991); Mark H. Rose, *Cities of Light and Heat: Domesticating Gas and Electricity in Urban America* (1995).

On the emergence of red-light districts, see Timothy J. Gilfoyle, *City of Eros: New York City, Prostitution, and the Commercialization of Sex, 1790–1920* (1992); Alecia P. Long, *The Great Southern Babylon: Race, Sex, and Respectability in New Orleans, 1865–1920* (2005); and Thomas C. Mackey, *Red Lights Out: A Legal History of Prostitution, Disorderly Houses, and Vice Districts, 1870–1917* (1987).

Notes

1. Willard Glazier, *Peculiarities of American Cities* (Philadelphia: Hubbard Brothers, 1886), 332.
2. Nicholas B. Wainwright, ed., *A Philadelphia Perspective: The Diary of Sidney George Fisher Covering the Years 1834–1871* (Philadelphia: Historical Society of Pennsylvania, 1967), 316.
3. Joseph C. Bigott, *From Cottage to Bungalow: Houses and the Working Class in Metropolitan Chicago, 1869–1929* (Chicago: University of Chicago Press, 2001), 118–121.
4. Roy Rosenzweig and Elizabeth Blackmar, *The Park and the People: A History of Central Park* (New York: Henry Holt, 1992), 62.
5. Howard P. Chudacoff, *Mobile Americans: Residential and Social Mobility in Omaha, 1880–1920* (New York: Oxford University Press, 1972).

CHAPTER 5

Newcomers and the Urban Core, 1865–1920

Today the American metropolis is separated into inner and outer parts. The division is a legacy from the social, economic, and technological changes that arose from the mid-nineteenth century onward. While the middle classes accompanied the trolley lines into the periphery and suburbs, working-class migrants and immigrants squeezed into older districts and transformed the walking city into the urban core. To those on the outside, the residential rings that surrounded business and manufacturing districts embodied the worst of American urban life because of the problems that were most visible there—poverty, crowding, crime, disease. Yet the inner city served necessary functions for those who lived there. It provided shelter and jobs. It eased newcomers into the urban-industrial world. And it created opportunities for mutual assistance within groups and social contact between groups.

Once a rural republic of farmers, the United States became a predominantly urban nation in the early twentieth century. The number of people living in American cities of eight thousand or more inhabitants rose from 6.2 million in 1860 to 54.3 million in 1920, by which time they made up more than half the U.S. population. Although an excess of births over deaths accounted for some of this population growth, most of the increase consisted of newcomers—people from rural America, foreign countries, or other American towns or cities. This migration resulted from both push and pull forces (see Table 5–1).

A variety of pressures pushed people to leave their farms and villages in the United States, Mexico, Europe, and Asia. Rural people everywhere felt their traditional livelihoods threatened by the worldwide expansion of communications, markets and capital. These vast abstractions became very real for farmers who were squeezed by falling international prices for crops, rising prices for provisions, high taxes and rents, and eviction from farmlands—while still struggling with the ancient woes of

TABLE 5–1 Population Composition of Major Cities, 1910							
		Foreign-Born White		Native-Born of Foreign or Mixed Percentage		Black	
	Total	Number	Percent	Number	Percent	Number	Percent
New York	4,766,883	1,927,703	40.4	1,820,141	38.2	91,709	1.9
Chicago	2,185,283	781,217	35.7	912,701	41.8	44,103	2.0
Philadelphia	1,549,008	382,578	24.7	496,785	32.1	84,459	5.5
St. Louis	687,029	125,706	18.3	246,946	40.0	43,960	6.4
Boston	670,535	240,722	35.9	257,104	38.3	13,564	2.0
Cleveland	560,663	195,703	34.9	223,908	39.9	8,448	1.5
Baltimore	558,485	77,043	13.8	134,870	24.1	84,749	15.2
Pittsburgh	533,905	140,436	26.3	191,483	35.9	25,623	4.8
Detroit	465,766	156,565	33.6	188,255	40.4	5,741	1.2
Buffalo	423,715	118,444	30.0	183,673	40.4	1,773	0.4
San Francisco	416,912	130,874	31.4	153,781	36.9	1,642	0.4
Milwaukee	373,857	111,456	29.8	182,530	48.8	980	0.3
Cincinnati	363,591	56,792	15.6	132,190	36.4	19,639	5.4
Newark	347,469	110,655	31.8	132,350	38.1	9,475	2.7
New Orleans	339,075	27,686	8.2	74,244	21.9	89,262	26.3
Washington	331,069	24,351	7.4	45,066	13.6	94,446	28.5

Source: 1910 U.S. Census.

agricultural life: drought, hard winters, and insect plagues. The same economic trends that made it harder to stay on the old farm made it increasingly easy to leave. Those who emigrated made use of the roads and railways, canals and steamships, post offices and telegraphs, banks and travel agencies—all products of and contributors to the quickening pace of global economic change.

Migrants left because there was somewhere else to go. In Europe and the United States, rural people were lured to nearby cities where they could live better lives than they could in the countryside. Some worked for a few months in local industries, then returned to the family farm when needed for planting and harvesting. But eventually many Europeans and Americans felt drawn to the growing industrial cities in the American Northeast and Midwest, which promised higher wages and more secure employment. Commercial and industrial growth generated new urban job opportunities, as did the physical growth of the city itself. Between 1850 and 1920, practically every major American city constructed or enlarged its basic facilities, all with the help of unskilled labor. Streets, bridges, water and gas systems, sewers, schools, and government buildings were built by and for the new city dwellers.

WAVES OF IMMIGRATION

Immigration to the United States can be considered to have three major waves. The first began in the 1840s, peaked in the 1880s, and ebbed thereafter. The second began in the 1880s, peaked between 1900 and 1910, and declined after 1924 when federal legislation closed the doors to the unrestricted influx. The third and largest—to be discussed in Chapter 10—began with the immigration reform legislation of 1965, gained force in the 1990s and has continued to the present.

The first wave consisted of five main groups: Irish Catholics, German Catholics, German Protestants, English Protestants, and Scandinavian Protestants. Also, before the Chinese Exclusion Act took effect in 1882, more than three hundred thousand Chinese entered the United States, settling mostly in the West. The new-comers built chains of migration, across which traveled relatives and friends to join them in the New World. Many immigrants were too poor to go beyond their port of arrival, or they found ready use for whatever skills they had. Thousands of European immigrants remained in the eastern ports of Boston, New York, Philadelphia, and Baltimore, or they ventured only a short distance to growing secondary cities such as Providence, Paterson, Newark, and Reading. Others plunged into the hinterland. From the 1850s on, Germans, Swedes, and Norwegians took up farming in the Old Northwest and the Plains. English, Welsh, and Scottish immigrants traveled inland to work in coal mines of Pennsylvania, West Virginia, Ohio, and Illinois. Chinese rail-road workers settled in towns along rail routes in California, Oregon, Utah, and Texas. A few migrated to the Midwest and the East, establishing nascent Chinatowns in metropolitan centers.

European newcomers also traveled on railroads into growing cities of the West, adding a foreign flavor not only to Great Lakes cities such as Cleveland and Chicago but to Minneapolis, Denver, and Los Angeles. In southwestern cities such as Los Angeles and San Antonio, the formerly dominant Mexican influence faded after the Civil War as European and Anglo-American newcomers became the majority. Often migrants settled in cities for no other reason than that their funds ran out, and they suffered the pangs of poverty as much in the West as their counterparts did in the East. But western towns offered opportunities for people with skills and resources, and many immigrants achieved success—Scandinavians in construction trades, Germans in brewing, English and Irish in jobbing and retailing. The commercial elite of western cities often included foreign-born members. Chinese entrepreneurs started cigar, shoe, and garment factories that competed with white-owned firms, and by the 1870s, these establishments were numerous enough to absorb many of the Chinese workers fired from factories as a result of anti-Chinese labor agitation.

Most immigrants in the second wave were poor and of peasant origins, like their predecessors, but they were much more numerous than those in the first wave. Some 2.8 million immigrants had arrived in the 1870s, the largest of any decade dur-ing the 1840–1880 period. When the second wave began in the 1880s, more than 5.2 million immigrants arrived; 8.8 million came between 1900 and 1910. Although large numbers of English, Irish, Germans, and Scandinavians continued to come, they were outnumbered by four new groups: Catholics from Eastern Europe,

Catholics from Italy, Jews from Russia and Eastern Europe, and Catholics from Canada. Other sources included Greece, Syria, Mexico, and Japan. By 1910, arrivals from Mexico were beginning to outnumber arrivals from Ireland, and thousands of Japanese had moved to the West Coast. During these years, immigrants were also streaming to other nations settled by Europeans—including Canada, Australia, and Argentina—but the United States attracted the most.

Many immigrants hoped to work in the United States for a while and return home in affluence. The vast majority of these changed their minds after settling in America, or never achieved the wealth they had expected. "After six months," said an Italian who arrived in 1907, "I wanted to go back. What held me was that I didn't have enough money to go back." Still there was a substantial current of return migration to Europe and Asia. Some even shuttled back and forth across the Atlantic and the Pacific to take advantage of seasonal wage differences. Return migration became especially feasible from the 1870s on, when steamships rendered ocean passage safer and faster and made more European and Asian ports accessible to America. It has been estimated that for every 100 aliens who entered the United States between 1820 and 1870, 10 to 20 left the country. The figures for 1870 to 1900 and 1900 to 1914 are 24 per 100 and 33 to 40 per 100, respectively.

Immigrants from both waves settled in cities, particularly in older, inner districts where they were close to job opportunities. Rather than arriving with vague

Trauma of Immigration.   The S.S. Patricia was one of many passenger ships that brought thousands of immigrants to American ports in the early 1900s. Arriving in New York City in 1906, this particular voyage brought more than 2,000 passengers who traveled in the horribly cramped under-deck steerage quarters.

dreams of streets paved with gold, many immigrants had been advised by prior migrants as to specific employment opportunities in specific cities. Heavy concentrations of foreigners appeared in New York's Lower East Side, Boston's North End, Chicago's West Side, Los Angeles's East Side barrio, and the inner wards of Cincinnati, St. Louis, Buffalo, and San Francisco. The second-wave immigrants were even more urban than the first. The Dillingham Commission of 1907–11, which in large part was responsible for perpetuating artificial and racialized distinctions between "new" immigrants and "old," reported that in 1920, 78.6 percent of those born in eastern and southern Europe lived in urban areas, compared with 68.3 percent of those born in northern Europe and the British Isles. Somewhat less skilled than the old immigrants, those arriving from new areas brought only their willingness to work. As one Italian immigrant woman explained, "I never have a lot of money, but I have my hands." These newcomers worked in the sweatshops and factories of larger cities and in the mills, slaughterhouses, construction gangs, and dock crews of most cities outside the South.

Although many immigrants stayed in the eastern port cities where they arrived (particularly New York), others spread across the continent. By 1920, Poles were the largest foreign-born group in Detroit and Toledo, Bohemians in Omaha, Italians in Youngstown, and Hungarians in Akron. Immigrants, together with their American-born children, dominated many cities. By 1890, three-fourths of St. Paul's population and four-fifths of Milwaukee's population were either foreign-born or native-born of foreign parents. Most southern cities in this period attracted more native migrants than foreign immigrants. Although Memphis's population had been 37 percent foreign-born in 1860, the foreign-born part of the population dropped to 15 percent by 1900.

Colonies of distinct nationalities formed quickly, called Little Italy, Bohemiantown, and similar names that identified neighborhoods with a particular ethnic group. Some neighborhoods became dominated by immigrant enclaves composed of Italians from the same province, Japanese from the same island district, or Russian Jews from the same *shtetl* (rural village). Whole villages were transferred from the Italian or east European countryside to New York, Philadelphia, and Chicago. Much of the population of Melilli, Sicily, resettled in Middletown, Connecticut; Chinese migrants of the Teng (or Ong) clan from Kaiping settled in Phoenix, Arizona. These localistic enclaves supported ethnic businesses, churches, mutual aid societies, fraternal associations, and newspapers. Community life, combined with the networks of kinship and friendship in the crowded neighborhoods, nurtured a sense of common identity.

Immigrants over time developed more inclusive identities. Regional loyalties coexisted for a while with an emerging sense of nationality or ethnicity. People from Mecklenburg and Wurttemberg gradually came to think of themselves as Germans, before they became German-Americans; and those from Calabria and Campania became Italians and then Italian-Americans. Regional differences persisted in politics and associations, but all Germans could read the same foreign-language newspapers, and Italians from different villages could take communion together.

The ethnic neighborhood was one of the strongest institutions of inner-city life, yet most of them were neither as monolithic nor as stable as people thought. Only rarely did one immigrant group constitute a majority of residents in an area. A careful study of the Near West Side of Chicago in 1895 found Poles, Bohemians, Russian Jews, Irish, Italians, and Germans all living in the same block. Individual buildings often held families from several countries, speaking different languages and filling the stairwell with the aromas of different cuisines. Even the most homogeneous neighborhoods were not as stable as they appeared. Residents typically scattered within a few years to other neighborhoods and other cities. The rapid turnover was not obvious to outsiders because the people moving in were of the same nationality as those moving out. A 1915 survey of Italian and Polish districts in Chicago revealed that nearly half the residents moved each year. And a study of Omaha at the turn of the century has shown that members of all ethnic groups who remained in the city fanned out from the central city into many outlying districts within the span of one generation. In some cities, principally New York and the congested industrial cities of the Northeast, pockets of single groups did persist, and when the immigrants moved, they transferred their whole colony to another district. But generally, residential experiences of immigrants involved dispersion into a number of ethnically mixed neighborhoods.

The ethnic community's major importance was commercial and cultural. In most places an area's institutions and enterprises, more than the people who actually lived there, identified it as an ethnic neighborhood. A certain part of town, familiar and accessible to a particular group, became the location of its churches, clubs, bakeries, meat markets, and other establishments. Some members of the group lived nearby, while others lived farther away but could travel there on streetcars or on foot. Thus some of the secondary business centers that formed at the intersection of mass-transit routes became locations of ethnic businesses and social activity. A Bohemiantown, for example, received its name because it was the location of Swoboda's Bakery, Cermak's Drug Store, Cecha's Jewelry, Knezacek's Meats, St. Wenceslaus Church, and the Bohemian Benevolent Association. Such institutions gave a district an ethnic identity even though the surrounding blocks were mixed and in flux.

The cohesiveness of immigrant groups affected the larger urban society as well as daily life in the inner city. In factories immigrants often segregated themselves in individual departments, perpetuating their separation by recruiting fellow ethnics into similar jobs. In the steel mills of Steelton, Pennsylvania, for example, native-born white Americans plus Irish and Germans procured the most skilled, highest-paying jobs, while African Americans, Croats, and Serbs clustered in the lowest-paying and most dangerous departments. On the job, wage earners of all types had similar interests in opposing exploitation by owners and managers and in obtaining better wages and safer and more secure working conditions. Off the job, many immigrants withdrew into their own social organizations, neighborhood saloons, and churches. The American Federation of Labor, the main labor organization in the late nineteenth and early twentieth centuries, was not interested in organizing unskilled workers, which in practice meant that black and immigrant laborers lacked representation. There were moments when groups of workers outside mainstream union organization crossed ethnic lines to work together in a strike. Steelworkers in McKees Rocks, Pennsylvania, in 1909; textile workers in Lawrence, Massachusetts, in 1912; copper miners in southeast Arizona in 1915—all built multiethnic coalitions that demanded recognition of workers' rights.

But in other circumstances, ethnic loyalties precluded cross-ethnic cooperation, and corporate use of Asian and African-American workers as strikebreakers weakened the solidarity of striking laborers. Ethnic and racial disunity has been a legacy of the American labor movement that has distinguished it from its European counterparts.

If the term *ghetto* is defined as a place of enforced residence from which escape is at best difficult, only nonwhites and Latinos in this era had a true ghetto experience. Wherever Asians and Mexicans immigrated, they encountered discrimination in housing, employment, and public accommodations. Though these groups often preferred to remain separate in Chinatowns and barrios, white Americans made every effort to keep them confined. In the 1880s the city of San Francisco tried to prohibit Chinese laundries from locating in most neighborhoods, and in 1906 its school board tried to isolate Japanese children in special schools. A 1907 federal law prohibited Japanese laborers from entering the country. Restrictive covenants kept blacks, Asians, and Chicanos from buying property in various areas. Chinese were refused service in barber shops, hotels, and restaurants. Chicanos were restricted to certain schools and specially designated sections of theaters.

Yet no group could live in isolation. Socially complex cities fostered contacts and exchanges between all people. Urban life altered old customs and spawned new institutions. The necessity of learning the English language, new patterns of employment, and the bustle of the streets all undermined attempts to re-create an unchanged Old World culture. Ethnic communities themselves were divided along class lines, between middle-class immigrants, who had arrived with greater educational and financial capital and thus were able to find employment and assume leadership, and working-class immigrants, who possessed fewer financial and educational resources. These divisions prompted debates within the ethnic community over Americanization versus cultural traditions and upward mobility versus labor solidarity.

Religious ties had at least the potential to draw fellow Catholics together and fellow Jews together. The second wave of migration made Catholicism the majority faith in many Northeastern cities. As they traveled westward, Poles and Czechs joined the established Irish and Germans to raise Catholic proportions in Buffalo, Cleveland, Chicago, and Milwaukee to 40 or 50 percent. Traditionally, geography determined parish boundaries, a system derived from Europe where most parishes contained only one nationality. But ethnic divisions complicated parish life in American cities. German Catholics felt neglected or slighted within heavily Irish parishes in the late nineteenth century, and resented the view of many Irish-American clergymen that the Church should help "Americanize" immigrants. They argued that Americanization would destroy German-American culture and, worse, would cause Catholics to lose their faith. Often reluctantly, the Irish-dominated hierarchy allowed the formation of "national" parishes with German-speaking priests, even within neighborhoods already served by older "territorial" parishes. National parishes proliferated in the early twentieth century to serve the needs of Poles, French-Canadians and other foreign-language Catholics. Neighborhoods with mixed populations often had multiple churches, with the territorial parish attended mainly by the Irish. For instance, nine separate Catholic churches stood within walking distance of each other in the Back-of-the-Yards neighborhood of Chicago by 1920. Irish, Germans,

Bohemians, Slovaks, Lithuanians, and Ukrainians each had a Catholic church of their own in that neighborhood; Poles had three, each with a distinctive character.

The newer immigrant groups, particularly the Italians, encountered some animosity from the established Irish and German Catholics. A strong tradition of anticlericalism among Italians limited their attendance at worship services and their willingness to support the Church financially. Moreover, some Americanized Catholics sneered at traditional religious practices among southern Italians, such as their lively celebrations of the feast of Our Lady of Mount Carmel, which unsympathetic observers considered signs of ignorant superstition bordering on paganism. Polish Catholics, on the other hand, were considered to be among the most religious of immigrants. They worshipped regularly and contributed generously. Polish Catholics constructed some of the most elaborate churches, with soaring towers, beautiful stained-glass windows and statuary, paid for with the hard-earned pennies of laborers and steelworkers.

In addition to forming churches, Catholics also developed a vast array of parochial schools, parish halls, rectories, and convents. These were often built and maintained by individual parishes, but dioceses and religious orders created services to serve Catholics from multiple parishes: hospitals, orphanages, colleges, and various social services. A Catholic family in difficulty often turned to their parish priest or to diocesan charities for help, rather than to non-Catholic relief agencies.

Jewish institution building in this period reflected a variety of religious and cultural practices. Children of earlier German Jewish immigrants had brought with them traditions of accommodation to German culture that included public assimilation and private household ritual practice. Many of them adopted Reform Judaism, a movement originated in the 1840s by German intellectuals who wished to reconcile Jewish religious traditions with secular, middle-class culture. Leaders such as Rabbi Isaac Mayer Wise of Cincinnati reformed the prayer book, anglicized the service, and loosened the rigors of ritual.

Unlike previous Jewish immigrants, Eastern European Jews came to the United States in desperation as much as in hope. Hundreds of thousands fled Russia in the late nineteenth and early twentieth centuries to escape intense anti-Semitism that included brutal pogroms, repressive laws, and efforts to force Jews off the land. When they crowded into American cities, they soon outnumbered their coreligionists whose ancestors had arrived earlier. The new arrivals were probably the most urbanized of all immigrant groups—in 1910, close to 85 percent of the Russian Jews in America lived in cities. New York City alone contained 1.5 million Jews, one of the largest Jewish populations in the world. Newcomers from Eastern Europe came from areas where traditional Jewish economic and cultural life had already been disrupted, and they carried with them a range of beliefs from religious orthodoxy to secularized progressive ideologies. Poverty-stricken and often illiterate, they were not always welcomed by the established German Jewish community. Rather than attend services at existing synagogues, Eastern European Jews typically formed their own congregations, usually orthodox. Like Catholics, Jews developed their own network of institutions, including charities, schools, colleges, recreational programs, and hospitals. They too faced discrimination and hostility from Protestants, especially as their numbers increased.

Other forces aided a breakdown of ethnic consciousness. Public schools drew urban children together across ethnic boundaries. Commercial amusements such as sports, vaudeville, and movies gave disparate ethnic groups common exposure to American mass culture, although different audiences responded to the experience in ways that in part reflected their various cultural traditions. As they could afford them, immigrants filled their homes with mass-produced cabinets that substituted for traditional dowry chests, and with plush upholstered American furniture and voluminous draping that replaced hand-crafted ornamentation. Chosen furnishings were part of immigrants' and their children's attempts to come to terms with American ways, to claim the good life that America promised, and to assert that they were at home in urban America.

RURAL AMERICANS MOVE TO THE CITY

Foreign immigrants were joined in the growing cities by a continuing influx of migrants from the American countryside. As the number of American farms almost tripled between 1860 and 1900, and mechanization boosted productivity, overproduction of staple crops forced prices downward. Meanwhile transportation, storage, and commission fees remained high, and costs of seed, fertilizer, manufactured goods, taxes, and mortgage interest drove many families deep into debt. Farmers were caught in a cycle in which the more they produced, the more prices fell because of oversupply. The future of farming belonged to large producers who could afford expensive machinery, crop specialization, and economies of scale. The impact of mechanization, the consolidation of landholdings, and the rise in farm tenantry pushed thousands of rural people toward the manufacturing cities of the Northeast and Midwest. Rural areas of several states, including New Hampshire, New York, Maryland, Ohio, and Illinois, suffered declines in population in the 1880s.

Movement off farms and into cities changed patterns of life in the countryside, particularly in the Old Northwest—Ohio, Indiana, Illinois, Michigan, and Wisconsin. In the last half of the nineteenth century, urban migration boosted growth not only in Detroit, Cleveland, Chicago, and Milwaukee but also in a host of secondary cities. Dayton, Toledo, Indianapolis, Fort Wayne, Grand Rapids, Kalamazoo, Rockford, La Crosse, Oshkosh, and many more cities brought the amenities of urban life closer to farm families. After 1896 rural free delivery gave easier access to letters, newspapers, advertisements, and catalogs, and after 1913 parcel post brought deliveries from big-city mail-order department stores such as Sears and Montgomery Ward. Still, rural emigrants streamed cityward; regional centers such as Atlanta, Los Angeles, San Francisco, and Seattle swelled, and upstart places such as Birmingham, Houston, Kansas City, and Albuquerque matched their growth rates. By 1900, 80 percent of Memphis's population came from the adjacent Mississippi or Tennessee countryside.

Plagued by economic exploitation, racial discrimination, and debt, black Southerners ventured away from their tenant farms to earn supplemental wages. Between 1880 and 1900, the African-American population of Memphis tripled and that of Chattanooga grew by 600 percent. Others followed water and rail routes into expanding commercial and industrial centers in the North. Once they reached their destination, they encouraged relatives and friends to join them, supplying them with information about wage rates and employment. Black communities in Northern cities grew especially quickly in the late 1910s, as newcomers were drawn by expanded job opportunities during World War I. In 1900, the three cities with the largest African-American population were all in the South: Washington, Baltimore, and New Orleans. By 1920, the two largest were New York and Philadelphia; Washington was third and Chicago was a close fourth. The 1910s marked the start of a 60-year mass migration that transformed the geography of America's black population. At the beginning, African Americans were an overwhelmingly rural, Southern people; by the 1970s, they were predominantly urban and a major presence in cities across the United States. Over these six decades, blacks made up a sharply increasing share of the population in Northern cities: typically ranging from 1 to 6 percent in 1910, and from 10 to 60 percent by 1980.[1]

Some rural migrants—white and black—were women who went alone to cities. Women who migrated to Chicago without families or relatives included native-born whites from the Midwestern hinterlands; African-Americans who migrated from Kentucky, Tennessee, Missouri, and Deep South states; and some foreigners, especially Scandinavians, Poles, Canadians, and Irish. These women were drawn to cities by the possibilities for paid labor and by new attractions of urban consumer pleasure. They also moved to escape familial dependence or, sometimes, abuse. Although the wages women could earn were not enough to support independent households, they found and created settings in boardinghouses and women's clubs such as the Young

Black Urban Laborers.   After the Civil War, freed slaves migrated to southern cities to reconstitute families and communities. This photograph shows African-American dock workers in the busy harbor of Charleston with the nearby and growing downtown in the background.

Women's Christian Association (YWCA) where they could stretch their earnings and gain companionship and support with which to confront the challenges facing women alone in a strange place.

Although African Americans resembled foreign migrants in their peasant backgrounds, urban destinations, and economic motivations, several factors distinguished them. In Southern cities, especially, they encountered increasingly strict practices of public segregation at the end of the nineteenth century and beginning of the twentieth, in conjunction with successful campaigns to disenfranchise African-American voters. In the North as well as in the South, they were generally excluded from factory work and thus were usually forced to take menial jobs. In Cleveland, 32 percent of the black labor force were engaged in skilled trades in 1870, but only 11 percent were so employed by 1910. Southern African-American males had a stronger grip on skilled trades than their Northern counterparts, owing to the relative absence of immigrant competition. In New Orleans, blacks remained numerous in the building trades well into the twentieth century, and in Savannah they doubled their representation in several trades between 1870 and 1880. Black women outnumbered black men in most cities, a reversal of the pattern among foreign immigrants. As factory and clerical jobs drew white women away from domestic service, African American women took their places. Thus, at least at this time, there was a greater demand for black female labor than for black male labor in cities, and a much larger proportion of black women than white women held jobs. Of all black males and females employed in the cities, two-thirds were engaged in domestic and personal service.

Education provided Northern blacks with what appeared to be the best path toward improving their circumstances, and they expressed their hopes for the future through high rates of school attendance. By 1920, in Pennsylvania, 84.5 percent of black males aged fourteen and fifteen were enrolled in school compared to 72 percent of adolescent males of foreign-born parents. Black adolescent girls were more likely to be attending school than immigrant girls. In New York and New Jersey cities, black school attendance rates also exceeded those of immigrant children.

Sometimes by choice but usually because of exclusion by white property owners, African-American migrants moved into predominantly black neighborhoods, which in nineteenth-century cities were characteristically scattered in several locations. In Washington, D.C., many migrants moved into houses facing alleys that formed into close-knit neighborhoods interlaced with ties of kinship and friendship. Historian Howard Rabinowitz has argued that in Atlanta, Montgomery, Nashville, Raleigh, and Richmond, patterns of segregation emerged during Reconstruction as a means of protecting black institutions in the face of white racial animosity.[2] African-American community organizations honeycombed the neighborhoods, where churches provided vital services of Sunday schools, adult night schools, welfare, and social activities as well as religious sustenance.

Larger, denser and more exclusively black ghettos developed in Northern cities during the Great Migration of the 1910s and 1920s. Increasing pressure on limited housing encouraged white real estate agents to organize protective associations that pledged not to sell homes in white neighborhoods to blacks. Some whites used violent harassment to scare away black families who did move in. Such efforts seldom worked in the long run. Whites who lived on the edges of expanding African-American neighborhoods typically fled, leaving their homes and apartments to be sold and rented to black occupants. By 1920, ten Chicago census tracts were more than three-fourths black. In Detroit, Cleveland, Los Angeles, and Washington, two-thirds or more of the African-American population lived in only two or three wards.

The ghettos bred frustration in the face of stunted opportunities, but they also provided space in which black culture could develop. Countless Southern migrants to New York City described the thrill of finding themselves at the heart of a vibrant black culture in Harlem. In all major cities, juke joints and honky-tonk dives nurtured musical expressions of the black experience. Each city had a few large black congregations of Methodists and Baptists, but numerous informal storefront churches, outgrowths of the Southern experience, sprouted everywhere and became fixtures of neighborhood life. New African-American leaders emerged in the cities, ranging from clergymen to small businessmen, educators, and doctors, proposing a variety of strategies for racial uplift in the face of widespread poverty and, in some cases, worsening discrimination, exclusion, and injustice. Some individuals and organizations sounded a new note of militancy after 1890. Their activities ranged from boycotts against segregated streetcars in the South to support for black entrepreneurship and retaliation against white violence in the North.

African Americans also formed mutual-benefit societies to provide a cushion for sickness, death, or unemployment. Many of these societies evolved into small insurance companies, owned by and serving the African-American community. By the early 1870s, Richmond supported more than four hundred such societies. Richmond's Independent Order of St. Luke, begun in 1867 by Mary Prout as a sickness and death benefit society for women, grew to a membership of one hundred thousand men and women in twenty-eight states under the leadership of Maggie Lena Walker, who in 1903 also established the St. Luke Penny Savings Bank. Between 1870 and 1890 Boston blacks joined veterans' organizations, social clubs, music clubs, literary associations, churches, political clubs, and protest organizations. All-black women's clubs enabled women who had left their original communities to continue to associate with one another for individual and collective advancement. These associations proved to be critical in extending the resources of family and kin to protect migrants from the harsh racial discrimination of urban life and to provide a base from which to protest racial exclusion. For example, in Atlanta in 1881, African-American washerwomen organized a Washing Society, through which they articulated group demands for higher and uniform prices for washing, and eventually mobilized more than 3,000 washerwomen to join them in a strike, inspiring similar efforts by hotel waiters and house servants. In this way, women's organizations redefined racial uplift as a collective strategy.

HOUSING AND HEALTH

As foreign and native migrants streamed into the inner regions of Northern cities, they pressed private housing markets beyond their capacities. In the late nineteenth century three out of every four city dwellers lived in rented quarters; in working-class districts the proportion was much higher. Population increases and rising land values drove up rents and tempted landlords to squeeze every penny from their tenants. The middle and upper classes could avoid this plight by moving to the outskirts, where they could find ample space for less cost. Needing to remain close to work and the assistance provided by ethnic communities, working-class families had to find a different solution. Countless families took in lodgers to help pay the rent. Often two or three families occupied a single three- or four-room flat.

Types of housing varied from city to city, and so did the levels of crowding. Since the eighteenth century, row houses had been the most common form of housing in central Philadelphia, and after the Civil War, builders made them smaller and packed more people into them. The new-style row house was only 16 feet wide, but a two-story building held four to six families. The same pattern appeared in Baltimore. In New England the predominant style was the three-decker—a narrow frame building consisting of three floors and a loft. Pleasant-looking, substantial three-deckers housed one family to a floor and often appeared in middle-class neighborhoods. But because they were an inexpensive type of housing to construct, three-deckers more frequently were located in working-class districts of Boston, Providence, Worcester, and other industrial cities. Here they housed two and three families to a floor and one each in the loft and cellar. In Chicago and St. Louis, two- and three-story wooden buildings, and later brick tenements, squeezed against each other, separated at best by a narrow walkway.

Immigrant Neighborhood Life. This photograph of a group of immigrants gathered behind a tenement in the Italian section of Providence, Rhode Island, in 1912, was taken by documentary photographer and reformer Lewis Hine. Hine's own caption for the photograph, "Housing Conditions. Rear of Republic Street," was probably intended to protest a back alley strewn with trash, festooned with laundry, and packed with people.

In Detroit, Milwaukee, Memphis, and Seattle, immigrants crowded into converted warehouses and into single-family dwellings split up for multiple-family occupancy.

New York City stood apart from the rest by having the most intensely crowded living spaces. But the development of mass housing influenced construction patterns in other cities and prompted the first concerted effort for housing reform. The city plan of 1811 set a standard lot size of 25 by 100 feet over most of Manhattan. Thereafter, these measurements rigidly determined the exchange of land and the size of buildings. In the early 1800s one of these lots might have contained a single row house or cottage inhabited by one or two families. Because the lot was so narrow, the house may have abutted adjacent buildings, leaving no room for side windows. But there was access to light in front and behind, and enough space to accommodate four to six people. By the middle of the century, increased demand may have encouraged the house's owner to convert it into a four-family unit, with two or three families living on the ground floor and one each in the attic and cellar. Because the house occupied only 40 or 50 feet of the length of the lot, there would have been room to build another house in the back yard, also holding four families. As this process of transformation spread across the city, congestion accelerated.

New York property owners met housing pressure from immigration in the 1860s and 1870s by razing old houses and replacing them with four- and six-story tenements. These buildings were usually 80 feet long and contained four apartments to a floor. Each building could hold a minimum of 16 to 24 families. Tenants usually shared an apartment or sublet rooms, so a single building would often contain nearly 150 people. A block filled with these buildings might contain 2,500 families. The population density of such neighborhoods was rarely equaled in even the most crowded European cities. Living conditions were abominable. Rooms were miniscule, some barely eight feet wide. Only those few rooms facing the front or rear had direct light and ventilation. Indoor plumbing was almost nonexistent; privies were located in cellars or along the alleys.

As the crowding, disease, and crime of the inner wards seemed to multiply with each new boatload of immigrants, middle-class observers were appalled by what they saw as a collapse of moral order. Tenements bred crime and immorality, the *New York Times* reported in 1876. "Young girls are found sleeping on the floor in rooms where are crowded men, women, youths, and children. Delicacy is never known, purity is lost before its meaning is understood."[3] The growing sense of alarm sparked investigations of inner-city life, and calls for regulating the practices of builders and landlords. Optimistic reformers were convinced that better conditions would result from heightened public consciousness and enlightened capitalism.

Housing reform originated in New York City. In 1864, the Council of Hygiene of the New York Citizens' Association undertook an investigation of housing and sanitary conditions to alert the public to the dangers of crowding and filth. Directed by Dr. Stephen Smith, a leading figure in the nation's public health movement, the council's investigation produced an indictment of slum housing. The report raised enough publicity that when a cholera epidemic threatened in 1866, the state legislature created a Metropolitan Board of Health and gave it authority to regulate housing and sanitary conditions through provisions of the Tenement House Law of 1867. This law required landlords to furnish minimum facilities for fire escape, ventilation to interior rooms, and indoor plumbing. The provisions were very weak (one privy per twenty inhabitants

and one water tap per building satisfied the requirements), and enforcement was difficult. But the law had symbolic value because it imposed public regulation on a landlord's
property rights, and it established a precedent for stronger codes in the future.

Meanwhile, other reformers were trying to reconcile housing improvement
with the aims of capitalism. Beginning in the 1850s, the New York Association for
Improving the Conditions of the Poor (AICP) advanced the idea of a model tenement, a type of housing in which investors would accept lower profits for the sake of
safer, healthier facilities and philanthropic service to the poor. In 1882, a group of
local businessmen invested $300,000 to construct the nation's first model tenement,
and in 1901, the Tenement House Committee of the Charity Organization Societies
of the City of New York sponsored a model tenement exhibit at the Pan American
Exposition in Buffalo. Advocates wanted to limit profits from model tenements to
5 percent, but few investors were willing to commit to such a figure and the idea
never came to widespread fruition.

The model-tenement idea was also responsible for the notorious dumbbell
tenement that spread across New York after 1879. The dumbbell, named for its shape
rather than its designer, was fashioned to meet provisions of the Tenement House
Law of 1879, which required that every room in new tenements have a window. It was
the winning entry in a contest to determine the best mass-housing plan to fit a 25-by-
100-foot lot. That the dumbbell design was an example of housing reform dramatizes
the tragic state of low-income housing in New York. Each tenement was five or six
stories high, with four apartments on each floor. An indentation on each side of the
building gave the dumbbell its shape. This indentation, when combined with that of
an adjacent dumbbell building, created an air shaft five feet wide. Ten of the fourteen
rooms on each floor had windows looking into the air shafts, which unfortunately
became receptacles for garbage, breeding places for vermin, and ducts for fire, noise,
and foul smells. Tenants on each floor shared the two water closets in the hall. The
dumbbell's major consequence was not comfort, but more crowding. Between 1880
and 1893, the density of New York's tenth ward, the heart of the immigrant-filled
Lower East Side, increased from 432 to 702 persons per acre. By 1893, most of the
ward's 75,000 inhabitants were packed into 1,200 tenements. The very word "tenement,"
which used to be a neutral term for any multifamily housing, now came to mean
substandard housing for the working class.

Continuing deterioration of inner-city housing conditions ignited new reform
crusades. The journalist Jacob Riis aroused public concern with his reporting and
photography of conditions in New York tenements, published in book form in 1890 as
How the Other Half Lives. Further investigations led by Lawrence Veiller, the nation's
first full-time professional housing reformer, resulted in passage of the Tenement
Housing Law of 1901. The new code replaced the dumbbell's air shaft with a longer,
more open court. It also required a separate water closet for each apartment, and it
provided stronger fire-protection measures. Significantly, however, these regulations
applied only to new buildings. The law included a few weak provisions to improve
light, ventilation, plumbing, and fireproofing in existing tenements, but it could not
effectively remedy the eighty thousand tenements throughout New York City.

Multistory tenements, dumbbell or otherwise, did not appear to any great
extent in other cities until the end of the century, but dilapidated shanties and cellar

dwellings multiplied everywhere as swelling populations flooded housing markets. The situation was particularly severe in Chicago, where landlords filled already cramped backyards with flimsy shacks called rear tenements. In Southern cities such as Charleston, much of the housing available to African Americans consisted of converted slave quarters that remained in yards and alleyways behind white-owned homes. In New Orleans, the more fortunate blacks occupied housing in back streets and alleys, while whites tended to live nearby along newly constructed avenues. Less fortunate black Orleanians made their homes in the "backswamp ghetto," a soggy region of shotgun shacks that was both gaining new land and subsiding below sea level, thanks to a powerful pumping system installed in 1899.

The New York housing reforms inspired similar efforts in other cities. Civic organizations sponsored investigations and exhibits, and they lobbied successfully for the establishment of housing commissions and regulatory codes in cities such as Baltimore, St. Louis, Chicago, Kansas City, San Francisco, Philadelphia, New Orleans, Los Angeles, and Washington. In some places reformers supported the removal of poor families from high-density central cities to less congested, more inexpensive land on the urban fringe. Assuming that their vision of the appropriate residential setting was inherently superior to what existed in the inner-city, reformers hoped that planned communities could grow up around industries that were locating outside city limits. Some applauded George Pullman's model factory town that opened in 1880 beside Lake Calumet, south of Chicago. The town of Pullman, Illinois, included rows of brick houses on tree-lined streets, all within walking distance of the sleeping-car factory, and, like the factory, owned by Pullman. Pullman also owned the hotel, the market house, an arcade building with shops and a theater, and even the church. The image of the town suffered when a major strike in 1894 revealed that residents were generally dissatisfied with Pullman's paternalism, and more specifically with his decision to cut wages without reducing rents. Thereafter, large corporations generally shied away from building decentralized new towns, and housing remained the prerogative of private real estate speculators. Small projects that were begun, such as the Russell Sage Foundation's Forest Hills Garden in Queens, New York, in 1911, could not reduce costs enough to attract working-class inhabitants. Decentralization, like housing codes and model tenements, never met the expectations of its proponents.

The strongest restraint on housing reform was the privatism that governed prevailing attitudes toward property. Americans have always considered the freedom to purchase, manage, and sell land and buildings as a sacred civil right. Any interference with this right constituted a threat to a cultural inheritance. Thus not only did landlords resist and evade housing codes (which tended to be poorly enforced anyway), but also reformers avoided interference with the housing market. Public agencies could neither demolish dilapidated and dangerous buildings nor construct adequate housing for low-income citizens. Eventually, by expanding their police powers and their privileges of eminent domain, governments began to assume greater responsibilities for providing public housing, as later chapters will show.

Although housing reforms improved inner-city neighborhoods only slightly, public health professionals and municipal engineers made cities safer and healthier. Concern over housing and public health had much in common. Countless surveys revealed that death rates in slum areas were two to three times those in other urban districts. Congestion and poorly constructed housing amplified the problems of urban life: ventilation, fire prevention, sewage disposal, water purification, and control of disease. Advances in engineering and medicine reduced dangers in almost all these areas, and legislative bodies were willing to use public police power to prevent threats to public safety. Significantly, these advances occurred most readily in cities because only cities had the resources and institutions that could make their implementation feasible.

Discoveries by European scientists convinced most doctors that tiny organisms called bacteria caused specific diseases, such as cholera, typhoid, diptheria, and tuberculosis. This evidence strengthened the link between sanitation and public health, and support for sanitation intensified as inner-city areas spread in the 1860s, 1870s, and 1880s. Efforts of men such as Edwin Snow of Providence and George E. Waring, Jr., of New York, who crusaded for public hygiene and for improved sewer systems, succeeded in reducing mortality rates in American cities. As knowledge of the germ theory became more common in the 1880s and 1890s, state and municipal health boards (many of which had been established in the aftermath of cholera, typhoid, and yellow fever epidemics that had ravaged cities during the nineteenth century) could apply scientific certainty to the enforcement of cleanliness regulations.

Increasing knowledge about the origins of diseases also fostered public activities in the field of preventive medicine. Beginning in the 1890s, a number of cities established diagnostic laboratories to analyze the incidence of certain diseases and to try to avert their spread. Meat and milk inspections were established. Health departments sponsored education programs to alert the public to the causes and prevention of disease. Newspapers, pamphlets, and school programs explained contagion, personal hygiene, and proper diets. Around the turn of the century various clinics and dispensaries were opened. They provided information on baby care and dental hygiene, and they offered assistance to those suffering from tuberculosis, venereal disease, and minor injuries. Although they brought needed services to many neighborhoods, especially in New York, the clinics and dispensaries functioned mainly as charity institutions. Restoring the health of the poor would reduce relief expenditures and might keep the epidemic diseases of poor districts from spreading to well-to-do neighborhoods.

Improvements in fire protection and in other utilities increased public safety. The Great Chicago Fire, which consumed nearly 1,700 acres in 1871, and the huge conflagration that swept Boston in 1872 were evidence that fire remained the principal threat to urban safety. Building codes, architectural designs, and professional firefighting forces began to lessen this danger. New buildings (too expensive for poor people) increasingly included fire walls, fire barriers, and steel-frame, fire-resistant construction. Much of the drive for better fire protection was spearheaded by the National Board of Fire Underwriters (NBFU), organized in 1866. The NBFU adopted a nationwide policy of drawing local maps, examining ordinances, and inspecting firefighting equipment as determinants of local insurance rates. This practice stirred cities to upgrade their building codes and fire departments. City governments purchased steam engines and pumping machinery and installed electric fire-alarm boxes, as well as expanded their fire-fighting personnel. In addition to fire protection, electricity (especially its use for lighting) and sewer construction promised new benefits in urban health and safety.

By the early twentieth century the United States had achieved the highest standards of mass urban living in the world. But neither the benefits nor the facilities reached all city dwellers evenly. By the 1870s, most municipalities had assumed responsibilities for constructing water and sewerage systems and for ensuring public health. But public responsibility virtually ended at the borders of private property. Landlords and builders who wanted water and sewers had to pay for connections between their buildings and the water main and trunk-line sewer. Owners of newly developed property were assessed for public improvements according to the amount of their land that abutted a street. Those who could afford such facilities, or whose tenants could absorb the costs in their rent, installed modern plumbing, heating, and lighting. But for those forced into high-density, low-quality dwellings, modern amenities were much scarcer. Inner-city landlords, eager to maximize profits, tried to avoid expensive improvements. And governments remained reluctant to enter the sanctum of housing construction and property management. Thus inner-city residents, most of them newcomers and most of them poor, were at the mercy of the housing market. Over time, some of the improvements in sanitation and housing construction trickled down to the poorest neighborhoods. For most people, however, the best solution was to escape, somehow to acquire a home beyond the inner core, or to pack up and take a chance that things would be better elsewhere.

COPING WITH INNER-CITY LIFE

People, crowded into too little space, created the problems in housing, health, and safety outlined above. But on the other hand, urban cores themselves transformed the everyday lives of their inhabitants. Unlike residents of the periphery or suburbs, whose environments consisted of detached single-family houses, inner-city residents seldom knew privacy. Blocks jammed with tenements, buildings housing a score of families, and apartments inhabited by a dozen people determined personal behavior and development. People had to endure the ways of others who lived close by. Toleration was not always easy; the strain from inadequate space and facilities tried tempers and created opportunities for misunderstandings. Domestic conflict and neighborhood fights were common. The shared spaces that helped generate sociability also created the conditions for violence. Observers from the middle class, accustomed to spacious surroundings and little public scrutiny, rarely understood how the circumstances of neighborhood life bred strong emotions that included shouting and fighting as a part of working-class coping mechanisms.

Crowding also complicated modes of living outside the tenements. In many areas each apartment building covered almost the entire lot on which it was built, leaving no room for recreational activity. Housing reformers urged that at least 35 percent of each residential lot be left open, but they could not undo the past and their guidelines were usually ignored. Unused space for yards and playgrounds remained scarce. Children were forced into the streets, where traffic interrupted their play and threatened their safety, or onto the roofs, where they found privacy but faced more danger. Adults who wished to escape the tenements frequented the neighborhood saloon, a custom that unnerved middle-class reformers. Yet by providing not only liquor but also newspapers, cards, free lunch, drinking water, and public toilets, saloons served inner-city men's needs. In working-class neighborhoods, bars were places where men relaxed, traded information, and organized activities from political campaigns to labor unions to funerals. Many workingmen used the saloon as a place to leave and pick up messages and meet friends, and as a bank, depositing money, cashing checks, or borrowing from the saloon keeper. In immigrant neighborhoods, men sometimes prevailed upon the saloon keeper to send money to their family back home. In spite of the drunkenness and occasional violence that it fostered, the neighborhood saloon proved to be one of the most durable features of the urban environment.

To afford minimal food and shelter, working-class families often pieced together an income from the labor of several family members. Women found that their household work had special economic value; the cost of feeding a family depended on women's skills in bargaining with grocers, fishmongers, and butchers. Women's skills at cajoling landlords could postpone when the rent was due. Women and children also exploited whatever opportunities presented themselves for generating income, such as cooking and cleaning for boarders and lodgers, washing laundry, peddling food, scavenging for fuel for the stove, and helping out in neighborhood shops.

In tenement sweatshops, whole families engaged in the production of clothing, cigars, artificial flowers, or foodstuffs, working long hours for low wages. Where it was available, women and children also did piecework manufacturing at home, finishing pants, linking jewelry chains, shelling nuts, or pulling lace threads for pennies an hour. One investigator found three- and four-year-olds aiding a cigar-making operation by straightening tobacco leaves and putting lids on boxes. Reformers were horrified to find women and children working at home because of the obvious exploitation and because such labor violated their norms of appropriate family life. Earning money while tending ongoing responsibilities for cooking and childcare exhausted homeworkers, but working together as a family at home was part of how working-class families taught their children to survive.

Residence in a single-family house rather than in quarters shared with others has been a deep-rooted American value. Historians who have investigated household patterns of past eras have discovered that this norm seldom occurred in urban cores. The great majority of families (kin groupings) were nuclear in structure, consisting only of the household head, spouse, and children all living in one place. But a large number of inner-city households (including all the people inhabiting one residential unit) contained lodgers and boarders. Evidence has revealed that at any point in time about one-fourth of all urban households contained nonfamily residents. Countless city dwellers boarded or lodged with others for at least a few years during their lives. The most common pattern was for young people, usually unmarried male migrants who had left their parents' household, to board with an older family whose children were grown. Sometimes, however, whole families boarded. Lodgers frequently stayed until they could obtain their own quarters.

Boarding houses and lodging houses also were common in cities. (Boarding houses served meals; lodging houses did not.) Though reformers and moralists decried the loneliness and degenerate behavior that they believed occurred in these settings, boarders and lodgers often made their own communities, including deep and lasting friendships that served as alternatives to family life for people who otherwise lacked family connections in the city. Inner-city neighborhoods containing clusters of boarding and lodging houses provided particular activities and institutions for the urban bachelor subculture that developed at the end of the nineteenth century. (In most cities, over 40 percent of all adult men were unmarried in 1890.) Unmarried men utilized the saloons, pool halls, cafés, barbershops, clubhouses, and other venues to cultivate a social life for themselves and to indulge in behavior, such as gambling, rowdiness, and sexual freedom that to some outsiders seemed to threaten social order but for the most part was relatively harmless. Unmarried women also formed peer group associations and, together with their bachelor counterparts, constituted a prime consuming group for new commercial entertainments such as amusement parks, dance halls, popular theater, and movies.

Middle-class and working-class families frequently took in boarders to help pay the rent. Immigrants and African-American migrants lodged newly arrived relatives and fellow villagers until they could establish themselves. Boarders were also often related to people in the households that lodged them, which meant that alleys and tenements that appeared to reformers as crowded horrors of social disorganization were more likely to be complex webs of kinship and friendship. Creating networks of mutual assistance by turning kin into neighbors was one of the ways that migrants shaped their residential space and enhanced their family resources. Housing reformers protested that boarding caused overcrowding and loss of privacy. Yet for those who boarded, the practice was highly useful. Boarding was a transitional stage of coping, providing boarders with a quasi-family environment until they set up their own households, easing migrants' struggle with anonymity in a strange city. And it gave the household flexibility, bringing in extra income to meet its needs.

In addition, approximately 15 or 20 percent of households included extended family members: parents, siblings, aunts, uncles, and cousins who lived as quasi-boarders. Often a family would take in a widow or unmarried sister or brother who would otherwise have had to live alone. Immigrants and migrants often doubled up with family who had preceded them to a city during the months or years while they were in the process of getting settled. Even when relatives did not share the same household, they often lived nearby. Tenements, triple-deckers, and duplexes were particularly well suited to the exchange of services such as shopping, child care, advice, and consolation. Women migrants particularly benefited from this exchange of assistance.

Obligations of kinship, however, were not always welcome or even helpful. Immigrant families often pressured last-born children to stay at home and care for aging parents, a practice that could stifle opportunities for education, marriage, and economic independence. As an aging Italian-American father confessed, "One of our daughters is an old maid [and] causes plenty of troubles. . . . It may be my fault because I always wished her to remain at home and not to marry for she was of great financial help." Tensions also developed when one relative felt that another was not helping out enough. One woman, for example, complained that her brother-in-law "resented the fact that I saved my money in a bank instead of handing it over to him." Nevertheless, kinship, for better or for worse, provided migrant families with an important set of resources for coping with the demands of urban life. Urbanization, industrialization, and migration did not crack the resilience of the family.

Although the city actually reinforced family life in several ways, the pressures of poverty and inner-city housing still threatened family solidarity. When they entered the urban job market, most migrant men and women took manual employment that was dangerous and physically wearing. Long hours of work in poor lighting and poor ventilation induced mental lapses that had harmful results. The incidence of industrial accidents was high, and there was no compensation to support families whose breadwinners or other members were killed or incapacitated. Moreover, men and women who worked eighty or ninety hours a week without proper rest and nourishment fell easy prey to tuberculosis, pneumonia, and other diseases. The death of the father of a working-class family at the age of thirty or thirty-five was a common occurrence. Widowhood among African-American and immigrant groups was more than a stereotype; it was a tragic reality.

Migration, city life, and poverty also touched children. The need for supplementary family income pressed many children into the labor market at early ages. Others, who did not have jobs but whose parents worked twelve to fourteen hours a day, roamed the streets away from adult supervision. Some of them became truants and petty thieves. Older youths joined gangs that cultivated peer-group solidarity but that also harassed merchants, antagonized police, and frightened neighborhoods with their defiant activities.

In spite of child labor, vagrant boys, and gang activity, most inner-city children went to public schools by the end of the nineteenth century. Yet here too problems arose, especially among immigrant generations. Children of foreign-born (or even of native-born rural) parents straddled two worlds. Although the public schools taught values of independence and self-made opportunity, parents often demanded that their children remain obedient and useful family members who would set aside self-fulfillment for the benefit of the entire family. Those who attended school assimilated more easily into the native middle-class cultural mainstream. Those who held on to their parents' values remained within their ethnic social structure and were generally less upwardly mobile.

Immigrant and African-American mothers had special roles in preserving ethnic and religious cultural traditions, maintaining family responsibilities in caring for kin, and contributing to a family economy. Mothers' rates of labor-force participation varied by race, ethnicity, husband's income, resources for caring for children at home, and urban occupational structure. In all cities black women mostly worked outside their homes as domestics. Italian wives worked with their children as family crews in vineyards and canning factories, and Mexican-American women joined with their families as farm laborers and in food-processing plants. Most unmarried daughters had opportunities for a wider range of jobs (as salesclerks, for example) than did their mothers, who were more constrained by maternal responsibilities and community norms. In some cities at least two-thirds of young women held paying jobs before marriage. Rates of labor-force participation after marriage varied, depending on class, ethnic group, and local economies.

Children lining up for work papers. Child labor provided an important component of family income in working-class neighborhoods. Here a group of children have lined up to receive work permits in 1911.

PATTERNS OF SOCIAL MOBILITY

At the end of the nineteenth century, beliefs remained strong that there was an open road from the bottom of society to the top, or at least to the middle. The expanding urban-industrial economy spun off new jobs, new markets, and new areas for investment. Although hard times punctured the booms with unprecedented frequency—there were serious, though temporary, economic declines in each of the four decades preceding World War I—the euphoria of expansion soothed harsh memories.

Yet dark clouds persisted. By the late nineteenth century the spread of slum decay, the power and impersonality of factories, and the widening gulf between rich and poor withered the dreams of many. In addition, the social complexity, churning neighborhoods, and competition for space and jobs prompted fears that immigrants were displacing native workers, depressing wage rates, blighting residential districts, subverting traditional morality, and threatening political order. Newspapers and pseudoscientific theories reinforced stereotypes of Italians as swarthy and stupid, Irish as lazy and drunkardly, and Jews as greedy and cunning. These beliefs plus activities of nativist organizations, such as the American Protective Association and the American Patriotic League, impeded immigrants' (particularly Catholics') chances for betterment.

A Market in an Immigrant Neighborhood.   This view of Hester Street on New York City's Lower East Side around 1900 scans a street lined with immigrant Jewish shops and peddlers. The photograph, showing confusion and clutter, also reveals the vitality of immigrant life in the city, an informality that is often viewed with nostalgia today.

Basically there were three ways a person could get ahead: occupational advancement (and the higher income that accompanied it), property acquisition (and the potential for greater wealth it represented), and migration to an area of better conditions and greater opportunity. These options were open chiefly to white men. Although many women were employed, owned property, and migrated, their social standing was usually defined by the men in their lives—husbands, fathers, or other kin. Many women improved their economic status by marrying men with wealth or potential, but other avenues were mostly closed. Men and women who were African-American, American Indian, Latino, or Asian-American had even fewer opportunities. Disadvantaged by institutional racism, these groups were expected to accept their inherited station.

To a large number of people, however, urban and industrial expansion of the late nineteenth century offered broad opportunities for occupational mobility. Manifold businesses were needed to supply goods and services to burgeoning urban populations. As corporations grew larger and centralized their operations, they required more managerial personnel. Although capital for a large business was hard to obtain, a person could open a saloon or small store for only two hundred to three hundred dollars. Knowledge of accounting could qualify one for white-collar jobs that sometimes paid better and were more secure than manual labor. Thus nonmanual work and the higher social status that tended to accompany it were possible.

Such advancement occurred often. To be sure, only a few trod the rags-to-riches route that men like Andrew Carnegie and Henry Ford traveled. Studies of the era's wealthiest businessmen have shown that the vast majority started their careers with distinct advantages: American birth, Protestant religion, better-than-average education, and relatively affluent parents. Yet considerable movement occurred along the path from rags to moderate success as men climbed from manual to nonmanual jobs or saw their sons do so.

Rates of occupational mobility in late nineteenth- and early twentieth-century American cities were slow but steady. To be sure, mechanization and new products pushed some callings into obsolescence, but expansion in other areas more than compensated for the contraction. In new, fast-growing cities such as Atlanta, Los Angeles, and Omaha, approximately one in five manual workers rose to white-collar or owner's positions within ten years—provided they stayed in the city that long. In older northeastern cities like Boston and Newburyport, upward mobility averaged closer to one in six in ten years. Some people slipped from a higher to a lower rung of the occupational ladder, but rates of upward movement almost always doubled downward rates. Immigrants generally experienced lower rates of upward mobility and higher rates of downward mobility than natives did. Still, regardless of birthplace, the chances for a white male to rise occupationally over his career or to have a higher-status job than his father had were relatively good.

It must be remembered, however, that what constitutes a better job depends on culture and an individual's definition of improvement. Many an immigrant artisan, such as a German carpenter or an Italian shoemaker, would have considered an office job demeaning and unproductive. People with traditions of pride in manual labor often encouraged their children to adopt their trade. As one Italian tailor explained, "I learned the tailoring business in the old country. Over here, in America, I never have trouble finding a job because I know my business from the other side [Italy]. . . . I want that my oldest boy learn my trade because I tell him that you could always make at least enough for the family."

Moreover, business ownership entailed risks. Rates of failure were high among shopkeepers, saloon owners, and so forth because business could be uncertain. Thus many manual workers sought security rather than mobility, preferring a steady job to the risks of ownership. A Sicilian who lived in Bridgeport, Connecticut, observed that "the people that come here they afraid to get in business because they don't know how that business goes. In Italy these people don't know much about these things because most of them work on farms or in [their] trade."

In addition to or instead of advancing occupationally, a person could achieve social mobility by acquiring property. But property was not easy to acquire in turn-of-the-century America. Banks and savings institutions were far stricter in their lending

Commerce Comes to a Residential Street.   A peddler displays his household goods for housewives' inspection and children's curiosity in Somerville, Massachusetts, near Boston in 1905.

practices than they would become after the 1930s, when the federal government began to insure real estate financing. Mortgage loans carried high interest rates and short repayment periods. Nevertheless a general rise in wage rates enabled many families to build savings accounts, which could be used as down payments on property. In northeastern cities, small building and loan associations financed home ownership for working-class families. Moreover, the simplified process for constructing cottages (see Chapter 4) enabled many blue-collar families to build their own homes.

Finally, every year millions of families tried to improve their living conditions by packing up and moving elsewhere. As early as 1847, a foreign visitor, amazed by American transiency, wrote, "If God were to suddenly call the world to judgement He would surprise two-thirds of the American population on the road like ants." The urge to move affected every region, every city. From Boston to San Francisco, from Minneapolis to San Antonio, no more than half the families residing in a city at any one time could be found there ten years later (see Table 5–2).

Social and geographical mobility did not eliminate poverty. Economic freedom and mobility produced greater distinctions between rich and poor, rather than more equality. Although few members of the middle class fell into the lower class, downward mobility did occur within the lower ranks, with somber results. Unemployment

TABLE 5–2 Percentage of Residents at Beginning of Decade Who Had Left by End of Decade

Decade	City	Percentage Who Had Left
1870–80	Atlanta	56
	Poughkeepsie, N.Y.	50
	San Francisco	52
1880–90	Boston	36
	Mobile	62
	Omaha	60
	San Francisco	50
1900–10	Omaha	59
1910–20	Boston	59
	Norristown, Pa.	41

Source: U. S. Census.

frequently ran high in industrial cities, and a breadwinner's loss of job or physical incapacitation could plunge a family into destitution. Additionally, myriad people entered urban society at the lowest levels and never rose. Thus absolute numbers of urban poor constantly expanded in spite of the opportunities that the urban economy promised.

As cases of dependency multiplied, public attitudes toward the poor hardened. Economy-minded officials and their middle-class supporters began to attack forms of outdoor relief. Believing direct grants of money and provisions encouraged pauperism, several city governments abolished outdoor relief by 1900, and others made such grants only in return for work. Poverty relief increasingly utilized institutions—poorhouses, almshouses, juvenile homes, and special homes for the blind, deaf, mentally ill, and physically handicapped. The trend was for states to assume management of these institutions, but efforts by state boards to change the poor into productive citizens usually fizzled. Increasing destitution exacerbated trends that had developed before the Civil War. The public was more anxious to remove "undesirables" from society than it was to help rehabilitate such people.

Reflecting the trend toward bureaucratic administration of all forms of organized activity at the end of the nineteenth century, private social welfare organizations emphasized coordinated, systematic efforts to relieve poverty. By the 1890s, many major cities contained a Charity Organization Society (COS) that organized communications among local charities, established agencies to find jobs for the unemployed, and sent agents to ascertain that every dependent was truly needy. These activities reflected the long-standing moralistic belief that individual weaknesses, such as drunkenness and laziness, caused poverty. Yet the investigations and close supervision of the poor stressed by the COS induced the conclusion that low incomes, low-quality housing, and inadequate sanitation, rather than individual failure, were responsible for dependence. The investigations led welfare agencies to support reforms to relieve the environmental problems afflicting the poor. These efforts slightly improved slum and factory conditions, but the public resisted large-scale change. The downwardly mobile and those immobilized at the bottom still had to fend for themselves.

The urban cores of industrial America were unusually volatile politically and socially in this time period. In the fifty years after the Civil War, urban areas suffered from increasing crime and civil discontent. Rising tensions between labor and capital generated violence in several cities in the 1870s and 1880s. More than fifty people were killed in Cincinnati in 1884 as the result of a three-day riot that burst out after an attempted lynching. New efforts to mobilize political support for immigration exclusion and racial disenfranchisement provided the context for an anti-Italian riot in New Orleans in 1891 and race riots in Wilmington in 1898, Atlanta in 1906, and Springfield, Illinois, in 1908, and flare-ups against Mexican immigrants in south-western and Pacific coast cities. As well, attacks on Chinese laborers united labor activists, small entrepreneurs and farmers, and opportunistic politicians in a full-fledged anti-Chinese movement, resulting in Chinese exclusion legislation and "anticoolie" associations that formed in various western cities. In 1871, a riot in Los Angeles ended with the murder of nineteen Chinese. And in 1885, mobs invaded Chinese sections of Seattle and Tacoma, burning down homes and destroying personal property. The violence prompted Washington's governor to request President Cleveland to send troops to restore order. Anti-immigrant and racist sentiments would continue to play a divisive role in labor and party politics for years to come.

But the extent of these incidents was much smaller than conditions might have warranted, because various "safety valves" relieved pressures of social unrest. First, geographic mobility left open a means of escape. America is not only a nation of immigrants, but a nation of migrants. If life was unsatisfactory in one place, the grass was always greener somewhere else. More important, nearly everyone could—and countless people did—seek greener grass in the cities. Migration patterns reversed Frederick Jackson Turner's theory that plentiful land in the West calmed urban tensions by drawing away the discontented. Instead, cities attracted those disappointed with farm life and those fed up with life in another city. To be sure, many dreams were wistful, and many migrants found only more of the same at their destination. But how was improvement to be measured? The worker who moved from the textile mills of Manchester, New Hampshire, to the grain mills of Minneapolis may not have increased his income, but he may have moved his family from a three-room dormitory apartment to a four-room rented house, and he may have paid a penny for a loaf of bread instead of two cents. Each city had its attractions, mythical and real. It took over a thousand dollars to start a farm but only a few dollars to buy a railroad ticket to Chicago or Kansas City. Why not give it a try?

Second, the existence and hope of upward mobility soothed the sores of urban dissatisfaction. As Stephan Thernstrom has written, "It is not equality of condition but equality of opportunity that Americans have celebrated."[4] In spite of the widening gap between rich and poor, the American economy left room for upward movement: if not at the top, then in the middle; if not for new entrepreneurs and industrialists, then for workers in new trades and services and for white-collar laborers in new commercial, industrial, and public bureaucracies. Even if there seemed to be no current hope of individual improvement, things might be better for the next generation. The big success story, the rise from bottom to top, was usually a myth. But improving one's status by taking a new job, acquiring some real estate, or buying a horse and wagon was altogether possible.

Thus mobility—whether geographic or socioeconomic—may have dampened class conflict in American cities. The ability of people to edge upward within or, occasionally, out of lower ranks meant that urban workers' expectations often were satisfied. For a poverty-stricken immigrant, a weekly wage and a home for the family represented genuine improvement over life in the old country. Such conditions gave many a feeling that they were part of the American dream, not outside of it.

The diversity of people, the intense social interactions, and the mobility along horizontal and vertical scales gave urban cores their dynamic quality. The migrant groups that peopled those cores each made their mark on urban culture: Italian and Mexican cuisine, Irish comedy, Yiddish theater, African-American jazz, and much more. Like their predecessors, newcomers in the nineteenth century changed the urban environment as much as they were changed by it. Ethnic, racial, and religious identity, key components of modern culture, derived from inner-city experiences. And in the half-century that followed the Civil War, the inner core provided not only the engine of social change but also the focus of most social and political issues.

Bibliography

For overviews of urban immigration, see John Bodnar, *The Transplanted: A History of Immigration in Urban America* (1982); Ronald Takaki, *A Different Mirror: A History of Multicultural America* (1993); and Takaki, ed., *From Different Shores: Perspectives on Race and Ethnicity in America* (1987).

Comparative studies of urban immigrant and African-American migrant groups include John Bodnar, Roger Simon, and Michael Weber, *Lives of Their Own: Blacks, Italians, and Poles in Pittsburgh, 1900–1960* (1982); Bradford Luckingham, *Minorities in Phoenix: A Profile of Mexican-American, Chinese-American, and African-American Communities, 1860–1992* (1994); and Iram Watkins-Owens, *Blood Relations: Caribbean Immigrants and the Harlem Community, 1900–1930* (1996).

Comparative studies of urban immigrants include Josef Barton, *Peasants and Strangers: Italians, Roumanians, and Slovaks in an American City, 1900–1950* (1975); Sucheng Chan, *Asian Americans: An Interpretive History* (1991); Roger Daniels, *Asian Americans: Chinese and Japanese in the United States Since 1850* (1990); Donna R. Gabaccia, *From the Other Side: Women, Gender, and Immigrant Life in the United States, 1820–1990* (1994); Gary Mormino and George E. Pozzetta, *The Immigrant World of Ybor City: Italians and Their Latin Neighbors, 1885–1985* (1987); and Judith E. Smith, *Family Connections: A History of Italian and Jewish Immigrant Lives in Providence, Rhode Island, 1900–1940* (1985).

Histories of specific immigrant groups include Hasia Diner, *Erin's Daughters in America: Irish Immigrant Women in the Nineteenth Century* (1983); Mario T. Garcia, *Desert Immigrants: The Mexicans of El Paso, 1880–1920* (1981); Steven Hertzberg, *Strangers Within the Gate City: The Jews of Atlanta, 1845–1915* (1978); Russell Kazal, *Becoming Old Stock: The Paradox of German-American Identity* (2004); Michael Leonardo, *Varieties of Ethnic Experience:*

Kinship, Class, and Gender Among California Italian-Americans (1984); Timothy Meagher, *Inventing Irish America: Generation, Class, and Ethnic Identity in a New England City, 1880–1928* (2001); Robert Orsi, *The Madonna of 115th Street: Faith and Community in East Harlem, 1880–1950* (1986); Dominic A. Pacyga, *Polish Immigrants and Industrial Chicago: Workers on the South Side, 1880–1922* (1991); and George J. Sanchez, *Becoming Mexican-American: Ethnicity, Culture, and Identity in Chicano Los Angeles, 1900–1945* (1993).

Other works relating to ethnicity and immigration include Andrew R. Heinze, *Adapting to Abundance: Jewish Immigrants, Mass Consumption, and the Search for American Identity* (1992);Yuji Ichioka, *The Issei: The World of First Generation Japanese Immigrants, 1885–1924* (1988); Mary Ting Yi Lui, *The Chinatown Trunk Mystery: Murder, Miscegenation, and Other Dangerous Encounters in Turn-of-the-Century New York* (2005); Ricardo Romo, *East Los Angeles: History of a Barrio* (1983); Virginia E. Sanchez Korrol, *From Colonia to Community: The History of Puerto Ricans in New York City, 1917–1948* (1983); Robert A. Slayton, *Back of the Yards: The Making of a Local Democracy* (1986); Mark Wild, *Street Meeting: Multiethnic Neighborhoods in Early Twentieth-Century Los Angeles* (2005); and Judy Yung, *Unbound Feet: A Social History of Chinese Women in San Francisco* (1995).

On interconnections between immigration and race, see Thomas A. Guglielmo, *White on Arrival: Italians, Race, Color, and Power in Chicago, 1890–1945* (2003); Noel Ignatiev, *How the Irish Became White* (1995); Matthew Frye Jacobson, *Whiteness of a Different Color: European Immigrants and the Alchemy of Race* (1998); David Roediger, *The Wages of Whiteness: Race and the Making of the American Working Class* (1991); and Roediger, *Working Toward Whiteness: How America's Immigrants Became White* (2005).

Nativism and racial exclusion have been explored by Thomas Almaguer, *Racial Fault Lines: The Historical Origins of White Supremacy in California* (1994); Charlotte Brooks, *Alien Neighbors, Foreign Friends: Asian Americans, Housing, and the Transformation of Urban California* (2009); Virginia Dominguez, *White by Definition: Social Classification in Creole Louisiana* (1986); Robert M. Fogelson, *Bourgeois Nightmares: Suburbia, 1870–1930* (2005); John Higham, *Strangers in the Land: Patterns of American Nativism, 1860–1920* (1955); and Ian Haney Lopez, *White by Law: The Legal Constitution of Race* (1996).

Studies of black migration, family, and residential patterns include James Borchert, *Alley Life in Washington: Family, Community, Religion, and Folklore in the City, 1850–1970* (1980); Lynne B. Feldman, *A Sense of Place: Birmingham's Black Middle-Class Community, 1890–1930* (1999); Robert Gregg, *Sparks from the Anvil of Oppression: Philadelphia's African Methodists and Southern Migration, 1890–1940* (1994); James Grossman, *Land of Hope: Chicago, Black Southerners, and the Great Migration* (1989); Louis M. Kyriakoudes, *The Social Origins of the Urban South : Race, Gender, and Migration in Nashville and Middle Tennessee, 1890–1930* (2003); Howard Rabinowitz, *Race Relations in the Urban South, 1865–1890* (1978); Touré F. Reed, *Not Alms but Opportunity: The Urban League and the Politics of Racial Uplift, 1910–1950* (2008); and Richard W. Thomas, *Life for Us Is What We Make It: Building Black Community in Detroit, 1915–1945* (1992).

On mutual aid associations, see José A. Hernandez, *Mutual Aid for Survival: The Case of Mexican Americans* (1983); Anne Meis Knupfer, *Toward a Tenderer Humanity and Nobler Womanhood: African American Women's Clubs in Turn-of-the-Century Chicago,* (1996); Ivan Light, *Ethnic Enterprise in America: Business and Welfare Among Chinese, Japanese, and Blacks* (1972); and Daniel Soyre, *Jewish Immigrant Associations and American Identity in New York, 1880–1939* (1997).

Changing patterns of ethnic and religious identity are discussed in Harold J. Abramson, *Ethnic Diversity in Catholic America* (1973); Paula Hyman, *Gender and Assimilation in*

Modern Jewish History: The Roles and Representations of Women (1995); Richard M. Linkh, *American Catholicism and European Immigrants (1900–1924)* (1975); and Randall M. Miller and Thomas D. Marzik, eds., *Immigrants and Religion in Urban America* (1977).

On housing reform, public health, and city services, see Robert B. Fairbanks, *Making Better Citizens: Housing Reform and the Community Development Strategy in Cincinnati, 1890–1960* (1988); Judith Walzer Leavitt, *The Healthiest City: Milwaukee and the Politics of Health Reform* (1982); Eric Monkkonen, *Police in Urban America, 1860–1920* (1981); Thomas J. Philpott, *The Slum and the Ghetto: Neighborhood Deterioration and Middle-Class Reform, Chicago, 1880–1930* (1978); Christine Rosen, *The Limits of Growth: Great Fires and the Process of City Growth in America* (1986).

Links between racism and public health have been examined in Susan Craddock, *City of Plagues: Disease, Poverty, and Deviance in San Francisco* (2000); Alan Kraut, *Silent Travelers: Germs, Genes, and the "Immigrant Menace"* (1994); Natalia Molina, *Fit to be Citizens? Public Health and Race in Los Angeles, 1879–1939* (2006); Samuel Kelton Roberts Jr., *Infectious Fear: Politics, Disease, and the Health Effects of Segregation* (2009); and Nayan Shah, *Contagious Divides: Epidemics and Race in San Francisco's Chinatown* (2001).

On urban women, see Ardis Cameron, *Radicals of the Worst Sort: Laboring Women in Lawrence, Massachusetts, 1860–1912* (1995); Sarah Deutsch, *Women and the City: Gender, Space, and Power in Boston, 1870–1940* (2000); Elizabeth Ewen, *Immigrant Women in the Land of Dollars: Life and Culture on the Lower East Side, 1890–1925* (1985); Alice Kessler-Harris, *Out to Work: A History of Wage-Earning Women in America* (1982); and Joanne Meyerowitz, *Women Adrift: Independent Wage Earners in Chicago, 1880–1930* (1988). On urban men, see Howard P. Chudacoff, *The Age of the Bachelor: Creating an American Subculture* (1999).

Residential and social mobility are examined in Howard P. Chudacoff, *Mobile Americans: Residential and Social Mobility in Omaha, 1880–1920* (1972); Stephan Thernstrom, *The Other Bostonians: Poverty and Progress in an American Metropolis* (1973); and Olivier Zunz, *The Changing Face of Inequality: Urbanization, Industrialization, and Immigrants in Detroit, 1880–1920* (1982).

Notes

1. Campbell Gibson and Kay Jung, "Historical Census Statistics on Population Totals by Race, 1790 to 1990, and by Hispanic Origin, 1970 to 1990, For Large Cities and Other Urban Places in the United States," Population Division Working Paper no. 76, U.S. Census Bureau, Feb. 2005 (http://www.census.gov/population/www/documentation/twps0076/twps0076.html).

2. Howard Rabinowitz, *Race Relations in the Old South, 1865–1980* (New York: Oxford University Press, 1978).

3. "Overcrowding in Tenement Houses," *New York Times,* Dec. 3, 1876.

4. Stephan Thernstrom, *The Other Bostonians: Poverty and Progress in an American Metropolis, 1880–1970* (Cambridge, Mass.: Harvard University Press, 1973), 256.

CHAPTER 6

Bosses and Reformers in City Politics, 1870–1920

ORIGINS OF THE MACHINE

Urban governments faced unprecedented challenges between 1870 and 1900. Massive migration and immigration created an urban population that was ethnically and racially stratified. Rapid industrialization, commercial expansion, and technological change recast social structure and reshaped economic relationships. Tensions between workers and corporate employers exploded in violent strikes. Overcrowding, ill health, poverty, substandard housing, and crime in poor neighborhoods fomented a crisis of public order. Between 1870 and 1900, many cities enlarged their boundaries by thousands of acres, and myriad new businesses, industries, and households strained existing services and created an urgent need for water, gas, street lighting, sewer systems, police officers, firefighters, teachers, streets, schools, and government buildings. How would these improvements be financed? Who among contending groups would determine public priorities?

Existing governmental forms appeared inadequate to these challenges. The municipal governments that had evolved during the urbanization of the early nineteenth century seemed to generate political chaos. After 1820, most city governments had copied the federal form: two legislative councils elected from districts (wards) and an executive (mayor) elected at large (citywide). Before 1850, most mayors could exert only limited control over municipal policy. Many mayors had ceremonial powers that entitled them to hand out keys to the city and cut ribbons, but they took only a minor role in administration. Many lacked power even to veto council ordinances. As the creators of cities, states jealously guarded their power over urban governance by limiting local taxing and bonding powers. Consequently, most cities had to expand their functions in piecemeal fashion by petitioning the statehouse for charter amendments. Also, as new needs called for new officials, a confusing array of boards and commissions piled on top of each other. Some were appointed by the governor, some by the mayor, some by the city council, and some were popularly elected. Jersey City's charter was amended ninety-one times in forty years, and at one time thirty separate boards administered public functions in Philadelphia.

Political leadership was fragmented by this governmental confusion and economic change. By the mid-nineteenth century, local-minded merchants, manufacturers, contractors, and real estate operators vied for political control in order to steer public policy in directions suited to their own interests. At the same time, businessmen involved in broader networks of transportation, banking, and communications withdrew from active involvement with municipal affairs. Expansion of voting rights after 1820 created a new electorate with new political goals and new kinds of political leaders, frequently self-made men who paid close attention to the concerns of their constituents. Political power, once based on general social deference, came to be based on party organization and mass partisan loyalty. Yet the leaders of the major political parties struggled to keep their organizations intact amid challenges by independent parties—the Free Soil, Know-Nothing, and numerous workingmen's parties—that emerged out of divisions over labor, temperance, and other issues.

Local politics was reshaped by the emergence of career politicians and partisan loyalties based on ward and neighborhood organization. The less affluent career politicians who replaced the wealthy in office boasted of the benefits they brought to their constituents. As the ward became the basic unit of political life, both career politicians and patrician leaders depended on these benefits to justify their claim to office. Career politicians, however, lacked the personal resources of patricians; instead, they used public money to help constituents, with the collusion of others who shared their goals. By the 1860s and 1870s, what insiders called "the organization" and what outsiders disparaged as "the machine" shaped politics in many large cities.

Machines were political associations, distinct from established government agencies. Acting as brokers among contending economic and political interests, they created a centralized authority that overcame the fragmentation of power within government itself. They succeeded at bringing a semblance of order to the city, but through methods that many observers found repugnant.

STRUCTURE AND FUNCTIONS OF THE MACHINE

Critics depicted political machines as monolithic mobs and bosses as despots who dictated every act, every crime. The images were seldom true. Despite the harsh exposés, city bosses functioned not as dictators but as executives, chairmen of boards, and brokers who coordinated whole hierarchies of smaller bosses. Their machines were coalitions that appeared homogeneous only because their leaders kept the parts well oiled, preventing friction and disintegration. Most big-city machines were federations of smaller machines organized at the levels of ward, precinct, and even block. It was not easy to keep order within these organizations. For example, throughout much of its early history Chicago changed so rapidly and spawned so many diverse power bases that a single citywide machine could not be formed until well into the twentieth century. On the other hand, the Tammany Hall machine in New York provided a foundation upon which political interests could combine throughout the nineteenth century.

Bosses controlled these coalitions only with the support and goodwill of others. Their power rested first on the lesser bosses who operated the machine's gears at the level of the ward or precinct. The ward and precinct bosses would not stay loyal for long if the city boss did not reciprocate by ensuring a flow of material benefits that could be distributed to constituents. Some of these benefits—such as jobs on a city street project—could be provided directly by the government officials who owed their election to the machine. Other resources had to be extracted from selected members of the business community, who cooperated only in return for favorable treatment of some sort: utility franchises, contracts, tax adjustments, favorable legislation, and so forth. From these somewhat shady deals, the machine amassed funds that could be distributed as charity, and gained leverage over private jobs for grateful constituents. Satisfied constituents provided the commodity upon which the whole system was based: votes on Election Day. Many bosses were immigrants or sons of immigrants, and they knew the inner city and its needs firsthand. They understood that working-class, immigrant voters would support the machine's candidates in return for the chance at a job, or a basket of coal, or even a glass of beer and a pat on the back.

The immigrant voters who supported the machine looked to politics not as the fulfillment of abstract ideals but as an extension of the family and communal economy. Bosses met some of the immigrants' daily needs, but in doing so they diminished the ability of immigrant voters to use politics as a tool for redressing economic griev-ances. In the 1880s, independent political initiatives by labor organizations directly challenged machine candidates. In 1886, in one of the most famous contests, Henry George, running on the United Labor Party ticket, narrowly lost the New York City mayoralty to Tammany Democrat and iron manufacturer Abram Hewitt, coming in far ahead of the third place candidate, Republican Theodore Roosevelt. But the collapse of labor politics by the mid-1890s left workers with little alternative to the major parties. In many circumstances, machines were actively antagonistic to the collective orientation of the labor movement, which threatened both the machine's electoral base and its business constituency. The rise of the machine contributed to a growing tendency in American political agitation to separate workplace concerns (relegated to unions) from community issues (left to an electoral fate).

Jobs were the big prizes handed out to loyal constituents. The enormous public and private construction within cities in the late nineteenth century meant that many jobs fell within the reach of public officials. Public works boards and inspectors could convince contractors and other employers to hire men faithful to the machine. Bosses could also provide constituents with jobs on the expanding public payroll. Men who received work as a result of machine influence were always reminded where their jobs came from. Some were required to express their appreciation by making a contribution to machine coffers. This was especially true for public employees— policemen, firefighters, teachers, clerks, and janitors. All were expected to remember the machine on Election Day.

Bosses also maintained popularity by offering forms of public benevolence. Through control of city officials, they appropriated funds for neighborhood improvements such as parks, playgrounds, and bathhouses. They took children on summer picnics and sponsored free days at the amusement park. They distributed turkeys and other food on Easter, Thanksgiving, and Christmas. Each boss had his own style. James Michael Curley, mayor and boss of Boston in the early twentieth century, wrote of how he would approach an elderly woman plodding down the street by saying to her, "A woman should have three attributes. She should have beauty, intelligence, and money." As he handed her a silver dollar he would add, "Now you have all three." Reformers protested these forms of what they called mass bribery. Yet no one else was interested in providing welfare in such a personal way.

Bosses mediated between inner-city residents and formal political and legal structures, convincing authorities to look the other way when a neighborhood saloon wanted to stay open after hours or on Sundays, or when gambling houses or other vice establishments needed relief from police harassment. More important, the boss intervened when a constituent ran afoul of the law. If arrested for intoxication, vagrancy, or assault, a neighborhood resident could call upon the boss to provide counsel and, in many cases, bail. This kind of intervention gave constituents a feeling that they were getting a break in an otherwise oppressive system.

Bosses cultivated popular support by making their power visible and accessible. They joined ethnic and neighborhood associations. They set up their own clubs, holding open house in informal offices, often saloon backrooms. They appeared at wakes and weddings, and offered cash to defray funeral expenses or to start a pair of newlyweds on the right foot. No wonder a boss's achievements, including the appearance of his name in the newspapers, reflected the glory of the neighborhood. National political issues were unimportant; a boss who became too interested in public land policy, or the amount of silver in national currency, soon lost his neighborhood following. In the streets and tenements local and personal issues came first. Here people measured a politician's success by two criteria: "He gets things done" and "He keeps his word."

The political machine required constant attention. As ward boss George Washington Plunkitt preached at the turn of the century, "[The boss] plays politics every day and night in the year, and his headquarters bear the inscription 'Never Closed.'" Help from charities and government agencies often required an assessment of the worthiness of welfare recipients, but for loyal constituents, bosses asked no questions. Martin Lomasney, boss of Boston's South End, once told reformer Lincoln Steffens, "There's got to be somebody in every ward that any bloke can come to—no matter what he's done—and get help. Help, you understand, none of your law and justice, but help."

Bosses helped to transform politics into a full-time professionalized service, and encouraged people served by bosses to expect government to attend to the problems of everyday life. Before social security, unemployment insurance, medicare, food stamps, and aid to families with dependent children, bosses and machines informally distributed relief and welfare. Many people even in the poorest circumstances never used these services, but many believed they could receive help if they needed it.

Not all immigrant groups were represented in machines. In most cities the Irish initially dominated machine politics, and they frequently attempted to defend their organizations from infiltration by outsiders, such as newer immigrant groups or

African-American migrants. In Boston, New Haven, and New York, the Irish took a disproportionate share of the patronage jobs, holding on with particular strength to the police force. In Chicago, New Orleans, and Detroit, Irish-dominated machines ignored Italians and Poles for many years, and only a few machines offered any favors or concessions to blacks. These outsiders were the truly disadvantaged, for they were excluded from whatever helpful services machines could render as well as from the larger society.

Machines did not depend on goodwill alone to ensure success at the polls. There were few legal constraints on the election process; most cities did not adopt voter registration laws or the secret ballot until the twentieth century. Repeat voting, false counting, stuffed ballot boxes, and other voting fraud were common occurrences. Politicians bought votes and used violent intimidation to insure election victories. Kansas City boss Tom Pendergast used a combination of fraud and bribery, backed by an organization and a police force employing local criminals, to produce a majority for a proposed railway franchise. Chicago ward boss Johnny Powers intimidated voters by threatening landlords and merchants with loss of licenses unless they supported him in his campaign for alderman. The use of various forms of coercion was the underside of machine politics.

Neighborhood constituents were one special-interest group served by political machines; the business community was the other. The urban boom of the late nineteenth century unleashed torrents of construction and commercial activity. The increased population and need for municipal services resulted in an expansion of public agencies to administer them. Machines in political power could control the letting of contracts for public works, such as streets, sewers, and government buildings. They could influence the granting of streetcar, gas, and electricity franchises. They could juggle tax assessments for favored property owners. They could select printers, banks, and other firms to receive city business. These privileges had their price: favored businessmen were expected to pay the machines for contracts and franchises. Outsiders called the practice bribery. Bosses called it gratitude. Often politicians padded public contracts so that chosen firms could kick back funds to the bosses and their treasuries. Outsiders called this graft. Bosses doctored the ledger to hide it.

There were two kinds of graft. Honest graft, or "boodle," was the kind of investment capitalism that maximized profits while eliminating risk. From their positions within government, machine politicians had an advantageous view of where lucrative investments in real estate and utility companies could be made. Moreover, they could set policies that would assure the success of such investments. George Washington Plunkitt illustrated this kind of graft.

> My party's in power in the city, and it's goin' to undertake a lot of public improvements. Well, I'm tipped off, say, that they're going to lay out a new park at a certain place. I see an opportunity and I take it. I go to that place and I buy up all the land I can in the neighborhood. Then the board of this or that makes its plan public, and there is a rush to get my land, which nobody cared particular for before.
>
>   Ain't it perfectly honest to charge a good price and make a profit on my investment and foresight? Of course it is. Well, that's honest graft.

Dishonest graft involved criminal activity such as shakedowns and payoffs from vice operations in return for protection from police harassment. This was the most sordid activity of boss politics, but it was difficult to avoid. Bosses were specialists in gaining exemptions from the law, and the line between who was to receive such favors and who would not was seldom drawn. Payoffs from gambling, prostitution, and illegal liquor sales provided the most accessible revenues for machines. Many bosses operated vice establishments themselves, and some entered politics from backgrounds in illicit activities. Kansas City's Tom Pendergast profited handsomely from his liquor and concrete businesses, and miles of excessive concrete paving still mark the city's landscape, but shaking down insurance companies made him vulnerable to federal prosecution, sending him to jail in 1939.

In addition to functioning as service agencies and dispensaries of political favors, machines provided one potential avenue of social mobility. Participation in politics particularly attracted some sons of immigrants, a restless generation. Their lack of skills, education, and capital frustrated their desires to move ahead in a supposed land of opportunity. They often felt the lash of discrimination and the chains of poverty. Yet their schoolbooks told them that government existed for the people, and machines offered them the opportunity to serve and be rewarded for their service. So they entered politics because the machine promised that the organization's success would also mean personal achievement. The magnetic force was the prestige that the machine could bestow, not only to the individual but to his family and his neighborhood, providing some of the support that enabled the boss system to withstand attacks for so many years.

SOME NOTABLE CASES

The essence of boss politics is best described by example. Sometimes a boss exerted power from an elected office. More frequently he pulled strings from backstage, attaching public officials to him by bonds of loyalty and patronage. Bosses could operate within the Republican as well as the Democratic Party, although most machines developed as Democratic because of that party's attraction for workingmen and immigrants. Democratic bosses felt no discomfort working out contracts and deals with Republican businessmen. All bosses pursued power and advantage; some showed more concern for their constituents, whereas others devoted more attention to dishonest graft and self-serving. Still, all bosses used politics as a vehicle for personalized service, and they dispensed political favors on a cash-and-carry basis.

Modern urban bossism was reared in New York's Tammany Hall. The Society of St. Tammany evolved from an Anti-Federalist social club in the 1790s into a political organization that courted the expanded working-class vote in the 1830s. During the depression that followed the Panic of 1837, the Tammany Club distributed food, fuel, and clothing to the city's poor. It continued its relief services into the 1840s, paying particular heed to the increasing numbers of Irish immigrants. By this time Tammany had become a powerful wing of the Democratic Party, and it used its charitable activities to win votes for its candidates. As the club acquired power, it exercised increasing control over local patronage. Party leaders consulted Tammany in the choice of candidates, and

"Who Stole the People's Money?"   This drawing by the famous political cartoonist Thomas Nast shows New York Tammany boss William M. Tweed and his henchmen trying to shift blame for the corrupt and excessive expenditures for building a courthouse in 1871. The corrupt alliance between machine politicians and certain businesses often stood at the center of early boss politics.

elected officials followed Tammany dictates in the distribution of government jobs, rewarding loyal members who worked for the club and the party.

William M. Tweed was the first Tammany leader to exert citywide power. Tweed rose from neighborhood gang leader to member of the New York City Council at age twenty-eight. Tweed's district elected him to the U.S. House of Representatives when he was thirty, but the debates of Congress bored him and he did not seek reelection. Instead, he returned to the city where in the late 1860s he used the Tammany machine to win control of the entire city administration and part of the state legislature. As chairman of Tammany, he boosted his associates into public office and created what became known as the Tweed Ring.

With his henchmen secured in office through various types of vote fraud, Tweed mounted an assault on the public treasury. In 1870, he used his influence over the state General Assembly to obtain a new charter for New York City. Among other things, the charter created a board of audit that would handle all bills paid by the city and county. With the mayor's office and board of audit in the hands of Tweed's allies, contracts could be padded and kickbacks demanded. Construction of a new county courthouse provided such an opportunity. Inflated appropriations totaled $12,500,000, including $7,500 for thermometers, $404,347 for safes, $41,190 for brooms, and $2 million for plastering. In contrast, a similar courthouse was built in Brooklyn at the same time for $800,000.

By 1871, at age forty-seven, Boss Tweed, bald and weighing three hundred pounds, reputedly was worth $12 million. He had a Fifth Avenue mansion, a Connecticut estate, and a steam yacht. But he always had enough money for others. In 1870, he spent $500,000 on the poor of the Seventh Ward and raised even more for the Catholic Church. And he willingly opened his wallet for Tammany candidates in need of campaign funds. Tweed recognized that in industrial America power and money were inseparable. He did not set the standards of his day. He merely embellished those established by ambitious businessmen.

Tweed's career collapsed in 1871, when the *New York Times*, acting on information divulged by a disgruntled sheriff, printed "reliable and incontrovertible evidence of numerous, gigantic frauds on the part of the rulers of the city." The exposés prompted formation of an investigating committee. Eventually several Tammany leaders were indicted, and Tweed was arrested and convicted on 104 counts of fraud and bribery. He died in prison in 1878.

The Tweed Ring left confusion and debt in its wake. Yet whatever his motives, Tweed oversaw important accomplishments. New York was growing too fast for existing institutions to meet its needs. Tweed's regime bypassed outmoded forms of administration. In doing so it built streets, granted franchises to transit and utilities companies, and developed Central Park. All the while, however, the boss and his henchmen lined their pockets at public expense.

Tweed was a personal boss, not an organizational leader like those who followed him. "Honest John" Kelly, who succeeded him as head of the machine, molded Tammany into a more efficient organization by centralizing decision making and appointing a more party-oriented breed of henchmen. After a brief hiatus Tammany candidates moved back into positions of power. In some ways Tammany Hall and similar machines elsewhere changed after 1880. Their graft and corruption became less flagrant, and they used the expanding municipal bureaucracy and the ever-pressing need for services to cement their influence. But machines still based their existence on numbers, jobs, and favors.

Richard Croker exemplified the late nineteenth-century boss. Born in Ireland in 1843, he sailed to the United States with his parents at the age of three. He grew up in the slums of lower Manhattan, dropped out of school when he was thirteen, and joined the Fourth Avenue Tunnel Gang. Here he learned the lessons that prepared him for his political career: discipline through loyalty, reputation through results, and leadership through strength. Using his forceful personality and pugilistic skill, Croker became the gang's leader and was recruited into Tammany Hall in the 1860s. He became Tammany's—and the city's—boss in the late 1880s.

An able politician, Croker could win a point with affable charm or with vicious attack; he also knew when to compromise. The reverence that the city's populace paid him was enormous. When he took his annual European vacation, thousands saw him off. When he attended the opera, the orchestra played "Hail to the Chief" while he took his seat. Unlike Tweed, Croker did not steal outright from the public treasury. Rather, he perfected the use of honest graft. By using control over city purchases and contracts, Croker could convince favored businessmen to grant stock in their companies to the boss and his associates or to offer tips on promising investments.

Honest graft could not sustain the whole machine, however. Croker welded his underlings to him by permitting them to participate in dirty graft. He generally overlooked the activities of his ninety thousand precinct workers—many of them policemen, firefighters, and other civil servants—as long as they carried their districts for Tammany candidates on election day.

Croker had many friends but also some enemies. In 1894, opponents managed to dent Tammany's power when a committee under the chairmanship of State Senator Clarence Lexow undertook an investigation of police corruption in New York City. The Lexow Committee's hearings—six thousand pages of testimony—detailed an extraordinary degree of police graft and accomplished just what Croker's enemies desired: disenchantment with the machine. But Croker stayed one step ahead. He sensed the public mood and resigned as Tammany's chairman so as not to be linked to an electoral defeat. The reformers' candidate for mayor, Republican merchant William Strong, won the 1894 election by forty-five thousand votes. After the election Croker sailed to England for a three-year vacation.

Strong and his police commissioner Theodore Roosevelt managed a few reforms, but their strict enforcement of the law made many people long for the looser Tammany days. In September 1897, with the Lexow revelations buried, Croker returned to New York and reestablished his control over Tammany. He was just in time. The state legislature had given the city a new charter that on January 1, 1898, would consolidate Brooklyn, Queens, Staten Island, and the Bronx with Manhattan. The winner of the 1897 mayoral election would administer a Greater New York City of more than three million people. Reformers entered Seth Low, president of Columbia University and former mayor of Brooklyn, as their candidate. Croker and the Democrats selected a political unknown, Judge Robert Van Wyck, and frankly aimed their campaign at the tenement districts, where reform crackdowns had been heaviest. Their slogan was "To Hell with Reform!" The strategy worked. The close election was decided by a Democratic landslide in the inner wards. Croker and Tammany again ruled the city.

Croker's triumphant return damaged his political savvy. First, he divorced his wife and moved into the Democratic Club on Fifth Avenue. Here he kept a court, forcing lieutenants to visit him in their best dress and to remain standing at dinner until the boss was seated. Then Croker tried unsuccessfully to lead his machine into state and national politics. He pressured his organization to run a Tammany candidate against Teddy Roosevelt for governor in 1898, and he backed William Jennings Bryan for president in 1900. In both instances Croker's ignorance of larger issues and his antagonistic speeches hurt him and his candidates. In addition, reformers revived public disaffection with the machine in New York City. An investigation exposed Croker's connections with a firm that furnished most of the city's ice and that was planning to double its prices to consumers. Croker's participation in the scheme was still honest graft, but it was the kind that directly drained the pockets of ordinary, working-class families. Moreover exposés revealed that dirty graft had again spread throughout the city. These occurrences loosened Croker's grip on his machine. When Seth Low defeated the Tammany candidate for mayor in 1901, Croker again sailed for England.

New York's "King Richard". Tammany boss Richard Croker, with top hat and boutonniere, had no reservations about his motives in running his powerful political machine. When a reformer asked Croker if he was working for his own interests, "King Richard" replied, "All the time, the same as you."

Croker had presided over some thirty-five district leaders. The career of one of these smaller bosses, Timothy D. Sullivan, illustrates an ethnic boss's political possibilities. "Big Tim" Sullivan was a second-generation immigrant, raised by his widowed Irish mother. Like Tweed and Croker, he left school and became the leader of a gang. His savvy and brawn gave him ready entry into Tammany Hall. He became a political prodigy and was elected to the state legislature in 1886 when he was twenty-three years old. He later served a term in the U.S. House of Representatives, but he could not stomach life in Washington and returned to New York after two years.

Back in New York, Sullivan secured control over the Lower East Side and Bowery districts by learning Yiddish and soliciting support from the Jewish immigrants who were replacing some of the Irish residents. He used political leverage to place his supporters on public payrolls and to open a string of profitable gambling halls. He also skillfully cultivated his personal appeal. He arranged bails, sent food and medicine to the sick, gave shoes to needy schoolchildren, and sponsored annual summer picnics. His Timothy D. Sullivan Association was a poor man's club that operated out of neighborhood saloons, distributing jobs, food, and other services. Sullivan built his machine on trust and loyalty. It was said that he was so well liked that his portrait hung in nearly every building in his district.

The Ward Machine in Action.   This photograph depicts one of many gatherings of the Timothy D. Sullivan Association, the political club run by ward boss "Big Tim" Sullivan of New York. Note that a political outing was generally an all-male event.

In his later years, Sullivan, who had become wealthy from investments in gambling enterprises and movie theaters, helped expand Tammany and the Democratic Party from their base of personal politics into support for social reform legislation. Deeply committed to the welfare of working-class people, Sullivan used his influence in the New York General Assembly to promote bills for the benefit of labor. He acted as mentor for Frances Perkins, then a lobbyist for the National Consumers' League and shortly to become a leading Progressive Era and New Deal reformer, and helped her pass a bill limiting working hours for women. Sympathetic to the crusade for women's suffrage, he also worked with Harriot Stanton Blatch, daughter of suffragist Elizabeth Cady Stanton, in support of women's political and economic equality with men. Sullivan's reform career was cut short in 1912, however, when he became ill and was committed to an insane asylum. He escaped but was apparently struck by a freight train and was found dead in a railroad yard. His funeral attracted more than twenty-five thousand mourners.

New York City provides the most colorful showcase for machine politics, but bossism flourished in many other cities as well. Philadelphia had "King" James McManes, a Republican who controlled the city's fiscal policies and electoral politics from the late 1860s until 1881. McManes achieved and exercised power by becoming the leading figure on a municipal board that superintended the city's gas utility. Using his authority over the distribution of jobs and letting of contracts, McManes influenced other city departments. He required city employees to kick back a portion of their salaries to his organization, and he manipulated elections for his own benefit. During his reign McManes reputedly earned two and a half million dollars, mostly from payoffs from favored contractors. Like other bosses, McManes alarmed opponents by his lavish expenditures of public funds. Between 1860 and 1880, Philadelphia's municipal debt swelled by 350 percent. Although much of the money facilitated the city's physical expansion, a number of Republican businessmen became outraged. They formed a Committee of One Hundred and joined local Democrats to defeat machine candidates in the 1881 elections. McManes retired to enjoy his private fortune, but even more effective boss rule returned to Philadelphia later in the decade, exploiting the reform campaign to centralize political authority and consolidating support with the state party organization.

Chicago had its own brand of machine politics. Practically every ward boss was an independent entrepreneur, each courting his constituency in his own style. Johnny Powers of the Nineteenth Ward was known as "The Chief Mourner" because of his attendance record at funerals. Michael "Hinky Dink" Kenna of the First Ward served free lunches in his saloon. His partner, "Bathhouse John" Coughlin, received his nickname for the kind of services he sponsored. "Blond Boss" William Lorimer worked to remove prejudices against Jews and other immigrants on Chicago's West Side. Although all but Lorimer were Democrats, no individual was able to construct one citywide machine. Carter Harrison and his son Carter II held the mayoralty off and on through three and a half decades and cultivated faithful support among immigrants by championing personal liberty—meaning toleration of drinking and gambling. But neither Harrison could overcome the independence of the ward bosses.

Still, machine politics in Chicago contained familiar features. Political power derived from voters and favors. City employees paid off the boss who got them jobs. Graft was common. Powers maintained a mutually profitable relationship with streetcar companies. Roger Sullivan, one of the most powerful bosses of early twentieth-century Chicago, specialized in granting favors to—and receiving gratuities from—banks and gas companies. The lack of a strong city boss, however, produced two extremes of instability. On one hand, it was somewhat easier for reformers to gain a foothold in Chicago politics because they did not have to battle a single, entrenched machine. On the other hand, because there were so many bosses, so many enemies, reformers found it difficult to mount a unified attack against every boss.

It is important to note that bossism was not confined to large cities. Small cities also needed leaders who could coordinate political power, mediate between immigrants and their new environment, and organize physical expansion. In Omaha, Tom Dennison built a Democratic machine that influenced local affairs for nearly three decades. Dennison used politics to protect his multimillion-dollar vice business. By appealing to immigrant voters of the inner wards (Dennison's saloons were often the only places where immigrant workers could cash their paychecks), Dennison could place his lieutenants in high offices and through them act as broker between the city government and the business community. As in other cities, the boss accumulated boodle from firms receiving city business. Dennison remained in power from the early 1900s to the late 1920s and retired to California a wealthy man.

Practically every major city experienced a period of boss rule. In Pittsburgh, Christopher Magee supervised a Republican machine that lasted for half a century. In San Francisco, Abe Ruef, whose Jewish ancestry and college training distinguished him from other city bosses, operated from within the Union Labor Party in the early twentieth century. Martin Behrman of New Orleans directed local affairs between 1900 and 1920 from his posts as mayor and as leader of the Democratic Choctaw Club. The Pendergast brothers, Jim and Tom, rose from Kansas City's river wards to rule the entire city from the late 1880s to the late 1930s. Edward H. Crump acquired power in Memphis around 1910 and did not lose control until the 1940s. Although he was never mayor, William F. "Billy" Klair dominated politics in the city of Lexington and in the Kentucky state legislature from the early years of the century to 1937. In Jersey City, Frank Hague ruled from 1917 to 1947 under the brazen slogan "I am the law." Like other bosses these men were coordinators, not dictators. They presided over federations, not over autocracies. Through key alliances with wealthy citizens and business interests, they offered a full range of services, from Thanksgiving turkeys to business franchises to gambling dens.

CITY GOVERNANCE AND MUNICIPAL REFORM

As early as 1860, lines in many cities were drawn in what would become characteristic political contests in the late nineteenth century: boss politics and the machine opposed by an elite minority organized under the banner of municipal reform. This latter group, which can be called municipal, or civic, reformers battled bosses in cities across the country by attempting to mold their own version of urban government. Mostly middle and upper-class, native-born, and Protestant, these people opposed immigrant-dominated political machines and offered various proposals to undercut bosses' power. To do so, they launched a campaign to alter municipal governance.

Though machines were often fragile alliances torn by internal rivalries, much of their political influence derived from the ward-based organization of city councils and boards of aldermen. In the mid-nineteenth century, the ward system, which resembles the geography-based representation of the U.S. House of Representatives, had begun to replace citywide representation, and most councilmen and aldermen were elected by voters of a certain ward. By 1900, the typical ward-elected representative was a modest saloonkeeper, retailer, artisan, or laborer who customarily lived and worked in the ward. Professionals and downtown businessmen were greatly outnumbered. Residential patterns guaranteed that some wards would be dominated by working-class Irish, others by Italians, and others by native-born Protestants. The ward system was also the vehicle through which workingmen's slates and later socialist tickets won representation on city councils. The council served as the neighborhoods' voice, the channel through which constituents obtained pavements, sewers, and water mains. By 1900, American cities included disparate neighborhoods with different social and ethnic orientations and diverse transportation, paving, and drainage needs, and city councils provided the forum for debate over urban expansion and its implications.

During the late nineteenth century, urban elites became alarmed as they observed immigrants and their representatives gaining ground in city councils and party organizations. To counter erosion of their authority, business and professional leaders organized themselves to intervene in the political process. Through chambers of commerce, boards of trade, and specially constituted good government and municipal reform leagues, these citizens sought to restore urban rule to the "better elements." Chambers of commerce were particularly active in promoting changes they felt would make the atmosphere of the city good for business, arguing that economic growth would eventually help the working classes. Political alliances of merchants, lawyers, and journalists, arguing that they were acting in the civic interest, constituted themselves into groups such as the Committee of Seventy in New York and the Committee of One Hundred in Philadelphia and offered reform candidates who succeeded in ousting the Tweed Ring in New York in 1871 and the McManes machine in Philadelphia in 1881, at least temporarily. These reformers blamed bosses for wasting taxpayers' money and polluting the American system. Eventually, these temporary alliances were replaced by municipal leagues with paid executives that competed with ward-based politicians and promoted what were considered to be better qualified candidates. These associations campaigned for cuts in expenditures and tax rates, drafted legislation, and endorsed charter revision.

An important means by which municipal reformers could recapture power involved was to shift authority from elected to appointed officials. Before the 1860s and 1870s, the city council had directly supervised municipal functions, determining appointments, hiring city employees, fixing policy, and deciding administrative details. By the 1880s and 1890s, as a result of some successes by municipal reformers, the supervisory role of the council had declined sharply, particularly in appointments and finances. New municipal charters, lobbied for by members of chambers of commerce and reform leagues, shifted authority to expert commissions and executive departments either appointed or elected by a citywide constituency that favored downtown business or professional interests. This was often accomplished with the help of state legislatures, frequently dominated by rural and business interests. New York City's reform charter of 1873, Boston's charter of 1885, and Baltimore's charter of 1898 all sharply limited aldermanic authority over public works, budgets, and police expenditures by substituting appointed commissions composed of specialists.

In the same years in which councils lost authority to special independent commissions, many mayors gained power through broadened use of the veto and expanded powers of appointment. Mayors, especially those elected when the general public became fed up with bosses' corruption and when reformers could mobilize middle-class voters behind candidates to challenge the machine, became the ones to initiate policy and to implement programs. Elected on a citywide basis, reform mayors were likely to be drawn from the ranks of bankers, manufacturers, wholesale merchants, large-scale real estate developers, and lawyers with old-stock social-register pedigrees. Such mayors were not likely to be among the city's wealthiest men, but they usually belonged to what Victorians called the better class of citizens. Downtown businessmen were also likely to hold the crucial post of city comptroller, where their fiscal orientation guided the auditing of city accounts and preparation of budgets. Independent commissions that governed municipal parks, libraries, and police departments tended to draw their membership from the same social strata. Most commissioners held long terms of office and were increasingly likely to be independent from elected officials.

Furthermore, the importance of elected officials as policymakers paled in the face of a new group of urban professionals: civil engineers, landscape architects, public health officials, and school administrators who supervised permanent urban bureaucracies that built and operated waterworks, designed and ran the parks, guarded public health and safety, and oversaw the education of millions of urban schoolchildren (see Chapter 7). Together the downtown businessmen and professionals, and the new municipal experts claimed that their vision of the city constituted the true public interest.

GOALS AND TACTICS OF MUNICIPAL REFORM

Municipal reform included a number of specific goals and tactics, most of which were touted as efforts to remove partisanship from politics and politics from government and to establish citywide rather than ward-based representation. In their attempt to dismantle party machinery, some civic reformers believed that they needed to limit suffrage. The commission appointed to investigate the Tweed Ring scandals recommended in 1878 that the vote be restricted to those who owned property. A leader in a campaign for municipal reform in Newport, Rhode Island, made the case in 1907 that universal suffrage failed to give property owners political power commensurate with their economic power: "The present system," he charged, "has excluded in large degree the representation of those who have the city's well-being most at heart." Rather than a government by the least educated, who he claimed were also the "least interested class of citizens," he proposed a system that gave majority representation to the city's wealthy citizens. As he put it, "It stands to reason that a man paying $5,000 taxes in a town is more interested in the well-being and development of his town than the man who pays no taxes." Although Northeastern and Midwestern municipal reformers looked with keen interest at legislation that had disenfranchised black and poor white voters in southern states, regulations that actually revoked immigrant voting rights never seemed politically feasible in cities because universal white-male suffrage was too deeply entrenched.

In many Southern cities, urban politics and civic reform were shaped by new racial and economic alignments. In Memphis, ward-based politicians struggled to meet local needs caused by post–Civil War economic contractions, competition for jobs between Irish immigrants and African-American migrants, new demands for services like street paving and police protection, and yellow fever epidemics in 1878–79 that drove multitudes of people out of the city. Severe budgetary problems gave wealthy taxpayers the opportunity to enlist the state legislature to overturn Memphis's home rule and replace the unlikely coalition of Irish, German, Italian, and African-American political leaders with a city commission dominated by a white commercial elite. The new government kept taxes low by providing services only in wealthy white neighborhoods. Even after Memphis regained home rule in 1893, the city maintained this form of municipal governance. In Charlotte, North Carolina, racial and class integration of city neighborhoods promoted broad participation in local government between 1865 and the 1890s. But then, a reform campaign of white supremacy and Democratic "redemption" successfully disenfranchised black and illiterate white voters, establishing upper-class political control and redrawing boundaries between different classes and races much more sharply.

Instead of limiting the franchise to property holders, municipal reformers in the North and West turned to strategies that would lessen the impact of immigrant and working-class voters without actually interfering with voting rights. Several of these strategies were designed to regulate elections and to make nominations and election procedures more uniform. By 1905, registration laws requiring residency and strict identification of a voter were on the books everywhere, and in the next fifteen years, localities set up election boards, tightened laws making it illegal to vote more than once, and tried to define legitimate use of campaign funds. Also, electoral reform strategies were designed to weaken party machines and to remove party politics from municipal administration. Because bosses thrived on ethnic neighborhoods and party loyalty, reformers tried to institute at-large (citywide rather than neighborhood-based) elections and nonpartisan ballots (no candidate could run for office under a party label) as a way of attacking the machines. Having to appeal to a large citywide electorate rather than one neighborhood or ethnic group would diminish the ability of candidates from ethnic and working-class districts to gain office. Large organizations such as civic leagues and business groups would have an advantage in influencing citywide elections and electing business candidates because they had resources to reach a large and diverse electorate.

Nonpartisan ballots symbolized reformers' claim that there was only one urban public interest, which businessmen best understood. Parties were not needed for public services to be provided as cheaply and efficiently as possible. Civic reformers contended that a city did not need a Democrat or Republican to build a school or lay a sewer; responsible local government was no place for party politicians. Yet removing party labels from election ballots, supposedly to cultivate civic loyalties rather than bloc voting, also had the effect of depriving working-class and ethnic candidates of party resources for campaigning and party employment. Few machine politicians could have stayed in politics without the party's help. Nonpartisan elections favored those who did not need party organization, men of wealth and social standing who restored their claim to office holding. Municipal reformers also campaigned for civil service along with at-large elections and nonpartisan ballots. Intended to destroy the machine's ability to provide employment to its foot soldiers, civil service provided presumably objective standards for hiring municipal employees, using written and oral examinations rather than party affiliation as the qualifying basis for city jobs.

Between 1900 and 1920, nonpartisanship, at-large elections, and civil service were successfully implemented in many cities. Municipal reform was less likely to penetrate large cities with complex electorates, where middle- and upper-class voters did not constitute an electoral majority; but smaller and fast-growing cities, usually in the Midwest and West, usually adopted reform provisions in their charters. Urban scholar Amy Bridges has argued that southwestern cities with a shortage of capital were particularly fertile ground for municipal reform. By emphasizing economic growth, using public policy to fulfill the needs of core business supporters, and excluding working-class ethnics from policymaking, reform politicians in cities such as Albuquerque, Phoenix, San Diego, and Dallas succeeded in getting themselves consistently reelected, and in installing commission and city manager governance, non-partisan elections, and civil service. Even in some big cities, reformers succeeded in getting nonpartisan at-large elections adopted: Los Angeles in 1908, Boston in 1909, Akron in 1915, and Detroit in 1918.

Municipal reform campaigns changed patterns of representation. The switch from ward to citywide electoral districts made it more difficult for ethnic and working-class wards and African-American neighborhoods to gain representation. Socialists in Dayton, Ohio, won 25 percent of the vote in 1909 and elected two aldermen and three assessors, but after a change to citywide elections, they failed to elect a single candidate even though their share of the total vote increased to 44 percent. The shift to citywide representation in Los Angeles prevented black and Mexican-American citizens from electing a single city council representative until the most recent period. And citywide elections in Pittsburgh in 1911 enabled upper-class businessmen and professionals to replace working- and middle-class representatives on the city council and school committee.

The orientation of most civic reformers was reflected in their commitment to applying principles of business management to cities. Trying to make the structure of urban governance match the model of the corporation, reformers proposed reorganizing cities to separate policymaking from administration either through a commission or a city manager form of government. The first city to adopt the business model was Galveston, Texas, where business and professional leaders had already secured a charter amendment from the state legislature that replaced ward representation with citywide elections. Businessmen on the council continued to be outvoted by a nonbusiness faction, but in 1900 emergency circumstances following a disastrous hurricane and flood enabled the state legislature to replace Galveston's city council with a commission of businessmen, each of whom administered a different branch of municipal affairs. The city adopted the commission form permanently and elected seven commissioners on a nonpartisan, at-large basis. In Nashville, conservative businessmen and Democratic Party leaders attacked the ward-based political system of Boss Hilary Howse, who had irritated them by spending public funds to improve the health, education, and welfare of ethnic and racial minorities. Charter reforms, establishing a commission government in 1913, led to Howse's ouster two years later. By 1915, 456 cities operated under commission governance.

The city manager form of government grew out of business reverence for expertise. In 1908, Staunton, Virginia, hired a city manager to administer local affairs in the place of a politically elected mayor. The idea spread slowly at first. But in Dayton, Ohio, John M. Patterson, the president of National Cash Register, working with the Chamber of Commerce and the newly organized Bureau of Municipal Research, began a campaign for charter reform that was enacted, finally, as a measure to aid recovery from the disastrous flood of 1913. Eventually the city manager plan was tried in larger cities such as Cleveland, Cincinnati, and Kansas City. This plan created a new separation of power. It usually provided for a small city council elected on a nonpartisan ballot that would determine policy and pass ordinances. The council would then appoint or hire a city manager, chosen for his (virtually all city managers were male) administrative and technical skills, who, like a corporate chief, would implement council policies and determine budgets. In some cases the mayor was retained and given mainly titular functions. By 1920, more than 150 cities had city managers. Business interests consistently campaigned for this reform. For example, the *Dallas News* promoted the plan in 1930 by asking, "Why not run Dallas itself on a business schedule by business methods under businessmen? . . . The city manager is the executive of a corporation under a board of directors. Dallas is the corporation. It is as simple as that. Vote for it."

The efficiency argument also produced a more controversial reform: municipal ownership of public utilities. Some reformers believed that regardless of the form of government, bribery and corruption would always fester as long as politicians could collude with big business at public expense. These reformers thought they could destroy bosses' financial resources and provide better services by replacing private franchises with publicly owned operations. City-owned water systems had been common since the mid-nineteenth century. Now, some reformers began to advocate public gas, electric, and transportation systems. Although by 1910 several hundred cities had experimented with this reform—including Cleveland, Detroit, and Chicago—public ownership succeeded mostly in smaller cities. Private investors disagreed about the benefits of public ownership, and many municipal leaders were frightened by the reform's popularity among socialists. Expenditures on public harbors, roads, and sewers won general acceptance because they stimulated economic growth. But when advocates of public utilities such as gas and electricity tried to supplant private operations, they frequently met strong opposition. Nevertheless, most city dwellers eventually accepted some form of public regulation of utility rates and services, even if public ownership proved unacceptable.

Some bosses were able to adjust to new structures of city governance and even use them for their own purposes. When a city commission government threatened to subvert Omaha boss Tom Dennison's control of the city in 1912, the boss did not fight public sentiment. He merely entered his own slate of candidates for the commission, who then dominated that body for the machine's benefit. Boss Ed Crump solidified his grip on Memphis in the same way when a new city charter established a commission form of government in 1909. James Michael Curley was able to use new citywide elections in Boston as a way of undermining the ward-based rivals with whom he was contesting for power.

The lines between some bosses and reformers blurred in late nineteenth- and early twentieth-century cities, when these bosses saw political advantages in supporting civic reforms, public ownership of utilities, and labor legislation that promised to help their constituents. For example, New York City's Big Tim Sullivan dashed to the statehouse in Albany to cast a decisive vote in favor of a bill limiting working hours for women to fifty-four a week. (He explained, "I had seen me sister go out to work when she was only fourteen and I know we ought to help these gals by giving 'em a law which will prevent 'em from being broken down while they're still young.") Republican boss George B. Cox of Cincinnati supported the secret ballot and voter registration, usually anathema to a boss, when he came under pressure from the suburban allies to whom he owed his initial election. Similarly, several big-city reform mayors moved beyond their initial goals of eliminating corruption to support social reforms desired by working-class, immigrant constituents. The mayoral careers of Hazen S. Pingree of Detroit, Samuel M. Jones of Toledo, and Thomas L. Johnson of Cleveland illustrate this pattern.

A Detroit shoe manufacturer, Pingree was drafted into the 1889 mayoral election by a group of Republican businessmen who wanted to rid Detroit of corruption. Pingree won the election by appealing to the city's German, Polish, and Irish voters. He immediately began to apply business principles of prudence and efficiency to government operations, and his success won him reelection in 1891. In his struggles to limit the rates and privileges of street-railway, gas, electric, and telephone companies, however, he began to shift his sympathies from businesses to ordinary people. When the depression of 1893–94 brought suffering to thousands of Detroiters, Pingree focused his administration directly on the welfare of the working classes. He bolstered relief agencies, authorized public works for unemployment relief, and cajoled merchants to keep prices low and not to lay off workers. During four terms as mayor, Pingree not only stopped corruption but also built parks and schools, instituted a more equitable tax structure, reduced utility rates, and spoke out for a graduated income tax and municipal ownership. Moreover, he ignored efforts to impose middle-class norms on others. He refused to enforce Sunday closing laws applying to saloons, and he tolerated gambling and prostitution. His administration became a model for reform mayors in other cities. Pingree's passion for the poor influenced administrators in other cities to assume greater social responsibilities, and his battles with utilities companies furnished other reformers with strong arguments for municipal ownership.

Samuel "Golden Rule" Jones served as mayor of Toledo from 1897 until his death in 1904, and Tom Johnson was mayor of Cleveland from 1901 until a narrow election defeat in 1909. Like Pingree, Jones and Johnson were successful businessmen who became social reformers. Both actively supported municipal ownership of utilities, and both stressed the need for social justice and equality. Johnson was influenced by the ideas of Henry George, whose book *Progress and Poverty* (1879) made considerable impact on reform thought around the turn of the century. George's proposal to eliminate social inequality by taxing profits that property owners unfairly received from the unearned increase of land values inspired Johnson and others like him to work for social and economic reform. Many of the programs supported by Jones and Johnson bordered on socialism and alienated their business allies. Yet, like Pingree, both mayors sought only to preserve what they believed to be the American tradition, not to change it. Their popular appeal and social welfare projects extended well beyond ordinary economy and efficiency, yet they envisioned their goals as the fulfillment of the American dream.

Pingree, Jones, and Johnson were the exceptions. Most municipal reformers aimed only to "throw the rascals out," and when successful, their "clean governments" often could not match the functions performed by political machines. Although reformers called for honesty and efficiency in government, they rarely mentioned social welfare. Behind their proposals was the notion that city government should provide a climate for economic growth through the provision of efficient administration. The city-as-a-business orientation provided a sharp contrast with socialist, social reform, and working-class ethnic demands to establish social programs aimed at improving the health, welfare, and living conditions of inner-city residents.

Civic reformers' self-righteousness moralism and obsessive budget cutting seldom addressed urban demands for jobs, housing, and better public health. Their attempts to apply business principles to politics commonly underplayed the complexities of business and political administration. A reformer, said Mr. Dooley, the fictional Irish commentator created by newspaper columnist Finley Peter Dunne in 1902,

> thinks business an' honesty is th' same thing. . . . He's got them mixed because they dhress alike. His idea is that all he has to do to make a business administhration is to keep honest men ar-round him. Wrong, I'm not sayin', mind ye, that a man can't do good work an' be honest at th' same time. But whin I hire a la-ad, I find out first whether he is onto his job, an' after a few years I begin to suspect he is honest too. . . . A man

, ought to be honest to start with an' afther that he ought to be crafty. A pollytician who's on'y honest is jus' th' same as bein' out in a winther storm without anny clothes on.

Thus municipal reformers may have succeeded in improving public administration by reducing corruption, lowering taxes, and shoring up local services. But their tendency to view urban society only in business and moralistic terms ignored long-term social problems and posed an incomplete substitute for the welfare functions of political machines.

Bibliography

Analyses of the relationship between urban political power and the provision of city services include Amy Bridges, *A City in the Republic: Antebellum New York and the Origins of Machine Politics* (1984); Robin Einhorn, *Property Rules: Political Economy in Chicago, 1833–1872* (1991); Terrence J. McDonald, *The Parameters of Urban Fiscal Policy: Socioeconomic Change and Political Culture in San Francisco, 1860–1906* (1986); and Jon C. Teaford, *The Unheralded Triumph: City Government in America, 1870–1900* (1984).

On labor politics in this period, see Leon Fink, *Workingmen's Democracy: The Knights of Labor and American Politics* (1983); Steven J. Ross, *Workers on the Edge: Work, Leisure, and Politics in Industrializing Cincinnati, 1788–1890* (1985); and Richard Schneirov, *Labor and Urban Politics: Class Conflict and the Origins of Modern Liberalism in Chicago* (1998).

Among individual machines, Tammany Hall has received the most attention from historians, including from Daniel Czitrom, "Underworlds and Underdogs: Big Tim Sullivan and Metropolitan Politics in New York, 1889–1913," *Journal of American History* 78 (September 1991): 536–58; David C. Hammack, *Power and Society: Greater New York at the Turn of the Century* (1982); Leo Hershkowitz, *Tweed's New York: Another Look* (1977); and Chris McNickle, *To Be Mayor of New York: Ethnic Politics in the City, 1898–1930* (1993). William L. Riordon, *Plunkitt of Tammany Hall* (1995) is a memoir of a boss and includes a perceptive introduction by Peter Quinn.

Other important studies are Steven P. Erie, *Rainbow's End: Irish-Americans and the Dilemma of Urban Machine Politics, 1840–1985* (1988); Philip. J. Ethington, *The Public City: The Political Construction of Urban Life in San Francisco, 1850–1900* (1994); Thomas W. Hanchett, *Sorting Out the New South City: Race, Class, and Urban Development in Charlotte, 1875–1975* (1998); Lisa Keller, *Triumph of Order: Democracy and Public Space in New York and London* (2008); Lawrence Larsen and Nancy J. Hulston, *Pendergast!* (1997); Peter McCaffery, *When Bosses Ruled Philadelphia: The Emergence of the Republican Machine, 1867–1933* (1993); Zane L. Miller, *Boss Cox's Cincinnati: Urban Politics in the Progressive Era* (1968); and Eugene J. Watts, *The Social Basis of City Politics: Atlanta, 1865–1903* (1978).

For perspectives on municipal reform, see Amy Bridges, *Morning Glories: Municipal Reform in the Southwest* (1997); James D. Bolin, *Bossism and Reform in a Southern City: Lexington, Kentucky, 1880–1940* (2000); Kenneth Finegold, *Experts and Politicians: Reform Challenges to Machine Politics in New York, Cleveland, and Chicago* (1995); Maureen Flanagan, *Seeing with their Hearts: Chicago Women and the Vision of the Good City, 1871–1933* (2002); Melvin G. Holli, *Reform in Detroit: Hazen S. Pingree and Urban Politics* (1969); Bradley R. Rice, *Progressive Cities: The Commission Government Movement in America, 1901–1920* (1977); Martin J. Schiesl, *The Politics of Efficiency: Municipal Administration and Reform in America, 1880–1920* (1977); and Lynette B. Wrenn, *Crisis and Commission Government in Memphis* (1998).

CHAPTER 7

Reforming the Social and Physical Environment, 1870–1920

IMPULSES OF SOCIAL REFORM

Urban bosses and municipal (civic) reformers confined their battles to the traditional political arenas: elections and the established institutions of government. But in the closing years of the nineteenth century and dawning years of the twentieth, other activists launched more broad-ranging campaigns to address the problems of urban life. The erosion of party loyalties—hastened by civic reforms such as tighter voter registration laws, secret ballots, and direct primaries—created new opportunities for pressure groups to exert influence. The growing power of manufacturers' organizations, labor lobbies, civic leagues, women's clubs, and professional associations made politics more fragmented, political combinations more fluid, and campaigns more issue oriented. Lobbying and coalition building supplanted older party channels, and reformers developed other methods to create and mobilize public opinion, such as sensationalistic journalism, celebrity picket lines, witness-calling investigations, referendum campaigns, and social science surveys.

Occasionally, maverick candidates such as socialists could win political office and reform coalitions could reshape urban politics. American socialists vigorously denounced urban inequality, poverty, and lack of welfare services, proposing their own remedies, which ranged from expanded public responsibility to hire the unemployed to municipal ownership of utilities and transportation. Municipal socialists were particularly visible in cities like Milwaukee, Reading, Schenectady, and Bridgeport, where socialist mayors were elected to office. In 1912 socialists held more than twelve hundred public offices in 340 cities and towns across the country. But the major thrust of reform was increasingly outside the political parties.

Men's political culture in the nineteenth century had been fervently partisan and widely participatory. As elections approached, throngs of men had marched through the streets in torchlight parades and cheered at mass meetings until they were hoarse—even if the campaign lacked exciting issues. The vitality of this culture waned near the end of the century, as upper-class and middle-class men abandoned partisan politics to working-class and ethnic machines and turned their interest to single-issue reform tactics. In so doing, these men found themselves in territory that women's voluntary reform associations had long occupied. As reformers tried to secure legislation to redress social problems by increasing the government's role in social welfare and economic life, men and women found themselves joining to achieve common goals. New ideas about government's broader social responsibility resonated with women's social concerns. Not surprisingly, then, female social activists played a major role in the articulation of urban reform, prior to their own direct participation as voters.

The liberal creed of the early nineteenth century had been laissez-faire, the belief that the natural order of things ensured equilibrium and that government ought not interfere with that natural order. But by century's end that faith had begun to dissolve. A broad phalanx of social reformers, ranging from wide-eyed humanitarians to calculating special interests, marched under a banner of public and private intervention to remove injustices from society. Their response to greed and individualism was community responsibility to promote the welfare of all. Historian Daniel Rodgers has described a shared language of social reform, influenced by goals and issues prevalent in Europe. The new thinking in America included a conception of social bonds that challenged older notions that success depended on strengths of individual character, that the economy was the product of individual calculations, and that governance was a matter of empowering the best men. This emphasis on public responsibility was expressed in a new interest in the social and physical environment, the discovery of what Rodgers termed "new forms of social sinning and corresponding new measures of social control," and an intense concern with community cohesion.[1] Social reformers also focused on protecting those whom they saw as victims of industrialization, such as women and child laborers, those injured by industrial accidents, the elderly, and unemployed people, and they pursued goals of industrial peace and cooperation.

Like civic reform, social reform grew out of changing economic and social conditions. Indeed, some social reformers were also civic reformers. It was based largely in the new middle class. Its membership consisted basically of men and women who were becoming specialists in expanding areas of law, medicine, education, social work, and other professions, as well as new-breed professionals in fields of business, labor, and agriculture. Their awakening professional consciousness encouraged them to apply their expertise to their environments. More important, it led them to support and to undertake scientific investigations of urban problems. From the 1870s onward, a number of different groups, mostly private and voluntary, sponsored formal examinations of aspects of urban life. These included surveys of public health and housing, studies of the incidence and location of poverty, and investigations of local corruption. One of the most striking qualities of early social science was the way in which the field tied scholarly methods to women's traditional community concerns. Agencies and organizations that were committed to social science methods provided women reformers with quasi-professional positions as investigators from which they carried domestic and social concerns into far corners of the city. By the turn of the century the methods and language of social science and women's role as social investigators had become institutionalized components of reform strategy.

The emphasis on investigation had two objectives. First, middle-class reformers were an inquiring generation: they felt a strong urge to know the facts. Many of them believed they had temporarily lost their ability to understand fast-growing, ever-changing urban society. Only by restoring that understanding could they soothe their sense of crisis and begin to formulate plans to improve present conditions. Second, reformers from new middle-class ranks had a strong faith in knowledge and conscience as reforming agents. Many believed that if the general public could be kept informed and if the major problems could be identified and exposed, an enlightened citizenry would rally behind programs to destroy injustice.

A new kind of journalism of exposure became a principal weapon in the campaign for reform. For nearly a century after the Revolution, few city newspapers gave more than a passing glance to local affairs. Most newspapers had limited circulation and acted as mouthpieces for a political party, focusing mainly on state, national, and international issues. But the decades following the Civil War witnessed an extraordinary popularization and proliferation of newspapers and magazines. The invention of the steam press, which could print copies much faster than the old hand presses, and increasing use of paper made of wood pulp instead of rags and linen enabled printers to produce copy much more cheaply and voluminously. The telegraph and telephone quickened the pace of communications and made information more accessible than ever before. To sell more newspapers, publishers began to replace political rhetoric with news and features. Journalists now created news as well as reported it. Circulation-hungry publishers such as Joseph Pulitzer, who bought the *New York World* in 1883, and William Randolph Hearst, who acquired the *San Francisco Call* in 1887 and the *New York Journal* in 1896, filled their pages with screaming headlines, sensational stories, and dramatic photographs. At the same time, literary magazines began to give way to more popular, cheaper periodicals, such as *Cosmopolitan, McClure's,* and *Everybody's,* whose circulations grew to hundreds of thousands.

Newspaper and magazine publishers tried to attract readers by exposing the scandals and injustices of contemporary society. Some articles were lurid and ill informed, but many others were based on careful investigation—a major standard of social science—and were designed to alert the middle-class public to the need for reform. A leading spokesman for this journalism was Jacob Riis, a Danish immigrant who worked for twenty years as a police reporter for the *New York Tribune* and later the *Evening Sun.* Riis rose to national prominence in 1890 with publication of *How the Other Half Lives,* an intimate, shocking portrayal of the lives and housing of poor people in New York. In a tone that was alternately sympathetic and indignant, Riis tried to alarm readers by describing "what the tenements are and how they grew to what they are." Using the camera as an instrument of reform and propaganda, the book included numerous photographs, many taken by Riis himself, which graphically illustrated the misery of "the other half." But, also, Riis posed and framed his photographs in a particular way to convey his personal, middle-class values of order and morality.

Other journalists stirred public attention with investigations of political abuses. Probably the most well-known reporter was Lincoln Steffens, whose seven articles on urban corruption in *McClure's* in 1902–3 were combined in a book titled *The Shame of the Cities*, published in 1904. Steffens was incensed by the unfair privileges that he saw pervading American society. Through exposure of the misrule that he observed in St. Louis, Pittsburgh, Minneapolis, and Philadelphia and through his review of the partial success of reform in Chicago and New York, Steffens appealed to mass sentiments of responsibility, indignation, and guilt. Steffens and other journalists meant their exposés to arouse the popular will and to revive democracy. As Steffens wrote in his introduction to *The Shame of the Cities*, "These articles, if they have proved nothing else, have demonstrated beyond doubt that we can stand the truth; that there is pride in the character of American citizenship; and that this pride may be a power in the land."

Attempts at reform also pervaded fictional writing. Novelists probed the impact of urban life on human character. The quest for power and wealth was depicted by Theodore Dreiser in *The Financier*, and by Frank Norris in *The Pit*, Stephen Crane's *Maggie, A Girl of the Streets*, and Upton Sinclair's *The Jungle* protested what they identified as the degradations of urban poverty. Sinclair's novel also exposed loathsome practices of Chicago's meat-packing industry and shocked Congress into passing a federal meat-inspection law in 1906. New opportunities, pleasures, and vulnerability for women in the city shaped the narrative frameworks of David Graham Phillips's *Susan Lenox, Her Fall and Rise* and Dreiser's *Sister Carrie* and *Jenny Gerhardt*.

African-American intellectuals also contributed to the literature of social reform. Memphis newspaper editor Ida B. Wells wrote editorials, essays, and pamphlets attacking the lynching of black men and exposing the use of dubious sexual accusations to serve as a cover for the real motivations of economic and political racism. W. E. B. Du Bois's book *The Philadelphia Negro* (1899) was a pioneering work of social science research that identified structural causes of poverty and identified important black political and economic contributions to the city. His eloquent book of essays, *The Souls of Black Folk*, (1903) used examples from African-American history, culture, and politics to educate readers on the "problem of the color line" and the black experience of "double consciousness."

In 1907–8, investigative social science and journalism combined to produce the most extensive catalog of modern urban life yet collected. Under the direction of Paul U. Kellogg, a professional social worker, and sponsored by the Russell Sage Foundation, the six-volume *Pittsburgh Survey* detailed the city's economic development and the social costs of industrialization. It particularly showed how political corruption and irresponsible business practices had contributed to Pittsburgh's problems of poverty, pollution, and inequitable tax structure. Kellogg and many like him in other cities strongly believed in the potential of reason and information as reforming instruments, investing their faith in the outrage of an informed public, but perhaps underestimating the strength of opposing forces.

REMEDIES OF SOCIAL REFORMERS

The activities of social reformers included a multitude of causes, ranging from religious humanizing of the Social Gospel movement to breadbasket issues of labor organizations. Such a variety of concerns does not fit a generalized interpretation that can categorize every program and personality. From an urban point of view, however, the most salient aspect of the reform movement was the attempt by middle-class individuals and groups to control and mitigate the problems of inner cities, where conditions seemed most menacing. In addition to the concerns with housing and health discussed in Chapter 5, and concerns with political process discussed in Chapter 6, social reformers' efforts in the inner city were concentrated in three major areas: moral and religious responsibility for social betterment, epitomized by the Social Gospel; the civic and cultural enlightenment of inner-city dwellers sponsored by educational reformers; and the settlement-house movement's drive to bridge cultural gaps and improve neighborhood life. Each of these areas opened new opportunities for women to participate in and influence public affairs, and activists in each area increasingly advocated government responsibility in refashioning a better urban society.

Religious and Moral Reform

During the 1870s and 1880s, a few clergymen of older Protestant sects reacted to social crises and labor struggles resulting from urbanization and industrialization by espousing a new interpretation of their religious mission. The Social Gospel, as this ethic came to be called, emphasized the humane aspects of Christianity. According to the Social Gospel the salvation of society replaced the salvation of an individual soul as the principal religious goal. Before the Civil War, Unitarian ministers such as Boston's William Ellery Channing and Theodore Parker had stressed the duty of Christians to attend to the needs of the poor. As problems of urbanization heightened after the war, this attitude spread and leaders of other Protestant sects tried to make their churches instruments of reform.

The leading figure of the Social Gospel movement was Washington Gladden, a Congregationalist minister in Columbus, Ohio. Gladden preached that modern Christians should seek salvation by attempting to realize the Kingdom of God on earth rather than worrying about the afterlife of their individual souls. Gladden, Walter Rauschenbusch, a Baptist minister and professor at the Rochester (New York) Theological Seminary, Josiah Strong, pastor of the Cincinnati's Central Congregational Church, Shaler Mathews of the University of Chicago Divinity School, and R. Heber Newton, a New York Episcopalian, stressed the social responsibilities of Christianity through good works and social betterment. Gladden supported arbitration as a means of achieving industrial peace between labor unions and employers. Rauschenbusch worked with Jacob Riis to obtain better living conditions for the poor. Other clergymen sponsored investigations and worked to improve conditions in slum districts.

Several socially conscious congregations, with help from wealthy members, established institutional churches in low-income neighborhoods. These churches offered nurseries, kindergartens, medical clinics, employment agencies, recreation centers, and adult education classes. The goal of all activities was service. As Josiah Strong wrote in

The Challenge of the City (1898), "Inasmuch as Christ came not to be ministered unto but to minister, the open and institutional church, filled and moved by his spirit of ministering love, seeks to become the center and source of all beneficent and philanthropic effort, and to take the leading part in every movement which has for its end the alleviation of human suffering, the elevation of man, and the betterment of the world."

The Social Gospel was particularly influential in advancing an environmental explanation of urban social ills. Gladden and Rauschenbusch believed that people were not intrinsically bad; rather, the conditions in which people lived corrupted them. Social Gospelers believed that by reforming the environment they could create a moral society. Dismayed by the greed of industrial capitalism, they poured their energies into the inner city, and through investigations, missions, and institutional churches they awakened a host of sensitive men and women to the needs and methods of social reform. A few Social Gospelers took radical approaches to the solution of urban problems. Boston's W. D. P. Bliss, for example, helped found the Society of Christian Socialists in 1889. The majority, however, were moderates, clergymen who felt guilty about their own and their churches' neglect of social problems and who reacted by trying to reorient the gospel into a more secular direction. The Social Gospel influenced some Catholics and Jews as well, and it also reached rural areas. But for the most part it evolved from the impact of urban problems on modern Protestantism.

Many Social Gospelers joined the drive to close down saloons. The temperance movement was not new to late nineteenth-century urban America. But after the Civil War the movement gathered fresh momentum, spurred by activists who believed they could improve conditions of the laboring classes by destroying the centers of immorality and political corruption. Temperance reformers were convinced that inner-city neighborhoods contained too many saloons. (They may have been right; by the 1890s, many districts had one saloon for every fifteen to twenty adult men.) Because competition was keen, reformers theorized, a drinking establishment could survive only by staying open after hours or by offering extra services such as gambling and prostitution. Such temptations, plus the addictive effect of liquor, caused men to squander their wages and weakened family life. Moreover, saloons were the bunkers of boss politics. Destroy the saloon and you remove the boss's base of operations.

The post–Civil War temperance movement was particularly fueled by the energies of native-born Protestant women. They joined the temperance crusade because it addressed the real problems of women victimized by alcoholic fathers and husbands and because as a social problem the issue of drink fell within women's traditional domestic concerns. Women's first activities were to stage marches, rallies, and prayer vigils to try to close saloons. Then temperance activism took organizational shape in the Woman's Christian Temperance Union (WCTU), the largest women's organization, founded in 1874 and with 245,000 members by 1911. Under Frances Willard's leadership, local chapters organized departments in areas such as labor, health, social purity, education, and eventually, suffrage, all under the banner of "home protection." The WCTU taught women how to translate domestic imperatives into political action, and local chapters were directly involved in electoral politics. The pressure group tactics of organizations like the Anti-Saloon League (founded in 1893), which ultimately resulted in state and national prohibition laws, shared a great deal with the reform strategies engineered by the WCTU.

Although temperance and prohibition attracted large numbers of rural enthusiasts who feared the city's evil ways, much of the leadership and financial support of these crusades came from city dwellers, largely native white Protestants who inhabited the outer wards. Some temperance advocates were willing to abandon total prohibition in favor of more pragmatic goals. They worked for enforcement of licensing

The Campaign for Prohibition.   This postcard appeal circulated by the Anti-Saloon League to "defend the home" by shutting down saloons utilizes the Woman's Christian Temperance Union's domestic rhetoric of "home protection," draping its native-born credentials (and stoking anti-immigrant feeling) in multiple American flags.

and closing laws, and they used pamphlets and public school programs to emphasize the dangers of liquor and the virtues of abstinence. In a few cities temperance reformers helped to establish local-option rules that permitted individual wards or precincts to vote themselves dry. The greatest successes occurred in Chicago, where, by 1908, almost half of the city was dry—mostly in the outer districts.

In the minds of many moral reformers it was a short step from the bottle to other temptations. Thus crusades against saloons often spread to gambling and prostitution. In most big cities, gambling dens and brothels were unofficially tolerated in red-light districts, where they operated with minimal police interference. But what Victorians had regarded as a "necessary evil," reformers regarded as the "social evil," a moral problem and a national menace. Cleveland, St. Louis, and a few other cities experimented with police registration and medical inspection of prostitutes rather than trying to abolish their profession. But most of the outcry about the "white slave trade" (the supposed kidnapping of young women for sale into brothels) triggered efforts to eliminate prostitution altogether.

Reformers' writings about prostitution reflected anxieties over unrestricted immigration, the anonymity of the city, the evils of liquor, the growth of what seemed to be an urban working-class culture far outside their control, and the changing role of women in society. The presence of women in public life had blurred the nineteenth-century distinction between "public" women, almost always synonymous with promiscuous women, and respectable wives and mothers. Female reformers saw prostitution somewhat differently, focusing on it as the symbol of sexual and economic exploitation. They condemned the pitifully low wages paid for women's work and identified prostitutes as the most victimized female labor. They hoped that eradication of prostitution would elevate the status of all women.

In the early 1900s, reformers in several cities established vice commissions to investigate prostitution and gambling and to recommend legislation. Reformers recommended four measures as remedies: (1) labor legislation to improve working conditions for women so that they would not be lured by adversity into prostitution; (2) education campaigns to alert the public to the dangers of venereal disease; (3) neighborhood recreational facilities to replace vice centers; and (4) nuisance and abatement laws by which citizens could obtain court orders to close down offensive establishments.

By the 1920s, however, technology enabled vice operators to circumvent most restrictive legislation. The automobile enabled gambling and prostitution to flourish in roadhouses outside city borders away from the law, and the telephone created the bookie and the call girl. In addition, the effect of legal crackdowns on prostitution was not to destroy it but to force prostitutes from the relative security of public brothels to the riskier act of streetwalking. Control of prostitution shifted from madams and prostitutes themselves to pimps and organized crime syndicates. Such changes meant that prostitutes faced new kinds of brutality from the police and from their new employers.

Educational Reform

Reformers had high hopes for using public schools as an agent of social reform. Education could be the key to instilling urban masses with reformers' standards of citizenship and democracy. However, late nineteenth-century critics of urban school systems charged that schools were disorganized, overcrowded, too vulnerable to political pressures from neighborhood interests, not effective enough in reaching immigrant children, and not relevant to the needs of modern industrial life. Before 1900, seldom more than two-thirds of school-age urban children attended classes— often because working-class families could not afford to withhold their children from the labor market.

An initial response to the problem of school attendance was the enactment of compulsory attendance laws, with truant officers mandated to enforce them. Such laws, passed in the 1870s and 1880s, along with increasing populations, caused enrollments to swell. Between 1870 and 1910, public school enrollments rose from 6.9 million to 17.8 million, and the number of public high schools increased from five hundred to ten thousand. These numbers confronted cities with problems of teacher shortages and inadequate buildings. New schools accounted for a large upsurge in bonded indebtedness in many cities during the last decades of the nineteenth century. Between 1860 and 1890, the number of normal (teacher-training) schools quadrupled, but they still could not meet the demand for teachers. Significantly, the increased demand opened up the profession to women, who now outnumbered men in the common schools. By paying women only half what they paid men (salaries of $600 to $700 per year for female teachers, $900 to $1,200 for males), school committees could increase teaching staffs without straining budgets.

The pressures on public school facilities and personnel would have been worse had it not been for the expansion of parochial education. Responding to the needs of growing numbers of Catholic immigrants, the Third Plenary Council, meeting in

A Progressive Schoolroom. By placing children, rather than subject matter, at the center of the learning process, school reformers helped make education more relevant to modern city life. This new approach also gave students freedom to participate in classroom activities, rather than forcing them to sit at rigid attention.

Baltimore in 1884, urged that each parish provide schools for its children. By the end of the century, nearly a million children were enrolled in Catholic elementary schools and several dioceses had established parochial high schools. By 1920, parochial schools enrolled between 20 and 40 percent of school-age children in cities with large immigrant Catholic populations like New York, Boston, Philadelphia, Chicago, and St. Louis.

Social reformers saw school problems as extending beyond enrollment to more basic questions of school organization and curriculum. Reformers' commitment to scientific efficiency led them, like the municipal reformers discussed in Chapter 6, to advocate centralized rather than ward-based school districts and professional rather than politically based administrators. A pioneer in administrative innovation was William T. Harris, superintendent of St. Louis public schools from 1867 to 1880. Harris believed that urban education should conform to new patterns of economic organization—meaning the factory—and he stressed the need for rigorous school administration and pupil discipline. He supported reforms such as graded schools, centralized policymaking, standardized curricula, and even uniform architecture.

To expand the reach of education into burgeoning immigrant neighborhoods, school systems experimented with kindergarten programs for very young children, modeled on the scheme of German educator F. W. A. Froebel, and with evening schools to teach English and civics to immigrant adults. Kindergartens stressed the importance of pleasant surroundings, self-activity, and physical training as a means of developing learning capacities. According to the editor of *Century Magazine*, they also provided "the earliest opportunity to catch the little Russian, the little Italian, the little German, Pole, Syrian and the rest and begin to make good American citizens of them." Proponents of evening schools claimed that their manual training programs would promote social mobility and economic efficiency and that their classes in English instruction would Americanize immigrants and shift their taste away from moving picture houses and vaudeville theatres to good literature. Some localities even attempted to make evening instruction compulsory for immigrants, so convinced were they of the necessity of extending the public school's outreach beyond the daytime classroom.

One of the most important educational innovations proposed by reformers was vocational training. By the early 1900s, scores of cities had established trade schools and vocational programs to train children in industrial skills. A 1910 survey located such programs in twenty-nine states, mostly in urban schools. Proponents of vocational education claimed that it would give students discipline and make schooling more relevant to everyday life. Philosopher John Dewey believed that vocational training would restore what industrial progress had eroded. "The invention of machinery, the institution of the factory system, and the division of labor have changed the home from a workshop into a simple dwelling place," he wrote. "While need of the more formal intellectual training in the school has decreased, there arises an urgent demand for the introduction of methods of manual and industrial discipline that shall give the child what he formerly obtained in his home and social life." But increasingly vocational education, soon accompanied by programs of vocational guidance, functioned to track working-class and immigrant children into manual work and to redefine the mission of education. Family, ethnic, and class background tended to determine the measures used to determine which program would best fit a child's future position in life.

By the 1910s, expectations for what urban education could accomplish were extraordinarily high. According to historian Robert Wiebe, educational reform reflected a belief that "the schools would facilitate the arrival of Social Rationality, preparing the nation for a higher civilization."[2] Even those reforms directed at the middle class—high schools, for example—revealed a strong belief in formal schooling as the best instrument for shaping American culture and for bringing order to heterogeneous urban society.

Settlements

The settlement-house movement became one of the most influential branches of urban reform. The idea originated in England, where a group of young intellectuals established themselves in a residence called Toynbee Hall in the London slums in 1884. There, these men and women sought to improve living conditions for working-class laborers by bringing them education and appreciation for the arts. At the same time, Toynbee Hall residents believed they could learn about life from the people they hoped to serve and thereby bridge the gap between classes. Toynbee Hall inspired a number of young Americans who were visiting or studying abroad, and several of them organized settlement houses when they returned to the United States. Stanton Coit started the Neighborhood Guild (renamed University Settlement) in a New York tenement apartment in 1886. Over the next few years Vida Scudder and Lillian Wald established other settlements in New York, Jane Addams and Ellen Gates Starr founded Hull House in Chicago, Graham Taylor opened Chicago Commons, and Robert A. Woods founded Andover House in Boston. By 1897, there were seventy-four settlements in the United States, and by 1910, more than four hundred.

Most participants in early settlements were young, middle-class, educated, religious-minded, and idealistic women and men disturbed by the social barriers between classes and frustrated by their own apparent uselessness in a society that cried for reform. Settlement workers had a strong desire to help, to apply their ideas of service (influenced by the Social Gospel) to the challenges of the city. They also had a strong investigative impulse, an urge to find out for themselves what urban society's problems were like.

Women particularly found new opportunities in settlements. Settlement work offered solutions to those young, college-educated women who felt they had no purposeful way to participate in "life," no outlet to apply their training. Replacing family roles with larger, public responsibilities, settlements fused social activism with conventional female concerns for nurture and sacrifice, and some women chose participation in reform as an alternative to marriage. A 1911 survey found that 53 percent of settlements surveyed housed women only. Even in those settlements containing both sexes, strong-minded, energetic women tended to dominate. The female communities established in these places created social and political networks that propelled settlement workers into leadership roles in early twentieth-century social and political reform agitation.

As residents of the inner city, settlement workers viewed problems of poverty firsthand, and they actively sought to improve living conditions for immigrants and

Settlement Houses as Urban Neighbors.　Settlement house workers hoped that educating young people would help create better citizens, and that children would encourage their families to join settlement house reform activities. Chicago's Hull House's initiatives included kindergartens, an employment bureau, an art gallery, libraries, English and citizenship classes, and theater, music and art classes. The actress Martha Scott is shown here playing the piano at Hull House and teaching singing to neighborhood boys.

other poor people. The settlement house itself became a hub of reform, acting as an educational center, information clearinghouse, and forum for debate. Settlement workers organized English and civics classes, amateur concerts and theatrical productions, and kindergartens. Jane Addams, Robert A. Woods, and Lillian Wald joined educational reformers in lobbying for public adoption of kindergartens, vocational training, school nurses, and playgrounds. Because one of their major goals was revitalization of inner-city neighborhoods, settlement workers strongly backed housing reforms and regulatory legislation. In the cause of labor reform, settlements offered rooms for union meetings, and settlement leaders Florence Kelley, Mary McDowell, Jane Addams, and Mary Simkhovitch spoke out in support of workers' rights.

These activities had a special meaning for the female participants, for they enabled women not only to take part in public affairs but also to develop new, paid professions for themselves. As settlement-house workers moved their efforts on behalf of child protection, neighborhood health care, poverty relief, and labor relations into the public arena, they prompted private humanitarians and government agencies to fund such paid positions as juvenile court and probation officers, school nurses, public health administrators, social workers, and factory inspectors. Often, because of their experiences, women settlement workers were hired for these positions, and they created a new professional culture that combined their desire to serve with a mission to make scientific knowledge about social problems understandable to the public. Lillian Wald, for example, was a school nurse who helped create the first independent public health nursing service and helped define nursing as a dignified profession independent from doctors. Florence Kelley used her background as an advocate for better factory conditions to become Illinois's first chief factory inspector.

The importance of the settlement movement lay in its flexibility and influence. Settlement workers were occasionally romantic and naïve; they could not always erase attitudes of condescension and paternalism toward immigrants, and they kept facilities for blacks separate from those for whites for fear of driving whites away. But they invested faith in urban social interaction, believing that immigrants did not have to shed their cultural backgrounds to become good Americans and that middle-class Americans could learn from immigrants as well as teach them. Settlements were based, remarked Jane Addams, "on the theory that the dependence of classes on each other is reciprocal."

An important contrast developed between white female reformers, who worked mainly in settlements of Northern cities, and black female reformers, who operated independently in both the South and, increasingly, in Northern cities. While middle-class white women worked for government-sponsored programs to help people in need—mainly immigrant and native-born working classes—African-American women, barred from white political institutions, raised funds from private donors and focused on aiding members of their own race. African-American female reformers engaged in such efforts as funding black schools, old-age homes, and hospitals, and they also worked for race uplift and the protection of black women from sexual exploitation. Their ranks included Jane Hunter, who founded a home for unmarried black women in Cleveland in 1911 and influenced the establishment of similar homes in other cities, and Nannie Burroughs, who established a school for black females in Washington, D.C.

Eventually the settlement movement succumbed to professionalization. After World War I, the houses lost their attractiveness and their functions were assumed by trained social workers, who brought more expertise to the slums but also more bureaucratic impersonality. As a result the poor came to be viewed as clients rather than as partners in the battle against poverty and decay. Yet for a full generation settlements provided hundreds of women and men with training and experience in social reform.

Experience in settlement houses, and especially the efforts in support of school nurses, building safety codes, health clinics, playgrounds, labor legislation, and other reform activities, prompted urban social reformers to believe in greater government responsibility to ensure social justice and welfare. But raising public consciousness and obtaining reform legislation were not enough. Because they served a clientele who often could not afford their professional services, settlement workers constantly searched for stable sources of funding. So reformers lobbied government at every level for the changes they wanted: they asked state governments to established publicly funded employment bureaus, county governments to hire probation officers to help juvenile delinquents, and municipal governments to build playgrounds construction and staffing.

Urban middle-class social reformers embraced the city. They believed that within the city lay the potential for human progress. As reformer Frederick Howe wrote in

1905, "The ready responsiveness of democracy, under the close association which the city involves, forecasts a movement for the improvement of human society more hopeful than anything the world has ever known." Along with the responsibility to help the masses, many social reformers also wanted to restore what they believed were traditional values of social deference and cultural purity. In this way, their spirit of service and sacrifice could easily be refashioned into condescension and paternalism, in many cases translating into support for immigration restriction and racial segregation. Many service-minded middle-class reformers wrongly assumed their perspective to be universally shared. As the fictional saloonkeepr Mr. Dooley candidly observed,

> [T]is a gr-reat mistake to think that annywan ra-ally wants to rayform. Ye niver heerd of a man rayformin' himself. He'll rayform other people gladly. He likes to do it. But a healthy man'll niver rayform while he has th' strenth. . . . But a rayformer don't see it. . . . [He] spinds th' rest iv his life tellin' us where we are wrong. He's good at that. On'y he don't unherstand that people wud rather be wrong an' comfortable thin right in jail.

What was service to some was meddling to others. Yet in spite of its limitations, social reform brought many changes to urban America, broadly constructing the foundation for the Progressive Era.

PLANNING AND ENGINEERING THE CITY

While social reformers, largely female and increasingly professional, tried to restore neighborhoods and social relations, various groups of males, professionals of another sort, tried to beautify the whole city and attend to everyday service needs of all city dwellers. Land use, sewerage and sanitation, streetlights, bridge and street building, and other such issues posed problems that required technological and professional, not political or humanitarian, creativity. In addressing these issues, American urban dwellers, especially the engineering profession, developed systems and standards of worldwide significance.

During the middle and late nineteenth century, efforts to create large, landscaped city parks had awakened people to possibilities of determining the mode and direction of future urban growth. By 1890, landscaping had merged with the new professions of architecture and engineering to create the City Beautiful movement, an attempt to improve life within cities by enhancing civic design. The City Beautiful blossomed at the World's Columbian Exposition in Chicago in 1893–94. This was the largest of a score of fairs held in American cities during the last quarter of the nineteenth century and early years of the twentieth. Heralded as commemorative expositions, these extravaganzas were usually organized to advertise a city's progress and opportunities. The 1893 fair marked the tercentennial of Columbus's 1492 voyage to the New World. Congress had chosen Chicago as the site because the city had made a remarkable recovery from its devastating fire of 1871. The fair's impressive exhibits of agricultural and industrial technology, plus its fantastic entertainments

The Brooklyn Bridge.   The Brooklyn Bridge, completed in 1883, was celebrated as an aesthetic and engineering marvel, its graceful arches and intricate steel cables bear testimony to the glories of technological progress and urban ascendancy.

(the Midway offered everything from a Cairo street to a Hawaiian volcano), offered spectators visions of an idealized future and a romanticized past.

More important, the Chicago exposition showed what planners could do if they had the chance. Daniel Burnham, a prominent architect and the fair's supervisor, mustered a battery of notables—including landscaper Frederick Law Olmsted and maverick architect Louis Sullivan—to plan a fully new city on Chicago's southern lakefront. More than seven thousand workers built a "White City," with neoclassical buildings, streets, sewers, a water system, and other services, all coordinated to a master design. The spacious, orderly, monumental character of the exposition in no way resembled the gray, smoky, teeming streets of most inner cities. Yet the White City captured the imaginations of civic leaders and inspired them to beautify their own communities. Most commonly the City Beautiful was translated into the construction of new public buildings and civic centers. Burnham, Olmsted's son Frederick Jr., Charles M. Robinson (an architect from Rochester whose many publications made him spokesman of the City Beautiful), and other planners were hired by cities to draw plans for new courthouses, libraries, and government centers.

In a few instances the City Beautiful movement generated projects that addressed the city as a whole, not just one part. In 1900, several planners who had been active in the Chicago fair were commissioned to prepare a plan for the beautification of

Washington, D.C. Their efforts left the city with a mall between the Capitol and the Potomac River, a number of new monuments, and Rock Creek Park, much of which had been envisioned by Pierre Charles L'Enfant a century earlier. In 1906, the Commercial Club of Chicago engaged Burnham and his associates to devise a comprehensive plan for the city. Their scheme, submitted in 1909 and accepted by the city council in 1910, shaped Chicago's development for the next five decades and became one of the most influential documents in the history of city planning. The Burnham Plan sought to create a "well-ordered, convenient, and unified city." In practical terms this meant improved transportation, accessible areas for public recreation, and provisions to control subsequent growth. The plan specified a new railroad terminal, an east-west boulevard, a civic center, lakefront parks and beaches, and large forest preserves around the city's borders. The project was expensive, and several of its more elaborate schemes had to be abandoned. Yet most of it was eventually realized, and its scope and innovation aroused nationwide fascination.

Burnham's motto was "Make no little plans. . . . Make big plans; aim high in hope and work." Yet few other cities could reproduce Chicago's accomplishments. In most places City Beautiful projects consisted of attempts to make commercial districts more attractive and profitable for business. Problems of poverty and social inequality were not their primary concerns. Burnham, Robinson, and others were not oblivious to social problems, but they claimed that improvements such as parks and sanitation would

"The Close of a Career."   Around the turn of the century, thousands of horses trod city streets and sometimes died of old age. Though their carcasses had some value, the dead animals created health hazards as well as disgusting sights. As this photographer seems to be suggesting, however, children playing on the street and adults going about their business became so accustomed to the sight that they ignored it.

correct imbalances. Their uncritical optimism—plus a faithfulness to the needs of private investment—limited the accomplishments of early planning. By the time of the St. Louis Exposition of 1904, the City Beautiful movement began to split, with some planners continuing to advocate aesthetics as the answer to urban problems and others involving themselves in planning that froze the divisions between uptown and downtown, center and suburbs, through the institutionalization of zoning and metropolitan and regional plans (see Chapter 8).

Even more relevant to the practical needs of urban dwellers than planning were issues of sanitation and health. In 1900, experts estimated that on average every resident of New York City annually produced 160 pounds of garbage (unused food and bones), 1,200 pounds of ashes (from stoves and furnaces), and 100 pounds of rubbish (discarded shoes, furniture, and other items). Europeans of that era generated only about half as much trash. At the same time, there were some three and a half million horses in American cities; each one produced about twenty pounds of manure and a gallon of urine daily. Moreover, each city had to dispose of a huge amount of human body wastes. In previous generations, most families and communities disposed of their waste by depositing it on the ground (simply throwing it away) or underground (in privy vaults). By the late nineteenth century, these methods threatened health and safety, and citizens were raising loud protests against inadequate refuse collection and disposal.

By 1880, most cities were switching to the use of water rather than land as a means of disposing of waste. A network of sewers used water from drains and runoff (such as from rain) to carry waste to a nearby river or lake. Depending on the proven theory that running water purifies itself, communities felt more secure in water-carrying methods, but at the same time their wastes were being passed on to become an increased problem for communities downstream. Thus it was not long before public health boards were advocating the new technology of filtration to enhance water purity. In addition, as bacteriology developed and identified the true causes of most diseases, some physicians and health officials urged cities to treat water supplies with chlorine that would destroy disease-causing germs.

By 1909, sewers served 85 percent of the population of cities with populations above 300,000 and 71 percent of those with populations between 100,000 and 300,000. Virtually all construction and control of these systems were under public auspices. Treatment through filtration and chemicals before water went into homes greatly lessened the threat of diseases such as typhoid fever and dysentery. Between 1890 and 1900 alone, the mortality rate for all diseases in the nation's twenty-eight largest cities fell by 19 percent. But physicians and engineers differed on what should happen to waste when it was discharged into waterways. To protect downstream communities, boards of health wanted state and federal governments to require treatment before discharge, but engineers, adhering to the theory that running water is self-purifying, argued that sewage treatment was unnecessary and too expensive. They said that each community could sufficiently protect itself by filtering its water at the place of intake. Between 1905 and 1914, cities such as Pittsburgh were successful in obtaining sewage treatment plants in instances where industrial and other solid wastes presented extreme nuisances, but for the most part the argument by engineers prevailed until well into the twentieth century. Today, most communities dispose of solid and hazardous materials in landfills and deep underground holes, but waste disposal remains a serious problem.

By the early twentieth century, urban dwellers had become more inclined to seek technological solutions to their practical problems, and more inclined to heed the advice of municipal engineers. Industrialization, with its daunting mechanical wonders and its obsession with efficiency, gave the public faith that technologically expert engineers not only could facilitate a city's expansion but also do so in a neutral way, above the petty frays of partisan politics. For their part, engineers, by creating professional bureaucracies, national organizations replete with conferences and professional journals, bolstered their reputations as trustworthy, impartial experts. By the early 1900s, engineers had become powerful figures in municipal administration, and it was no coincidence that the first city managers, in Staunton, Virginia, and Dayton, Ohio, were engineers.

In spite of these successes, however, the challenge of dealing with industrial pollution would fray the confidence in technological solutions and expert neutrality. Regulatory strategies in matters of smoke divided the interests of corporate employers, industrial workers, and homeowners. In Cincinnati, for example, the impetus for controlling smoke emissions from coal-burning locomotives came from middle-class women intent on protecting homes and children from the intrusion of industrial dirt. But the burden of enforcing regulations once they were created fell on railroad employees, forcing the battle over smoke and soot to be fought out between the railroad company, the union, the civic elite, municipal officials, middle-class women, and working-class men. Throughout the twentieth century industrial pollution posed a singularly intractable urban problem.

REFORM BECOMES PROGRESSIVISM

The period between 1895 and 1920, when reform activism spread through almost all facets of American life, is known as the Progressive Era. Progressivism was not a single movement; it involved shifting coalitions of reformers operating on a number of fronts. Some progressive reforms, particularly those involving government reorganization and railroad regulation, were adopted from the Populist movement of the 1890s. Most progressive issues, however, were national and derived from urban problems. The Progressive Era culminated three decades of urban reform; its issues had been the concerns of civic and social reformers for some time. Progressivism in the cities distinguished itself from earlier urban reform by the strategic contribution of national organizations, led by like-minded reformers from different cities; the importance of female urban reformers; and the increased focus on government as guarantor of justice and welfare.

Nationwide reform activism was the product of several ingredients. In large part it grew from reformers' basic optimism in their causes. No problem seemed too complex; no geographic area too large. Failure and frustration on the local level had not dampened reform ardor; these only made national programs more imperative. National organization was driven by the impulse for standardization and professionalization characteristic of new middle class confident expertise. And certainly faster and easier communications by mail, rail, telegraph, and telephone aided intercity contacts, just as they facilitated the growth of economic links that stretched between regions. Large numbers of urban reformers now carried their causes to the national level and provided progressive movements with their intellectual and organizational bases.

One of the earliest of these organizations was the National Municipal League, organized in Philadelphia in 1894 by the First Annual Conference for Good City Government. The league attracted a number of civic reformers, and it included 180 affiliated societies by 1895. At first members favored the types of elitist reforms that business and professional groups had supported in the 1870s and 1880s—civil service, stronger vice laws, tighter fiscal policies. But the depression of the 1890s catalyzed broader concerns about urban society and prompted organizations such as the National Municipal League to consider more comprehensive reform programs. In 1899, the league consolidated its various governmental proposals into a model city charter that provided for home rule, a strong mayor, civil service, and ceilings on taxing and bonding powers. In 1916, members drew a revised model charter that included a combined commission-manager plan, nonpartisan elections, and shorter ballots. Also some, though not all, league members became advocates of municipally owned city services.

The model charters, support for municipal ownership, and other programs signaled the league's recognition that electing the best men and passing regulatory legislation were no longer adequate to remake the city. Civic reform needed a plan that could be formulated and supported nationally. Although no city adopted a model charter verbatim, the league's recommendations had considerable influence on local charter committees for the next several decades. To aid the planning process, bureaus of municipal research, often supported by self-interested corporate donors, provided important information and lobbying services to public officials and municipal reformers.

The desire for coordinated programs also characterized other national reform organizations. The National Civic Federation, founded by business liberals in 1900, organized local branches and enlisted prominent leaders to mediate in labor disputes. The federation also campaigned nationally for a moderate version of workmen's compensation and other forms of social insurance. In 1904, Florence Kelley and other social reformers launched the National Child Labor Committee, which campaigned for passage and enforcement of laws restricting child labor. Such restrictions had long been the goal of female reformers concerned about the welfare of working-class children and the conditions of tenement sweatshops. The Child Labor Committee also drafted a bill prohibiting child labor, which passed Congress in 1916, only to be overturned by the Supreme Court. The formation of the Federal Council of Churches of Christ in 1905 climaxed the Social Gospel movement. At its first annual conference in 1908, the council adopted a platform calling for improved housing, educational reform, government-sponsored poverty relief, better working conditions in factories, unemployment insurance, minimum wages for manual workers, and equal rights for all.

In 1910, Lawrence Veiller succeeded in combining various housing reform groups when he convinced the Russell Sage Foundation to sponsor the National Housing Association. Settlement workers helped to found the National Child Labor Committee and the National Playground Association of America, and in 1911 they organized their own National Association of Settlements. In 1909, architects, engineers, and reformers concerned with urban congestion and city planning formed the National Association of City Planning, forerunner of the American City Planning Institute (today called the American Planning Association). In 1906, proponents of vocational training organized the National Society for the Progress of Industrial Education, whose board of managers included efficiency expert Frederick W. Taylor, settlement-house leaders Jane Addams and Robert A. Woods, the president of American Telephone and Telegraph Company, and the head of the Union of Electrical Workers. After 1900, municipal employees formed specialized associations of the National Associations of Port Authorities, the Municipal Finance Officers Association, the American Association of Park Superintendents, the National Conference of Mayors, and the Conference of City Managers. This complex network of specialized organizations helped to develop reform agendas and a communications and lobbying network that financed and organized reform on a national scale.

By the early twentieth century national progressive reformers revealed a distinctive approach to social and political problems. Their tone was less indignant and less moralistic than that of reformers of the 1870s and 1880s. At the same time, the character of reform shifted from elitist paternalism—the idea that the best men should govern—to bureaucratic control—the belief that experts and specialized agencies should determine policies. Urban progressives' faith in scientific methods blinded them to the contradictions between democracy and social engineering. Thus they could advocate more trust in the people and more popular involvement on the one hand while they worked for centralized power and impersonal bureaucratic administration on the other. Moreover, they confused the independence of experts and bureaucrats with neutrality, when in fact impersonal government agencies became as self-serving as the boss-led machines that reformers wished to replace. Progressive reformers were unable to transfer their own values to all of urban society. They had expected opposition from entrenched economic interests, but had failed to recognize the tenacity of competing working-class cultures and institutions. Nonetheless, the progressives' impassioned commitment both to social reform and scientific expertise left a lasting legacy to the modern era.

THE RISE OF URBAN LIBERALISM

The Progressive Era reforms relying on an ideology of government intervention to ensure the safety and promote the welfare of its citizens—involving labor and welfare issues, regulation of big business, and electoral reform—have been labeled as urban liberalism. The proponents of urban liberal reforms emerged directly from the cities, produced by the sometimes blurred boundaries between boss politics and urban reform noted in Chapter 6. During the Progressive Era, politicians from immigrant and working-class districts, often aided by the resources of political machines, won seats in state legislatures and in Congress. Although their numbers remained too small for them to wield legislative power alone, these urban lawmakers frequently were able to coalesce with reform-minded colleagues to produce some of the era's most important measures.

Urban workingmen had long been at the forefront of campaigns for legislation promising safer working conditions, collecting labor statistics, and creating workmen's compensation. During the Progressive Era, representatives of the ethnic working classes, including machine politicians, successfully pushed for passage of these and other reform measures. New legislation provided widows' pensions, limited the hours of labor, regulated tenement housing, and mandated better conditions in factories and sweatshops. In New York, many of these laws grew out of the Factory Investigation Commission hearings instituted after the tragic Triangle Shirtwaist Company fire in

New York City in 1911 in which 145 women workers were killed. Robert F. Wagner and Alfred E. Smith, graduates of Tammany Hall politics, chaired this commission, and they and their fellow Democrats introduced nearly all of the 56 welfare laws passed as a result of the commission's recommendations. Irish-American Democrats from Jersey City and Newark strongly supported workmen's compensation and factory-safety bills in the New Jersey legislature. Cleveland's immigrant-based Democrats pushed for welfare legislation in the Ohio legislature. Politicians with urban ethnic constituents supported similar issues in other Northern and Midwestern states, with mixed success. Their efforts were fruitful only when they worked in cooperation with other groups sympathetic to workers' concerns, but in each instance urban ethnic representatives exerted considerable influence on reform legislation.

Less successfully, these same lawmakers also backed measures to strengthen unions, regulate big business, and equalize tax burdens. Urban Democratic leaders often rose out of the ranks of organized labor and became strong advocates for the rights of unions to organize, bargain, and strike. In 1911, for example, Boston representatives to the Massachusetts Senate supported a bill permitting strikers to picket. Urban lawmakers generally favored government regulation of big business rather than breaking up trusts, because workers believed regulation was the surest means of stabilizing economic conditions and ensuring job protection. These Democrats particularly favored government control over the rates and services of public utilities, upon which working classes depended. Many of them supported municipal ownership of utilities and streetcar

Philadelphia Streetcar Strike. In 1909 and 1910, a series of bloody riots occurred as a result of a strike against the monopolistic Philadelphia Rapid Transit company. The public, incensed by muckraking articles exposing the company's arrogance, joined in sympathy with the workers, with men and boys attacking trolley cars and ripping up track while women and girls cheered them on. Such labor action prompted many reformers to advocate arbitration as a means of settling disputes and avoiding violence.

companies. For example, Edward F. Dunne, Democratic mayor of Chicago and governor of Illinois in the early twentieth century, backed measures to provide for municipal ownership of several utilities in Chicago. Though these measures were defeated, Dunne was able to create a public utilities regulatory commission in 1913. Urban legislators also worked to shift tax burdens to those best able to pay by supporting inheritance taxes, stronger enforcement of intangible property taxes, and, most of all, a graduated federal income tax. In New York, Massachusetts, New Jersey, Ohio, and other states, urban Democrats backed the Sixteenth Amendment to the Constitution, which established congressional power to levy an income tax, because they viewed it, in Robert Wagner's words, as "a tax on plenty instead of necessity. It will lighten the burdens of the poor."

Lawmakers with working-class and immigrant constituencies also promoted political changes that promised to bolster popular control of government. They opposed the kind of electoral reforms promoted by civic reformers, such as nonpartisan elections, civil service, short ballots, and at-large candidates, because such issues did not aid working people in need. But working-class ethnic interests often did favor broadening participation in government by establishing initiatives and referendums, recalls of appointed officials and judges, women's suffrage, and direct election of U.S. senators. Although urban machines initially opposed giving women the right to vote, by the 1910s many inner-city leaders, including those of Tammany Hall, were backing women's suffrage in hopes of luring women into the Democratic Party. And urban ethnic working classes also could lend support to measures such as city commissions and direct primaries when it proved politically profitable to do so.

Immigrant-stock lawmakers associated with urban liberalism did not support Progressive-Era moral reform. In fact they actively fought key aspects of the middle-class moral reforms such as prohibition, Sunday closing laws, and other attempts to control personal liberty. Their opposition insisted on cultural pluralism, expressing the idea that in a heterogeneous society differing groups have a right to maintain their own customs and values as long as they did not harm anyone. The types of measures that new-stock urban lawmakers did favor—those establishing government responsibility for ensuring social welfare and those directed toward opening up political and economic opportunities—have become principal components of national reform from the Progressive Era to the present.

Bibliography

For selected works on Progressivism, see John D. Buenker, *Urban Liberalism and Progressive Reform* (1973); Alan Dawley, *Struggles for Justice: Social Responsibility and the Liberal State* (1991); Maureen Flanagan, *America Reformed: Progressives and Progressivisms, 1890s–1920s* (2006); Michael McGerr, *A Fierce Discontent: The Rise and Fall of the Progressive Movement in America, 1870–1920* (2003); and Daniel T. Rodgers, *Atlantic Crossings: Social Politics in a Progressive Age* (1999).

For local studies, see James J. Connolly, *The Triumph of Ethnic Progressivism: Urban Political Culture in Boston, 1900–1925* (1998); Edward Shannon LaMont, *Politics and Welfare in Birmingham, 1900–1975* (1995); Don Doyle, *Nashville in the New South, 1880–1930* (1985); William Issel and Robert W. Cherny, *San Francisco, 1865–1932: Politics, Power, and Urban Development* (1986).

On women's centrality to Progressive reform, see Maureen Flanagan, *Seeing with their Hearts: Chicago Women and the Vision of the Good City, 1871–1933* (2002); Glenda Elizabeth Gilmore, *Gender and Jim Crow: Women and the Politics of White Supremacy in North Carolina, 1896–1920* (1996); Robyn Muncy, *Creating a Female Dominion in American Reform, 1890–1935* (1991); Kathryn Kish Sklar, *Florence Kelley and the Nation's Work* (1995); and Sharon E. Wood, *The Freedom of the Streets: Work, Citizenship, and Sexuality in a Gilded Age City* (2005). See also Mary Lethert Wingerd, *Claiming the City: Politics, Faith, and the Power of Place in St. Paul* (1999).

On settlements, see Allen F. Davis, *Spearheads for Reform: The Social Settlements and the Progressive Movement, 1890–1914* (1967); Jean Bethke Elshtain, *Jane Addams and the Dream of American Democracy* (2002); Elizabeth Lasch-Quinn, *Black Neighbors: Race and the Limits of Reform in the American Settlement Movement, 1890–1945* (1993); and Eleanor J. Stebner, *The Women of Hull House: A Study of Spirituality, Vocation, and Friendship* (1997).

On cleanliness, Daniel Eli Burnstein, *Next to Godliness: Confronting Dirt and Despair in Progressive Era New York City* (Urbana: University of Illinois Press, 2006); Marilyn Thornton Williams, *Washing the Great Unwashed: Public Baths in America.*

On moral reform and reformers, see Paul S. Boyer, *Urban Masses and Moral Order in America, 1820–1920* (1978); Elizabeth Alice Clement, *Love for Sale: Courting, Treating, and Prostitution in New York City, 1900–1945* (2006); Perry Duis, *The Saloon: Public Drinking in Chicago and Boston, 1880–1920* (1983); Regina Kunzel, *Fallen Women, Problem Girls: Unmarried Mothers and the Professionalization of Social Work, 1890–1945* (1993); Alecia P. Long, *The Great Southern Babylon: Sex, Race, and Respectability in New Orleans, 1865–1920* (2004); and Ruth Rosen, *The Lost Sisterhood: Prostitution in America, 1900–1918* (1982).

On reforms affecting children, see Dominick Cavallo, *Muscles and Morals: Organized Playgrounds and Urban Reform, 1880–1920* (1981); David Hogan, *Class and Reform: Schools and Society in Chicago, 1880–1930* (1985); David Nasaw, *Children of the City: at Work and at Play* (1985); Stephen Robertson, *Crimes against Children: Sexual Violence and Legal Culture in New York City, 1880–1960* (2005); David B. Tyack, *The One Best System: A History of American Urban Education* (1974); David B. Wolcott, *Cops and Kids: Policing Juvenile Delinquency in America* (2005).

On planning, see M. Christine Boyer, *Dreaming the Rational City: The Myth of American City Planning* (1983); Howard Gillette, Jr., *Between Justice and Beauty: Race, Planning, and the Failure of Urban Policy in Washington, D.C.* (1993); Stanley K. Schultz, *Constructing Urban America: American Cities and City Planning, 1800–1920* (1989); William H. Wilson, *The City Beautiful Movement* (1989).

On the influence of technology on the urban infrastructure and environment, see Martin V. Melosi, *Garbage in the Cities: Refuse, Reform, and the Environment, 1880–1980* (1981); Melosi, *The Sanitary City: Urban Infrastructure in America from Colonial Times to the Present* (1999); Melosi, ed., *Pollution and Reform in American Cities, 1870–1930* (1980); Harold L. Platt, *The Electric City: Energy and the Growth of the Chicago Area, 1880–1930* (1991); Mark H. Rose, *Cities of Light and Heat: Domesticating Gas and Electricity in Urban America* (1995); David Stradling, *Smokestacks and Progressives: Environmentalists, Engineers, and Air Quality in America, 1881–1951* (1999); and Joel Tarr, *The Search for the Ultimate Sink: Urban Pollution in Historical Perspective* (1996).

Notes

1. Daniel Rodgers, "In Search of Progressivism," *Reviews in American History* 10 (December 1982), 125.
2. Robert Wiebe, *The Search for Order, 1877–1920* (New York: Hill and Wang, 1967), 157.

CHAPTER 8

Cities in an Age of Metropolitanism:
The 1920s and 1930s

NEW URBAN GROWTH

The 1920 federal census marked a milestone in American history: it revealed that for the first time a majority of the nation's people (51.4 percent) lived in cities. This revelation, though, can be misleading: the bureau defined a city as a place inhabited by at least twenty-five hundred people—hardly a rigorous criterion. Nevertheless, the 1920 tallies had symbolic importance: they confirmed that America had evolved into an urban society. The city, not the farm, had become the locus of national experience.

The agrarian way of life had been waning ever since urbanization accelerated early in the nineteenth century. To be sure, the demise was far from complete by the 1920s. Several social reform movements and much political rhetoric looked nostalgically backward to the simple virtues of an imagined past. But everywhere signs pointed to an urban ascendance. A precipitous drop in commodity prices after 1920 spun small farmers into distress. Convinced that there was a better life elsewhere, an estimated six million Americans gave up the land in the 1920s and poured into cities like Pittsburgh, Detroit, Chicago, Denver, and Los Angeles.

So many Southerners moved from farm to city that the South became America's most rapidly urbanizing region (in terms of proportionate population growth), after nearly a century of lagging behind the rest of the nation. Memphis, Atlanta, and Chattanooga experienced extraordinary expansion. Birmingham, Alabama, a burgeoning steelmaking center in the late nineteenth century, developed a diverse industrial, commercial, and service economy in the 1920s. This expansion attracted workers and their families from all over the South, who boosted the population of Birmingham's metropolitan area from 310,000 to 431,000 during the decade (the population of the city proper was 260,000 by 1930). Smaller cities, many of them created by textile companies that had left New England to take advantage of low-wage Southern labor and readily available hydroelectric power, also helped boost the urban population of the South to thirteen million by 1930.

The most visible contingents of native migrants from World War I onward were the millions of African Americans who moved into Northern and Southern cities. Pushed off tenant farms by failures in the cotton fields and attracted by jobs in labor-scarce cities, black families packed up and boarded the trains for Memphis, New Orleans, Chicago, Detroit, Cleveland, and New York. African Americans comprised already 90 percent of Birmingham's unskilled work force by 1910, half of the iron- and steel workers, and 70 percent of the ore miners by the 1910s and 1920s. When the war cut off the influx of cheap foreign labor, some northern companies began to hire black labor. Short-term migration in search of wages in turpentine camps, sawmills, cottonseed oil mills, and other industries tied to agriculture began to acculturate young African-American men to industrial labor. Young black women similarly ventured into nearby cities and towns to find work as domestics.

By the time that World War I created increasing demand for labor in northern cities, thousands of African-American men and women were ready to mobilize family and personal networks, giving up the dream of autonomy based on landownership in exchange for the promise of full citizenship emanating from northern urban life and industrial employment. By 1920, four-fifths of the country's African Americans residing outside the South lived in cities. As migrations continued during the 1920s, New York's African-American population increased from 152,000 to 328,000, Chicago's from 109,000 to 234,000, Philadelphia's from 134,000 to 220,000, Detroit's from 41,000 to 120,000, and Cleveland's from 34,000 to 72,000. African Americans constituted between 5 and 10 percent of the population of each of these places. This migration continued into the 1930s as New Deal crop subsidies paid to landowners prevented tenant farmers from making their customary living.

Agrarian depression was only part of a broader phenomenon. Mining and other extractive industries as well as agriculture were receiving a diminishing share of national wealth, while retail and service establishments were mushrooming. An ever-larger white-collar, urban middle class became increasingly influential in local and national affairs. At the same time, some critics added a disdain for rural society to a general cynicism toward social conventions. Edgar Lee Masters's *Spoon River Anthology* (1915), Sherwood Anderson's *Winesburg, Ohio* (1919), Sinclair Lewis's *Main Street* (1920), and Thomas Wolfe's *Look Homeward, Angel* (1929) assaulted the drabness of village and small-town life. The term "hick" became a widely used derogatory adjective, equating something clumsy or stupid with the farm. Much of the contempt for rural life represented a larger revolt against what writers called Puritan moralism—a revolt reflected in the popularization of the writings of Austrian psychoanalyst Sigmund Freud. But the debunking of the sturdy yeoman and small-town folkways also underscored a cultural shift that accompanied the city's rise to numerical superiority.

During the 1920s, urbanization took place on a wider front than ever before. Maturing industrial economies boosted the populations of many areas, particularly steel, oil, and automobile centers such as Pittsburgh, Cleveland, Detroit, Akron, Youngstown, Houston, Tulsa, and Los Angeles. New commercial and service activities primed expansion in regional centers such as Atlanta, Cincinnati, Nashville, Indianapolis, Kansas City, Minneapolis, Portland, and Seattle. The most exceptional growth, however, occurred in warm-climate resort cities. As the prime beneficiary of the Florida real estate explosion of the twenties, Miami attracted thousands of land speculators and home builders. Between 1920 and 1930, the population of Miami ballooned from 29,571 to 110,637. Tampa and San Diego doubled their populations during the twenties.

The flood of European immigrants suddenly dried up in the 1920s. After World War I, nativist arguments for restricting immigration gained broader support. By 1919, reformers who had formerly opposed restriction were convinced that the melting pot had not worked and that many immigrants—particularly those from southern and eastern Europe—stubbornly resisted assimilation. Labor leaders, fearful that a new flood of unskilled aliens would depress wages, looked at the high post-war unemployment rates and increased their longstanding support for restriction. At first, businessmen opposed the rising clamor out of self-interest: they hoped that a new surge of foreign workers would not only aid industrial expansion but also cut wage rates and curb unionization. But by 1924, when Congress was debating whether to close the doors more tightly, many industrialists were willing to support restriction because they discovered that mechanization and native migration from farm to city enabled them to prosper without foreign-born labor. Congressional acts of 1921, 1924, and 1929 successively reduced the numbers of immigrants who could be admitted annually. A racially motivated system of quotas, based on the number of descendants from each nationality living in the United States in 1890, severely limited immigrants from southern and eastern Europe, the very groups who had dominated urban cores since 1880.

The laws left the doors open only to those coming from Western Hemisphere countries. Mexicans now became the largest foreign group entering the country. Many came to work in the fields and vineyards of the Southwest, but others streamed into the region's booming cities. By the end of the 1920s, Chicanos made up more than half the population of El Paso, slightly less than half that of San Antonio, and one-fifth that of Los Angeles. Other Mexicans found employment in the automobile factories of Detroit and the steel mills, tanneries, and meat-packing plants of Chicago and Gary. By 1930, more than 15 percent of Mexican immigrants lived outside the Southwest. Mexican women took work in cities as domestics and in textile and food processing factories. Crowding into old barrios or forming new ones, Mexican immigrants often lacked decent city services such as sanitation, schools, and police protection. But the barrio community provided an environment where immigrants could sustain customs and values of the homeland and develop institutions to protect themselves from the uncertainties of urban life. In the same period, Puerto Ricans began to arrive on the American mainland in significant numbers, primarily settling in neighborhoods in Brooklyn and Manhattan, identified by their bodegas (grocery stores), restaurants, and boardinghouses. Social and cultural diversity continued to be a distinctive quality of urban life that distinguished cities most sharply from the relative homogeneity of rural and small-town social relations.

Chicago's Comiskey Park. This crowd lined up outside of Chicago's Comiskey Park to cheer for White Sox symbolizes how higher productivity and shorter work hours gave people spendable income and more time for leisure activities. The park's original capacity to accommodate 32,000 fans was expanded in 1927 to seat 52,000.

Many of the neighborhoods in which Latino immigrants settled were multi-ethnic in their early years. As institutional and ethnic discrimination limited Latinos' access to other neighborhoods, the growing Latino populations of Los Angeles, El Paso and other cities increasingly concentrated in distinct barrios. An increasing reliance by realtors on the use of real estate covenants, by which white property owners pledged not to sell homes to members of racial and/or ethnic minorities, helped sharpen lines of segregation from the 1920s onward, more tightly confining Mexicans, Asians, African Americans, and Jews to certain neighborhoods.

Urban America's coming of age was proclaimed by the establishment of its own academic discipline. The study of city life was formalized at the University of Chicago's school of sociology, where Robert E. Park and Ernest W. Burgess trained scholars to draw relationships between city people and their environment in much the same way that biologists examined interactions between plants and animals and their surroundings. The Chicago school's approach to the city was known as human ecology. According to this theory, the cultural dimension of human life and the forms of communication it facilitated were what held communities together. Migration to cities, said the Chicago sociologists, severed traditional forms of communication and community and created a disorganized society that isolated individuals amid rapid change.

The Chicago sociologists believed that they could understand the chaos of the city by studying its various "natural areas"—types of communities they identified as downtowns, slums, ethnic neighborhoods, suburbs, and artists' colonies, that formed as people adapted to the urban environment. Thus sociologists set out to collect data—numbers, characteristics, maps, ratios, interviews, and the like. The data then reinforced the general theory that neighborhood communities had become the cores of individual and group life in the city and that these communities held the keys to people's adjustment to urban society.

These ideas were central to such studies as Burgess's concentric-ring thesis, which depicted urban growth in terms of a series of concentric zones radiating outward from the urban core; Harvey W. Zorbaugh's *The Gold Coast and the Slum* (1929), which outlined the life patterns of contrasting neighborhoods; Louis Wirth's *The Ghetto* (1928), which probed the development of a single residential type; Frederick Thrasher's *The Gang* (1927); and Roderick D. McKenzie's *The Metropolitan Community* (1933). These scholars often failed to identify relationships within families and among neighbors that inner-city residents preferred to keep invisible to outsiders, and critics have charged that their emphasis on neighborhood looked nostalgically backward toward an imagined pre-urban village. Still, the Chicago school's commitment to urbanism as a legitimate field of inquiry, like the census milestone, unmistakably marked the city's importance in twentieth-century culture.

SUBURBANIZATION AND METROPOLITANISM

Ironically, at the moment that urban life had achieved ascendancy in the United States, important patterns of suburban development challenged the city's economic viability and political centrality. For one thing, industry began to decentralize. Electric power gave factories greater flexibility in location and made possible the assembly line, which required sprawling one- and two-story plants, not compact multistory ones like those in the city. Corporations increasingly located beyond city limits, where land was cheaper and tax burdens less onerous. Factory jobs proliferated in industrial satellite suburbs such as East Chicago and Hammond outside of Chicago, Lackawanna outside of Buffalo, East St. Louis and Wellston near St. Louis, and Norwood and Oakley beyond the Cincinnati city limits. Henry Ford moved his own auto production factory outside of Detroit to Highland Park in 1910. The proportion of factory employment located within city limits began to decline, an ominous foreshadowing of the massive deindustrialization that would afflict cities in the second half of the century.

As industry decentralized, suburban areas resisted urban attempts to annex them to the central city. Upper-class residential suburbs had opposed central-city annexation since the late nineteenth century, but now corporate leaders exerted economic and political influence in local governments and in state legislatures to assure that the political independence of suburbs would be maintained. As one suburban editor explained, "Under local government we can absolutely control every objectionable thing that may try to enter our limits, but once annexed we are at the mercy of City Hall." As sharper racial, ethnic, and class divisions separated city and suburbs, new laws made incorporation easier and annexation more difficult, and suburbs were able to gain access to improved services without annexation. Newer southern, midwestern, and southwestern cities were able to continue to annex suburban areas, ensuring that urban growth would continue. But older cities came to be ringed by incorporated suburbs that emphasized their distinctiveness from cities rather than their ties to them.

When industry moved out of the central city, many white workers followed to be near their jobs. The availability of inexpensive automobiles (by 1908, twenty-four American companies produced cars at relatively low prices) allowed even more workers to reside beyond and between the reaches of urban mass transit. Less expensive suburban house lots afforded white workers an opportunity to build their own modest bungalows, and engage in domestic production, raising vegetables and animals to supplement wages. African Americans created suburban enclaves in Lincoln Heights and Chagrin Falls, Ohio; LeDroit Park outside of Washington, D.C.; New Bern, Raleigh, and Durham, North Carolina; Evanston, Illinois; Mt Vernon, New York; and East Orange, New Jersey. Suburbs such as these contained space for black families to provision their own tables by raising vegetables and chickens and to continue reliance on extended kin for childcare and emotional as well as financial support.

Suburban expansion in the 1920s owed much to the automobile and its related industries. Real estate interests, the construction industry, the auto, rubber, and oil industries joined automobile owners in pressing for new roads to facilitate high-speed travel. Automobile wheels destroyed whatever was left of older, lower-speed gravel surfaces. But smoother pavements and wider streets encouraged even more urban residents to invest in automobiles, generating more traffic and demands for additional roads. The building of expressways and parkways encouraged still further suburban migration.

In 1920, the growth rate of suburbs exceeded that of the cities for the first time. Among the most rapidly growing suburbs in the 1920s were Elmwood Park, Berwyn, and Wilmette near Chicago; Beverly Hills and Inglewood near Los Angeles; Grosse Point and Ferndale near Detroit; and Cleveland Heights and Shaker Heights near Cleveland. Of seventy-one new towns incorporated in Illinois, Missouri, and Michigan in the 1920s, two-thirds were suburbs of Chicago, St. Louis, or Detroit. Many were residential communities for the upper and the middle classes, and others were industrial and mixed-use suburbs where factory workers constituted a fifth or more of the population. Both commercial agriculture and industrial suburban belt settlements sprung up south and east of Los Angeles. In the 1920s, the Los Angeles community of Watts, initially a labor camp for the Pacific Electric Railroad, was home to blacks, Mexicans, European immigrants and native born whites, settled in different sections of town. Although other early working-class suburbs housed diverse groups, suburban populations were overwhelmingly likely to be racially homogenous.

Retailing followed the migration of people to the suburbs. Older secondary business centers at streetcar transfer points were replicated by those springing up at major highway intersections. Neighborhood banks, movie theaters, office buildings, branches of major department stores, and chain stores such as Woolworth's, Kresge's, and Walgreen's brought the amenities of downtown to the periphery. The twenties also witnessed the birth of the country's first suburban shopping center. In 1922, Jesse C. Nichols, a Kansan versed in land economics, built the Country Club Shopping Center as the commercial hub of his huge real estate development in Kansas City. A few years later Sears Roebuck and Company began to build stores in outlying districts to reap sales from growing suburban populations. The major proliferation of shopping centers would occur following World War II (see Chapter 9), but throughout the twenties and thirties, doctors, saloon keepers, restauranteurs, and independent merchants followed clients and customers out to expanding residential areas until business districts speckled every quadrant of a city's metropolitan area. By the time of the economic collapse in 1929, the population of the suburbs was growing twice as fast as that of central cities. The more that industry and retailing decentralized, the more roads were built; the more roads that were built, the more automobiles became a social and economic necessity for suburban residents.

Streetcars, once marvels of progress, began to decline in the 1920s. After World War I, the cumulative effect of publicized abuses by streetcar franchises, strikes by streetcar employees, and accidents was that streetcars lost public support during precisely the period when companies were seriously strained by postwar inflation, overextended lines, and competition from automobiles. Millions of Americans continued to depend on mass transit to get to work, but by the end of the decade the number of white mass-transit riders began to decline, leaving public transportation in some cities increasingly dependent on African-American riders. As automobile use made central-city streets more congested, streetcars and the buses that began to replace them could no longer provide a convenient ride to work, and the farther away a commuter lived from downtown, the more benefits accrued from car travel. In the 1920s, cars counted for between 20 and 30 percent of daily traffic into central business districts even in congested cities such as Boston, New York, and Chicago, and as much as 50 to 66 percent in smaller cities like Kansas City, Milwaukee, and Washington, D.C. Streetcar revenues began to fade, and even with rate increases, the companies could no longer earn enough to meet operating expenses.

Instead of mass transit, city and state governments invested heavily in street improvement, traffic regulation, and new road construction. Highway building has been subsidized by government in a way that mass transit, considered a private investment, has never been. By the 1920s, street and highway construction constituted the second largest item in municipal and state budgets. Between 1915 and 1930, the city of Chicago widened and opened 112 miles of streets at a cost of $114 million. New York City parkways built between 1923 and 1937 opened up for development seventeen thousand acres around the city. Urban road building failed to relieve congestion in the central business district or even keep pace with the spread of auto use, but it did encourage car travel, overloading streets and thoroughfares as soon as they were built and ultimately stimulating travel that avoided the central business district altogether.

Although cities were unable to secure much direct assistance from state capitals or from Washington in meeting local traffic needs during the twenties, urban interests were successful in influencing the evolution of national highway policy. Early in the twentieth century, urban merchants and industrialists had organized the Good Roads Association because they believed that more and better highways would aid

The Age of the Skyscraper. A workman sits on the end of a beam and bolts together the framework of the Empire State Building. Completed in 1930, this skyscraper operated with huge financial losses during the first six years of the Depression.

business. But among the most influential advocates of federal assistance were agrarian interests, such as the National Grange Association, which wanted to improve transportation between farm and market. The first attempt to initiate federal aid to highway construction reflected this rural base: an unsuccessful 1902 bill called for a federal Bureau of Public Roads that would have assisted states in building roads in rural areas only.

It was not long, however, before metropolitan interests helped to swing federal highway policy to an urban axis. By 1915, increasing truck traffic gave urban businessmen stronger arguments for the construction of arteries to aid freight transportation between cities rather than to help farmers bring their crops to market. The Roads Aid Act of 1916, the first legislation to create federal responsibility for highway improvement, revealed a tension between support for arterial commerce between cities and aid for farm-to-market routes. The act authorized the secretary of agriculture to make matching grants to state highway departments for the improvement of post roads. World War I demonstrated the nation's need for trunk highways, especially after the Council for National Defense was forced to use trucks to relieve rail congestion. As a result, Congress passed the Highway Act of 1921, which provided federal aid to primary state roads that would contribute to a system of connecting interstate highways. More important, the act created the Bureau of Public Roads, which by 1923 was planning a national highway system that would connect all cities of fifty thousand or more inhabitants. The new highway complex reflected the emerging dominance of metropolitan interests in national affairs.

At the same time that manufacturing was relocating outside the city, the proportion of communications, finance, management, clerical and professional services situated in downtown increased. The spreading out of factories on the periphery and the proliferation of skyscraper office buildings downtown accelerated the trend of separating production from corporate administration. The massive corporations expanded by vertical and horizontal integration made such a separation advantageous, and transportation between offices and factories via streetcars and highways plus communication over the telephone made separation possible. By 1929, the editors of *The American City* could count 377 buildings at least twenty stories tall. Although New York claimed nearly half of the nation's skyscrapers, Syracuse, Memphis, and Tulsa also boasted of their own. Just as factories and railroad stations symbolized prosperity and growth in nineteenth-century cities, skyscrapers offered visual proof of progress in twentieth-century cities. Corporate offices, along with the banks, law offices, and advertising agencies that serviced them, now towered over downtown streets. Cleveland's 52-story Terminal Tower, Chicago's 36-story Tribune Tower, and New York's 102-story Empire State Building represented the reorientation of downtown space in the transition from industrial to corporate city.

Competition from suburban shopping districts and the reorganization of downtown threatened major department stores, which found sales slipping by the 1920s. To recoup revenues, stores went to great lengths to entice customers to shop downtown. According to historian William Leach, "The department store became a zoo (Bloomingdale's and Wanamaker's in New York had enormous pet stores), a botanical garden (floral shops, miniature conservatories, roof gardens), a restaurant (some of the major stores had lavish restaurants bigger than any other in their cities), a barber shop, a butcher shop, a museum (gift and art shops, art exhibits), a world's fair, a library, a post office, a beauty parlor."[1] Downtown nightclubs, movie palaces, cabarets, and restaurants could afford premium space only by charging high prices and cultivating a following among the wealthy and those aspiring to an expensive lifestyle. Older neighborhoods near high-rent sections continued to be characterized by a mix of commercial, industrial, and residential space. But as office towers replaced factories, small retail businesses, apartments, and tenements that had previously occupied the downtown, streamlined buildings and specialized land use defined what was valuable in the central city. Older, more varied neighborhoods came to be seen as slums.

Acceptance of the new spatial specialization and especially of a suburban mentality dominated the thinking of political, social, and physical reformers who planned cities and formulated policy from the 1920s until the 1960s. A commitment to decentralization implicit in its title characterized the Regional Planning Association of America (RPAA). Convened in 1923, the RPAA included among its members architect and former settlement-house worker Clarence Stein and fellow architect Henry B. Wright, plus intellectuals Lewis Mumford and Benton McKaye. Wright and Stein asserted that uncontrolled expansion was causing unnecessary congestion and that decentralization would relieve pressures of housing and traffic. Following the English model of Ebenezer Howard's Garden Cities—new, planned communities with limited populations and surrounded by open land—the RPAA tried to prove the merits of decentralization by planning two projects near New York City. In 1924, it sponsored Sunnyside, a limited-dividend housing corporation in Queens planned by

Wright and Stein and intended for low-income residents. Radburn, New Jersey, a genuine garden city, was begun in 1928 on a large tract seventeen miles from New York. Although Sunnyside and Radburn won much publicity for their advanced design, both were too expensive to build to offer a feasible model for low-income housing or a solution to the problems of urban overcrowding.

Impulses toward decentralization did not halt with Sunnyside and Radburn, however. In the 1930s, New Deal faith in the beneficial effects of modern suburbanization prompted Rexford Tugwell, head of the U.S. Resettlement Agency, to plan a network of garden suburbs that he visualized as Green-Belt cities. These were to be of limited size (about ten thousand people), located on the outskirts of metropolitan centers, surrounded by farms and open lands, built with federal funds, and leased to cooperatives of local residents. Tugwell hoped that his Green-Belt cities would relieve slum congestion, provide low-cost housing, and rebuild community cohesion. Tugwell planned twenty-five Green-Belt cities, but only three were actually built: Greenbelt, Maryland, north of Washington, D.C.; Greenhills, near Cincinnati; and Greendale, southwest of Milwaukee. Private developers' opposition to plans to house low-income people in Green-Belt communities, and to government-sponsored planned communities in general, squelched the program. For example, building and loan associations in Milwaukee sued to prevent Greendale from being built. In 1938, the Resettlement Administration was abolished, and after World War II the government sold the communities to nonprofit corporations.

Regional planning was popular among planners, but seldom implemented. The New York Regional Plan was presented in 1931, and surveys were also taken for the metropolitan areas of Philadelphia, Chicago, Boston, San Francisco, Los Angeles, and Cleveland. Civic leaders held conferences and appointed commissions to discuss regional problems of highways, land use, and water supplies, but political and economic rivalries and suburban insistence on political independence prevented substantive reforms such as consolidation of cities with their surrounding territories. Schemes to combine city and county governments by Cleveland, St. Louis, and Seattle were defeated, and efforts to integrate planning in Cook County, Illinois (the Chicago region), were

A Green-Belt Town.   Left, a plan of Greendale, Wisconsin, prepared in 1936 by the Department of Suburban Resettlement of the U.S. Resettlement Administration. Right, a photograph of a Greendale neighborhood in 1939.

tabled. Whenever it was implemented, regional planning had the effect of certifying growth as inevitable and celebrating the automobile as the best possible means of transportation, undervaluing possibilities for controlled growth and mass transit.

More narrowly defined planning strategies such as zoning and traffic control, popularized in the 1920s and 1930s, hardened the divisions between cities and suburbs. Zoning is a type of local police power that restricts certain types of buildings or land use to certain districts of the city. Copied from Germany, it was originally intended as a means of achieving stability in existing districts and orderly growth in newer regions. The earliest comprehensive zoning ordinance was passed by New York in 1916 to prevent skyscrapers and garment-industry lofts from encroaching on the fashionable Fifth Avenue retail district. Some cities, mostly in the South, had previously attempted to use racial zoning ordinances to divide white from black neighborhoods, but they were blocked by the Supreme Court in *Buchanan v. Warley* (1917).

By 1924, every major city, plus hundreds of smaller cities, had established zoning regulations. The laws generally controlled heights of buildings, determined boundaries of commercial and residential zones, and fixed density limitations. The U.S. Supreme Court upheld zoning in *Village of Euclid, Ohio v. Ambler Realty Co.* (1926), a landmark case that had consequences for future urban land-use policies. The court ruled valid a local law that zoned a parcel of land as residential and that prevented a property owner—in this case, the Ambler Realty Company—from using residentially zoned land for industrial purposes. According to the Court, zoning was a legitimate use of police power under which local government had the authority to abate a nuisance. This decision gave local governments much stronger powers against formerly sacred property rights, but zoning proved to be no panacea for urban ailments. Zoning laws primarily protected the interests of real estate developers and owners of commercial property by ensuring that residential or commercial zones would not be invaded by unwanted features such as multiple-family dwellings and factories. Thus, their effect was to preserve the status quo. Zoning maps could not renovate dilapidated housing, abolish want and crime, or improve the quality of life for all city dwellers. In the decades ahead, zoning rules that limited the development of inexpensive housing would commonly be used to exclude "undesirable" people from the suburbs, including racial minorities. Zoning became a tool of exclusion that still governs land-use patterns today.

Despite the increasingly rigid distinction between urban and suburban space, "automobility" allowed more people to travel freely in and out of the city. On weekends, thousands of cars pierced the countryside, carrying picnicking and sightseeing families, many of whom thought that farmers' fields were appropriate places for pitching tents and disposing of tin cans. Service stations, motor camps, and tourist restaurants sprouted along highways, and as farmers relied more heavily on automobiles for travel to purchase necessary supplies, small crossroads market centers lost their general trade and service functions to larger towns. With access to urban stores, goods, and services, farm families became less culturally isolated from urban life.

These regional networks formed metropolitan districts—regions that included a city and its suburbs. In 1910, the Census Bureau gave the concept official recognition by identifying twenty-five areas with central-city populations of over 200,000 as metropolitan districts. By 1920, the total of metropolitan and near-metropolitan districts had grown to fifty-eight, and together they contained two-thirds of the nation's urban population. By 1930, there were ninety-three cities with populations of over 100,000. The rise of urban America had been eclipsed by the metropolitan age.

CITIES AND CONSUMER CULTURE

The mass-consumer culture that characterized the nation in the 1920s concentrated in cities. City dwellers, now a majority of the country's population, more than ever provided workers and consumers for expanding industry and related services. American industrialists utilized new mass-production techniques to market a dazzling array of goods that many white-collar and skilled workers' families could afford. Installment buying allowed people to purchase automobiles, radios, washing machines, vacuum cleaners, refrigerators, and phonographs. Advertising helped to make acquisition desirable by celebrating consumerism in newspapers, magazines, radio, billboards, and motion pictures. Advertising strategies shifted from merely developing the brand-name loyalty to associating the possession of these products with states of well-being and the lack of them with inadequacy.

Advertisers aimed their campaigns mainly at the more affluent urban market, as rural families were falling behind in purchasing power. Between 1920 and 1929, farmers' share of the national income dropped from 16 percent to 9 percent, while incomes of urban skilled industrial and white-collar workers expanded. Moreover, the proportion of urban dwellings wired for electricity rose from 10 percent in 1920 to over 50 percent by 1930, whereas even at the later date few farmhouses had electricity. Thus most household appliances, vanguards of the new materialism, could be sold initially mainly to urban and suburban families.

Advertisers claimed that refrigerators, washing machines, stoves, canned goods, and ready-made clothing would transform housework and liberate wives from constant drudgery. Though running water and gas or electric stoves lightened housewives' burdens by freeing them from the necessity of hauling water and stoking fires, other new household conveniences actually failed to cut time spent in housework because rising standards of cleanliness kept women just as busy. Washing machines enabled housewives to wash their family's clothes frequently rather than sending them out to commercial laundries; vacuum cleaners changed rug cleaning from a once-a-year to a weekly or daily task. The decentralization of retailing made marketing more time consuming because goods previously available downtown now had to be purchased at stores scattered throughout the suburbs. Whether working as domestic producers or as domestic consumers, urban women with children at home found household responsibilities continuing to weigh heavily on them.

Leisure activities were another type of consumption mostly supported by city dwellers. A mania for sports, movies, and music gripped every city. Passionate interest in sports had been building since the late nineteenth century. In 1923, 300,000 fans attended the six-game World Series of baseball between the New York Yankees and the New York Giants. In 1926, the attendance of 130,000 at the first Jack Dempsey–Gene Tunney heavyweight championship prizefight in Philadelphia broke all records. Each week millions of sports enthusiasts practiced baseball in sandlots and filled tennis courts, golf links, and beaches.

The rise of show business paralleled the rise of sports, maturing with the growth of cities. Shrewd promoters turned vaudeville into big business, presenting magic and animal acts, juggling stunts, comedy (especially ethnic humor), and song and dance. Playing continuously for hours, vaudeville's variety made it attractive to mass audiences, including families. Music halls, cabarets, and nightclubs brought performers and audiences closer together, dancing to new kinds of ragtime and jazz band music in an informal setting that celebrated pleasure and a more explicit sexuality.

Motion pictures also attracted enormous crowds in the 1920s. During the banner years from 1927 to 1929, weekly movie attendance reached an estimated 110 million people—at a time when the nation's total population was just over 120 million and total weekly church attendance was under 60 million. Many moviegoers were country folk who streamed into the Bijou on Main Street in a thousand towns and villages. But many more were city dwellers who stood in line for one of the six thousand seats in Roxy's in New York or in one of the ornate Balaban and Katz movie palaces in Chicago. Silent movies could attract a linguistically diverse urban audience, although by 1927 familiarity with English was widespread enough for the introduction of sound in *The Jazz Singer* to make movies even more appealing. Mass spectacles such as Cecil B. de Mille's *The Ten Commandments* (1923), sexually charged romances such as *The Four Horsemen of the Apocalypse* (1920) and *The Sheik* (1920), and slapstick comedies, which often poked fun at authority, were widely popular to a

The Palatial Urban Movie Theater. Movie fans crowd the sidewalk in front of the opulent Warners Theater in New York, August 6, 1926, for the opening of *Don Juan*, starring John Barrymore. Note the lavish use of electricity for air conditioning as well as for lighting.

variety of different class and ethnic audiences. African-American audiences in big cities also viewed Hollywood films, sometimes from separate balconies reserved for people of color. They patronized films depicting familiar cultural dilemmas such as those made by the popular African-American filmmaker Oscar Michaux, shown on a circuit of independently owned and sometimes black-owned "race" theaters (for black audiences only) from New York to Texas, which also showcased African-American musical and vaudeville performers. Movies helped to popularize urban culture as national culture by presenting scenes involving diverse city people such as wise-cracking and worldly working-class characters, including a range of ethnic and racial types.

Radio brought the new world of entertainment and advertising directly into urban homes in the 1920s. By 1930, radios were a fixture in approximately 40 percent of all American households, and radio production had become a billion-dollar industry. Stations sprouted in hundreds of cities. In Nashville, a local insurance company pioneered new marketing techniques by operating its own radio station to sell its product through advertising and by creating a new entertainment institution, the Grand Ole Opry, as the station's chief listener attraction. In 1926, a network of stations was formed by the National Broadcasting Corporation, and in 1927, the federal government created the Federal Radio Commission, which distributed broadcasting licenses and frequencies among 412 cities. National radio broadcasting linked people living distant from one another in new ways, enabling listeners to share a common experience with a national audience, and radio advertising brought the message of consumption into every listening household.

Los Angeles Suburbanization.   This photograph of Whittier Boulevard in Los Angeles, California, illustrates the interconnections among automobiles, electrification, and suburbanization in the 1920s.

A new emphasis on spending, consuming, and playing replaced older values of frugality, hard work, and self-denial; external characteristics of personality substituted for internal strength of character. The glitter and glamour of city life beckoned from the urban settings that radio and films projected. Cars, new goods and services, and nightlife infused cities with an expansionist spirit. But by mid-decade, dark clouds were gathering. Speculation in securities was draining private capital from mortgage markets and pushing the costs of home ownership beyond the reach of many families. Housing construction ebbed in both the inner cities and the outskirts. As prices for land and buildings soared, real estate operators used inflated paper profits as security on loans obtained for stock market speculation. Moreover, advertising and consumer credit had created huge demands for products, but demands themselves could not raise buying power. To be sure, the new prosperity had lifted the wages and living standards of urban workers, but a rising proportion of private incomes was spent on interest payments for installment purchases, instead of on goods and services. The economy of the urban nation was teetering on a weakening base—a base that crumbled in 1929.

CITIES AS A CULTURAL BATTLEGROUND

Commercial amusements drew on diverse cultural traditions for their popular appeal. African-American music, dance, and minstrelsy humor were utilized in the creation of "respectable" forms of entertainment in white-supported urban commercial amusements such as vaudeville theaters, dancehalls, and movie theaters. White suburbanites trekked to Harlem nightspots to hear the hottest African-American jazz bands, and New Orleans–born Italian-American Louis Prima played jazz trumpet and performed with his orchestra for African-American audiences at the Apollo Theater in New York and the Howard Theater in Washington, D.C. Much of American popular music emerged out of a process of cultural exchange and mixing. For example, the first published blues to reach a wide audience, "Memphis Blues," was originally written by the African-American W. C. Handy, classically trained as a composer and also a veteran of the black minstrel tent show circuit, as a campaign song for Memphis's political boss Ed Crump. As well, immigrant Jewish singers Fannie Brice and Sophie Tucker and African-American dancer and comedian Burt Williams won loyal followings on the vaudeville circuit, although often their humorous appeal depended on perpetuating demeaning stereotypes of their own group experience. In less respectable bars and brothels in the South and Southwest and in vice districts in cities such as New Orleans, Kansas City, and Memphis, the lines of formal racial segregation blurred, and musical traditions from white and black Southern culture mixed with local Italian, Polish, and Latin ethnic traditions to produce popular jazz, blues, and "hillbilly" music.

Urban commercial culture's potential for undermining older patterns of separation and for mixing ethnic groups and races was a source of great concern to some urban residents. The disruptive potential of commercial culture seemed to converge with new possibilities of independence and vulnerability for the thousands of country-born young men and women moving to cities. Issues like prohibition, union organizing, and immigration restriction sharply divided urban populations, and lynchings and race riots bared deeper tensions lying beneath surface accommodations. The city in the 1920s was often a battleground as various groups within the population struggled for social and cultural authority.

The triumph of national prohibition in 1919 and rebirth of the Ku Klux Klan (KKK) after 1915 seemed to be last gasps of fading rural resistance to urban civilization. However, important segments of city populations contributed to the initial successes of these campaigns, while other urban groups brought about their ultimate failure. Although rural groups, particularly small-town Methodists and Baptists, had been in the vanguard of the crusade against alcohol, a number of urban interests also supported the Great Cause. With the exception of Episcopalians and Lutherans, prohibition was supported by the cities' middle-class Protestants, most of whom lived in outlying neighborhoods or suburbs. These Protestants linked liquor to poverty, vice, and corruption. They believed that enforced abstinence would improve worker efficiency, fortify family life, and blunt the power of political machines.

Enforcement of the law worked well at first. The Volstead Act, which provided for enforcement of the prohibition amendment, forged new links between local police and federal agents in the attack against bootlegging. But it proved impossible to dry up the cities. Large numbers of people refused to renounce the bottle, and speakeasies blossomed in cities across the country. Smuggling and illegal distilling were increasing rapidly by the mid-twenties. Local authorities proved unable or unwilling to enforce the law effectively, and even federal enforcement was sporadic, undermanned, and inept.

Crime blossomed into a big business, organized much like any other big business. Organized crime had already adopted business techniques by the early twentieth century that included coordinated management, payrolls, and modern communications. But in the twenties the public desire to evade prohibition gave crime syndicates new opportunities to consolidate and centralize. In New York, Chicago, Detroit, Cleveland, Kansas City, Buffalo, New Orleans, San Francisco, and other cities, big-time criminals expanded from illegal activities into labor racketeering and control of small businesses, such as restaurants, barbershops, and dry cleaners.

The most notorious feature of organized crime in the 1920s was the use of extortion and murder to win customers and eliminate competition. Merchants who refused to accept gang-controlled business, such as slot machines or bootleg beer, or who refused to pay protection money, were beaten and their property was destroyed. During the twenties, Chicago, New York, Kansas City, and Detroit witnessed hundreds of gangland killings, almost all of which went unsolved. Between 1925 and 1928, over four hundred gang-related bombings of business establishments occurred in Chicago alone. Rivals who contested a gang leader's will were assassinated, and their bodies, feet encased in cement slippers, were dumped into nearby rivers and harbors. In Chicago, a dispute over the bulk of illegal liquor traffic burst into violent war when henchmen of crime boss Johnny Torrio murdered archrival Dion O'Banion in O'Banion's florist shop in 1924. Torrio and his lieutenant, Al Capone, were considerate enough to send a basket of flowers to O'Banion's lavish funeral, but the gesture failed to console the florist's gang, now led by Hymie Weiss. The gang went on a bullet-filled rampage, driving Torrio into retirement, and Capone assumed full control of Torrio's legions. Combat raged for more than four years, climaxing on St. Valentine's Day, 1929, when Capone's agents, posing as policemen, trapped seven members of the O'Banion gang in a North Side garage and executed them with submachine guns. By this time Capone ruled the Chicago suburb of Cicero and had spread his influence from bootlegging into a huge network of rackets that included ninety-one trade unions. He was earning over $100 million a year, and his flamboyant habits made him as famous as Charles Lindbergh and Babe Ruth. He was not yet 32 years old.

Other factors besides prohibition contributed to the rise of big-time crime. Trucks and automobiles gave criminals and illegal commerce new mobility. Submachine guns and other weapons inherited from World War I made crime more threatening. And the times themselves had given birth to an indiscriminate worship of swagger. Organized crime provided a ladder of social mobility, a means of making it for immigrants and other groups forced to live on the margins of society. A 1930 report of 108 crime leaders in Chicago revealed that 32 were Italian, 31 Irish, 22 Jewish, and 13 African American. By supplying liquor, gambling facilities, and prostitutes, organized crime served a consuming public. Thus Al Capone defended himself as an ordinary businessman. "All I do is to supply a public demand," he once remarked. "I do it in the best and least harmful way I can."

By 1933, Capone was in jail and prohibition was repealed by the Twenty-First Amendment. The return of legal liquor swept away most of the bootlegging but left behind more sinister underworld activities that had accompanied the growth of organized crime in the twenties—extortion, racketeering, and narcotics (activities in which gangsters created demand far more than they served existing needs). These areas gave the underworld its future.

Race relations became explosive when the unprecedented Great Migration of African-American migrants from 1915 onward unsettled prior patterns of racial accommodation. Tensions over housing shortages, inflation, black voting strength, the labor movement's unsuccessful initiatives amid postwar labor surpluses, and new antiunion offensives inflamed racial hostilities along the shifting boundaries separating black from white residential areas. A race riot in East St. Louis in 1917 erupted when some African Americans, having been beaten repeatedly by white gangs, shot into a police car. In the dusk they had mistaken it for another Ford automobile containing white joyriders who had shot up black homes earlier in the evening. In 1919, a race riot in Longview, Texas, occurred after some African Americans shot whites who entered their neighborhood seeking a teacher who had reported a recent lynching to the African-American newspaper, the *Chicago Defender*.

In the summer of 1919, race riots broke out in twenty-six cities. The worst violence occurred in Chicago, where vicious violence erupted after whites stoned to death a black youth swimming off a Lake Michigan beach after he had drifted into water unofficially reserved for whites. When the city was finally quieted, 38 people had been killed (23 blacks and 15 whites), 520 were injured (342 black and 172 white), and 1,000 black families were left homeless by arsonists and vandals. Riots erupted in cities as diverse as Omaha, Knoxville, Charleston, and Washington, D.C. The 1921

riot in Tulsa, Oklahoma, one of the deadliest outbreaks in the nation's history, originated when a crowd of armed African Americans assembled before the courthouse to
prevent the lynching of a black arrested for allegedly attacking a white girl. Some
African Americans shot at the white police and civilians who attempted to disperse
them. Whites then destroyed a 34-block area of black residences and killed almost
300 people.

Unlike previous race riots in which African Americans had been relatively pas-
sive victims of white mob action, the typical pattern in all these blowups was retaliation against white acts of persecution and violence. Whites perceived this retaliation
as an organized, premeditated conspiracy, which then unleashed the armed power of
white mobs and police. In the face of overwhelming numerical superiority, African-
American resistance collapsed fairly early during the riots, especially in the South.
Still, the riots left deep scars and divided communities.

Partly in response to race riots and threats, thousands of African Americans in
northern cities joined movements that called for black independence. The most
influential of these black nationalist groups was the Universal Negro Improvement
Association (UNIA), headed by Marcus Garvey, a fiery and flamboyant Jamaican
immigrant who believed that blacks should separate themselves from a corrupt white
society. Proclaiming, "I am the equal of any white man," Garvey cultivated racial
pride through mass meetings and parades. His newspaper, the *Negro World,* refused
to publish advertisements for hair straighteners and skin-lightening cosmetics, and
his Black Star Shipping Line intended to help blacks emigrate to Africa. The UNIA
declined in the mid-1920s when the Black Star Line went bankrupt (unscrupulous
dealers had sold it dilapidated ships) and when antiradical fears prompted government prosecution (ten of the organization's leaders were arrested on charges of anar-
chism, and Garvey was deported for mail fraud). Nevertheless, the organization had
attracted a huge following in New York, Chicago, Detroit, and other cities, and
Garveyites would resurface in later years as civil rights leaders.

White fears of African-American urban migration were one of the forces underlying the reemergence of the KKK in this period. Urbanization and industrialization in the
South seemed to feed a new expression of what historian Nancy MacLean has identified as reactionary populism. This sentiment included extreme racism and nativism,
militant sexual conservatism, and hostility toward both big capital and working-class
radicalism.[2] These were the sentiments of the crowd in Atlanta that in 1915 lynched Leo
Frank, a Jewish northern-born factory supervisor, accused of murdering Mary Phagan,
a thirteen-year-old white girl who worked in his factory. They were also the defining
elements of the revived KKK unveiled two months later by William J. Simmons, an
Atlanta evangelist and insurance salesman, at a ceremony attended by many purportedly
involved in the Frank lynching. Simmons extended the racist mission of the Klan to
include the purification of Southern culture, and he revived the hoods, mystical rituals,
and tactics of terror and intimidation of its forerunner.

The Klan grew slowly until 1920, when Simmons hired two public relations
experts, Edward Clarke and Elizabeth Tyler, to recruit members. By sending agents
into Masonic Lodges and other organizations, Clarke and Tyler built membership to a
figure between two and four million by 1924. Using threatening assemblies, violence,

Ku Klux Klan on Parade. For a brief period of time, the revived Ku Klux Klan attracted large numbers of disaffected urban dwellers in the Midwest and Northwest as well as in the South. Note the phalanx of women at the head of this parade held in Washington, D.C.

and political pressure, the Klan for a time wielded frightening power in Arkansas, California, Indiana, Ohio, Oklahoma, Oregon, and Texas. Although, like its predecessor in the 1860s and 1870s, the new Klan vowed to maintain forever white supremacy, its constitution also pledged Klansmen "to conserve, protect, and maintain the distinctive institutions, rights, privileges, principles, traditions, and ideals of pure Americanism," and added anti-immigrant, anti-Catholic, anti-Jewish, and antifeminist venom to its racist poison. From 1921 onward, Klansmen paraded, harangued, and assaulted in the name of Protestant morality and Anglo-Saxon purity, meting out vigilante justice to bootleggers, wife beaters, and adulterers; forcing schools to adopt Bible readings and stop teaching the theory of evolution; and campaigning against Catholic and Jewish political candidates.

Although the Klan flourished in rural districts and small towns of the West and South—areas where people feared and distrusted the city—it also enjoyed success in metropolitan areas. Historian Kenneth T. Jackson has estimated that half the Klan's membership lived in cities of over fifty thousand people. Detroit, Atlanta, Indianapolis, Memphis, Philadelphia, Portland, and Denver had sizable contingents. Chicago, with an estimated fifty thousand Klansmen, contained the largest operation in the country. The urban Klan thrived in the zone of emergence, the belt of modest neighborhoods that separated the inner core from the periphery. Here, working-class and lower-middle-class white Protestants, one step removed from the slums, grew increasingly apprehensive when blacks, Catholics, and Jews began to press upon housing markets in nearby neighborhoods. Many white families, still on the lower rungs of the socioeconomic ladder, grasped for some means of soothing their anxieties and reinforcing their identification with "100 percent Americanism."

In cities, Klansmen often turned to politics rather than relying on parades, cross burnings, and lynchings to achieve their goals. Usually operating within one of the two major parties rather than independently, the KKK was partially successful in influencing local elections: it helped to elect a Republican mayor in Indianapolis and Democratic mayors in Denver and Atlanta. But after 1924, racked by scandals and dissidence, the Invisible Empire swiftly declined. The Klan waned locally because its political machinations failed to bring substantive results. Politics provided the only avenue by which nativists could translate 100 percent Americanism into policy, but even the election victories produced only short-term effects. Moreover, by the midtwenties Catholics and Jews, along with liberal Protestants, could outvote the Klan. By 1930, the Klan had submerged into the current of intolerance that has flowed beneath the stream of American history.

Besides joining movements for moral purity such as prohibition and the KKK, perplexed, native-born city residents also provided a base of support for religious fundamentalism. A literal interpretation of the Bible and unquestioning faith provided not only a means to salvation but also a comforting defense against what these individuals saw as a materialistic, hedonistic urban society. The most famous religious clash of the decade occurred in Dayton, Tennessee, in July 1925. Here, at the trial of John Thomas Scopes, a high school biology instructor arrested for teaching the theory of evolution, city leaders encouraged a showdown between fundamentalists and modernists, the unquestioning religion of the country against the scientific higher criticism of the city. The prosecution enlisted the counsel of William Jennings Bryan, self-proclaimed defender of the faith, and the defense obtained assistance from big-city lawyers Clarence Darrow, Arthur Garfield Hays, and Dudley Field Malone. Although the jury found Scopes guilty of breaking a Tennessee law prohibiting instructors in state-supported schools from teaching that humans had descended from lower orders of animal, it was a Pyrrhic victory for the fundamentalists. Scores of newspaper reporters conveyed the circus-like event to a national audience and made the trial an object of ridicule, especially after Darrow cross-examined Bryan and bared all the ambiguities of literal interpretation of the Bible. Afterward, humorist Will Rogers remarked, "I see you can't say that man descended from the ape. At least that's the law in Tennessee. But do they have a law to keep a man from making a jackass of himself?"

It appeared, then, that cosmopolitan urban culture could shrug off the challenge of rural old-time religion. Yet at the same time, pietistic fundamentalism, with its holiness and Pentecostal churches, was surging in cities across the country. In part this upswing accompanied the move of African Americans to cities. African Americans transplanted their churches from the rural countryside and looked to them for solace and affirmation. The majority of urban fundamentalists were white, however. Like the KKK, urban fundamentalist churches drew much of their membership from groups caught between the middle and lower classes. Many were rural migrants attracted by the friendliness, lack of dogma, and closeness to God that the various storefront churches and revivalist tabernacles promised.

Most leaders of these churches were professional evangelists, charismatic figures who operated outside of regular Protestant denominations. Using the pageantry of the new advertising age, they attracted huge followings and stirred up a revivalistic fervor. In Los Angeles, Aimee Semple McPherson, the widow of a missionary, established the Four Square Gospel Temple, where she produced extravaganzas of religious vaudeville. Sister Aimee's lavish services, flowing gowns, and moving sermons captivated thousands of newly arrived Midwesterners and Southerners. Her Sunday evening "shows for the Lord" were broadcast by her own radio station, KFSG, throughout Southern California each week. Similar enterprises appeared in other cities. They included Clinton H. Churchill's Evangelistic Tabernacle in Buffalo, Paul Rader's Chicago Gospel Tabernacle, Katherine Kuhlman's Denver Revival Tabernacle, E. J. Rolling's Detroit Metropolitan Tabernacle, T. H. Elsner's Philadelphia Gospel Tabernacle, Karl Wittman's Tabernacle in Toledo, and Luke Rader's River Lake Gospel Tabernacle in Minneapolis. Most of these churches had their own radio programs and newspapers, Bible camps, and foreign missionaries.

Fundamentalist churches, along with prohibition and the Klan, were part of a larger organizational impulse that pervaded all of urban society. City populations were too large and diverse to sustain a unified sense of community that many believed once existed in small towns and villages. In a fragmented society people turned to new forms of association that revolved around interest-group identities. Memberships in middle-class organizations such as Rotary, Kiwanis, Lions, Elks, and women's clubs swelled during the twenties. Football, baseball, and basketball games brought people together in new forms of community identification. Community chests, which were campaigns for support of local welfare projects, increased in number from twelve in 1919 to 363 in 1930. Each of these activities and associations reflected a type of social adjustment to the new urban society, where tight-knit communities no longer existed and where people tried to bring order to the complexities of group and personal loyalties. The impulses of group organization had always been characteristic of the city, but the tensions and self-consciousness of the years between World War I and the Depression heightened the search for identity.

URBAN POLITICS IN THE 1920s

Urban governance in the 1920s reflected a readjustment to these new allegiances and organizations. To be sure, bosses and reformers still contested for the reins of power, but now both had to be more sensitive to the changing electorate. For one thing the curtailment of European immigration, by World War I and later by legislated restriction, shut off one important source of urban population growth. Newcomers still poured into many cities, but these were poor rural Southerners, African-American and white, and migrants from Mexico and the Caribbean. At the same time, the children of immigrants who had arrived during the early 1900s were growing up. In 1907, the year of the heaviest foreign influx, two-thirds of all school-age children in the nation's thirty-one largest cities had foreign-born fathers. During the twenties these children became voters, workers, and parents. Their impact upon urban politics and society now bore considerable weight.

In the 1910s and early 1920s, it was usually the Democratic Party that recognized the potential of these trends and drew the strongest ethnic support. The first ethnic politician to enter the arena of national politics was New York's Alfred E. Smith—legislator, governor, and the nation's first Catholic presidential candidate. Smith's early career almost duplicated the backgrounds of the Tammany bosses who ruled the city during his youth. Born to Irish parents on New York's Lower East Side, Smith left school at an early age to support his widowed mother. Smith's toughness and ambition led him into Tammany Hall, where he rose rapidly within the organization and within the Democratic Party. In 1903, he won a seat in the state legislature, where he managed to satisfy Tammany chieftains and at the same time ally with prominent progressive reformers such as Robert F. Wagner and Frances Perkins, supporting welfare and labor-reform legislation. Smith ran successfully for governor of New York in 1918 and served from 1919 to 1921 and again from 1923 to 1928.

Smith's political successes and broad appeal made him a logical presidential candidate. His attempt to win the Democratic nomination in 1924 failed, but in 1928 he could not be denied. His campaign against Republican Herbert Hoover was vigorous and boisterous, stressing labor reform and an end to prohibition. Although both candidates tried to avoid religious issues, bigots managed to hurl some malicious barbs at Smith's Catholicism. But prosperity was the major issue. Hoover and his party readily accepted credit for the good economic times, and Smith was badly beaten at the polls. Nevertheless, the voting returns revealed some suggestive results. In almost every major city, Smith drew a significantly higher proportion of the total vote than had any other Democratic presidential candidate for the past generation. For the first time since 1892, the Democrats carried several large cities in the presidential election. Hoover and the Republicans managed to retain majorities in places like Indianapolis, Akron, Kansas City, and Portland where native white Protestants still predominated, but Smith carried immigrant cities such as Providence, Jersey City, New Orleans, Milwaukee, and St. Paul. Although successes of Democratic candidates for national office in off-year elections were not consistent enough in the cities to justify calling 1928 the year of the "Smith revolution," his candidacy nevertheless signaled the emergence of urban ethnic America as a strong factor in presidential politics, a factor that reinforced the census returns.

THE GREAT DEPRESSION

After nearly a decade of optimistic economic expansion, something uncharacteristic happened to the American nation in the autumn of 1929: a wildly plummeting stock market dissolved $30 billion of personal wealth and pushed the country into a decade of deprivation. In retrospect, the signs of imminent decline seem clear. Farmers had been suffering long before 1929. The construction industry had weakened after 1926. Automobile manufacturers and related industries had overextended production relative to the general public's buying power. Unbridled speculation, encouraged by irresponsible banking practices, had created huge paper profits that masked the economy's shakiness. The stock market crash bared these weaknesses, and during the last weeks of October an era of expansion gave way to an era of

Hooverville, Seattle, 1933.   Men and women who found themselves jobless and homeless as economic conditions worsened during the Depression built squatter settlements such as this one on the outskirts.

depression. American cities endured considerable trauma in the ensuing decade. But economic collapse pulled them and the federal government into a new alliance, one in which Washington became the dominant partner. The American economic system depended heavily on a national network of cities, and government could not ignore how vital that network had become. During the 1930s, urban problems became national problems.

Just as (or perhaps because) prosperity in the 1920s had been most visible in the cities, economic crisis struck city dwellers with particular severity. The effects came slowly, however. At first the Depression seemed far away, a temporary setback that bankrupted a few New York investors. Workingmen in Minneapolis and Houston joked about frantic stockbrokers jumping out of hotel windows, and advertisers in Atlanta and Los Angeles continued to celebrate the virtues of credit and consumerism. But the crash generated a brutal recession that gradually deepened in every city. Factories and stores cut back payrolls. In Chicago, Cleveland, Milwaukee, and Grand Rapids, teachers went without paychecks for months. In New York City, the International Apple Shippers Association sold crates of surplus apples to six thousand unemployed workers, who then peddled the fruit at five cents apiece. Relief rolls in Detroit swelled while automobile assembly lines slowed to a snail's pace.

Everywhere savings accounts dwindled, insurance policies lapsed, and mortgage payments fell delinquent. Families were forced to consume less. Private loans and IOUs circulated widely.

The major source of hardship was unemployment. The Depression spun a vicious cycle: the more the business community contracted production in order to economize, the more people it threw out of work, and the more it diminished the nation's purchasing power. By 1932, about a quarter of Americans were jobless. The figures were astronomical in big cities: one million unemployed in New York, 600,000 in Chicago, 298,000 in Philadelphia, 178,000 in Pittsburgh, and 105,000 in Los Angeles. The weight of unemployment fell most heavily on the unskilled, the young, and people of color. Employers laid off those who were needed least, and many factory owners downgraded skilled workers so they could fill unskilled jobs. Local surveys revealed that joblessness among people in their late teens and early twenties ran twice as high as among other age groups. Much of the unemployment resulted from the fact that young people entering the job market for the first time simply could not find work. Although African Americans were able to retain jobs in some industries—meat packing, for example—the aphorism "last hired, first fired" rang true. A census of unemployment in 1931 found that in fourteen of sixteen Northern and Western cities the percentages of African Americans out of work were much higher than those of whites. In Chicago, Pittsburgh, and Philadelphia, rates of joblessness among employable African Americans reached 50 percent and higher.

The displacements of the Depression saddled local governments with unprecedented responsibilities. In November 1929 President Herbert Hoover called upon governors and mayors to initiate public works projects to provide jobs for the unemployed. In 1930, Hoover appointed the Emergency Committee for Employment, reorganized in 1931 as the Organization on Unemployment Relief, to encourage local communities to care for their jobless citizens. But at the same time, he emphasized the need for balanced budgets that he believed would stabilize all levels of the economy.

Municipal governments responded quickly. Even before the stock market crash, Cincinnati city manager C. O. Sherrill organized a committee to survey possibilities for public works, job training, and job placement. After the onset of the Depression other cities copied the Cincinnati model. By the end of 1930 the seventy-five largest cities were spending $420 million annually on public works projects. Yet even the most generous efforts failed to keep people out of bread lines and off the relief rolls. In 1929, Detroit spent $2.4 million on relief; in 1931, it spent $14.9 million. Over those same two years, relief expenditures rose from $620,000 to $2.9 million in Milwaukee, and from $582,000 to $3.5 million in Philadelphia.

The problem for cities was basically a financial one, but underlying that were serious political and ideological issues. The Depression caught municipalities between two millstones. On one side the need for services hiked costs of government operations, while on the other side unemployment and falling business reduced municipal tax revenues. One of the most universal problems was property tax delinquency. In 1930, among the 145 cities with fifty thousand or more inhabitants, about 11 percent of local taxes went unpaid. By 1933, the rate had reached 25.2 percent. To collect more revenue some cities, such as Dayton and Des Moines, agreed to accept late payments without penalizing the delinquents. But business leaders charged that such breaks only encouraged irresponsibility among taxpayers. Other cities spent budgets based on anticipated full collection of tax revenues, and made up the shortfall by going deeper and deeper in debt.

On top of revenue problems lay financial burdens inherited from the past. During the expansion years of the early 1900s, and especially during the 1920s, cities had borrowed extravagantly through bond issues that came due in the 1930s. Unable to make payments on either principal or interest, many cities defaulted. Others were able to meet their obligations only by depleting their sinking funds—emergency monies to be used only in the last resort. As a result, the value of municipal bonds held by investors plunged. By 1933, bond issues of Detroit and of Greensboro, North Carolina, were worth forty cents on the dollar. Local officials were quick to point out that rates of default by municipal governments were much lower than those by private corporations. Nevertheless, the financial problems of cities affected a greater number of people. In 1932, during the depths of the Depression, many people became distrustful of failing banks and hoarded so much currency that the amount in circulation declined precipitously. The shortage became so acute in the South that a few cities—Richmond, Knoxville, and Atlanta, for example—began to print their own scrip to pay public employees and relief recipients.

Cities' failures to meet their debt obligations raised cries for state control of local finances that echoed the charges of fiscal irresponsibility that reformers had leveled at boss-ridden city governments in the 1870s and 1880s. The real tug, however, was less between city and state than between those who advocated prudence and those who favored more debt and liberal public spending. Many civic leaders, such as Milwaukee's socialist mayor Daniel W. Hoan and the members of the International City Managers' Association, believed that public funds should be conserved to protect the solvency of local governments. They adopted a pay-as-you-go policy toward relief projects, approving only those that would not drain the public till. Others, such as mayors Frank Murphy of Detroit and Fiorello La Guardia of New York, preferred to spend whatever money was available and borrow more for relief, even if it meant reducing other municipal services. Both policies—economizing and spending for relief—severely limited the activities of those departments deemed nonessential. Between 1929 and 1933, total expenditures by parks and recreation departments in 795 cities and towns decreased by 50 percent. Public parks programs in Fall River, New Bedford, Providence, and San Antonio were completely eliminated; the parks were saved only by private donations.

The drive to economize produced some beneficial results. For example, to conserve funds Fresno, California, and New Haven, Connecticut, combined previously separate parks and recreation departments. More important, city and county departments were merged to create more centralized administration to meet metropolitan needs. The Chicago Park District, created by the Illinois state legislature in 1933, consolidated the nineteen independent park districts of the Chicago area under one board. Cincinnati's welfare responsibilities were absorbed by Hamilton County, and in New Jersey and New Hampshire, state agencies assumed welfare functions formerly handled by their various cities. In other places, city and county health departments were combined.

Public and private agencies everywhere struggled through the Depression's early years, groping for ways to meet the intense demand for relief. During the fall of 1931 the National Association of Community Chests and Councils, following President Hoover's suggestion, raised $85 million for relief in cities and towns throughout the nation. That sum was hopelessly inadequate. As the Depression continued to deepen, many families who had teetered on the margins of subsistence for two or three years succumbed and applied for relief. Faced with mounting hardship and shriveling revenues, even the most resourceful municipalities began to run out of funds. In cities with over 100,000 people, per capita government spending dropped from $78 in 1929 to $67 in 1933, while per capita expenditures on relief rose from $0.90 to $2.94.

Inevitably, cities looked to Washington for help. In May 1932, at the invitation of Mayor Murphy, twenty-six mayors met in Detroit and appealed to the federal government for $5 billion to finance public construction projects. This group became the nucleus of the United States Conference of Mayors (USCM), the first permanent organization formed to bring urban concerns before the president and Congress. By making Washington the focus for urban lobbying activities, the USCM opened a new era in American urban history. Frustrated by rural-dominated state governments and overcome by economic and social pressures, urban officials came to believe that the road to relief led to the federal government.

Washington approached urban problems gingerly, however. President Hoover rejected the mayors' request but did approve the Reconstruction Finance Corporation (RFC), an agency that loaned money to banks, railroads, and other big businesses in hopes that stabilizing these institutions would enable recovery to filter down to the rest of society. Later the RFC was authorized to make loans to local government agencies for some projects. Money trickled into the cities at a very slow pace, however, and the bankers who increasingly assumed control as cities defaulted on debt payments could offer little help except to institute further retrenchment. Moreover, the RFC failed to bring relief to the unemployed, who needed it most. Hoover vehemently opposed direct assistance and squelched congressional proposals for public works projects designed as unemployment relief. Instead, he continued to push voluntaristic efforts.

Mayors, city managers, and other civic leaders did not uniformly favor greater assistance from the federal government. A number supported Hoover's policies, and they accepted the RFC as a meaningful reform. Yet, with their local economies and services continuing to collapse, by the fall of 1932 many leaders began to ponder the possibilities if the Democratic presidential candidate, New York's governor Franklin D. Roosevelt, should win and carry out his promise for a "new deal."

When Roosevelt did win, cities were quick to revive their pleas and the new government was quick to respond. In time *a* new deal became *the* New Deal: the legislative and administrative measures generated by Roosevelt and his advisers to bring about relief, recovery, and reform. Roosevelt launched his programs quickly; within one hundred days he had instituted measures affecting banking, agriculture, industry, and conservation. These measures affected cities only indirectly, if at all. In fact, several New Deal measures revealed a bias against cities. For example, a back-to-the-land intent was clearly part of the Subsistence Homestead Division, a program inaugurated in 1933 to remove inner-city residents to some one hundred government-sponsored rural communities.

Yet New Deal policymakers did accept the fact that cities had become the principal centers of national life. To be sure, concern was directed not so much at urban life itself as toward the ways in which urban problems existed as part of the national economic crisis. Still many of the bills that were passed and the agencies that were created grew out of the urban experience, where thrift, self-help, and rugged individualism had always shared the stage with mutual benefit and public responsibility. The effect, if not the intent, of the New Deal was to meet traditional needs of city dwellers.

Relief and Welfare

Unemployment loomed as one of the most serious problems facing FDR when he assumed office. Its impact upon cities had been devastating. By 1933, unemployment rates approached 40 percent in Chicago, 30 percent in New York, and 26 percent in Cincinnati. Roosevelt responded first by proposing the Federal Emergency Relief Administration (FERA). Created by Congress in May 1933, the FERA distributed $500 million to the states for direct relief. Although the program was not explicitly designed to aid city dwellers, 42 percent of the 1933 appropriations were spent in five heavily urbanized northern states.

By the winter of 1933–34, almost eight million families, comprising twenty-eight million individuals, were receiving federal relief. The heads of nearly half of these households were enrolled in work-relief projects sponsored by the Civil Works Administration (CWA), an agency created in November 1933 to give jobs to the unemployed. Before it was dismantled and absorbed by the FERA in April 1934, the CWA pumped a billion dollars into the economy and carried millions of people through the winter, providing them with incomes to purchase needed goods and services. Many of

Working for Uncle Sam. The many projects in which WPA workers participated included fixing roads and cleaning up after a flood. The agency not only supplied needed unemployment relief to the jobless during the Depression but also aided thousands of communities with its public works projects.

the CWA's 400,000 projects were located in, and directly benefited, cities. CWA workers built five hundred airports and improved many more. Many of the fifty thousand teachers employed by the CWA offered adult education classes in city schools. Millions of construction workers developed city parks, dug city swimming pools, and laid city sewer lines. Moreover, wages paid for CWA jobs were spent in business-starved city establishments—barbershops, shoe stores, drugstores, and clothiers. The Public Works Administration (PWA), a similar work-relief agency, also proved beneficial to cities. It built a new water-supply system in Denver, a municipal auditorium in Kansas City, and thousands of schools and hospitals across the country.

In 1935, the Roosevelt administration responded more radically to continued cries for more jobs and security. Congress created the Works Progress Administration (WPA) to finance public projects, many of which were located in municipalities. The WPA included over two and a half million workers on its payrolls by 1936. Under the guidance of Harry Hopkins, the WPA filled needs that had been neglected or postponed by private enterprise and civic initiative. Between 1936 and 1941, almost one-fifth of the nation's work force was employed by the WPA at one time or another. WPA workers built almost 600 airports and landing fields, 500,000 miles of roads and streets, 100,000 bridges and viaducts, 500,000 sewerage connections, and 110,000 libraries, schools, auditoriums, stadiums, and other public structures. Like the FERA and CWA, many WPA projects pumped new life into civic improvement. Indeed, the U.S. Conference of Mayors, now headed by New York's Fiorello La Guardia, strongly influenced the size of WPA appropriations by pressing urban needs before the White House.

The Social Security Act, passed in August 1935, had a more permanent impact than did the relief agencies. The act created programs of old-age insurance, unemployment insurance, and federal assistance to the blind, the disabled, and dependent children. The full consequences of these programs were not felt at the time, but the Social Security Act set a momentous precedent for the nation and its cities. Care of

City Streets as Playgrounds. Russell Lee's 1941 photograph shows how children in Chicago's South Side made do with whatever play space they could appropriate.

the aged and the distressed was now accepted as a national rather than a local concern, and the path had been broken for a long line of antipoverty programs that would follow. Collective responsibility for the relief and prevention of poverty, long a major issue of urban growth, had been nationalized.

Housing

Between 1929 and 1935, new housing construction shriveled to almost nothing and the specter of eviction threatened millions of home owners. Between 1926 and 1933 the number of annual mortgage failures quadrupled, and by the latter date home mortgages were being foreclosed at the rate of one thousand per day. In New York City alone, 186,000 families were served eviction notices during eight months ending in June 1932. By 1933, 70 percent of building trades workers were on relief.

These circumstances made housing an early concern of the New Deal. The Roosevelt administration adopted a two-pronged approach: an insurance program to stabilize financial conditions for homeowners and mortgage lenders, and publicly sponsored construction and slum clearance to improve housing conditions for the poor and boost employment in the building trades. Both programs influenced subsequent urban growth. Mortgage insurance made possible a massive wave of suburbanization after World War II. Public housing and slum clearance brought the federal government into the urban core. As well, however, the two-tiered housing policy had strong racial consequences. Mortgage insurance mostly aided white families eager to escape central cities for the suburbs, while housing assistance to the poor implied that poor people, especially people of color, belonged in areas separate from more privileged urban dwellers.

During its first one hundred days, the New Deal Congress created the Home Owners Loan Corporation (HOLC) to bail out endangered homeowners and stabilize mortgage markets. The HOLC almost exclusively served urban interests. (The Emergency Farm Mortgage Act, passed a month earlier, was designed to prevent rural foreclosures.) The HOLC was empowered to refinance private loans with government money carrying interest of 5 percent, giving borrowers fifteen years to repay. The loans were to enable homeowners to escape foreclosure, pay taxes, and make needed repairs. The HOLC did not reduce a person's debt, but it did save millions from defaulting. In three years of lending, the HOLC granted $3 billion in loans to one-fifth of the nation's nonfarm households and held about one-sixth of all urban home mortgage debt. In keeping with prevailing biases against inner-city ethnic and racial minorities, however, the HOLC established appraisal criteria that rejected financing in "redlined" neighborhoods that were dense, aging, or occupied by people of color.

Mortgage relief was only a stopgap measure; it did little to aid either the construction industry or housing markets. Thus at FDR's instigation, in June 1934 Congress passed the National Housing Act, which created the Federal Housing Authority (FHA), an agency to insure loans made by private lending institutions to families wishing to renovate or build homes. Over the next six years the agency underwrote $4.25 billion for the modernization of 3 million existing units and the construction of over 600,000 private homes. The FHA drastically revised the nature of mortgage lending and by doing so initiated a new housing trend in metropolitan areas. Because the FHA would guarantee a borrower's mortgage (the borrower had to pay only a small fee for the insurance), lending banks could reduce the interest rates to as low as 4 percent and could stretch out loans to twenty-five or thirty years. These new terms contrasted sharply with the loans of five to seven years and interest rates of 6 to 12 percent that had been common in the preceding half-century. Thus long-term, federally insured mortgages made home building and home owning much easier than in the past. In effect, federal mortgage insurance created subsidies for low-density, detached, owner-occupied single-family housing, virtually excluding other types of dwelling units. FHA terms in effect denied benefits to black people and in general deflected investment money away from the central city and encouraged flight to the suburbs because families could finance a new home in a development springing up along a highway outside the city more inexpensively than they could repair or modernize an older building in an inner-city neighborhood.

Both the HOLC and FHA offered little to the one-third of the nation whom President Roosevelt described as ill-housed, ill-clad, ill-nourished. The plight of these groups raised to national dimensions the specter that had haunted urban reformers for a century: the slum. By amplifying local decay, the Depression alerted even the most economy-minded leaders to the costs of physical deterioration. Early in 1930, studies of Cleveland and Boston revealed that maintenance of city services in slum areas was much more expensive than in other districts. Such studies galvanized new efforts to abolish blight and provide low-income groups with adequate housing. These had been longstanding reform goals, but the new component was the belief that projects should be financed with public funds. For decades most Americans had cast only a cursory glance at the impressive public renewal projects in European cities such as Paris, Glasgow, Vienna, and Berlin. By the 1930s, however, many civic leaders were able to view fiscal and physical decay as part of the same problem, and they paid more attention to European precedents.

In the summer of 1933, the Emergency Housing Division was attached to the PWA. This agency financed local projects for slum clearance and for construction of low-cost housing. The work was done by private contractors, and the projects were intended to provide job relief for people on PWA rolls. In four years the PWA Housing Division financed about fifty projects. The first was in Atlanta, where workers leveled eleven slum blocks and replaced them with Techwood Homes, a group of low-rent apartments. Other slum-conversion projects included Lakeview Terrace in Cleveland, Jane Addams Homes in Chicago, and Williamsburg Houses in Brooklyn. PWA funds financed construction of some twenty-two thousand dwelling units. Yet most projects failed to help those in need. Rents averaged twenty-six dollars per month, still too high for the working-class families whose incomes were under a thousand dollars a year. Clearance programs only pushed these people deeper into the slums.

The obstacles to housing programs were political. As in the past, public officials were reluctant to lead government, whether local or national, into the hallowed region of housing construction and maintenance. Even President Roosevelt preferred that Congress support private rather than public housing. Opposition to direct federal participation won the upper hand in 1935 when a U.S. district court, in the *Louisville Lands* case, ruled that the federal government could not condemn private property for low-cost housing. Although subsequent court action reversed the ruling, the original decision had the effect of steering federal programs away from direct involvement and toward indirect grants-in-aid or loans to municipalities, which could then use the funds at their own discretion.

This, in effect, was the strategy adopted by the U.S. Housing Authority (USHA), created by the Wagner-Steagall Housing Act of 1937. Passed by Congress only after Senator Robert F. Wagner of New York, long a champion of public housing, had secured the reluctant support of FDR, the bill authorized $500 million for loans and grants to state and local authorities for slum clearance and housing developments. The law stipulated that tenants in USHA units be in the lowest income third of the population, and it particularly benefited African Americans. Some 47,500 federally financed, low-cost dwelling units, nearly a third of those built in northern and southern cities, were occupied by black families in segregated projects. Critics charged that USHA-sponsored public housing was undermining the private market, but most of the accusations were false. Without the aid of public funds, private enterprise was unable and unwilling to construct modern, low-cost housing. Units built under the USHA averaged $2,720 in cost, about 25 percent less than privately erected housing but still too high for the poorest families. It razed more substandard housing than had any other program in the previous half-century, but it only dented the problem. Millions of families still lacked decent housing, and federal policies helped to enforce the color line even in the face of major population movement.

Public concern with housing during the New Deal era split into two points of view, each with its own constituency. On one side stood philanthropists, social workers, economic liberals, tenants, and unions who wanted government to take responsibility

African-American Housing During the 1930s. These shanties in a black neighborhood in Atlanta typified the quarters that the U.S. Housing Authority attempted to replace.

Home Life in the 1930s.   During the Depression, newspapers and radio broadcasts played important roles in providing home entertainment. Note the clothing styles and furniture of this middle-class household.

for removing slums and assuring a supply of decent housing. The Wagner-Steagall Housing Act of 1937 defined a slum as "any area where dwellings predominate which, by reason of dilapidation, overcrowding, faulty arrangement or design, lack of ventilation, light or sanitation facilities, or any combination of these factors, are detrimental to safety, health, or morals." Slum-clearance reformers adopted this definition to reinforce their belief that government must assist people to achieve better health, safety, and morals by sponsoring slum clearance and construction of low-cost housing.

On the other side stood landowners and business owners who worried about falling property values and rising taxes. Their concern was with blight, the deterioration in an area that made it no longer profitable to maintain or improve. These people were concerned with profits rather than with social conditions. Their motives were not pure greed; they simply believed that if an area was economically viable, its effects would benefit all groups. Thus they sought government aid, in the form of loans and clearance projects, to stimulate private investment. They opposed public housing because it interfered with private enterprise. Passage of the Housing Act crystallized these two points of view and began a debate that influenced federal policies concerning urban renewal and redevelopment after World War II.

POLITICAL AND SOCIAL LIFE IN THE 1930s

The New Deal etched its mark on cities in other ways as well. The National Recovery Administration (NRA) mustered local producers and consumers behind industrial codes of fair trade and price limits, and it encouraged labor organization by guaranteeing collective bargaining. The Wagner National Labor Relations Act, passed in 1935 after the Supreme Court had dissolved the NRA, rescued and reiterated the NRA labor provisions, clearing the way for future unionization drives in many occupations, including municipal employees. The NRA, the Wagner labor bill, and the Fair Labor Standards Act of 1938 were not aimed at cities, but they did implement some of the goals of over half a century of urban reform: minimum wages, maximum hours, and an end to child labor and sweatshops. Still, many African Americans and women workers were excluded from social security coverage and minimum wage provisions because these did not extend benefits to waiters, cooks, hospital orderlies, janitors, farm workers, or domestics. Other NRA codes allowed pay differentials based on gender, so that women's minimum wages were frozen at a lower rate than those for men. An unprotected low-wage labor market for blacks and women in cities was the result.

The Depression years also left a legacy of urban protest. As early as 1930 in Chicago, Los Angeles, and Philadelphia, the unemployed had marched on city hall, agitating for jobs and fighting evictions. In 1932 fifteen thousand black and white unemployed World War I veterans and their families made a historic journey to Washington, D.C., demanding immediate payment of veterans' bonuses due in 1945. Chicago schoolteachers protested budget cuts by pulling down the 1933 World's Fair flag and storming City Hall. The Congress of Industrial Organizations (CIO) used the sit-down strike to mobilize broad-based community support for unionization; unorganized groups as diverse as laundry workers in Chicago and dime-store clerks in Detroit also sat down to protest unfair working conditions. In Northern cities, blacks protested the persistence of racial discrimination by boycotting stores as part of Don't-Buy-Where-You-Can't-Work campaigns and organizing tenants' unions to fight high rents. In 1939, in Chicago, social activist Saul Alinsky began to apply the principles of labor organizing to neighborhoods, setting up a model for community organizing with the Back of the Yards Neighborhood Council. Depression-era protest gave a generation of urban residents experience with organizing that would be a frequently utilized resource in the years to come.

New Deal programs had been committed to getting Americans spending again, and the decade of the 1930s shows the remarkable resilience and even expansion of consumer values despite economic collapse. For example, passage of the Rural Electrification Act brought electricity to isolated rural households and helped bring urban conveniences such as appliances and radios into the countryside, lessening the distinction between city and farm. Attendance at baseball and football games, which dropped between 1930 and 1935, revived later in the decade. Big-city tabloids tripled their circulation during the thirties, mostly by publicizing human interest stories such as the kidnapping of the son of Charles A. and Anne Morrow Lindbergh, the birth of the Dionne quintuplets, and the killing of bank robber John Dillinger.

Radio's importance increased in the 1930s, especially after FDR began to broadcast his "fireside chats," reaching out to many Americans with sets in their living rooms. After 1933, much daytime radio programming consisted of soap operas such as "Stella Dallas," "Guiding Light," and "Search for Tomorrow," which translated social distress into individual domestic tales of woe, making housewives feel less alone and that their problems were not unique. Movies also thrived in the 1930s. Although a third of the nation's movie houses closed in the early years of the Depression, remaining movie theaters offered reduced prices, ladies' nights, sneak previews, and raffles to keep up attendance. Horror films like *Dracula* (1932), *Frankenstein* (1932), and *King Kong* (1933), adventure films such as *Mutiny on the Bounty* (1936), historical films evoking a bygone era such as *Gone With the Wind* (1939), and animated fantasies such as *Snow White and the Seven Dwarfs* (1937) attracted audiences of eighty-five million viewers per week. Urban settings became especially prominent in several of the film genres popular in the 1930s, and in turn, the films embedded images of urban life in the popular imagination. Screwball comedies often included scenes of sophisticated urban night life. Backstage musicals centered on the promise of bright lights and urban performance opportunities. Gangster films and related hard-boiled detective films familiarized an urban milieu of alleys, rain-soaked streets, and inner-city tenements.

Deprivation and fiscal collapse did not dim the appeal of mass culture; indeed they often encouraged the search for escape. The Parker Brothers' successful board game Monopoly enabled would-be entrepreneurs to make a killing in real estate when economic conditions all but prohibited such results in real life. Urban consumers continued to dictate popular tastes across the country. Although consumption patterns in some ways sharpened distinctions between people, in other ways they helped to create a shared culture that had the potential to cut across ethnic and

Movies Dreams, 1939.   The world Hollywood created in films was all the more compelling in the Depression. A photographer working for the Farm Security Administration captured this image of a young boy in Memphis, Tennessee, outside the entrance to a movie house on Beale Street.

racial lines, promising a better life, which gave new meaning to Americanism and new legitimacy to workers' demands for wage increases and unionization as the path to job security. The consumer culture's focus on leisure time instead of working time paralleled the divisions between home and work, and between suburb and city, that were the hallmark of the metropolitan era.

Meanwhile, the New Deal shifted urban political loyalties. By the mid-thirties, two-thirds of the populations of the eleven cities with over a million inhabitants were first- or second-generation immigrants, most of whom had few loyalties to rugged individualism and few scruples about state interference in their lives. These were the same people who had come to expect assistance in times of need from their leaders and who had exerted strong influence on the development of an urban liberalism. Franklin Roosevelt responded to these ethnic city dwellers more than had any previous national leader. During Roosevelt's early career in New York politics, boss Big Tim Sullivan had told him, "The people who had come over in steerage . . . knew in their hearts and lives the difference between being despised and being accepted and liked." As president, FDR remembered this advice. He exuded warmheartedness, and his New Deal agencies offered direct relief with a minimum of questions. Thus political support flowed to FDR because the effects of many of his national programs resembled what bosses and machines traditionally had done on the local level. Important New Deal personalities such as Rexford Tugwell, Harry Hopkins, Frances Perkins, Robert F. Wagner, and Harold Ickes had backgrounds in urban reform, and they helped shape federal programs into a national urban policy during the thirties.

Urban voters voiced their reactions to the New Deal in the presidential election of 1936, and Roosevelt won a resounding victory by carrying every state but Maine and Vermont. Support for FDR was particularly strong in the cities. The nation's ten largest cities contributed one-third of Roosevelt's eleven-million-vote margin over Alfred M. Landon. Smaller places such as Duluth, Gary, Scranton, Canton, and Youngstown that had supported Hoover in 1932 gave nearly three-fourths of their votes to FDR. In 1936, six million more voters went to the polls than in 1932, and it has been estimated that Roosevelt attracted five million of them. Immigrants and their children, who had responded to Al Smith's candidacy in 1928, moved solidly behind FDR. A new segment of the electorate, urban black voters, joined the Democratic fold. Although the New Deal in many ways failed to remedy racial problems, it had at least dispensed relief with less discrimination than had any previous government effort. As a result, African Americans broke their ties with the party of Abraham Lincoln and joined FDR's camp. African Americans in Chicago, Cleveland, Detroit, and Philadelphia, who had supported Hoover in 1932, now swung to the Democrats and became important fixtures of the party's national base.

New Deal programs and political realignments created a changing environment for boss politics. The most powerful urban leaders survived and flourished during the New Deal: Crump of Memphis, Hague of Jersey City, Pendergast of Kansas City, and Kelly of Chicago. Although a number of bosses originally supported Al Smith for the Democratic nomination in 1932, almost all accepted Roosevelt by the time of the election. FDR maintained good relations with these men, and they often turned to the president for assistance.

Yet the New Deal did alter the nature of boss politics in important ways. The Christmas turkeys, burial money, summer outings, and free shoes for schoolchildren no longer made an impact in the widespread trauma of Depression conditions. The federal government's assumption of responsibilities for offering relief and insuring security had the potential to scale down the bosses' power. To be sure, many New Deal benefits were filtered to the needy through local politicians, but the recipients knew the jobs and cash were coming from Washington. Equally important, by fostering the growth of organized labor the New Deal indirectly chipped away several functions of bossism. Under the CIO and other unions, more laborers than ever before had access to jobs, protection on the job, and unemployment compensation. Moreover, union halls offered new social centers to workingmen, sometimes replacing saloons. Union leaders organized picnics, speeches, and other affairs that had previously been the prerogative of political machines. Because the labor vote became an increasingly important political force, craft and industrial unions commanded the attention of city halls, state capitals, and Washington.

On the other hand, the New Deal gave some bosses new opportunities. By directing CWA, WPA, and other money to local projects, the federal government created new sources of patronage jobs, paid with federal funds but controlled by local leaders. Particularly in cities such as Pittsburgh and Chicago, where ward and precinct representation had not been replaced by city councils or city commissions elected at-large, the reinvigorated Democratic Party offered employment possibilities to many people. In Pittsburgh, the New Deal helped Democrats oust Republicans from power and install Democrat David Lawrence as a powerful boss. In Boston, Mayor James Michael Curley and his successors used New Deal programs to reward the party faithful, especially Irish-stock voters. Although they supported Roosevelt and benefited from his policies, Boston politicians continued to be guided more by local conditions and ethnic rivalries than by national New Deal philosophy. Elsewhere, local political traditions, such as a commitment to states' rights, conservative Democratic leadership, and disdain for relief, moderated the impact of New Deal programs. In Baltimore, city officials provided only minimal unemployment assistance, conditional on means testing, low wages, and inferior working conditions to all workers but especially to white women and African-American men and women. Atlanta, Birmingham, Memphis, and New Orleans were reshaped by the ways that federal programs were used to resettle African Americans in downtown areas while home improvement loans facilitated white suburban flight.

As bosses adjusted to increased federal influence at the local level, their intermediary functions became more important. Only those bosses who recognized the need for new flexibility could survive after the New Deal. They could still control patronage, nominations for political office, and elections, but to do so meant acquiring a broader image. The best-known mayor of the New Deal era, and the one who epitomized the merger of machine politics and social reform, was Fiorello La Guardia of New York, a former insurgent congressman who could outduel any machine politician in popular appeal. Born in the Lower East Side of New York, La Guardia spent his youth in Arizona, where his Italian immigrant father was a bandmaster for the U.S. Army, and his young manhood in southeastern Europe, where he worked for a U.S. consulate. In 1906, he became an interpreter on Ellis Island, the famous entry station for immigrants coming to the New York port. Here young La Guardia acquired firsthand experience with the plight of newcomers to the American city. He attended New York University Law School at night and entered politics. Squeezing his way up through the Republican Party, he won a seat in Congress in 1916, where he quickly gained notoriety as a people's advocate. He then made some frustrated attempts to unseat Tammany Hall from power in New York City and finally was elected mayor on a Fusion-Republican ticket in 1933, after Jimmy Walker, the scandal-tainted Democratic mayor, had been removed from office.

La Guardia immediately became a national spokesman for the urban cause. Along with Mayor Murphy of Detroit, he took a leading role in the newly formed U.S. Conference of Mayors. In New York, La Guardia's fiery, dynamic personality won him great affection, particularly from the city's many ethnic groups. As one reporter wrote,

> "La Guardia is melting-pot America-first-generation Italian-American, with a Jewish great-great grandparent. . . . The Mayor is adept in all branches of political fanfaronade: he can lead the Fire Department Band, he can dress up in a sand-hog's helmet to inspect new tunnels, he can step into the pitcher's box on opening day at the Yankee Stadium and cut loose with a high hard one in the general direction of home plate."

As mayor, La Guardia not only succeeded in obtaining large shares of PWA and other federal relief funds but also started a local program of public works and slum clearance, restored the city's credit, improved public facilities, obtained a new city charter, and initiated low-rent public housing. He was reelected twice, serving until 1945.

By the end of the 1930s the rising prominence of cities in national affairs had prompted new initiative on the local and metropolitan levels. Planning commissions revived projects postponed by the Depression. Responding to new pressures from automobile traffic, New York, Los Angeles, Detroit, Pittsburgh, and Cleveland planned or constructed belt highways and freeways, often with the aid of federal funds. Still, however, efforts of local planners, builders, and scholars paled beside the activity of the federal government. The New Deal had tightened the federal-city knot, and local officials were reluctant to loosen the bonds. Skeptics like Harold Buttenheim, editor of *The American City,* warned that Uncle Sam was becoming Boss Sam, but most urban leaders accepted federal programs and appropriations without fear of interference by Washington in local affairs. It is significant that at this time the federal government sponsored the first national study of urban life. In 1937, the Committee on Urbanism within the National Resources Committee, a branch of the Department of the Interior, published a report entitled *Our Cities: Their Role in the National Economy.* This study, headed by Clarence Dykstra, former city manager of Cincinnati, was intended as a complement to the report of the Country Life Commission, which had examined rural society for President Theodore Roosevelt three decades earlier. In its foreword the National Resources Committee clearly recognized the central themes of the evolution of America as an urban nation:

> The city has seemed at times the despair of America but at others to be the Nation's hope, the battleground of democracy. Surely in the long run, the Nation's destiny will be profoundly affected by the cities which have

two-thirds of its population and its wealth. . . . The failures of our cities are not those of decadence and impending decline, but of exuberant vitality crowding its way forward under tremendous pressure—the flood rather than the drought.

The report urged the federal government to pay more attention to the needs of city dwellers. After a brief history of American urbanization, it cataloged the nation's unsolved urban problems (no less than thirty-six of them) and presented a list of recommendations. The solutions proposed nothing new. They included public housing for low-income groups, more planning, increased and more equitable welfare services, slum removal, streamlined local governments, and more research. But the fact that these suggestions were being offered by the federal government presaged a new era in the country's urban history.

Bibliography

Overviews which cover urban growth in this period include Janet Abu-Lughod, *New York, Chicago, Los Angeles: America's Global Cities* (1999); Rosalyn Baxandall and Elizabeth Ewen, *Picture Windows: How the Suburbs Happened* (2000); Robert Fogelson, *Downtown: Its Rise and Fall, 1880–1950* (2001); David Goldfield, *Region, Race, and Cities; Interpreting the Urban South* (1997); Kenneth T. Jackson, *Crabgrass Frontier: The Suburbanization of the United States* (1985); and Jon C. Teaford, *City and Suburb: The Political Fragmentation of Metropolitan America, 1850–1970* (1979).

Local studies include Greg Hise, *Magnetic Los Angeles: Planning the Twentieth Century Metropolis* (1997); Thomas W. Hanchett, *Sorting Out the New South City: Race, Class, and Urban Development in Charlotte, 1875–1975* (1998); Patricia Everidge Hill, *Dallas: The Making of a Modern City* (1996); Char Miller, *On the Border: An Environmental History of San Antonio* (2001).

Recent studies of early working-class suburbs include Margaret Crawford, *Building the Workingman's Paradise: The Design of American Company Towns* (1995); Matt Garcia, *A World of Its Own: Race, Labor, and Citrus in the Making of Greater Los Angeles, 1900–1970* (2001); Becky M. Nicolaides, *My Blue Heaven: Life and Politics in the Working-Class Suburbs of Los Angeles, 1920–1965* (2002); and Andrew Wiese, *Places of Their Own: African-American Suburbanization in the Twentieth Century* (2004). On middle and upper class suburbs, see Michael Ebner, *Creating Chicago's North Shore: A Suburban History* (1988); Margaret Marsh, *Suburban Lives* (1990); Zane Miller, *Suburb: Neighborhood and Community in Forest Park, Ohio, 1935–1976* (1981); Carol O'Connor, *A Sort of Utopia: Scarsdale, 1891–1981* (1982); and William S. Worley, *J. C. Nichols and the Shaping of Kansas City* (1990).

On automobiles and their impact, see Jeremiah B.C. Axelrod, *Inventing Autopia: Dreams and Visions of the Modern Metropolis in Jazz Age Los Angeles* (2009); Paul Barrett, *The Automobile and Urban Transit: The Formation of Public Policy in Chicago, 1900–1930* (1983); Scott L. Bottles, *Los Angeles and the Automobile: The Making of the Modern City* (1987); Mark S. Foster, *From Streetcars to Superhighways: American City Planners and Urban Transportation, 1900–1940* (1981); Clay McShane, *Down the Asphalt Path: The Automobile and the American City* (1994); Peter D. Norton, *Fighting Traffic: The Dawn of the Motor Age in the American City* (2008); and Martin Wachs and Margaret Crawford, eds., *The Car and the City: The Automobile, The Built Environment, and Daily Urban Life* (1991).

On regionalism and decentralization, see Joseph C. Arnold, *The New Deal in the Suburbs: A History of the Greenbelt Town Program, 1935–1954* (1971); and Daniel Schaffer, *Garden Cities for America: The Radburn Experience* (1982).

On the spread of new patterns of consumption and leisure, see Robin F. Bachin, *Building the South Side: Urban Space and Civic Culture in Chicago, 1890–1919.* (2004); George Chauncey, *Gay New York: Gender, Urban Culture, and the Making of the Gay Male World, 1890–1940* (1994); Howard P. Chudacoff, *The Age of the Bachelor: Creating an American Subculture* (1999); Ann Douglas, *Terrible Honesty: Mongrel Manhattan in the 1920s* (1995); Ronald Edsforth, *Class Conflict and Cultural Consensus: The Making of a Mass Consumer Society in Flint, Michigan* (1987); Nan Enstad, *Ladies of Labor, Girls of Adventure* (1999); Lewis A. Erenberg, *Steppin' Out: New York Nightlife and the Transformation of American Culture* (1981) and Erenberg, *Swingin' the Dream: Big Band Jazz and the Rebirth of American Culture* (1998); Chad Heap, *Slumming: Sexual and Racial Encounters in American Nightlife, 1885-1940* (2009); William Howland Kennedy, *Chicago Jazz: A Cultural History, 1904–1930* (1993); Michael A. Lerner, *Dry Manhattan: Prohibition in New York City* (2007); David Nasaw, *Going Out: The Rise and Fall of Public Amusements* (1993); Kathy Peiss, *Cheap Amusements: Working Women and Leisure in Turn-of-the-Century New York* (1986); Burton W. Peretti, *The Creation of Jazz: Music, Race, and Culture in Urban America* (1992); the essays on Tin Pan Alley, the blues, and jazz in Rachel Rubin and Jeffrey Melnick, ed., *American Popular Music* (2001); David Stowe, *Swing Changes: Big Band Jazz in New Deal America* (1994); and William R. Taylor, *In Pursuit of Gotham: Culture and Commerce in New York* (1992).

On the transformation of the urban household, see Susan Porter Benson, *Household Accounts: Working-class Family Economies in the Interwar United States* (2007); and Susan Strasser, *Never Done: A History of American Housework* (1982). On sports, see Steven A. Reiss, *City Games: The Evolution of American Urban Society and the Rise of Sports* (1991). On early radio and movies, see Michele Hilmes, *Radio Voices: American Broadcasting, 1922–1952* (1997); Lary May, *The Big Tomorrow: Hollywood and the Politics of the American Way* (2000); and May, *Screening out the Past: The Birth of Mass Culture and the Motion Picture Industry* (1980); and Gregory A. Waller, *Main Street Amusements: Movies and Commercial Entertainment in a Southern City* (1995). For the development and effects of urban crime, see Humbert S. Nelli, *The Business of Crime: Italians and Syndicate Crime in the United States* (1976).

On nativism in this period, see John Higham, *Strangers in the Land: Patterns of American Nativism, 1860–1925* (1955). On the revival of the Ku Klux Klan, see Kathleen Blee, *Women of the Klan: Racism and Gender in the 1920s* (1991); Kenneth T. Jackson, *The Ku Klux Klan in the City, 1915–1930* (1967); Shawn Lay, *Hooded Knights on the Niagara: The Ku Klux Klan in Buffalo, New York* (1995); Shawn Lay, ed., *The Invisible Empire in the West: Toward a New Appraisal of the Ku Klux Klan in the 1920s* (1992); and Nancy MacLean, *Beyond the Mask of Chivalry: The Making of the Second Ku Klux Klan* (1994). On the Scopes trial, see Edward J. Larsen, *Summer for the Gods: The Scopes Trial and America's Continuing Debate Over Science and Religion* (1997).

Ethnic and racial boundaries are discussed in Ronald H. Bayor, *Neighbors in Conflict: The Irish, Germans, Jews, and Italians of New York City, 1929–1941* (1979); Elizabeth Clark-Lewis, *Living In, Living Out: African-American Domestics and the Great Migration* (1994); Juan R. Garcia, *Mexicans in the Midwest, 1900–1932* (1996); Cheryl Lynn Greenberg, *Or Does It Explode? Black Harlem in the Great Depression* (1991); Earl Lewis, *In Their Own Interests: Race, Class, and Power in Twentieth-Century Norfolk, Virginia* (1991); John T. McGreevy, *Parish Boundaries: The Catholic Encounter with Race in the Twentieth-Century Urban North* (1996); and George J. Sánchez, *Becoming Mexican-American: Ethnicity,*

Culture, and Identity in Chicano Los Angeles, 1900–1945 (1993). Race riots are discussed in David Allen Levine, *Internal Combustion: The Races in Detroit, 1915–1926* (1976); Tim Madigan, *The Burning: Massacre, Destruction and the Tulsa Race Riot of 1921* (2001); and William Tuttle, Jr., *Race Riot: Chicago in the Red Summer of 1919* (1970).

The depression in the cities is discussed in Jo Anne E. Argersinger, *Towards a New Deal in Baltimore: People and Government in the Great Depression* (1988); Richard O. Davies, *From Metropolis to Megalopolis: A History of Urban America Since 1930* (1980); William H. Mullins, *The Depression and the Urban West Coast, 1929–1933: Los Angeles, San Francisco, Seattle, and Portland* (1991); Harvard Sitkoff, *A New Deal for Blacks* (1978); Douglas L. Smith, *The New Deal in the Urban South* (1988); and Charles H. Trout, *Boston: The Great Depression and the New Deal* (1977).

On the history of public housing, see John F. Bauman, *Public Housing, Race, and Renewal: Urban Planning in Philadelphia, 1920–1974* (1987); John Bauman, Roger Biles, and Kristin Szylvian, *From Tenements to the Taylor Homes: In Search of an Urban Housing Policy in Twentieth Century America* (2000); Arnold Hirsch, "Containment on the Home Front: Race and Federal Housing Policy from the New Deal to the Cold War," *Journal of Urban History* 26, no. 2 (January, 2000): 158–189; and Gail Radford, *Modern Housing for America: Policy Struggles in the New Deal Era* (1996).

On politics in the Depression years, see Roger Biles, *Big City Boss in Depression and War: Edward J. Kelly of Chicago* (1984); Lyle W. Dorsett, *Franklin D. Roosevelt and the City Bosses* (1977); and Bruce Stave, *The New Deal and the Last Hurrah: Pittsburgh's Machine Politics* (1970). For an engaging memoir of the period, see James Michael Curley, *I'd Do It Again* (1957).

On labor, civil rights, and neighborhood organizing in the 1930s, see Lizabeth Cohen, *Making the New Deal: Industrial Workers in Chicago, 1919–1939* (1990); Karen Ferguson, *Black Politics in New Deal Atlanta* (2002); Robert Fisher, *Let the People Decide: Neighborhood Organizing in America* (1984); Michael Honey, *Southern Labor and Black Civil Rights: Organizing Memphis Workers* (1993); Sanford D. Horwitt, *Let Them Call Me Rebel: Saul Alinsky, His Life and Legacy* (1989); Robin D. G. Kelley, *Hammer and Hoe: Alabama Communists during the Great Depression* (1990); Kelley, *Race Rebels: Culture, Politics, and the Black Working Class* (1994); and Patricia Sullivan, *Days of Hope: Race and Democracy in the New Deal Era* (1996); Victoria W. Wolcott, *Remaking Respectability: African American Women in Interwar Detroit* (2001).

Notes

1. William Leach, "Transformations in a Culture of Consumption: Women and Department Stores, 1890–1925," *Journal of American History* 71 (September 1984): 326.
2. Nancy MacLean, "The Leo Frank Case Reconsidered: Gender and Sexual Politics in the Making of Reactionary Populism," *Journal of American History* 78 (December 1991): 920–21.

CHAPTER 9

The Emerging "Urban Crisis," 1941–1975

Prosperity returned to the United States in the 1940s as World War II accomplished what the New Deal could not. Wartime military spending launched a thirty-year period of economic growth that produced unprecedented affluence. Yet the social and political trends established in the 1930s had potent long-term effects. The new power of industrial labor unions, abetted by federal protections, ensured that prosperity was broadly shared. Workers' incomes grew rapidly during the 1940s and continued to rise through the next two decades. The promise of well-paid jobs in industry set off a new wave of migration to cities, particularly by African Americans and whites from the rural South. Federal housing policies encouraged a surge in white homeownership after the war, mostly in suburbs. Ironically, the affluence and high expectations in the postwar decades contributed to what was called an "urban crisis." Millions of whites moved to suburbs, along with many businesses, while poorer African Americans crowded into the deteriorating neighborhoods left behind. The bitter racial conflicts accompanying this transition had barely begun to subside when a recession and financial crisis hit the Northeastern and Midwestern cities in the 1970s. By 1975, many cities were losing jobs, population, and their optimism about the future.

THE IMPACT OF WORLD WAR II ON CITIES

The vigorous federal activity during the 1930s paled in comparison to the extraordinary mobilization during the war years, 1941 to 1945. Military spending spurred urban growth on the West Coast; coalitions of politicians and business boosters, who even before World War II had made their cities the locations of naval bases and the aircraft industry, aggressively lobbied for more military bases and repair facilities. Southern cities also experienced a surge of federal money, as shipyards boomed along the Gulf Coast from New Orleans to Mobile, and airplane assembly plants bustled in the Dallas and Atlanta areas. Military installations brought rapid growth to the Norfolk-Hampton Roads area of Virginia and even to sleepy old Charleston.

The war put America back to work. In 1944, at the war's height, only 1.2 percent of the labor force was jobless, compared to 25 percent or more in the depths of the Depression and 19 percent as recently as 1938. Washington funneled $175 billion in contracts to various corporations between 1941 and 1944. Corporate profits doubled between 1939 and 1943; wages and salaries rose more than 135 percent. The federal bureaucracy swelled from 1.1 million workers to 3.4 million. FDR's "soak the rich" tax policies in combination with full employment achieved some redistribution of income from the wealthiest downward.

Wartime economic opportunities drew throngs of newcomers to live and work in industrial cities. Mobile, a military and shipbuilding center in Alabama, saw its population grow by 65 percent from 1940 to 1944. Its housing, businesses, streetcars and even sidewalks were overcrowded; such basic services as police, water, and garbage collection were overwhelmed. Industrial cities outside the South drew a mass migration of about 1.6 million African Americans in the 1940s, more than the total migration of the previous thirty years. African-American men and women quit work as sharecroppers, domestic servants, and menial employees in restaurants, dime stores, laundries, and hospitals to seek the better working conditions, higher pay, and union benefits of industrial employment. Mexican immigrants also seized new economic

Little Tokyo, Los Angeles.   During World War II, Japanese Americans were removed from their homes and detained in camps outside major urban centers, ostensibly for security reasons. As a result, communities such as this one lost their vitality but rebounded quickly after the war ended.

opportunities despite persistent discrimination. Reversing its Depression policy of repatriation, the government began in 1942 to admit Mexicans to the United States as *braceros* on short-term work contracts for farm and industrial labor. More than fifteen thousand Mexican workers relocated to Chicago. In Los Angeles, thousands of Mexicans found shipyard jobs when before the war none had been available. Similarly, displaced white coal miners and marginal farmers from the hills of West Virginia and Kentucky left to work in the war industries of Detroit, Cleveland, Columbus, and Cincinnati. Yet military service soon drew so many men away to Europe and the Pacific that much of the industrial labor was performed by women. More than six million women entered the labor force during the war, mostly in cities where they found jobs ranging from typing to shipbuilding. Among female workers, 75 percent were married and two-thirds were mothers.

Cities hummed with vitality during the war, with multiple work shifts keeping people on the streets day and night. Nightlife was active. Swing bands reached their height of popularity, blues and jazz musicians played in many venues, and dance halls, nightclubs, bars, and restaurants were filled with war workers and soldiers on leave and with spendable cash. Movie theaters were packed, attracting weekly audiences of 85 million by 1945.

The wartime upheaval produced social tensions and violent conflicts. African Americans and whites competed for defense jobs and scarce housing in both the North and the South. They bumped against each other in overcrowded schools, buses, parks, and beaches, violating white Southerners' expectations of segregation. Some white workers staged walkouts to protest black hiring and promotion. Black membership in civil rights organizations such as the NAACP soared, suggesting new confidence in resisting discrimination. Other minorities asserted themselves as well and faced ugly resentment. When Mexican-American youths in Los Angeles flouted wartime clothing rationing by wearing "zoot suits"—outfits with exaggerated padded shoulders and tapered pants identified with black urban jazz culture—some white servicemen on leave responded with outrage. During a week of rioting in June, 1943, servicemen assaulted and stripped zoot suiters in a symbolic attempt to display their dominance.

The zoot suit riot was just one of the many conflicts that erupted in cities across the country in the spring and summer of 1943. White workers in Mobile went on a two-day rampage in May, attacking any blacks they could find, after seven black men took skilled shipbuilding positions. The worst riot bloodied Detroit in June, after blacks and whites clashed on a bridge between the city and Belle Isle Park. Undeterred by police, white mobs roamed the city attacking blacks, who in turn hurled rocks at police and hauled white passengers off streetcars. The violence left 25 blacks and nine whites dead, and more than 700 injured. In August, a riot in Harlem began with a confrontation between a white policeman and an African-American soldier. Rumors of an assault on the serviceman prompted blacks to respond with looting and vandalism.

Despite public prohibitions on homosexuality, wartime sex-segregated environments expanded the opportunities for same-sex relationships. Far from the watchful eyes of home, men and women with homosexual longings found relationships with others in war jobs and war housing. Many large cities already offered meeting places, especially bars, that enabled the public expression of homosexual identities. Some places encouraged mingling among a variety of patrons; others specifically served a homosexual clientele. By the 1940s, gay bars could be found not just in the metropolitan centers of San Francisco, Chicago, and New York, but also in smaller cities such as San Jose, Denver, Kansas City, and Buffalo. Despite the hazards posed by morals legislation, the bars provided a haven for gay culture. By the 1950s small groups of homosexuals began organizing for political and civil rights. Other homosexual groups gathered around arts and cultural institutions, where they helped to define urban cosmopolitanism.

Wartime federal spending encouraged migration to the suburbs and the "Sunbelt," the region encompassing the Southwestern states and most of the old Confederacy. Between 1939 and 1945, the federal government built an average of $2.5 billion worth of industrial buildings every year, more than double the average for private industry. Lacking adequate space in crowded cities, most of these plants located in suburbs. At war's end, these facilities were turned over to private industry, often at nominal cost. In this manner, federal construction regionalized the national economy, making southern and western metropolitan areas the locations of defense and aircraft industries. With help from defense industries and from research and development associated with them, the economies of Phoenix, Tucson, Albuquerque, San Diego, Los Angeles, and San Francisco expanded substantially in the war years and after. Southern cities such as Houston, Nashville, Birmingham, and Huntsville also continued to benefit disproportionately from federal defense spending, thanks to the power of Southern congressmen. As the Southern writer William Faulkner exaggerated in 1956, "Our economy is no longer agricultural, our economy is the Federal Government."[1]

Building on their wartime growth, the booming cities of the Sunbelt also captured a large share of new, non-military industries such as petrochemicals, information technology, and retirement communities, as well as some older manufacturing such as clothing and auto parts. Efficient air conditioning made the region's summer heat more endurable. A band of fast-growing communities extended across the country's southern tier, among them the metropolitan areas of Tampa, Miami, Jacksonville, Atlanta, Dallas–Fort Worth, and the southern coast of California. Houston, with fewer than 600,000 people in 1950, exceeded 1.2 million by 1970; Phoenix rose from barely 106,000 to 582,000. By 1980, the majority of Americans lived in the South or the West. Meanwhile, northern metropolises such as New York, Pittsburgh, Detroit, and Cleveland grew minimally or lost population. Sunbelt cities found that their rapid growth was a mixed blessing. It left them heavily dependent on automobiles and vexed by housing shortages. The media made New York a feared city for its muggings and murders, yet in the late 1970s the homicide rates of Atlanta and Houston doubled that of New York. Phoenix, once a haven for people suffering from respiratory ailments, saw its clear air turn smoggy from all the new cars, trash, and pollen-producing landscape plants.

POSTWAR SUBURBAN GROWTH

Servicemen returning from war faced severe housing shortages in the cities, but found assistance from the expanded federal government. The Serviceman's Readjustment Act of 1944, also called the GI Bill, made low-interest home loans available to military veterans. These, combined with FHA mortgage insurance, helped subsidize suburban real estate development. New housing starts climbed from 326,000 in 1945 to over one million in 1946 and two million by 1950. Developers such as Levitt and Sons erected whole communities of nearly identical houses with mass-production techniques. By 1948, the Levitts were turning out 150 houses per week, completing one every fifteen minutes in their new community of Levittown outside New York City. Efficient mass production allowed the Levitts and their imitators to sell their homes for considerably less than individually built houses, making home-owning more affordable. Fewer than one-third of Americans had owned their homes in 1930, but nearly two-thirds would do so by 1960. Comparatively little single-family housing was built within cities, where open land was scarce and FHA mortgages more difficult to obtain. In the Chicago area between 1945 and 1959, more than 75 percent of all new housing units were located in the suburbs.

Housing development was shaped by discriminatory lending practices, encouraged by the federal government. In the late 1930s, the federal Home Owners' Loan Corporation mapped the creditworthiness of neighborhoods across the nation. The maps, which identified areas where real estate loans were most likely to be repaid, explicitly favored suburban areas of newly built single family homes. Urban neighborhoods with older housing, with mixed incomes, or with "undesirable" ethnic groups such as Jews or Italians, were given low ratings. Neighborhoods that housed blacks were deemed to be the worst investments and were marked as red on the maps. Adopted by private bankers and reinforced by the Federal Housing Administration's *Underwriting Manual,* these "red-lining" criteria encouraged racial segregation through the 1940s, 1950s, and early 1960s. In one extreme example, a developer in Detroit found that the FHA would not back mortgages for his all-white subdivision until he built a thick concrete wall, six feet tall and half a mile long, to separate his property from a nearby black area. Cities that had an intricate patchwork of black and white neighborhoods now divided into much larger racial sectors. In Charlotte, for instance, the northwest side grew more heavily black while the southeast side and adjacent suburbs developed into a solidly white region. Local zoning ordinances further encouraged the separation of low-rent districts (disproportionately occupied by blacks) from areas of large, single-family homes. Though the Supreme Court's 1948 decision in *Shelley v. Kraemer* made it impossible to enforce restrictive covenants, unspoken agreements among real estate agents kept all but the most economically secure and assertive black families from buying homes in white areas. The effect of all these discriminatory practices was to exclude blacks from the new communities and to deny them the tax benefits and equity that came with homeownership.

Most suburban developments were racially exclusive, and whites wanted to keep them that way. When California in 1963 passed a fair housing law to ban racial discrimination, the law was attacked as an infringement on the rights of property owners. Conservatives gathered signatures for a state initiative prohibiting all fair housing measures at the state and local levels. The proposition passed with overwhelming support from white homeowners. In the white blue-collar Los Angeles suburb of South Gate bordering mostly black Watts, 87.5 percent voted for the measure.

Nonetheless, white Americans were not the only ones living in suburbia. Black working-class settlements such as Inkster, Michigan, and Chagrin Falls Park, Ohio, were already in existence, and a few new developments were built for the black middle class. Many metropolitan areas featured one model "integrated" suburb where black and white middle-class families co-existed comfortably, such as Shaker Heights near Cleveland.

American mass culture celebrated an idealized vision of suburban domesticity: happy neighborhoods of single-family homes where breadwinner fathers and home-maker mothers found personal satisfaction in family life and consumerism. In *Life* magazine's special 1956 issue on American women, the most space was devoted to a "typical" suburban woman, aged thirty-two and mother of four. A high school gradu-ate who had married as a teenager, *Life's* model mother sewed her own clothes, enter-tained fifteen hundred guests a year, and was supported by her husband's middle-class income. "In her daily rounds she attends clubs or charity meetings, drives the chil-dren to school, does the weekly grocery shopping, makes ceramics, and is planning to learn French," *Life* revealed as it followed the housewife from domestic chores to social events. Born in the Depression, most suburban homemakers appreciated the security and standard of living represented by a suburban lifestyle. A Gallup poll taken in 1962 reported that "few people are as happy as a housewife." But the poll also predicted future changes when most women interviewed revealed hopes that their daughters would have more education and marry later than they did.

The suburban boom came with high environmental costs. Cities had always existed in precarious relationship with nature, gobbling up open areas and natural resources while making themselves vulnerable to floods and storms. But the new mass construction of suburban housing had special environmental impact. Developers who erected hundreds of homes at a time used powerful earth-moving equipment to level hills, fill wetlands, and clear vegetation; the resulting soil erosion contaminated streams. Also, the new homes had to be built with septic tanks because many new tracts lacked connection to sewage lines. Seepage of human waste and soap suds from poorly constructed septic systems polluted groundwater. The architecture of new homes, many of them one-story "ranch" style with no basement, increased the use of energy for heating and cooling.

Much of the suburban expansion would not have occurred had not federal high-way construction provided access to rural land for development. In 1947, Congress authorized a 37,000-mile national highway network, including nearly three thousand miles of roads in or near major cities. Following a scheme of a hub (downtown) with spokes fanning out from the center and a beltway circling the city on the outskirts, federal roadbuilding redefined downtown as a commercial center with direct access to and from suburban areas. Cities also funded their own freeways. During the early 1950s, New York laid out the Cross-Bronx Expressway, Detroit began construction of the John Lodge and Edsel Ford superhighways, and Chicago built the Congress (later Eisenhower) Expressway. By 1956, there were an estimated 376 miles of freeways in the nation's twenty-five largest cities and at least 104 additional miles under con-struction. The Interstate Highway Act of 1956 strengthened these patterns. Justified as a means to aid intercity travel for purposes of civil defense, and to ease downtown

Highway Cloverleaf. This 1962 shot of an intersection between two interstate highways in Los Angeles shows clearly the engineering feat required to build high-speed limited access freeways amidst existing neighborhoods. The freeways enabled new configurations of cross-town travel between home, work, and recreation, but the community reorientation, loss of housing and local businesses, and disruption that resulted as highways sliced between blocks permanently altered local patterns of social and economic interchange.

traffic congestion, federal funds spent on highways swelled from $429 million in 1950 to $2.9 billion in 1960. Road construction cut huge gashes through neighborhoods, parks, and downtowns. Boston's John F. Fitzgerald Expressway, wrote one critic, created a "tangled web of old streets, ramps, and parking lots shadowed in gloom beneath the elevated structure."[2] Highways in Atlanta and Miami forced massive relocations of black people and served as barriers separating black and white neighborhoods.

The Postwar Housing Expansion.   Signs in an undeveloped section outside San Diego advertise the types of housing and government support for financing that invigorated suburbanization after World War II.

Beltway road construction and increased reliance on trucking for intercity freight traffic provided incentives for industrial relocation to suburban areas. By the 1960s, new factories lined peripheral highways, boosting suburban tax bases at the cost of central cities, and siphoning jobs out to the periphery. Between 1947 and 1954, the number of manufacturing plants in Chicago suburbs doubled; there was a 220 percent rise in factory jobs in suburban Detroit. In 1957, Massachusetts completed a freeway encircling Boston, and by year's end ninety-nine plants employing seventeen thousand people had located along the highway. Between 1954 and 1963, in the twenty-four metropolitan areas with populations greater than one million, the central cities lost more than five hundred thousand jobs while their suburbs were gaining 1.5 million. Some communities developed industrial parks, outlying tracts zoned exclusively for industry.

Retail development followed the residential expansion and sometimes even preceded it. Shopping centers offered suburbanites ready access to branches of the major downtown department stores, as well as drugstores, groceries, movie theaters, restaurants, banks, specialty shops—all with plenty of free parking. Revisions in the federal tax code in 1954 made commercial development even more profitable, contributing to the creation of 22,000 shopping centers between then and the late 1970s. State and municipal governments further subsidized shopping center construction through tax abatements and public financing of roads. Suburbanites initially used shopping centers for convenient short trips, and preferred making major purchases at the flagship department stores downtown, where they expected to find the best selections and prices. But shopping centers increasingly drew stores and customers away from the central city. While retail sales in the Cleveland metropolitan area rose more than 15 percent between 1958 and 1963, downtown sales dropped by nearly that amount and two major department stores closed.[3] Fully enclosed shopping malls, pioneered by the construction of Southdale mall near Minneapolis in 1956, became the major metropolitan marketplaces, replacing the public space of down-town streets with privately owned and controlled interiors. The glittering malls became new objects of boosterism as each year chauvinists from a different commu-nity boasted that they had the biggest. Thus outward movement generated its own momentum. Access to superhighways attracted residents, who in turn lured busi-nesses, who then brought jobs and more enticement for residential development.

More Americans than ever lived in metropolitan areas, but now they were mainly in the suburbs. Of the nation's two hundred million people, the 1970 census revealed, seventy-six million inhabited suburban areas, sixty-four million lived in central cities, and sixty million lived in nonmetropolitan areas (the stagnant rural districts and shrinking small towns). Almost three-fourths of the nation's total hous-ing stock had been built since 1940, two-thirds of it single-family homes, the major-ity in suburbs. The suburban population was growing ten times faster than that of central cities. Since 1950, Chicago and New York City had lost population while their suburban rings grew by 117 percent and 195 percent respectively. Detroit's popula-tion fell by 20 percent as its suburban population expanded by 206 percent. Similar patterns held in Boston, Cleveland, St. Louis, Minneapolis, and Pittsburgh. The only cities that continued to grow were southern and western cities that expanded by annexation. Even in these places, suburban growth overtook central-city increases. Dallas's and Houston's populations grew by 94 percent and 104 percent, but their suburbs grew by 107 percent and 330 percent.

Suburbs continued to house both blue-collar and white-collar workers, but sel-dom in the same neighborhood. Suburban communities ranged from wealthy, exclu-sive towns in Marin County near San Francisco to heavily ethnic and working-class Cicero, Illinois, and Hamtramck, Michigan. But as local zoning regulations enforced plot and house size and prohibited multiple dwellings, communities stratified more than ever before along class and racial lines. Only 5 percent of the nation's black pop-ulation in 1970 lived in suburbs. Racial division between cities and suburbs was increasingly obvious: whites on the outside, people of color on the inside.

RACIAL TRANSITION IN URBAN NEIGHBORHOODS

The pace of African American migration accelerated after the war, and white urban residents struggled to maintain the formal and informal practices of segregation that had previously allowed them to dominate urban institutions and neighborhoods. Approximately five million African Americans left the South between 1950 and 1970, mostly for the cities of the Midwest and Northeast. Many of them had been displaced from rural areas by the mechanization of cotton harvesting. They encountered con-tinued housing shortages in Northern cities, as many landlords in white neighbor-hoods refused to rent to them. African Americans packed instead into established black areas, sometimes doubling up with friends or relatives, sometimes renting tiny apartments carved out of larger units, cellars, and garages. The overcrowded build-ings deteriorated quickly from poor maintenance, threatening the safety of their res-idents. Rats that thrived amid the squalor frequently bit children. Tenement fires

Middle Class Black Suburbanites in Parkchester Village, Richmond, California.   After World War II, increased competition for scarce housing sparked tensions between blacks and whites. Parkhester Village was planned to be a model racially integrated housing development, designed to remedy both the scarcity and the tensions, but no white families moved in.

from 1947 to 1954 killed 235 Chicagoans, many of whom had gotten lost in the smoke within confusing "rabbit warrens" of subdivided rooms. Nonetheless, the shortage of housing for African Americans guaranteed that substandard units could continue to be rented, often at higher rates than prevailed in white neighborhoods.

While population densities rose in black neighborhoods, housing shortages subsided in nearby white neighborhoods. Though many of these neighborhoods had grown shabby during the hard times of the Depression, the return of prosperity raised hopes of better times ahead. Families were able to afford cars, radios, home improvements, and the new television sets. White working-class neighborhoods, particularly those with large numbers of Catholics, had developed a strong sense of community. Tensions that had once divided white ethnic groups had eased to the point where intermarriage was growing more common. Anchored by the church, by parish schools thriving amid the postwar baby boom, and by a cluster of local businesses, the neighborhood seemed to many of its residents to be a stable, self-contained world. Yet there were signs of impending change. Neighbors were dismayed to see many young adults relocating to the suburbs once they could afford to do so. The remaining population was older and poorer, a trend that threatened the viability of the local businesses and institutions.

The process of racial transition was painful for both whites and blacks, but in different ways. Most whites were convinced that a neighborhood could not be successfully integrated. This was to some extent a self-fulfilling prophecy: the arrival of the first black family set off a panicked exodus for a new white neighborhood within the city or the suburbs. Yet there were stronger forces at work than the racism of individual white neighbors; everyone was trapped by the logic of a segregated housing market. Realtors belonging to the National Association of Real Estate Boards were prohibited by their code of ethics from initiating the racial transition of a neighborhood. They simply would not show homes in exclusively white neighborhoods to black homebuyers. The effect of this practice was to maintain stark racial boundaries within cities. As the surging black population spread out from the crowded ghetto, it did so in an orderly progression, block by block. Whites in nearby neighborhoods could see it coming.

As an expanding area of black settlement approached a white neighborhood, potential homebuyers viewed the white area as a poor investment and banks grew reluctant to provide mortgages. Landlords had trouble finding tenants even at reduced rents. A growing number of apartments and homes stood vacant, while pessimistic property owners neglected to do basic maintenance. Finally an enterprising real estate agent not affiliated with the local real estate board would offer to buy a home or apartment building for a generous price, obviously with the intention of housing African Americans. Once the first sale had been made, and the racial transition underway, people owning property on that block would try to sell at whatever price they could get, for fear that they would get nothing if they waited too long. Many shared the sentiment that "I'm not going to be the first one to sell to a black, but I'm sure not going to be the last."[4] Neighborhoods often passed within a few years from all white to almost all black.

Real estate speculators made hefty profits through this process of "block busting," buying at reduced prices and then renting at inflated levels to blacks desperate for housing. Black homebuyers were doubly exploited. Because many white homeowners did not want to sell directly to blacks, and because banks often refused to provide mortgages, speculators served as intermediaries who resold houses on installment contracts with high interest rates. Black families could lose their entire investment if they missed installments, and then the speculator could sell the property again. Black families who struggled with high housing costs were often forced to rent out part of their home or skimp on maintenance, recreating the conditions that they had tried to escape by leaving their old neighborhood. By then, the process had rolled on relentlessly to further blocks.

Responses to the new migrants varied among white groups. In some Boston neighborhoods, Jewish residents were willing and able to relocate to new communities. Jewish congregations that had stayed intact through previous moves within the city now constructed new, modern synagogues in the suburban areas where their members were settling. In contrast, Catholic parishes were rooted in place. Territorial parishes (as opposed to the smaller number defined by ethnicity) were bounded by precise lines, within which each church served as the unifying center of neighborhood life. Catholics grew up in a culture that linked neighborhood and parish through such practices as street processions on feast days. Expecting stability, they had made heavy investments both in their homes and in the construction, maintenance and operation of elaborate stone churches, parochial schools, parish halls, and convents. The flight of Irish, Italian, German, and Polish Catholics threatened institutions left behind in neighborhoods now filled with African Americans, who were mostly Protestant. The Church hierarchy tried to keep Catholics from abandoning their parishes. It sponsored neighborhood improvement efforts and home loan programs, and some clergymen urged coexistence with the black Protestant newcomers. Yet many parish priests and laymen doubted that peaceful integration was possible. In Detroit, reported a church volunteer, "we have situations where . . . a priest will insist 'we have no problems' while their parishioners are busy out throwing rocks or attending Homeowner's meetings organized to threaten Negro citizens."[5]

The first blacks to move into a white neighborhood could expect abusive language, threats, and vandalism of their homes or cars. For example, Josh and Barbara Hargrave encountered ferocious opposition in 1959 when they bought a house two blocks inside a white district in the West Garfield Park neighborhood of Chicago. Crowds of up to four thousand people gathered on three successive nights, some throwing stones and bricks at the Hargraves' house. The real estate broker who sold them the house received death threats. An unusually vigorous police response squelched the violence outside the Hargrave home, and the neighbors changed tactics. Many of them joined a larger "United Property Group" dedicated to keeping blacks out of West Garfield Park. They and other members of the group held block meetings to maintain unity, and posted "Not for Sale" signs at the homes to discourage blockbusters. Despite these efforts, white resistance quickly collapsed throughout West Garfield Park. The neighborhood was 16 percent black in 1960, and between 65 percent and 85 percent black by 1965.[6]

Many cities underwent dramatic shifts in racial composition as blacks replaced the dwindling white population. Few cities outside the South had black populations of more than 15 percent in 1940. By 1970, blacks made up a third of the population of Cleveland, Detroit, and Philadelphia, and were the majority in Newark and Washington, D.C. (see Table 9–1). Other nonwhite groups achieved a significant presence as well. As early as 1930, Mexicans and Mexican Americans constituted more than half the population of El Paso, slightly less than half of San Antonio, and one-fifth of Los Angeles. Their numbers increased after 1940 in the Southwestern cities and in Chicago. Puerto Ricans accounted for about 8 percent of New York's population by 1960. Other growing minority populations included Cubans in Miami, and Asians in San Francisco, Los Angeles, and New York. The numbers of new immigrants from Latin America and Asia would rise sharply after 1965, because of a major reform of U.S. immigration laws.

The desegregation of public schools in the late 1950s and 1960s further threatened whites' presumptive control of institutions and neighborhoods. The legality of racial segregation had been undermined in 1954 by the U.S. Supreme Court's famous decision in *Brown v. Board of Education of Topeka*, but public officials in the South vowed "massive resistance." School systems that attempted to desegregate encountered strong opposition from white parents and political leaders. In 1957, angry

TABLE 9–1 Central-City, Black, and Metropolitan Populations for Selected American Cities, 1940 and 1970

City	1940 Central City	Blacks	Metro Area	1970 Central City	Blacks	Metro Area
Atlanta	302,288	104,533	558,842	496,973	255,051	1,390,164
Baltimore	859,100	165,843	1,139,529	905,759	420,210	2,070,670
Boston	770,816	23,679	2,209,608	641,071	104,707	2,753,700
Buffalo	506,775	17,694	958,487	462,768	94,329	1,349,211
Chicago	3,396,808	277,731	4,569,643	3,366,957	1,102,620	6,978,947
Cincinnati	455,610	55,593	787,044	452,524	125,000	1,384,851
Cleveland	878,336	84,504	1,267,270	750,903	287,841	2,064,194
Dallas	294,734	50,407	527,145	844,401	210,238	1,555,950
Denver	322,412	7,836	445,206	514,678	47,011	1,227,529
Detroit	1,623,452	149,119	2,377,329	1,511,482	660,428	4,199,931
Houston	384,514	86,302	528,961	1,232,802	316,551	1,985,031
Indianapolis	386,972	51,142	460,926	743,155	134,320	1,109,882
Kansas City (Mo.)	399,178	41,574	686,643	507,409	112,005	1,256,649
Los Angeles	1,504,277	63,774	2,916,403	2,816,061	503,606	7,032,075
Louisville	319,077	47,158	451,473	361,472	86,040	826,553
Memphis	292,942	121,498	358,250	623,530	242,513	770,120
Miami	172,172	36,857	267,739	334,859	76,156	1,267,792
Milwaukee	587,472	8,821	829,629	717,099	105,088	1,403,688
Minneapolis	492,370	4,646	967,367	434,400	19,005	1,813,647
Nashville	167,402	47,318	257,267	447,877	87,876	541,108
Newark	429,760	74,965	1,291,416	382,417	207,458	1,856,556
New Orleans	494,537	149,034	552,244	593,471	267,308	1,046,470
New York	7,454,995	458,444	8,706,917	7,894,862	1,668,115	11,571,899
Philadelphia	1,931,334	250,880	3,199,637	1,948,609	653,791	4,817,914
Pittsburgh	671,659	62,216	2,082,556	520,117	104,904	2,401,245
Portland (Ore.)	305,394	1,931	501,275	382,619	21,572	1,009,129
Providence	253,504	6,388	695,253	179,213	15,875	789,186
Rochester	324,975	3,262	438,230	296,233	49,647	882,667
St. Louis	816,048	108,765	1,464,111	622,236	254,191	2,363,017
Salt Lake City	149,934	694	211,623	175,885	2,135	557,635
San Francisco	634,536	4,846	1,461,804	715,674	96,078	3,109,519
Seattle	368,302	3,789	593,734	538,831	37,868	1,421,869
Washington, D.C.	663,091	187,266	967,985	756,510	537,712	2,816,123

Source: U. S. Census.

white mobs and Arkansas National Guardsmen blocked the entrance of the first black students into Little Rock's all-white Central High School. President Eisenhower had to use federal troops to escort the nine black teenagers into the school and to patrol the halls for the rest of the year. State and local officials in Little Rock and in Norfolk, Virginia, shut down their schools in 1958–59 to delay integration. A more common response among white Southern parents was to enroll their children in all-white private academies. City schools outside the South had long been unofficially segregated as well; schools in black neighborhoods were almost all black, and those in white neighborhoods were almost all white. The chronically underfunded black schools grew even more crowded as newcomers poured into the ghettos. White parents resisted the integration of their neighborhood schools in the same spirit as they resisted the integration of their neighborhood housing.

The conflict over school integration dragged on into the 1970s, now focusing on the issue of "forced busing." The Supreme Court ruled in *Swann v. Charlotte-Mecklenburg Board of Education* (1971) in favor of achieving school integration by busing students to and from schools in distant neighborhoods. Some of the fiercest resistance came not in the South, but in Boston. Boston's School Committee had responded to the continued African-American migration by using techniques of district gerrymandering and student transfers to keep white schools white. After a long campaign by black parents for improved education, culminating in a lawsuit, Federal District Court Judge Arthur Garrity ordered the School Committee to begin a program of desegregation and busing in the fall of 1974. White neighborhoods organized to protest, holding rallies, motorcades, and boycotts. Black students were the targets of violent attacks before the tensions subsided. A 1974 U.S. Supreme Court ruling pointed to a durable solution for whites trying to escape school integration. In *Milliken v. Bradley,* the court ruled against busing students across district lines to achieve racial balance between schools in Detroit and those in its suburbs. Together, the various court rulings seemed to declare school integration to be mandatory within each city but unnecessary for the metropolitan area as a whole. Whites seeking segregated schools could find them by moving to white suburbs, a further federal incentive for "white flight."

URBAN RENEWAL AND ITS CONSEQUENCES

The trends of suburbanization and racial transition loomed over every effort to rebuild central cities. Downtowns had suffered from neglect during the hard times of the 1930s and the wartime shortages of the early 1940s. Downtown St. Louis presented a depressing view of deserted buildings, while New York, Chicago, Philadelphia, and Boston were also said to be "rotting at the core." Indeed, commercial space in some downtowns became so worthless during the Depression that property owners demolished numerous buildings to create parking lots. By 1939, a driver in Bridgeport, Connecticut, could "park his car where once stood a theater, an ice cream plant, a Turkish bath house, a livery stable, a hotel, the telephone building and a couple churches."[7]

Business leaders and city officials in the 1940s feared that once prosperity returned after the war, the antiquated city core would be bypassed in favor of new suburban development. They talked of the deterioration of property in and around the central business district as if it were a disease, called "blight." Only radical surgery could stop the spread of this "blight" (some people said "cancer"). They hoped that a massive program to tear down old buildings and replace them with new ones could restore the downtown to health. In the process, city officials also hoped to address problems of poor housing conditions, housing shortages, and inadequate highway access. All of this would require money—government money.

The federal government became involved as an extension of its public housing work. The Housing Act of 1937 had committed the federal government to financing public housing. In securing that legislation, champions of public housing such as social workers and labor leaders had sought public housing for a broad range of urban residents with only so much slum clearance as was necessary to provide the building sites. The National Association of Real Estate Boards (NAREB) and organizations that supported private housing lobbied against any public housing at all, claiming that it was a socialist interference with the private market. Instead, real estate interests and builders supported government subsidy for private redevelopment of "blighted" areas in inner cities. Though it called public housing a socialist interference with the private housing market, the real estate lobby demanded government intervention to acquire blighted property, demolish the buildings, and subsidize the redevelopment of the land for private profit. NAREB argued that this kind of renewal would expand municipal tax bases and reinvigorate downtowns. Conservative opponents failed to stop the 1937 Housing Act but limited its scope and managed to tilt its emphasis from public housing to slum clearance. Public housing constructed during the war years was designated for the use of war workers.

In 1945, Senators Robert Wagner of New York, Allen Ellender of Louisiana, and Robert A. Taft of Ohio cosponsored a bill that set a goal of 1.25 million new housing units a year to be built for all social classes during the next ten years. The proposal included government loans and subsidies for the construction of 810,000 public housing units. Conservative real estate interests again resisted, but public housing advocates had strong support in Congress. After prolonged and often heated debate, including a fistfight between two elderly congressmen, the legislation finally passed in the spring of 1949. The Housing Act of 1949 was a compromise that contained several measures: slum clearance, public housing, and expanded mortgage insurance through the FHA. Title I of the bill established the principle of urban redevelopment, committing federal funds to the clearance of slums by local redevelopment agencies. Through a method of subsidy called a "write-down," the properties would then be sold at a loss to private developers who would presumably "renew" the area. The law mandated that redevelopment programs be "predominantly residential." But this term could mean *either* that areas earmarked for redevelopment had to be at least 50 percent residential before they were cleared *or* that new construction in cleared residential areas had to include 50 percent residential units—*not necessarily both.* Thus redevelopment projects could level residential areas labeled slums and replace them with office buildings, shopping complexes, luxury apartments, and parking lots—land uses intended to raise property values, increase tax revenues, and restore economic vitality.

Title II of the bill greatly increased the availability of FHA mortgages, a boon to the private housing market. Title III authorized 810,000 units of public housing over the next six years. The AFL, CIO, U.S. Conference of Mayors, veterans' groups, and the NAACP strongly supported Title III. Public housing advocates were skeptical of the redevelopment provision of Title I but believed that a compromise that included Title III was the only way public housing could be achieved. On the whole, liberal supporters viewed the passage of the 1949 Housing Act as a triumph. The act committed the nation to providing "a decent home and suitable living environment" for every American family, and it created a powerful mechanism for transforming urban land use. But the law soon brought disappointment to its advocates.

In 1951, Robert Moses, the New York City planner, park commissioner, and highway builder, showed how a local power could redirect the act's intentions. Moses wanted to build a coliseum and luxury housing at Broadway and 57th Street. Because he could show that the area included a few run-down tenements sheltering three hundred people, Moses defined it as "predominantly residential" and used federal urban redevelopment funds to gain control of more than two square blocks of thriving commercial property. His action demonstrated that the 1949 Housing Act could be used to redevelop business districts rather than to house the urban poor.

Revisions made by Congress in 1954 turned the law further in that direction. The 1954 revisions were primarily intended to replace "redevelopment" with "renewal," which meant allowing the renovation of some buildings instead of tearing them all down. This change enabled cities to use federal support to upgrade residential neighborhoods that were not utterly dilapidated. For instance, urban renewal funds made possible the successful rehabilitation of Philadelphia's historic Society Hill district. ("Renewal" subsequently became the umbrella term for both renovation and slum clearance). The amendment also let cities use 10 percent of federal funds for projects that could not be called predominantly residential even under the loose definition established in 1949. Further revisions in 1959, 1961, and 1965 progressively boosted the nonresidential proportion to 35 percent.[8] The federal housing acts thus became important means of supporting downtown revitalization projects, even projects that involved no housing.

Even before 1949, renewal projects had been launched using state, municipal and private funds. The goal of downtown revitalization had drawn together local coalitions of politicians, businessmen, labor unions, and planners who favored economic growth over social reform. Pittsburgh was the model for many of these growth coalitions. The steel city's business and political leaders had feared in the early 1940s that corporate headquarters would flee their grimy downtown after the war. Richard K. Mellon, heir to a huge corporate fortune, brought together leaders of the city's major businesses to form the Allegheny Conference on Community Development in 1943. Mayor David Lawrence worked closely with this group, supported by downtown merchants, real estate interests, and construction trades. Together, they orchestrated the Pittsburgh Renaissance, a downtown redevelopment program that cleared railroad yards and commercial blight to create a park, six high-rise office structures, a luxury hotel, and underground parking garage in the 1950s. (A campaign to reduce the city's choking smoke also helped). Similarly, New Orleans mayor DeLesseps

Skyscraper Construction. While housing starts boomed in the suburbs during the 1950s, the roar of construction also vibrated through central business districts. This view shows iron workers on the thirty-second floor of an office tower in Manhattan in 1954.

Morrison joined the business community in constructing a downtown civic center. In St. Louis, a businessmen's association known as Civic Progress allied with Mayor Raymond Tucker, labor unions, and religious groups to support a $110 million bond issue that cleared downtown areas for expressways, bridges, and hospitals. To undertake these projects, local governments lured private investment money with generous property tax breaks, thereby sacrificing immediate revenue in hopes of future growth.

In Boston, pro-business mayor John Hynes initiated the West End Project, which demolished a dense slum housing twenty-six hundred families and replaced it with high-rise luxury apartments. His successor, John Collins, worked together with a powerful group of downtown business leaders called "The Vault" to push forward the campaign for a "New Boston." Collins hired Ed Logue, an energetic urban renewal executive, to oversee a federally supported program that ultimately subjected 10 percent of the city's land area to redevelopment. Projects in the 1960s included the construction of a huge parking garage under Boston Common, the Prudential Center office complex and a convention center to the southwest of the downtown, a City Hall and government office towers in place of the sleazy Scollay Square entertainment district, plus redevelopment of the waterfront with high-rise luxury apartments. Critics charged that Boston's urban renewal was black and ethnic removal, and indeed the areas designated for slum clearance included parts of the multiethnic West End, the racially mixed South End, and Lower Roxbury, a major African-American community. Urban renewal in Boston intensified the competition between the city's working-class whites and blacks over the diminishing number of low-rent apartments, heightening the tensions that would explode in the busing conflict of the 1970s.

Richmond's downtown businessmen and city leaders organized a Greater Richmond movement, calling for freeways to be built through the city and for a larger, more exclusively commercial downtown. Though Richmond was well on its way to gaining a black majority, a city government controlled by the white elite successfully used federal renewal funds to remove black residents from locations desired by white businessmen. In Miami, urban renewal replaced black housing with government office and community college buildings, a sports arena, and high-rise apartments. San Francisco's redevelopment efforts disrupted the city's produce market, its Japanese neighborhood, its major African-American neighborhood, and a variety of other low-rent sites. In almost every instance, then, urban redevelopment negatively affected people of color. By the end of the 1950s, nearly 9 out of 10 families that were compelled to move because of urban renewal and redevelopment were nonwhite.

Meanwhile, because congressional conservatives successfully cut appropriations for public housing, barely 200,000 of the proposed 810,000 units were actually completed by the original target date of 1955. The real estate lobby conducted a massive campaign to hold local referenda on public housing, defeating the issue twenty-five of thirty-eight times. In Los Angeles, Mayor Fletcher Bowron and the city council backed a public housing plan to construct ten thousand dwelling units at a cost of $110 million. One of the largest projects was to be located in Chavez Ravine, a 315-acre area near downtown and settled by Mexican Americans and Chinese Americans. Architects designed a series of new, mostly low-rent apartments for the parcel, from which the residents were evicted. Bowron's public housing program was supported by local unions and by various groups representing churches and veterans, yet it was strongly opposed by business interests. The antihousing forces prevailed. By late 1951 the majority of the city council agreed to cancel the project. Chavez Ravine was finally developed in 1957 when Los Angeles signed a contract with Walter O'Malley, owner of the Brooklyn Dodgers, who built a stadium for his baseball team.

Where public housing was built, legal battles and neighborhood conflict over its location meant that many years passed between land clearance and the completion of new dwellings. Nobody by the late 1950s seemed to want a public housing project built in their neighborhood. Public housing advocates had not anticipated the intense neighborhood hostility to the projects. The earliest projects in the 1930s and 1940s had been welcomed by many working-class whites as well as blacks, while middle-class liberals hoped that the projects would contribute to an improvement in urban living conditions. Public housing stayed in great demand throughout the 1940s and the projects had not yet gained the stigma of being for poor blacks. Indeed, Chicago housing officials scrupulously tried to fill each apartment complex with tenants who matched the racial composition of the area; projects in black areas were for blacks, projects in white areas were for whites, projects in mixed areas were racially integrated. The neighborhood composition rule proved difficult to maintain in the

Pruitt-Igoe Housing Project.   Once one of the nation's most acclaimed public housing complexes, the Pruitt-Igoe project in St. Louis, built in 1954, came to symbolize the unworkable qualities of poorly designed low-income housing. After futile efforts to overcome its deficiencies, demolition began in 1972 and was completed in 1974.

late 1940s, as black applicants filled long waiting lists while potential white tenants found more alternatives in the private market. Rather than keep units vacant during a housing shortage, Chicago officials reluctantly allowed the black population of the Frances Cabrini Homes to surpass the original 20 percent limit, reaching 40 percent by 1949. Black tenants occupied two-thirds of Chicago's public housing by 1955 and 85 percent by 1959. In New York, the racial composition of public housing changed during the 1950s from two-thirds white to one quarter white. Low-income blacks displaced by slum clearance continued to seek public housing, while higher incomes and greater residential options limited the numbers of eligible white applicants. Once public housing became associated with impoverished black residents, it became much more politically contentious to build a project in a white neighborhood. Sympathetic to demands of white constituents, and worried about the white racial violence, political leaders in the 1950s limited most new public housing projects to established ghettos, and increased their density by building high-rise towers. The Robert Taylor Homes, the largest of these housing complexes, consisted of 28 sixteen-story towers on a two-mile long strip of land in Chicago's South Side ghetto, separated from a nearby white neighborhood by an enormous expressway. There as in many other cities, public housing became an instrument of segregation. Virtually all of the 27,000 tenants in 1965 were black.

By the 1960s, the results of urban redevelopment efforts disappointed those who had hoped to solve the problems of downtown decay and slum housing. Slum clearance and highway projects had eroded the cities' tax base by destroying thousands of small businesses. Redevelopment had disrupted lively neighborhoods, Jane Jacobs complained in *The Death and Life of American Cities* (1961), and replaced them with deserted concrete plazas. Cities had used slum clearance as a segregationist tool, particularly in the South where they removed black enclaves from larger white neighborhoods. Urban renewal through 1967 had displaced more than 400,000 families, and federally supported urban highway projects another 330,000.[9] Displaced people had crowded into previously undisrupted neighborhoods and hastened their deterioration. Fewer public housing units were built than promised. The total number of completed units did not reach 810,000 until 1969, 20 years after the passage of the Taft-Ellender-Wagner Act. Worse, the public housing projects proved not to be havens of modern living and social harmony—as their advocates had hoped—but America's dumping grounds for its most impoverished citizens. Cheaply built to begin with, they deteriorated quickly because of inadequate maintenance and abuse by tenants. They became notoriously crime infested. Revitalization thus carried high social costs, borne disproportionately by the poor, and it failed to stop the flight of businesses and affluent whites from the city.

CURRENTS OF PROTEST

Government's limited success in coping with urban change contributed to the political struggles of the 1960s. For different reasons, blacks, working-class ethnics, and members of the white middle class during that tumultuous decade began losing faith in the power of government to solve social problems. As Americans questioned the political compromises inherent in the New Deal coalition, increasingly contentious positions took shape.

African Americans' struggle for racial justice was at the center of many conflicts that dominated urban and national politics in the postwar era, and it influenced everything else. The movement had started to gain force in the 1940s, with pressure for an end to job discrimination. The 1941 March on Washington movement resulted in opening defense industry jobs to black workers and establishment of a federal Fair Employment Practices Commission. Left-leaning labor unions also pushed for better treatment of black workers. Though the black migration to cities had opened some new opportunities, discriminatory hiring had kept most African Americans in jobs that were exhausting and poorly paid. In the enormous Sparrows Point steel mill near Baltimore, blacks were segregated into unskilled work units in the grimy "basic steel" side of the plant; relatively few were allowed to take jobs in the heavily white "finishing side" that offered more opportunities for advancement. Despite efforts by some steel union officials, the plant was not fully desegregated until the 1970s, and then only acrimoniously under court supervision. Hiring practices in Detroit's automobile factories were inconsistent, with some plants seemingly "lily white" into the 1960s, and others employing hundreds of black workers. Blacks who did find work were disproportionately assigned to jobs that were less skilled, unpleasant, or unhealthy—such as spraying paint on car bodies. Though the United Automobile Workers' national leadership was at the forefront in supporting civil rights efforts, local union leaders and the white rank and file were unreliable allies. Some staged spontaneous "wildcat" strikes to protest the hiring or promotion of blacks.

Like the struggle for fair employment in industry, the effort to desegregate public accommodations in the South largely focused on urban settings. Urban African Americans had the strength in numbers to sustain civil rights protests, and they could draw on the resources of NAACP chapters, churches, and sometimes black colleges. Also, racial segregation had historically been most intense in the cities. The defense of white supremacy in an anonymous urban environment depended more on formal restrictions than in the countryside or small town where inequality was acted out through the daily encounters of people who knew each other. Thus, it was in the city of Montgomery, Alabama, that blacks organized the famous 1955 boycott that ultimately helped end segregated seating on public transportation. From that boycott emerged the Southern Christian Leadership Conference and its charismatic young leader, the Reverend Martin Luther King, Jr. After the bus boycott ended with federal court orders to desegregate, similar efforts were organized in Atlanta, Birmingham and other Southern cities. In 1959 and 1960, a "sit-in" movement initiated by black college students willing to risk arrest worked to demand equal treatment in stores, restaurants, and lunch counters. Again, the movement began in cities: in Oklahoma City, Miami, and most famously at the Woolworth's lunch counter in Greensboro, North Carolina. The success at Greensboro inspired sit-ins to desegregate lunch counters in Nashville, Tallahassee, Houston, and all across the South. King himself helped lead the effort in Atlanta.

These grass roots struggles against racial injustice and urban poverty were reinforced by liberal Democratic policymakers in Washington. President John F. Kennedy promised civic leaders federal aid for urban needs such as schools, medical care, mass transit, and planning. Kennedy's Committee on Juvenile Delinquency initiated several projects that organized slum communities to work out solutions to their own problems, a tactic that later became central to the War on Poverty. Seizing the political initiative in the shock following Kennedy's assassination, the new president Lyndon B. Johnson prodded Congress in 1964 to pass the Civil Rights Act, outlawing racial discrimination in public accommodations, employment, and federal programs. In the Voting Rights Act of 1965, Congress authorized federal agents to register voters who had been illegally denied suffrage. Johnson and his advisers mounted an extensive attack against urban problems, particularly against poverty. In 1964, Johnson pressed Congress to pass the Economic Opportunity Act, which created the Office of Economic Opportunity (OEO) to oversee an agenda designed to end domestic poverty: Job Corps, a skill-training program; Head Start, an educational boost for preschool children with disadvantaged backgrounds; Volunteers in Service to America (VISTA), a domestic Peace Corps; and the Community Action Program, which encouraged "maximum feasible involvement" of neighborhood residents in policy planning. Other legislation provided federal funds to expand the food-stamp program, build more public housing, and modernize hospitals.

In 1966, the Johnson administration launched the Model Cities program, a new variant of renewal that directed federal funds to districts where locally elected boards designed plans to improve neighborhood housing, health, education, and employment. The Model Cities program's emphasis on neighborhood participation often stirred conflict among community organizations, professional politicians, social workers, and planners over whose ideas should prevail. Though federal officials tried to approve only those Model City projects that would not undermine locally elected officials, many projects had the opposite effect. For example, OEO-financed programs mobilized both black and Chicano activists in San Antonio to demand control over projects within their own communities. In Chicago, the OEO approved $900,000 to support a job training program run in part by the Blackstone

Rangers youth gang, much to the chagrin of mayor Richard J. Daley. In Oakland, community activists took control of the board overseeing local antipoverty programs, and used it as a political base to "organize the poor" against the white power structure. Community participation in antipoverty efforts strengthened an already vigorous culture of grassroots organizing in that city, and produced bitter conflicts with City Hall until the mayor persuaded state and federal officials to shut down the Oakland program in 1971.

By the late 1960s, neighborhood activists were vigorously challenging the progrowth consensus of public officials and private developers. Community activists organized opposition to redevelopment projects, which stood as the most visible agent of displacement and housing shortages. In San Francisco in 1967, blacks protested destruction of the thriving commercial and residential Western Addition neighborhood by forming a broad-based community organization and picketing the Redevelopment Authority office, seizing the stage at public hearings, and lying down in front of bulldozers. In Boston in 1968, community activists in renewal neighborhoods occupied redevelopment offices and built a tent city to dramatize displacement of poor families previously housed there. In Gary, Indiana, industrial pollution from steel mills vital to the city's economy engendered opposition, first from middle-class homeowners, then from unions demanding occupational health and safety, and finally from black residents who were forced by discriminatory practices into the most polluted neighborhoods and unhealthiest jobs.

Antipoverty programs heightened poor people's determination to assert their rights, including a right to receive welfare. Aid to Families with Dependent Children (AFDC), the federally assisted program of poor relief, was nothing new, having been created in 1935 by the Social Security Act. But in its early years, its use had been limited by the stigma against accepting charity. Even into the early 1960s, only about a third of eligible families drew AFDC benefits. The increased public attention to poverty, and the example of the Civil Rights movement, encouraged a new mood of entitlement among welfare applicants in the mid 1960s. Greater numbers of poor people began asking for benefits, sometimes demanding them. Welfare rights organizations, often led by civil rights activists, mustered recipients to disrupt welfare offices from Boston to San Francisco, and stage demonstrations for more money. The numbers of people on AFDC rose from 4.3 million in 1965 to 10.8 million in 1974, with the greatest growth coming between 1967 and 1971, by which point 90 percent of eligible families were receiving the benefits. The welfare budget of New York City alone was $1.4 billion in 1970. One out of ten residents in the nation's twenty largest metropolitan areas now received some form of public relief. The continuing migration of poor blacks from the South also contributed to the increase in city welfare rolls.

Activists' demands for justice inspired African Americans who were frustrated by the slow progress in ending discrimination and disillusioned with the ideal of interracial brotherhood preached by Martin Luther King. Many blacks were impressed particularly by the uncompromising stance of the Nation of Islam (Black Muslims), led by Elijah Muhammad. Strongest in big cities outside the South, the Black Muslims in the 1950s built a culture that promoted spiritual renewal, self-discipline, and economic self-sufficiency. Malcolm X emerged in the late 1950s as the

Segregation in Action. Throughout cities in the South, African Americans were forced by law as well as by custom into separate facilities, including, as the sign above this couple's heads reveals, the rear of buses. Long-standing tensions over discriminatory treatment of black riders on the buses in Montgomery, Alabama, prompted seamstress and local NAACP chapter secretary Rosa Parks to refuse to yield her seat in to a white person, sparking the 1955 Montgomery bus boycott and resulting legal challenge to segregation in public transportation. *Source*: Marion Palfi, *Somewhere in the South*, 1946–49. Gelatin silver print, 24.2 × 19 cm. © Center for Creative Photography, The University of Arzona.

Muslims' most prominent spokesman, militantly criticizing the mistreatment of African Americans. "You need somebody who is going to fight," Malcolm once asserted in response to King's philosophy of nonviolence. "You don't need any kneeling or crawling in." Though Malcolm was assassinated in 1965, his spirit of defiance was taken up by young civil rights activists such as Stokely Carmichael, who in 1966 energized crowds by calling for "Black Power." The Black Panther Party for Self Defense, founded that year in Oakland, voiced black separatist rhetoric and patrolled black neighborhoods with guns to resist brutality by the white police. By 1970, the Panthers claimed nearly 5,000 members in cities from San Diego to New Haven. Much of their work involved free breakfast programs for children, free medical testing for sickle cell anemia, and other community services, but it was the image of the defiant black man with a gun that fueled the imagination of African Americans—and the nightmares of many whites.

The Challenge of Civil Rights. Martin Luther King, Jr., leads a march down Columbus Avenue in Boston, Massachusetts, in 1965. Note the broad support for civil rights and integration that the banners and marchers proclaim.

The hopes raised among urban blacks by the movement for racial justice were undercut by the federal reluctance to keep expanding antipoverty efforts as the American war in Vietnam grew more costly. By 1967, the United States was spending $27 billion a year for the war in Vietnam, compared to $2 billion for the War on Poverty. Far more devastating, though, were the profound changes in the urban economy. In the same years that blacks finally gained greater access to employment, education, and public accommodations, industrial jobs were disappearing from the cities of the Northeast and Midwest. Industries were drawn to suburbs where there were tax advantages, open land, and easy highway access. Many shifted operations to distant small towns, or to the South and West, to find tax advantages and non-unionized workers willing to accept lower wages. Others used automation as a way to reduce their need for labor. Detroit lost more than 134,000 manufacturing jobs between 1947 and 1958. In Chicago, jobs in manufacturing firms declined by a quarter of a million between 1947 and 1972. The city ceased to be the "hog butcher to the world," as meatpackers relocated their operations to smaller towns and cities further west. Philadelphia, Pittsburgh, and Buffalo also suffered, as did smaller manufacturing cities such as Trenton, New Jersey, whose civic pride had been expressed in an enormous sign: "Trenton Makes, the World Takes." African Americans were hit particularly hard by the loss of urban manufacturing jobs; lacking seniority, they were often the first to be laid off. They also found it harder than whites to relocate to the suburbs when the jobs moved there. The unemployment rate among Detroit's blacks was more than double that of whites. Further, the number of entry level jobs in industry shrank amid the continued African American migration to Northern cities, thus denying black newcomers the opportunities that had greeted European immigrants a half century earlier.

Despite their undeniable progress in achieving an end to legal segregation in the South, blacks in Northern cities saw many reasons for frustration. In every city conditions seemed the same: inadequate housing, inferior schools, and unemployment. Many blacks who had achieved some success were still excluded from finding housing in white neighborhoods. Meanwhile, the urban renewal efforts continued to disrupt black neighborhoods, and the War on Poverty was clearly a lower priority than the growing war in Vietnam.

Black frustration exploded in the mid 1960s in urban riots throughout the United States: Los Angeles, San Francisco, Portland, Kansas City, Omaha, Chicago, Milwaukee, Atlanta, Miami, Nashville, Cincinnati, Dayton, Cleveland, Rochester, Philadelphia, New York, Boston, and many more. The riots of these years followed a common pattern. They often began with incidents of police brutality, which provoked attacks on white-owned property and stores. Unlike previous racial violence, these riots did not involve confrontations between blacks and whites over contested neighborhoods. Most deaths and injuries occurred in clashes between rioters and police. Most of the dead were black men. Investigators estimated that 10 percent or more of the ghetto populations of Detroit, Newark, and Watts (Los Angeles) participated to some extent in those cities' riots. Police were unable to contain the enormous crowds that pillaged neighborhood stores, while firefighters struggled amid barrages of rocks, bottles and sometimes bullets to put out fires set by arsonists. The Kerner Commission, appointed by President Johnson to investigate the causes of the riots, speculated that "what the rioters appeared to be seeking was fuller participation in the social order and material benefits enjoyed by the majority of American citizens. Rather than rejecting the American system, they were anxious to obtain a place for themselves in it." Many blacks referred to the riots as "revolts," a consequence of unrelenting inequality. Unsympathetic whites questioned the sincerity of the protestors.

A huge wave of rioting swept through the United States in the summer of 1967. Following a confrontation between a black cabdriver and white policemen, protestors in Newark fought with police and looted stores. Through five days of violence, rioters took control of nearly half the city and set numerous fires; 27 people died. An even more destructive riot exploded days later in Detroit. By the time Army paratroopers and National Guardsmen restored order, 43 people were dead, 7,000 arrested and many neighborhoods badly damaged by fire. The following year was still worse. The assassination of Martin Luther King on April 4, 1968, sparked a nationwide upheaval that struck at least 80 cities. Chicago and Washington, D.C. suffered some of the most intense destruction. In Chicago's West Side ghetto, mobs rampaged along the major commercial streets smashing store windows, looting, and setting fires. Only nine people died, despite Mayor Richard J. Daley's statement that police should "shoot to kill any arsonist," but block after block of West Side businesses was gutted by fire. Horrified by what had happened to his city, Daley ranted publicly about the failure of the schools to maintain discipline and the failure of the police to shoot enough arsonists and looters. His intemperate remarks further alienated many African Americans, but drew thousands of admiring letters from white conservatives throughout the United States.

The urban upheavals succeeded in directing public attention, and some public spending, to the problems faced by low-income urban blacks. They also represented for many participants an unforgettable moment of empowerment as they expressed their outrage against persistent injustice. Nonetheless, the long-term effects were grim. In addition to all the deaths and injuries, the riots caused lasting physical damage to the neighborhoods in which the protestors lived, and hastened the departure of those who could afford to leave. Many of the looted businesses never reopened, depriving the remaining residents of convenient shopping opportunities and jobs. The collective violence—by protestors and by police—fed the growing polarization of American politics. It seriously weakened the liberal coalition that sustained the War on Poverty.

CHANGES IN URBAN POLITICS

African American protests—ranging from peaceful marches to battles with police—had widespread political effects. Black leaders used experience in civil rights protests and antipoverty organizations as a stepping stone to greater political power. Nearly one-fourth of all blacks elected to city positions and state houses of representatives between 1964 and 1977 had gained political experience from working in community action programs. In many cities, blacks won representation on city councils for the first time. By 1974, black mayors had been elected in six major cities: Atlanta, Cleveland, Detroit, Gary, Los Angeles, and Newark. The Rev. Jesse Jackson rose to national prominence through his leadership of Operation Breadbasket, an offshoot of the civil rights movement that pressured white businesses to hire black workers and black contractors. "We are going to see to it," Jackson stated in 1969, "that the resources of the ghetto are not siphoned off by outside groups. . . . If a building goes up in the black community, we're going to build it. And we're going to stop anyone else from building it." Jackson would later campaign for president in the 1984 Democratic primaries.

The movement for racial justice set the terms for other forms of urban community protest. The rhetoric of Black Power inspired the politicization of the Young Lords, a Puerto Rican gang in Chicago. Under the leadership of Jose "Cha Cha" Jimenez, the Young Lords made peace with their rival gangs and urged them to turn their anger "against the capitalist institutions that are oppressing us."[10] The Young Lords organized opposition to the white gentrification of Chicago's Lincoln Park neighborhood, and then formed a coalition with the Black Panthers and a left-wing gang of white Appalachians called the Young Patriots. From Chicago, the Lords expanded to New York City and then to Philadelphia, Newark, and Bridgeport. They sponsored efforts to remove garbage from the streets, called attention to police brutality, and led a takeover of a dilapidated New York hospital in 1970 to demand better medical care.

The gay rights movement, another form of interest group activism, adopted the strategy of confrontation as well. The Stonewall uprising in June of 1969 marked the beginning of the modern gay rights movement. A routine New York police raid on the Stonewall Inn, a gay bar in Greenwich Village serving a racially and economically mixed group of patrons, encountered unprecedented resistance from the bar patrons as well as from a crowd gathered outside. The protests escalated into full-scale riots in which dozens were arrested and many injured over several nights. Coming at the end of a decade and a half of civil rights agitation, Stonewall triggered a protest movement that borrowed heavily from tactics and language of radical social and political change. As news of the riot spread, groups of homosexuals in other cities organized demonstrations and organizations demanding an end to the multiple bonds of discrimination based on sexuality.

The confrontational tactics and riots of the 1960s provoked strong conservative reaction and eroded the Democratic Party's base of support among the white working class. Conservatives in the 1960s found a way to voice their opposition without directly expressing racial animosity. Lumping social protest movements together with riots and crime, Republican presidential candidate Barry Goldwater and Alabama Democrat George Wallace spoke of a crisis of "law and order." This proved to be a powerful slogan.

The crime issue had been building for a long time. Concerns about juvenile delinquency arose during World War II, and again during the 1950s. Some of this concern was a reaction by adults against an emerging youth-oriented culture that seemed part of a broader challenge to the family-centered way of life. Explanations of juvenile delinquency blamed a wide range of perceived dangers to domesticity, including inadequate parental supervision, rising divorce rates, violent comic books, and rock and roll. Rock and roll was a new musical form building on the urban cross-fertilization of rhythm and blues, country, polka, zydeco, and Latin music. The rock and roll shows which attracted teenage crowds to listen to the new music were the only entertainment with demonstrable capacity to fill the downtown theaters. In the Los Angeles area, even where working-class neighborhoods to the east of the city continued to be divided by race and class, white, black, and Mexican-American teenagers in the 1950s and 1960s escaped on weekends to public dance halls and performance venues that featured rock and roll shows, like the El Monte American Legion Stadium, and found a rare public space enabling intercultural and interracial exchange. Similar trends occurred in other metropolitan areas. But the mixing of black and white performers and teenagers made the live shows seem too socially explosive, and municipalities shut them down rather than capitalize on their potential for drawing crowds downtown.

The fears about rock may seem ridiculous in retrospect, but real juvenile delinquency did appear to be growing during this period. Despite the unreliability of statistical evidence, the issue drew considerable attention in the news media, in book-length studies, movies such as *Blackboard Jungle* and *Rebel Without a Cause*, and in the Broadway musical *West Side Story*. The media and the public viewed juvenile delinquents mainly as white ethnics who sassed their teachers, vandalized property, and fought street battles. This stereotype started to shift in the late 1950s to focus on urban blacks. White racists blamed black crime on innate inferiority and immorality, while liberals thought that the problem would subside as racial discrimination decreased. President Kennedy established a delinquency commission in 1961 that studied youth crime and developed responses such as experimental community programs in New York and New Haven. Officials in the Kennedy and Johnson administrations came to treat delinquency as a social problem that could be addressed in part by attacking poverty. Juvenile delinquency continued to rise as children from the postwar baby boom entered their teenage years, but public attention was grabbed by a surge in more serious violent crime throughout the United States.

Rates of violent crime such as robbery and homicide doubled between 1960 and 1969, a frightening trend affecting rural areas, small towns, and suburbs as well as big cities. Explanations at the time included the rising number of men in the crime-prone ages of 15–24, an increase in gun ownership and use of drugs such as heroin. Conservatives blamed liberal judges and criminally inclined blacks. President Lyndon Johnson responded by launching a "War on Crime." He declared himself determined to see that "every woman and child in this Nation can walk any street, enjoy any park, drive on any highway, and live in any community at any time of day or night without fear of being harmed."[11] Johnson's War on Crime—which provided modest federal assistance to local police—was even less successful than his war in Vietnam. Homicides in New York City, which totaled only 314 in 1957, had risen to 681 in 1965, the year Johnson declared war on crime. That annual rate doubled again by 1971, when 1,513 people were murdered in New York. The nationwide robbery rate grew by 153 percent in the late 1960s. While murders captured headlines and raised public apprehension, the aging white population that remained in central cities felt particularly vulnerable to muggings by young African Americans. Indeed, in a trend that troubled many liberals, blacks accounted for two of every three robbery arrests.

In the year following the 1965 Watts riot in Los Angeles, former movie actor Ronald Reagan used the "law and order" issue to win election as governor of California. The votes of working-class whites helped him decisively defeat the Democratic incumbent. George Wallace, the aggressively segregationist Alabama governor, drew surprising support from working-class white Northerners when he sought the Democratic nomination for president in 1964 and when he ran as a third-party candidate for president in 1968. Wallace usually avoided racist rhetoric in these campaigns, instead emphasizing "crime in the streets" and "violence in the cities." His support in 1968 faded away as Republican Richard Nixon took up the issue himself and rode it to power.

Once in office, Nixon did not stop the stream of federal dollars into cities, but he did try to channel it in new ways. His administration ended the Model Cities program, which had become an irritant to local officials. In 1973, Nixon halted the urban renewal program and imposed a moratorium on the use of federal funds for public housing construction. He proposed instead allowing state and local governments more flexibility to spend federal money on programs of their own choosing. Nixon pushed forward the Housing and Community Development Act of 1974, which included a program of "Community Development Block Grants" to localities. In place of the massive slum clearing projects of the 1950s, the block grants supported numerous smaller efforts to rehabilitate neighborhoods and improve local facilities. In place of public housing, Section 8 of this act provided for rent subsidies that tenants could use to find apartments in privately owned buildings. Public housing projects had by then developed an exaggerated (but not altogether inaccurate) reputation as crime-ridden breeding grounds of social pathology. The St. Louis Housing Authority was already demolishing its Pruitt-Igoe complex, which had begun as a celebrated model of housing design and ended as a symbol of failure.

More important to cities than these policy changes was the severe recession that hit the nation during Nixon's second term. In 1973 and 1974, an Arab embargo tripled the price of oil. The resulting energy crisis, with its soaring prices for fuel and long lines at gas stations, momentarily revived the attractiveness of mass transit. Some suburbanites began to question their commitment to automobiles and reconsidered the advantages of downtown living. But on the whole the rise in oil prices was a further blow to the cities, particularly in the cold Northeast and Midwest. High-cost fuel drove up inflation and unemployment and interrupted economic growth, which had obviously been lagging already for several years. New office towers stood empty in New York and Chicago. Housing starts dropped from 2.4 million in 1972 to 1.5 million in 1974. The automobile industry suffered as Americans began buying fuel-efficient imports instead of the gas guzzlers from Detroit. Manufacturers in major cities continued to lay off workers and close plants. Detroit lost more than 50,000 industrial jobs between 1967 and 1977, while Philadelphia lost more than 100,000.

Unable to raise taxes without driving out businesses, yet overwhelmed by the mounting needs among their inhabitants, the older cities spiraled into financial crisis. New York City, the financial capital of the world, desperately struggled in 1974 and 1975 to obtain loans that would keep it out of bankruptcy. It finally obtained crucial loan guarantees from the federal government in late 1975, but only after submitting numerous proposals to President Gerald Ford, Nixon's successor. One of Ford's refusals had occasioned the inflammatory headline in the *Daily News:* "Ford to City: Drop Dead." Cleveland would actually default on its debts three years later, after voters rejected tax increases.

It was hard to find much optimism in the mid 1970s that American cities would recover. ". . . The decline has gone too far," one prominent commentator told a newsmagazine in 1975. "Our society [has] decided it's cheaper to turn our old cities over to the poor and buy them off with welfare."[12] More than 100,000 housing units in New York were abandoned between 1970 and 1975. Much of the city's South Bronx area was destroyed in an epidemic of fires set by landlords seeking insurance payments and tenants seeking emergency aid; in 1974 alone, there were 12,300 fires in that neighborhood. Horror filmmaker John Carpenter wrote a screenplay, "Escape from New York," set in a future Manhattan that had become a hellish prison colony. (It was eventually filmed in the crumbling city of East St. Louis and released in 1981).

Nevertheless, though it was hard to see it at the time, in some ways America's older cities were finally turning a corner. True, crime continued to rise through the late 1970s and 1980s, suburbanization continued, industrial jobs kept dwindling, and poverty intensified in some neighborhoods. Yet many of the conditions that created the urban crisis had come to an end. Blacks in cities throughout the nation began to benefit from the new opportunities created by the civil rights movement. Racial tensions relaxed somewhat, and riots grew uncommon. Slum clearance ceased to disrupt so many neighborhoods. After years of delay, the major downtown redevelopment projects now contributed to a resurgence of white-collar employment that offset the loss of factory jobs. Some central neighborhoods saw definite signs that affluent people were starting to return. All these changes would bring both benefits and new problems in the years ahead.

Bibliography

For an overview of this period, see Carl Abbott, *Urban America in the Modern Age: 1920 to the Present* (1987); Barry Bluestone and Bennett Harrison, *The Deindustrialization of America: Plant Closings, Community Abandonment, and the Dismantling of Basic Industry* (1982); Lizabeth Cohen, *A Consumer's Republic: The Politics of Mass Consumption in Postwar America* (2003); John Findlay, *Magic Lands: Western Cityscapes and American Culture After 1940* (1992); Kenneth Kusmer, "African Americans in the City Since WWII: From the Industrial to the Postindustrial Era," in *The New African American Urban History*, Kenneth W. Goings and Raymond A. Mohl, eds. (1996): 320–68; Christopher Silver and John Moeser, *The Separate City: Black Communities in the Urban South, 1940–1968* (1995); and Jon C. Teaford, *The Twentieth-Century American City: Problem, Promise, and Reality* (1986).

On the impact of World War II on cities, see Beth Bailey and David Farber, *The First Strange Place: Race and Sex in World War II Hawaii* (1994); Allan Bérubé, *Coming Out Under Fire: The History of Gay Men and Women in World War II* (1990); Dominic Capeci, Jr., *The Harlem Race Riot of 1943* (1977); Capeci, Jr., *Race Relations in Wartime Detroit: The Sojourner Truth Housing Controversy, 1937–1942* (1984); Dominic Capeci, Jr., and Martha Wilkerson, *Layered Violence: The Detroit Rioters of 1943* (1991); John D'Emilio, *Sexual Politics, Sexual Communities: The Making of a Homosexual Minority in the United States, 1940–1970* (1983); Marilynn S. Johnson, *The Second Gold Rush: Oakland and the East Bay in World War II* (1993); Roger Lotchin, *The Bad City in the Good War: San Francisco, Los Angeles, Oakland, and San Diego* (2003); Lotchin, *Fortress California, From Warfare to Welfare* (1992); Mauricio Mazon, *The Zoot-Suit Riots: The Psychology of Symbolic Annihilation* (1984); Robert Spinney, *World War II in Nashville: Transformation of the Homefront* (1998).

On the impact of federal public policy on cities, see John F. Bauman, *Public Housing, Race, and Renewal: Urban Planning in Philadelphia, 1920–1974* (1987); Ronald Bayor, *Race and the Shaping of Twentieth Century Atlanta* (1996); Adam Cohen, *American Pharoah: Mayor Richard J. Daley: His Battle for Chicago and the Nation* (2000); Arnold Hirsch, *Making the Second Ghetto: Race and Housing in Chicago, 1940–1980* (1983); Douglas Massey and Nancy Denton, *American Apartheid: Segregation and the Making of an Underclass* (1993); Wendell Pritchett, *Brownsville, Brooklyn: Blacks, Jews, and the Changing Face of the Ghetto* (2002); Thomas Sugrue, *The Origins of the Urban Crisis: Race and Inequality in Postwar Detroit* (1996); and Forrest R. White, *Pride and Prejudice: School Desegregation and Urban Renewal in Norfolk, 1950–1959* (1992).

On highway building, see Richard Longstreth, *City Center to Regional Mall: Architecture, the Automobile, and Retailing in Los Angeles, 1920–1950* (1997); and Mark Rose, *Interstate: Express Highway Politics, 1941–1956* (1979). On progrowth coalitions and urban-renewal programs in various cities, see Roger Biles, *Richard J. Daley: Politics, Race, and the Governing of Chicago* (1995); Robert Caro, *The Power Broker: Robert Moses and the Fall of New York* (1974); John Mollenkopf, *The Contested City* (1983); Jon Teaford, *The Rough Road to Renaissance: Urban Revitalization in America, 1940–1985* (1990); and David Tucker, *Memphis Since Crump: Bossism, Blacks, and Civic Reform, 1948–68* (1980). On the emergence of rock and roll from diverse musical roots, see Reebee Garofalo, *Rockin' Out: Popular Music in the USA* (1997); and George Lipsitz, *Rainbow at Midnight: Labor and Culture in the 1940s* (1994).

New work on suburbanization, black and white, includes Robert Fishman, *Bourgeois Utopias: The Rise and Fall of Suburbia* (1987); Matt Garcia, *A World of Its Own: Race, Labor, and Citrus in the Making of Greater Los Angeles, 1900–1970* (2001); Sylvie Murray, *The Progressive Housewife: Community Activism in Suburban Queens, 1945–1965* (2003); Becky Nicolaides, *My Blue Heaven: Life and Politics in the Working Class Suburbs of Los Angeles, 1920–1965* (2002); Adam Rome, *The Bulldozer in the Countryside: Suburban Sprawl and the Rise of American Environmentalism* (2001); Andrew Wiese, *Places of Our Own: African-American Suburbanization Since 1916* (2004); and William H. Wilson, *Hamilton Park: A Planned Black Community in Dallas* (1997). On the new domestic suburban ideology, see Stephanie Coontz, *The Way We Never Were: American Families and the Nostalgia Trap* (1992); and Elaine T. May, *Homeward Bound: American Families in the Cold War Era* (1988). On the suburban origins of the New Right, see Lisa McGirr, *Suburban Warriors: The Origins of the New American Right* (2001).

On postwar civil rights activism, see Martha Biondi, *To Stand and Fight: The Struggle for Civil Rights in Postwar New York City* (2003); Albert S. Broussard, *Black San Francisco: The Struggle for Racial Equality in the West* (1993); William Chafe, *Civilities and Civil Rights: Greensboro, North Carolina, and the Black Struggle for Freedom* (1980); Gretchen Lemke-Santangelo, *Abiding Courage: African-American Migrant Women and the East Bay Community* (1996); Shirley Ann Moore, *To Place Our Deeds: The African-American Community in Richmond, California, 1910–1963* (2000); Glenda Alice Rabby, *The Pain and the Promise: The Struggle for Civil Rights in Tallahassee, Florida* (1999); James R. Ralph, *Northern Protest: Martin Luther King, Jr., Chicago, and the Civil Rights Movement* (1994); Robert O. Self, *American Babylon: Class, Race and Power in Postwar California* (2004); Jeanne Theoharis and Komozi Woodward, ed., *Freedom North: Black Freedom Struggles Outside the South, 1940–1980* (2003); Heather Thompson, *Whose Detroit: Politics, Labor, and Race in a Modern American City* (2001); and Bobby M. Wilson, *Race and Place in Birmingham: The Civil Rights and Neighborhood Movements* (2000). On the 1960s riots, see Gerald Horne, *Fire This Time: The Watts Uprising and the 1960s* (1995). See also Edward Escobar, *Race, Police, and the Making of a Political Identity: Mexican Americans and the Los Angeles Police Department, 1900–1945* (1999)

On the emergence of protest based in neighborhood organizations, see Robert Fisher, *Let the People Decide: Neighborhood Organizing in America* (1994); Robert Halpern, *Rebuilding the Inner City: A History of Neighborhood Initiatives to Address Poverty in the United States* (1995); Mandi Isaacs Jackson, *Model City Blues: Urban Space and Organized Resistance in New Haven* (2008); Ira Katznelson, *City Trenches: Urban Politics and the Patterning of Class in the United States* (1981); and Lloyd H. Rogler, *Migrant in the City: The Life of a Puerto Rican Action Group* (1986). On antihighway movements, see William E. Borah, *The Second Battle of New Orleans: A History of the Vieux Carré*

Riverfront Expressway Controversy (1981) and Gordon Fellman in association with Barbara Brandt, *The Deceived Majority: Politics and Protest in Middle America* (1973). On welfare, see Michael B. Katz, *The Undeserving Poor: From the War on Poverty to the War on Welfare* (1989) and Katz, *In the Shadow of the Poorhouse: A Social History of Welfare in America* (1986); Alice O'Connor, *Poverty Knowledge: Social Science, Social Policy, and the Poor in Twentieth Century U.S. History* (2001); and Jill Quadagno, *The Color of Welfare: How Racism Undermined the War on Poverty* (1994).

On the Sunbelt and Snowbelt, see Carl Abbott, *The Metropolitan Frontier: Cities in the American West* (1981); Abbott, *The New Urban America: Growth and Politics in Sunbelt Cities*, rev. ed. (1987); Richard M. Bernard, ed., *Snowbelt Cities: Metropolitan Politics in the Northeast and Midwest Since World War II* (1990); Richard M. Bernard and Bradley R. Rice, eds., *Sunbelt Cities: Politics and Growth Since World War II* (1983); Franklin J. James, *Minorities in the Sunbelt* (1984); Bradford Luckingham, *The Urban Southwest: A Profile History of Albuquerque, El Paso, Phoenix, and Tucson* (1982); Randall M. Miller and George E. Pozzetta, eds., *Shades of the Sunbelt: Essays on Ethnicity, Race, and the Urban South* (1988); Raymond A. Mohl, ed., *Searching for the Sunbelt* (1989); and Deborah Dash Moore, *To the Golden Cities: Pursuing the American Dream in Miami and Los Angeles* (1994).

Notes

1. David Goldfield, "The Urban South in World War II," in *Region, Race, and Cities: Interpreting the Urban South* (Baton Rouge: Louisiana State University Press, 1997), 253.
2. Jon C. Teaford, *The Rough Road to Renaissance: Urban Revitalization in America, 1940–1985* (Baltimore: Johns Hopkins University Press, 1990), 163.
3. Teaford, *The Rough Road to Renaissance*, 130.
4. Kenneth D. Durr, *Behind the Backlash: White Working-Class Politics in Baltimore, 1940–1980* (Chapel Hill: University of North Carolina Press, 2003), 100
5. John T. McGreevy, *Parish Boundaries: The Catholic Encounter with Race in the Twentieth Century Urban North* (Chicago: University of Chicago Press, 1996), 139.
6. Amanda I. Seligman, *Block by Block: Neighborhoods and Public Policy on Chicago's West Side* (Chicago: University of Chicago Press, 2005), 169–175.
7. Teaford, *The Rough Road to Renaissance*, 19; Alison Isenberg, *Downtown America: A History of the Place and the People Who Made It* (Chicago: University of Chicago Press, 2004), 137.
8. Bernard J. Frieden and Lynne B. Sagalyn, *Downtown, Inc.: How America Rebuilds Cities* (Cambridge: MIT Press, 1989), 23.
9. Ibid., 29.
10. Jimenez, quoted in Jeffrey O.G. Ogbar, *Black Power: Radical Politics and African American Identity* (Baltimore: Johns Hopkins University Press, 2004), 178.
11. Johnson, quoted in Michael W. Flamm, *Law and Order: Street Crime, Civil Unrest, and the Crisis of Liberalism in the 1960s* (New York: Columbia University Press, 2005), 51.
12. George Sternlieb, quoted in Robert A. Beauregard, *Voices of Decline: The Postwar Fate of U.S. Cities*, 2nd edition (New York: Routledge, 2003), 204.

CHAPTER 10

New Hope and New Concerns in the American City

New York City did not "drop dead" from its 1975 fiscal problems, despite the ominous newspaper headline. It not only recovered but reached new heights of visible affluence in the decades ahead. Yet the grudging federal response to the fiscal crisis, and some of the underlying economic conditions, represented the new climate in which American cities found themselves in the late twentieth century. President Ford's successors allowed federal priorities to continue drifting away from urban issues, reversing the 40-year trend of strong government engagement with social welfare and urban revitalization. Though the nation's economic woes eased temporarily in 1977–1978, and then more decisively in the 1980s and 1990s, the collapse of urban manufacturing continued. The United States and its cities were experiencing an historic restructuring of their economies, comparable in scope to the industrialization of the nineteenth century. The abstract forces of economic globalization had plainly visible effects on the city. Rusting chains held shut the doors of empty factories, as manufacturing shifted to lower-wage countries; meanwhile, skyscraper construction heralded the growth of the financial and service sectors. Combined with the dismantling of New Deal social programs, the changing economy dramatically increased the distance between rich and poor people—as well as between thriving and struggling cities.

DEINDUSTRIALIZATION AND FINANCIAL CRISIS

Conventional explanations for New York's and other cities' fiscal problems blamed excessive wages paid to municipal employees and excessive welfare doles to malingering cheaters. But the causes ran much deeper. The core of New York's fiscal crisis was the loss of 542,000 jobs when offices, plants, and stores moved to the suburbs and the Sunbelt between 1969 and 1976. Losses of tax revenue inevitably ensued. Economists estimated that if those half-million jobs were still providing income for New Yorkers, the city would have received $1.5 billion in extra tax revenues and there would have been no fiscal crisis.

New York was not alone. The industrial cities of the Midwest and Northeast had begun losing significant numbers of manufacturing jobs in the 1950s, initially because of relocation either to the suburbs or to the Sunbelt. The decline slowed during the prosperous 1960s, but the 1970s began a long wave of plant closings and layoffs that destroyed much of what remained of the industrial base in what came to be called the "Rust Belt," the old industrial heartland of America, stretching from New England west through Pennsylvania and the Great Lakes region. American manufacturers were finding it difficult to compete with cheaper, high-quality foreign imports of clothing, shoes, automobiles, and other products. Japanese car makers in particular began cutting into the domination of the U.S. auto market by the "Big Three"— General Motors, Ford, and Chrysler. The massive scale of de-industrialization was deeply discouraging to organized labor, public officials, and ordinary citizens. In New York, the number of manufacturing jobs dropped from 757,000 in 1972 to 328,000 in 1992. (See Table 10–1). The once-thriving garment industry was decimated as jobs moved to the sweatshops of Asia. Chicago also lost more than half of its remaining manufacturing jobs during that 20-year period, as enormous steel mills shut down abruptly. Layoffs hit tens of thousands of autoworkers in Detroit.

Deindustrialization did not immediately seem to affect the Sunbelt in the same way. Indeed, manufacturing jobs continued to grow in Los Angeles, Houston, and other Sunbelt cities into the 1980s, partly because these areas were quite successful at winning defense contracts. Los Angeles benefitted also from the rapid growth of trans-Pacific trade, which boosted its financial sector and the sprawling port facilities of Los Angeles and Long Beach, the two largest ports in the United States. Houston thrived as a center for the oil industry, chemical manufacturing, and space exploration. The Sunbelt region as a whole continued its rapid growth through the rest of the century. As in previous decades, manufacturers liked its relatively low wages and low taxes. Retirees and vacationers were drawn by its warm climate. California, Texas, Florida, Nevada, Arizona, Colorado, Utah, Georgia, and North Carolina all grew

TABLE 10–1 Manufacturing Employees in America's Six Largest Cities (in thousands)

	1972	1977	1982	1987	1992	1997	2002
New York	757.6	609.7	529	436.1	328.2	208	143.2
Chicago	430.6	366	277	220.6	186.9	130.4	97.6
Los Angeles	280.1	315.6	327.6	301.9	240.9	186.8	162.2
Philadelphia	202.6	157.5	125	95.9	73.2	47.9	42.9
Detroit	180.4	153.3	105.7	102.2	62.2	47.5	38
Houston	108	147.4	174.6	112.8	124.4	104.2	88

Cities ranked by total 1970 population. *Sources:* U.S. Census Bureau, *County and City Data Book* for 1977, 1983, 1988, 1994, 2000, and 2007; U.S. Census Bureau, *1992 Census of Manufactures, Geographic Area Series.*

quickly during the late twentieth century, and most of this growth was in the cities and suburbs. By 2000, six of the nation's ten most populous cities lay in territory once held by Mexico: Los Angeles, Houston, Phoenix, San Diego, Dallas, and San Antonio. San Jose, a computer technology center, joined the list by 2005, replacing Detroit as the tenth largest city in America.

Deindustrialization in the Rust Belt in the 1970s and 1980s devastated both the old industrial giants like Detroit and Cleveland, and smaller centers of heavy industry like Flint and Gary. Youngstown, Ohio, was hit particularly hard. The Mahoning River valley had once been lined with steel mills and other heavy industries along a 25-mile strip through Youngstown and northwest to Warren, thanks in part to the region's abundance of high-quality coal. Tens of thousands of Poles, Hungarians, Italians, Slovaks, and African Americans had flocked to work in the blast furnaces and open hearths. In the 1920s, the Mahoning Valley surpassed Pittsburgh as the leading steel-producing region in the United States; smokestacks spewed the "black gold" of soot, a sign of prosperity, over the surrounding landscape. Youngstown itself never lost its gritty image as a hard-drinking, rough-and-tumble city, but unionization and the resulting high wages enabled many workers to buy their own homes in the postwar era, some in suburban areas. In 1977, the Youngstown Sheet and Tube Company announced the closing of the valley's largest industrial complex, the Campbell Works. Despite frantic local efforts to save jobs, the Campbell Works shutdown was followed within the next five years by the closing of four other steel mills, until an estimated 50,000 jobs had been eliminated and unemployment reached nearly 25 percent. Steelworkers who had taken pride in their work felt the layoffs as a blow to their sense of self-worth; many grew depressed, and some turned to alcohol or drug abuse. The economic cost was staggering. Amid an epidemic of bankruptcies and foreclosures, much of Youngstown's housing grew dilapidated, then fell vacant, and then burned down or was demolished. The city's population crashed from 141,000 in 1970 to 96,000 in 1990. The owners of the steel mills tore most of them down in the 1980s to avoid paying property taxes, until in 1997 the last of Youngstown's great steel plants, the Jeannette Blast Furnace, was demolished by explosives and hauled off for scrap. A CBS news reporter called the city a "symbol of the failure of American industry." Prisons replaced steel as Youngstown's new growth industry.[1]

Thousands of unemployed workers in Ohio and Michigan lost hope and moved out in the late 1970s and 1980s. Some simply packed whatever belongings would fit into their car or camper and drove off looking for a place where they could start over. Expecting to find work in Texas, many were surprised to find themselves still unemployed and living out of their cars; a downturn in the oil industry had boosted unemployment there too in the early 1980s. Yet they kept coming in such numbers that the president of the Texas AFL-CIO held a press conference to warn them away ("Texas Union to Yankees: Stay Out!" read a Dallas headline). Populations dropped sharply in many Rust Belt cities.

The closing of factories in the 1970s damaged the property tax base on which most Rust Belt cities relied, while unemployment created economic hardships and a rising demand for social services. City governments struggled to avoid tax increases by reducing expenses. But to meet service obligations such as road maintenance and education, and to honor union contracts, officials often had to overspend their budgets. They escaped deficits by borrowing from the city's cash flow, hoping to repay such loans from anticipated revenues due the following year. The next year, however, they found it necessary to borrow again. In this way, cities accumulated large debts that were difficult to repay. A sudden emergency could collapse the system and trigger fiscal crisis. In 1979, for example, cleanup from a massive snowfall cost Chicago an unanticipated $72 million. Once this bill was paid, however, the city lacked cash to meet normal obligations, including its payroll. Only an emergency loan and sharp tax hike forestalled major catastrophe.

As a result, cities became increasingly dependent on federal money. The percentage of local budgets funded by Washington grew from 5.1 percent in 1970 to 12.9 percent in 1975. In 1967, federal aid accounted for only 1 percent of St. Louis's budget and 2.1 percent of Buffalo's. By 1978, federal aid accounted for 54.7 percent and 69.2 percent, respectively. Government aid also made up one-fourth to one-half of operating revenues of Baltimore, Philadelphia, Phoenix, Cleveland, and Detroit. Cities had set themselves up for a new crisis if federal urban policy should shift or wither—as it soon did.

THE DECLINE OF FEDERAL URBAN POLICY

The federal–city relationship, which had originated during the New Deal in the 1930s and expanded during the Great Society of the 1960s, began to dissolve in 1974 with passage of the Housing and Community Development Block Grant Act. This measure signaled a retreat from the war on poverty. Instead of mandating spending on specific inner-city problems, these grants gave local officials more discretion over how to spend federal revenue-sharing funds. Pledging that the act would avoid excessive federal regulation, President Ford announced that cities would have greater certainty about the level of funding they could expect and that local officials could concentrate on broad programs of community betterment rather than applying for money for small-scale, individual projects. Revenue-sharing funds could be used for almost any purpose— public works, salaries, law enforcement, housing, job training. A formula based on population density, age of housing supply, and extent of poverty would ensure that needy cities received proportionately more than cities that were better off. In practice, smaller communities, especially suburbs, benefited the most from revenue sharing. Federal grants enabled suburbs to undertake new projects such as roads and sewage treatment without raising taxes. But big city officials had to spend most of their grants to avoid severe budget cuts necessitated by loss of tax revenues and to sustain Great Society programs threatened by loss of federal funds and by soaring inflation.

In winning the 1976 presidential election, Jimmy Carter, a rural Georgia Democrat, had promised to help America's cities with a "comprehensive" urban program. Big-city mayors, especially the increasing numbers of African-American mayors, intended to cash in on these promises. The US Conference of Mayors proposed that $20 billion be spent for a "national urban investment program" to address such diverse problems as employment, health care, crime, welfare, housing, and transportation. Carter, however, diverged from urban leaders over several ideological

Reopening of Historic Faneuil Hall Market. Finishing touches are added to a cake celebrating the reopening of historic Faneuil Hall Market in 1976 as an upscale marketplace, developed by James Rouse. The market's restaurants, food stalls, shops, and boutiques attracted tourists and suburbanites to downtown Boston.

issues. Whereas mayors focused on getting increased federal spending in inner cities, Carter sought a mix of federal aid and fiscally conservative measures to spur private investment. His proposed urban policy would maintain popular programs such as Urban Development Action Grants, provide fiscal relief to cities in crisis, and initiate a $1 billion public works program. It called for giving tax breaks to businesses that hired the long-term unemployed or set up shop in impoverished areas, and for creating an urban development bank that could give urban businesses loans they were unable to secure on the open market. Though the proposal fell short of what urban leaders had hoped, it was still too much for Congress, which tilted more than ever toward suburban interests.

The defeat of Carter's urban policy in Congress marked the end of an era of significant federal spending earmarked for cities and the beginning of collective urban belt-tightening. The political support for an ambitious federal urban policy was eroding. Middle-class Americans, reeling from the impacts of inflation and a stalled economy, were losing faith in governmental programs. The political mood of the nation was growing more conservative, and would continue to shift in that direction under the new Republican administration of Ronald Reagan that took office in 1981.

Reagan, the former governor of California, believed that the way to reinvigo-rate the free market was to shrink the size of the federal government and to slash taxes. Reagan's supporters had been instrumental in the politics of middle-class tax revolt, white backlash, and distrust of big government. Feeding on this energy, Reagan focused on bolstering the suburban upper and middle class, claiming that their economic gains would eventually "trickle down" to the urban poor. He claimed that federal aid to cities had actually made matters worse. "The Federal government cannot develop the flexible, broad range of policies and partnerships needed to rebuild and revitalize urban life," declared a 1982 policy statement issued by his administration. "Neither can it guarantee a city's long-term prosperity. All too often the promise of such guarantees has created a crippling dependency rather than initia-tive and independence. It will now be the responsibility of local leadership, working closely with the private sector and the city's neighborhoods, to develop a strategy for the survival and prosperity of the country's cities."[2]

In keeping with this philosophy, Reagan reduced federal aid to cities and social programs that provided a safety net for the urban poor. He won Congressional approval during his first term for deep cuts in welfare, food stamps, and child nutri-tion. In 1987, he canceled federal revenue sharing, which had disbursed $85 billion over its fourteen-year existence and touched more municipalities than any other leg-islation in history. A drastic shift had taken place.

DUAL CITIES: RICH AND POOR IN A CHANGING ECONOMY

Parts of the American economy began to recover in 1983. White-collar jobs in finance and management expanded both in number and in pay. Reagan's deregula-tion of the banking industry freed entrepreneurs to develop high-risk, high-return investment strategies, starting a long-term boom in the financial sector that lasted (despite some slumps) until the collapse of 2008. Financiers made huge profits in forms of speculation such as junk bonds and later hedge funds and subprime mort-gages. Top-level corporate managers grew increasingly wealthy from rapidly rising salaries and other forms of compensation. Many developed princely lifestyles with opulent city apartments, multiple vacation homes, and private jets. Limousines and luxury cars ferried them around New York City between the residential Upper East Side and the Wall Street financial district, and in the evenings to cultural events at Lincoln Center or to dinners at staggeringly expensive restaurants.

Meanwhile, blue-collar industrial jobs continued to leave the Rust Belt cities. Wages stagnated or declined in many of the factories that remained, as workers accepted pay cuts in order to keep their jobs. Workers with no college education or special training found their opportunities more limited than in the heyday of union-ized industry. The new entry-level jobs created by economic growth typically fell short of the wages, benefits, and job security of the vanished industrial jobs. By the time Reagan left office in 1989, social and economic divisions were apparent everywhere, especially in cities. Journalists and social scientists increasingly returned to the older metaphor of a "dual city" to describe a polarization of wealth reminiscent of the nineteenth century. Tom Wolfe's best-selling 1987 novel, *The Bonfire of the Vanities,*

Orioles Park at Camden Yards, Baltimore.   Opened to great acclaim in 1992, this new baseball stadium represents the attempt to revive community identification with a professional baseball team by recreating the look and feel of an earlier era in which the scale of things seemed more manageable.

tried to capture this disparity in a story of an arrogant Wall Street bond trader charged with running over a black teenager in his Mercedes.

Wolfe's story was fictional but New York City's economic stratification was very real. In the period from 1977 to 1986, income dropped sharply among the bottom 20 percent of the city's households, and soared among the top 10 percent. The image of a city divided between hyper-consuming rich whites and an impoverished black "underclass" overlooked a more complicated situation in which income disparities increased within each racial group. Still, as the social scientists John Mollenkopf and Manuel Castells wrote in 1991, "the dual city metaphor has the virtue of directing our attention to the new inequalities that define the postindustrial city, just as depictions of 'How the Other Half Lives' defined the emerging industrial city a century ago." The thriving corporate and financial sectors of the economy benefitted a core of upper-income corporate managers far more than the "disorganized periphery that ranges from Chinese or Dominican women garment workers or restaurant workers through native-born black male civil service professionals to West Indian building tradesmen, and even to white women clerical workers."[3]

The rising inequality in wealth was a nationwide phenomenon whose causes went beyond tax cuts for upper-income people and cuts in social services to the poor. Income disparity continued to rise sharply after Reagan left office. By the early 2000s, nearly 45 percent of total income went to the richest 10 percent of the population, a rate that had not been seen since the 1930s. "We're no longer a middle-class society, in which the benefits of economic growth are widely shared," the economist Paul Krugman observed. The polarization of wealth reflected both the shift in federal priorities toward helping the affluent, and a dramatic change in the global economy in the 1970s and subsequent decades. Manufacturers based in wealthy, high-wage nations were relocating production to lower-wage nations, either by opening their own plants there or by sub-contracting. Meanwhile, certain financial hubs in America, Europe, and Asia emerged as "Global Cities" that wielded increasing international power.

Economists have identified a number of causes for global economic restructuring. Some have emphasized the effects of the "information revolution" in improving the speed and productivity of some forms of work, and in facilitating long-distance communication. For instance, the increased use of computers, connected by the Internet, has made it easier to coordinate manufacturing in a factory thousands of miles from the central office. Although improved communication has encouraged the shift of manufacturing to underdeveloped countries, it has also enabled corporate and financial offices to remain within the United States. Further, computer-assisted financial transactions allowed the continued growth of the New York Stock Exchange, the Mercantile Exchange of Chicago, and the Chicago Board of Trade. Despite their declining importance as manufacturing centers after 1970, New York and to a lesser extent Chicago grew ever more important as "command centers" for global capitalism, as Janet Abu-Lughod and others have shown. The corporate offices, banks, and international financial institutions (as well as related accounting and law firms) all generated high-paying jobs in their host cities. They also created a much larger number of jobs at lower levels of pay, including clerical positions that offered some opportunities for advancement, along with exploitive janitorial jobs and temporary positions as data entry typists. Their demand for more office space created plenty of work for the building trades.

Intermodal cargo transportation was another important technological reason for global economic restructuring. The technology in this case—a metal box, originally a truck trailer—was simple and familiar; the innovation came from the way in which it was used. Malcom McLean, the owner of a large trucking company, developed the idea of keeping goods packed in the same standardized shipping containers that could be towed by truck to the port, stacked by a giant crane onto the deck of a ship, and eventually loaded back on a truck (or flatbed rail car) for transport to their final destination. At the time McLean launched his first container ships in 1956, most cargo was still being loaded and unloaded by hand each time it changed transportation modes (such as from truck to ship), a time-consuming and expensive process. Containerization allowed McLean's Sea-Land Corporation to gain a growing share of international shipping in the 1960s. As other companies switched to intermodal shipping containers, waterfronts dominated by longshoremen in Manhattan and San Francisco lost business to mechanized port facilities in Elizabeth, New Jersey, and Oakland, California. Waterfront jobs grew scarce in many older ports, some of which had been maritime hubs for hundreds of years. On dozens of once-busy piers, the only sound was the distant noise of street traffic and the slap of water against rotten pilings. Less visible but more important, the decline in shipping costs helped imports from overseas compete with American-made goods.

Mixed-Income Redevelopment in Chicago. In 1997, Chicago's Housing Authority began taking down the massive high-rise public housing of the Cabrini Green Homes, visible in this photograph in the upper right corner, and replacing them with mixed income townhouses and apartments built by private developers, 30 percent of which must be offered to low-income families. The strategy aimed to break up highly concentrated poverty areas by re-establishing mixed income neighborhoods.

Shifts in international trade policies also contributed to global economic change. The United States since 1947 has pushed for a relaxation of barriers to trade, and particularly for reducing import duties designed to protect industries from foreign competition. It persevered in this policy despite the loss of auto assembly, steel, and textile jobs in the 1970s, in the belief that greater trade would eventually mean greater prosperity for everyone. Northern Mexico was among a number of world regions that expanded their export-oriented economies in the late twentieth century. In towns and cities along the U.S. border, women working for low wages in Mexican "maquiladora" factories assembled American-made components for export back to the United States. The maquiladoras were further assisted by the North American Free Trade Agreement (NAFTA), which took effect in 1994. The nominally communist People's Republic of China emerged as a formidable industrial power in the 1990s, when its normalization of trade relations with the capitalist nations allowed it to produce a widening range of goods for export. Walmart, the world's largest retailer, cut back its "Made in America" promotional strategy as it became obvious that far more of its goods were produced in China. Not just textiles and shoes, but even some of the production of computers and computer components—once thought to be a U.S. specialty—shifted to China in the 2000s. Chinese manufacturers undercut the Mexican maquiladoras, which declined slightly, but by 2008 the Chinese were themselves losing some business to Vietnam and Bangladesh where the price of labor was still lower.

Most economists believe that the shift toward freer world trade has benefitted the U.S. economy as a whole, although the effects on manufacturing employment remain debatable. Regardless of the cause, manufacturing employment is now declining not just in the Rust Belt but throughout the United States. As late as the mid-1980s it still seemed that "deindustrialization" did not affect Sunbelt cities such as Los Angeles and Houston. Since then, both cities have lost manufacturing jobs, and the Sunbelt joined the rest of the nation in deindustrializing during the 2000s. The temptation of profits in the financial world led some corporations to shift their capital out of lower-yield manufacturing, closing factories even if they were not losing money. Fewer than 13 million manufacturing jobs remained in the United States in 2006, down more than five million since 1996.

The scarcity of manufacturing jobs was just one reason for the growth of dense concentrations of poor people in some urban neighborhoods. The rise in poverty concentration began in the early 1970s, because of declining incomes of the poor and the exodus of middle-income families leaving inner-city neighborhoods. Mixed-income black neighborhoods turned into high-poverty neighborhoods, marking them as dangerous places that many people wanted to avoid—black as well as white. Most of the remaining businesses closed, and jobs disappeared. People who still lived in the neighborhoods were increasingly isolated from the social and economic networks that had helped earlier generations rise from poverty.

Homelessness increasingly marked the urban landscape after 1980. The decline in affordable housing resulted from demolition and gentrification in downtown neighborhoods as well as from government retrenchment. In 1970, there were a few more cheap apartments than needy renters: 6.2 million renters and 6.5 million apartments. But by 1995, there were 10 million needy renters and just 6 million low-rent apartments. More than a third of those lacking permanent housing were mentally ill people, released from homes and hospitals by the Reagan administration's cuts in federal aid and by a trend toward removing people from institutions. Long-term homeless men and women became familiar sights on city sidewalks, panhandling for change, sleeping in sheltered doorways, mumbling incoherently, or pushing shopping carts containing their possessions. Some squatted in vacant buildings or camped beneath highway overpasses. City governments responded with varying degrees of assistance and compassion. New York City cracked down on panhandling and other "quality of life" infractions in the 1990s, encouraging a decline in visibly homeless people in the Midtown business and entertainment district. By 1998 in San Francisco, on the other hand, 16,000 homeless individuals wandered the streets on any given day, attracted by the city's mild climate and tradition of social consciousness. The homeless population included increasing numbers of families, especially those headed by women, unable to derive sufficient income and cast adrift by cuts in housing subsidies. The burden of the shortage of affordable housing and the resulting homelessness fell heavily on children, who composed 40 percent of the poor by the year 2000, a proportion even higher in African-American, Latino, and new Asian immigrant populations.

Drug use expanded throughout American society in the 1960s and 1970s, affecting suburbs, rural areas and especially cities. The drug epidemic in the 1980s amplified an emerging epidemic of Acquired Immune Deficiency Syndrome (AIDS), which had already traumatized the male homosexual community. Passed to victims through infected intravenous needles as well as through infected body fluids exchanged during sexual contact, AIDS became a major urban public health concern.

Gentrification of an Inner-City Neighborhood. The houses along Montgomery Street in Baltimore, shown here in different stages of restoration, attracted middle-class professionals to the old Federal Hill neighborhood, just one block from Baltimore's Inner Harbor. Also nearby were the newly built Maryland Science Center, National Aquarium, and the restaurant- and shop-filled Harborplace.

At its peak around 1994, the disease had killed more than 50,000 people in New York City alone, and was continuing to kill them at a rate of nearly twenty a day. By then, more than 10,000 had died of AIDS within the much smaller city of San Francisco; nearly everyone in the city's gay community had lost someone they knew.

The spread of crack cocaine in the mid-1980s brought severe consequences to some neighborhoods. Easily addictive, crack became an entrepreneurial bonanza in neighborhoods with few other economic opportunities. Street gangs in the 1980s evolved into powerful organizations that ran much of the urban drug trade and effectively controlled many impoverished neighborhoods. In Chicago, for instance, the Black Kings (BK) had initially been little more than a loose organization of a few thousand teenagers and young men who engaged in small-scale crimes; they were held together by a vague doctrine of racial solidarity and a shared enjoyment of late-night partying. In the mid-1980s, older gang members who had served prison time turned the Black Kings into a tightly focused drug trafficking operation, as the sociologist Sudhir Venkatesh has found. Tenants in the low-rent Robert Taylor Homes felt increasingly threatened by the presence of the gang members, who refused to defer to established tenant leaders. Outside the buildings, tenants no longer felt comfortable relaxing on benches; inside, they risked harassment as they passed through the lobbies and stairways to reach their apartments. Gang members and drug users broke into vacant apartments and converted them to crack dens. A core group of nearly 200 BK members worked in Robert Taylor in the early 1990s as dealers, lookouts, or as makers and packagers of crack cocaine, while peripheral members stepped in whenever core members were in jail. Gunfire echoed through the vast, empty courtyards in intermittent wars between BK and the rival Sharks, who controlled one end of the complex. Rather than attempt to resist the gang's power, some tenants agreed to store guns and drugs in exchange for small payments or guarantees of safety. BK members cultivated good will by hosting summer cookouts with free food and beer, and occasionally helping tenants with small gifts of cash.

Crime rates—the number of serious crimes per 100,000 people—actually leveled off nationwide after their explosive growth from 1964 to 1974. Still, crime remained persistently high with a few ups and downs; several years of decline in the early 1980s was reversed amid the crack epidemic in the late 1980s. Along with "quality of life" concerns such as homelessness and graffiti, crime created a sense of increasing danger and disorder in urban society. Fears of being mugged were heightened by sensational news coverage of relatively rare incidents in which people were murdered or raped in public places by strangers. Television shows and movies also encouraged the perception that cities in general—rather than particular neighborhoods—were falling into chaos. New York City was the city that symbolized urban crime to many Americans. Its sensational crimes—from the Kitty Genovese murder in 1964 to the "Central Park Jogger" rape in 1989—were often given huge national attention, thanks in part to the major media outlets based there. The reality didn't seem too far from the image by 1990, when more than 2,200 homicides and 112,000 robberies were committed in New York. Despite the disproportionate attention paid to affluent victims, those who suffered the worst crime rates were the residents of high-poverty areas.

PRIVATIZATION, GAMBLING, AND TOURISM

Unable to count on increases in federal aid, city governments after 1975 struggled to find creative solutions to their continuing financial problems. Leasing city services to private contractors offered several mayors a tempting way to save money in the 1980s and 1990s. The U.S. Postal Service had been privatized, and numerous schemes for turning over management of public housing, toll roads, prisons, and airports to private companies circulated at state and local levels. By contracting out services, cities could escape fast-rising employee wage, benefit, and pension costs and avoid having to buy expensive equipment for tasks as varied as data processing and snow removal. The prospect of privatization could also force public workers to be more efficient. For example, the city of Phoenix required its own employees to bid against private firms for residential trash collecting. City workers initially lost these contracts but then streamlined their operation and won them back.

Estimates of savings to a city from privatization ranged up to 20 percent. Consequently, more and more cities began considering it. In the early 1970s, as a result of generous federal aid, Chicago, under the powerful Mayor Richard J. Daley, had over 44,000 people on the city payroll. By 1991, the payroll under his son, Mayor Richard M. Daley, had shrunk to 38,500, and the younger Daley was seeking ways to reduce it further. By contracting out jobs such as sewer cleaning, addiction treatment, towing away abandoned cars, and custodial service for city buildings, Daley hoped to prevent tax hikes and budget deficits. But privatization was controversial. Public employee unions naturally objected, and racial minorities expressed fears that the private sector could not be prevented from discriminatory hiring practices as readily as the public sector could. Critics charged that politicians could too easily award contracts to friends and campaign contributors, or that fraud would increase when services were released from strict public supervision.

Several cities considered generating new revenues through legalized gambling. Since their inception, American cities have been centers for gambling, and though it was almost always illegal, urban leaders have alternated between tolerating some modicum of gambling and trying to eliminate it. In the post–World War II era, only the state of Nevada officially allowed gambling, and Las Vegas was the only city to base its economic growth on gambling and the tourism that accompanied it. By the 1970s, however, fiscal shortfalls were tempting public officials to reconsider the jobs and tax revenues gambling could create. Several states revived lotteries, which during the colonial period had been used to raise revenue. New Jersey legalized casino gambling in the fading resort town of Atlantic City. The first casino opened there in 1978, followed by a boom in hotel building and entertainment—though not without the destruction of low-rent neighborhoods and an increase in crime. Changes in Nevada law allowed Nevada-based gambling businesses to branch out into other states, so several Las Vegas casino operators rushed to open resorts in Atlantic City. Investment companies and pension fund managers supplied the capital needed to build new gambling resorts in both cities, and large hotel chains like Hilton and Ramada entered the casino business as well.

Gambling spread to cities and Indian reservations scattered across the United States in the 1980s and 1990s. "Riverboat" gambling was legalized by several states, allowing floating casinos to operate in such desperately poor cities as Gary, Indiana, and East St. Louis, Illinois. Land-based casinos opened in Detroit and New Orleans. But the increased number of casinos spawned fears that there would be diminishing returns from an excess of casinos relative to the gambling population and that the economic returns hid social costs. Some economists estimated that for every job that legalized gambling created two disappeared because consumers who lost money gambling would cut back on spending in other areas such as buying clothes or getting haircuts.

Tourism and entertainment became an increasingly important part of the economies of some cities. Starting in the 1970s, planner and developer James Rouse began renovating inner-city markets and port districts with remarkable success. His restoration of the Quincy Market–Fanueil Hall area, the hub of Boston's commercial activity in the eighteenth and nineteenth centuries, and of Baltimore's Inner Harbor district attracted throngs of local residents as well as tourists to the shops, restaurants, and general urbane ambience that these places offered. The success of these places—and the older examples of Pike Place Market in Seattle and Ghirardelli Square in San Francisco—inspired the creation of "festival markets" in Milwaukee, St. Louis, Miami and other cities, some designed by Rouse himself. Many of these combined the re-use of historic buildings with a sanitized atmosphere reminding some critics of Disneyland. Less elaborate clusters of theme restaurants attracted diners to previously unappealing areas near the central business districts of Philadelphia and Chicago. In the 1990s, a number of cities assisted private organizations in creating new amusement attractions: Chattanooga built a spectacular new aquarium, Cleveland opened the Rock and Roll Hall of Fame, and Detroit's refurbished theaters and other cultural attractions formed an expanded entertainment district. The growing Detroit nightlife, boasted Mayor Kwame Kilpatrick, showed that doomsayers were wrong "when they said in 1974, 'The last person out of Detroit, please turn off the lights,' and when they said Detroit was dead."

In Las Vegas, new casino complexes in the 1990s added theme park features to the familiar gambling resort, in an effort to expand the city's appeal to vacationing families. Three "mega-resorts" opened in Las Vegas in 1993 alone: the Luxor, Treasure Island, and the MGM Grand, the world's largest hotel at the time. Older casino hotels were blown up to make room for additional mega-resorts. Breaking out of the business model set by previous casinos, the mega-resorts drew a much larger share of their revenue from shopping, merchandizing, dining, theme park rides, night clubs, concert arenas, and conference centers. One of these resorts, the "New York New York Hotel and Casino," was built as a pastiche of New York City landmarks, with reduced-scale replicas of the Statue of Liberty, Empire State Building, and Brooklyn Bridge.

The real New York City, another leading tourist destination, had gained a Rouse festival market called "South Street Seaport" in the 1980s. It moved further in the theme park direction in the 1990s with the transformation of the entertainment district centered on Times Square. The intensely congested district was in many ways the symbolic heart of New York City, and claimed to be "the crossroads of the world." It was the scene pictured on millions of postcards, and televised into millions of homes each December 31 when the dropping of a lighted ball marked the beginning of the New Year. Every day, tourists thronged to the surrounding Broadway theaters, clogged the gum-encrusted sidewalks, and stood stunned by a barrage of sensations: a blaze of enormous advertising, a cacophony of taxi horns, and the smells of exhaust and hot pretzels. By the 1980s, this epitome of urban energy had become a symbol of urban decay. Many of the theaters and storefronts on 42nd Street offered pornography or "live girls." Crime was rampant. Drug dealers openly sold marijuana to passersby. Mayors Edward Koch and David Dinkins pushed forward an ambitious 42nd Street Development Project in the 1980s and 1990s that, despite considerable skepticism, ultimately dislodged the sex business from the core of Times Square and brought in new theaters, theme restaurants, and office towers for major media companies. Under Mayor Rudolph Giuliani, the area finally re-emerged in the late 1990s as a more family-friendly tourist attraction; the crowning achievement in this respect was the arrival of the Walt Disney Company, which opened a theater and a Disney Store. Critics charged that "Disneyfication" had destroyed the area's authenticity, but tourists loved it.

City governments in the 1990s invested hundreds of millions of dollars in building convention centers and sports stadiums to encourage the tourist trade, despite limited evidence that these investments would pay off. Owners of sports teams learned that they could gain public funding by threatening to move to a different city, damaging the prestige of the place they abandoned. The threat was quite real. Los Angeles, Cleveland, Houston, Hartford, and metropolitan Minneapolis all lost major league football or hockey teams in the 1980s and 1990s. Baltimore, Cleveland, and several other cities helped build new ballparks to retain their baseball teams and to promote tourist-related development. Even New York City felt vulnerable to the New York Yankees' repeated threat to move to New Jersey; in the 2000s, the city and state governments finally agreed to spend millions of dollars to help prepare the site for a new Yankee Stadium, demolish the old one, and build a new train station nearby. The city provided similar assistance for a new stadium project for the New York Mets.

THE FEDERAL GOVERNMENT AND THE CITIES IN THE 1990S AND 2000S

George H. W. Bush, Reagan's successor, did little to alter Reagan's policies. During his one term in office, from 1989 to 1993, some optimists hoped that domestic social programs would benefit from a "peace dividend" after the collapse of communism in Eastern Europe and the break-up of the Soviet Union. But that money never materialized. Instead, Bush focused his energy on foreign policy and particularly on a war against Iraq.

An uprising in Los Angeles in late April and early May of 1992 briefly turned public attention to urban issues during Bush's final year in office. Exposing deep-seated tensions from racism and police brutality against minority communities, the uprising's immediate spark was the acquittal of four police officers who had been videotaped violently subduing an African-American man, Rodney King, during an arrest. Abetted by youth gangs, some enraged blacks and Latinos destroyed whole city blocks in South Central Los Angeles and spread violence and fear into surrounding communities, including Hollywood. In all, more than thirty-five people were killed, most of whom were shot by the police, and $2 billion worth of property was destroyed. Like the uprisings of the 1960s, the 1992 violence focused attention on abject poverty and anger among racial minorities in all cities as well as in Los Angeles. The riots jarred Americans who had mostly been content to reap the rewards of economic prosperity and to stand by as minorities and poor people suffered. According to one pollster, 61 percent of Americans now thought the nation was spending too little on inner cities, compared to just 35 percent four years earlier during the height of the Reagan Revolution.

Bush's response to the rioting was to blame the Great Society programs initiated in the 1960s, while Vice President Dan Quayle blamed the immorality of its participants. Said Quayle, "I believe the lawless anarchy which we saw is directly related to the breakdown of family structure, personal responsibility, and social order." After some partisan squabbling, the President and Congress approved some half-hearted urban aid legislation that actually did little to aid cities. In the absence of a constructive national response, the most important effect of the riot was to spread a sense of pessimism about the future of Los Angeles among its Anglo population. The 2000 census found that the city of Los Angeles had lost 200,000 non-Hispanic white residents since 1990 and the metropolitan area as a whole had lost 458,000.[4] Fast-growing metropolitan areas in the interior west—such as Phoenix, Tucson, and Las Vegas—received many of the people who left Los Angeles in the years following the riots.

Bush lost the 1992 presidential election to a Democrat from Arkansas, Bill Clinton. Clinton seemed somewhat more liberal than Bush, but in many ways his administration continued the trend of diminishing federal efforts to address urban social programs. In May of 1993, Clinton announced a plan to establish 110 "empowerment zones." This plan essentially revived Ronald Reagan's proposal for "enterprise zones" that were supposed to promote private sector investment in the nation's most impoverished neighborhoods by reducing taxes and reducing federal regulation of businesses that located there. By the late 1990s, the seventy-two urban empowerment zones supported by the federal government had generated almost $4 billion in private investment, a 200 percent return on the federal program of $2 billion. Whether or not this trend could be attributed to Clinton's efforts, it did help many people find jobs.

In the fall of 1996, Clinton signed a massive welfare reform bill that was sponsored mostly by conservatives and opposed by liberals and big-city mayors. The legislation dismantled the 62-year-old federal welfare system and turned it over to state governments, imposing only the barest minimum of guidelines. Based on the premise that previous measures fostered dependency, the new decentralized system focused on getting welfare recipients off relief and into the workplace. It relied on two principles. The first held that limited benefits would prevent welfare from becoming a way of life. The other assumed that uneducated single mothers needed support in order to find jobs and achieve stability. The policy flowing from these principles created new work rules, penalties, and time limits for welfare payments but also expanded certain services. For example, the Wisconsin welfare system required its recipients to be employed thirty hours a week in order to collect benefits. Recipients who broke the rules were cut off. In addition, no one could receive benefits for longer than five years. At the same time, however, the state made a more concerted effort to find work for welfare recipients and created public service jobs for those who could not find work. Other states pursued different paths to reach the same goals. Fortunately, a booming national economy at the time reduced unemployment and increased the earnings of low-wage workers, making it somewhat easier for families to make the transition away from welfare. Nonetheless, critics argued that the new pressure to find work of any sort would confine welfare recipients to dead-end jobs with no hope of receiving the training to move up the occupational ladder. Others feared that penalties were too strict and rules too hard to follow. What might happen when the economic boom ended remained uncertain.

The Clinton administration also implemented an important reform of public housing, introduced during the preceding Bush administration. Under the Housing Opportunities for People Everywhere (HOPE VI) program, federal grants would fund the demolition and assist in the partial replacement of "severely distressed" public housing projects. The program particularly targeted large complexes of high-rise towers. When they had been planned and built in the 1950s and 1960s, these projects had been touted as offering modern, high-rise living as an alternative to the outmoded, shabby slums in which poor people lived, but by 1990s the projects themselves were seen as the problem. They had not only deteriorated from neglected maintenance, but had become isolated pockets of intense poverty that bred all sorts of social ills. Advocates of HOPE VI, including housing secretary Henry Cisneros, argued that the high rise projects should be replaced by mixed-use, mixed-income developments that would be integrated physically and socially into the surrounding neighborhoods. The program reflected a change in the philosophy of urban design to what was called "The New Urbanism," which included smaller-scale buildings set close to the streets—improved versions of the sorts of neighborhoods found throughout cities before the postwar slum clearance efforts.

Under HOPE VI, the federal Department of Housing and Urban Development (HUD) granted nearly $400 million from 1996 through 2003 to demolish 57,000 housing units, mostly in high-rise buildings. By 2006, HUD had approved $5.8 billion in revitalization grants to rebuild these areas in partnership with private developers. Many of the HOPE VI developments featured rowhouses, some sold at market rate and others occupied by former public housing tenants. Among these developments were replacements for some of Chicago's notorious housing projects: the Robert Taylor Homes, the Henry Horner Homes, Stateway Gardens, and the sprawling Cabrini-Green housing project. Built between 1943 and 1962, Cabrini-Green had become one of the most decrepit, crime-ridden, and drug-infested neighborhoods in any city. Developers built condominiums and town houses intended to accommodate a mixed-income population, with families receiving public rent subsidies living nearby to owners of top-of-the-line residences. Low-income tenants had to pass a background check for criminal record and drug use, but families eager for better housing than the "projects" could offer worked hard to make themselves qualified for occupancy. Far fewer low-cost housing units were constructed on the site than were needed; still, the experiment of blending neighbors of differing incomes, providing at least some worthwhile public housing, and at the same time accommodating more affluent people eager to live near the shops and restaurants of the city's "Old Town" offered a more vibrant option to what had preceded it.

Economic growth and the destruction of the high rise projects helped break up the dense concentrations of poverty in troubled neighborhoods. In 1990s, 15 percent of all poor people lived in high poverty neighborhoods, but ten years later, only 10 percent did. This decline was most significant in Midwestern and Southern cities like Detroit, Chicago, and San Antonio. Poverty concentrations remained unchanged in older Northeastern cities. At the same time, poor residents moved into the inner ring of older suburbs in Chicago, Detroit, Cleveland, and Dallas. Black people were still more likely to live in high poverty neighborhoods than other poor people, although their proportions fell from 30 pecent in 1990 to 19 percent in 2000. There was still plenty of poverty—it was just somewhat more scattered than before.

Clinton and his housing secretary, Cisneros, pushed to raise homeownership rates among moderate-income Americans, particularly African Americans and Latinos. Under pressure from the administration, Fannie Mae, the largest underwriter of home mortgages, relaxed its restrictions so that more families could qualify for federally insured loans. It reduced down payment requirements and encouraged banks to lend to "subprime borrowers" whose income and credit history were not good enough to qualify for conventional loans. Clinton further encouraged people to buy houses by getting Congress to approve tax breaks on profits from sales of housing. Partly because of these changes, as well as the booming economy of the 1990s, more than 67 percent of American families were homeowners by the time Clinton left office, up from 64 percent in 1994.

Clinton's effort to encourage homeownership was enthusiastically expanded by his successor, George W. Bush, the son of the former president. In keeping with his philosophy of encouraging people to rely on their own enterprise in the free market, Bush pushed Fannie Mae to direct more of its lending to lower-income home buyers. He persuaded Congress to approve up to $200 million a year to help first-time home buyers make down payments. He also encouraged private corporations to find innovative ways to lend to people who might not otherwise qualify for loans. "Subprime" mortgages proliferated in this atmosphere of public encouragement and minimal regulation. The homeownership rate briefly reached 69 percent, before dropping amid a wave of foreclosures in 2007 and 2008. Suffering from job losses or otherwise unable to pay their monthly bills, hundreds of thousands of home owners defaulted on their mortgages, especially in the states of California, Florida, Nevada, and Arizona where home prices had risen quickly. Detroit, Cleveland, and some other Rust Belt cities also suffered, even though their housing prices had not grown nearly as quickly in the years before the crash. As many as 15,000 houses stood vacant in Cleveland by early 2009, mostly the result of foreclosures. Scavengers stripped abandoned buildings of anything valuable, and squatters camped in the empty shells. As the extent of the housing crisis became evident in 2008, subprime lenders were criticized for predatory practices of lending to unqualified buyers on terms that made repayment difficult. Still, Bush's political strategist Karl Rove defended the administration's support for subprime mortgages, which he said "did provide an opportunity for people, a lot of whom are still in their houses today."[5]

REVITALIZATION AND GENTRIFICATION

Until the housing bubble burst, economic growth and a frenzied pace of real estate investment contributed to the revitalization of many urban neighborhoods in the 1980s, 1990s, and 2000s. One unlikely success story was the South Bronx. Formerly a blue-collar community of European immigrants, the South Bronx section of New York City experienced "white flight" in the 1960s as African Americans and Puerto Ricans moved in. The Bronx grew increasingly poor in the 1970s amid rapid deindustrialization; 300 companies went out of business or left the Bronx between 1970 and 1977, taking 10,000 jobs with them. The South Bronx in particular became one of the country's most devastated urban districts, racked by crime, drug use, and poverty. It lost more than half its population between 1970 and 1980.

Some dedicated residents did stay behind, however, and they formed a neighborhood organization to improve local conditions. They called their non-profit organization the Banana Kelly Community Improvement Association, named after a crescent-shaped section of Kelly Street near their homes. Formed in 1977 to protect three buildings from demolition by the city, the association first consisted of thirty families who began working on their own to rehabilitate the neighborhood. Using the motto "Don't move, improve," they obtained loans to renovate the buildings. In the process, they learned firsthand about construction, management, and financing without help from outside consultants. Their success convinced the city to turn over more abandoned South Bronx buildings to the association. Eventually, Banana Kelly built up a staff of ninety-two people and a multimillion-dollar budget. The association managed fifty-two structures, aiding thousands of residents in buying and improving apartment buildings, restoring fifty million dollars of property to the tax rolls, building a pediatric clinic, running an adult job-training program, funding a task force against crime and drugs, and providing low-interest loans for businesses locating in the community. The association not only oversaw the rehabilitation of buildings but also carefully screened prospective tenants and trained them to participate in community matters. The association provided loans for residents to start their own enterprises, develop management skills, and create jobs.

Thanks in part to community associations like Banana Kelly, the deterioration of the South Bronx slowed and began to reverse. In the late 1980s, the city of New York launched a $5.1 billion program to rehabilitate all the buildings—both occupied and vacant—that had fallen into the city's possession for non-payment of taxes. The city, community groups and private developers all encouraged homeownership as part of their effort to improve residential neighborhoods. One symbolically important change took place in the Charlotte Street neighborhood, which had become nationally famous when President Carter toured it in 1977 to see urban decay at its worst. The South Bronx Development Organization turned the rubble-strewn, vacant land into a suburban-style neighborhood of tree-lined streets and ranch houses in the 1980s. By the time President Clinton visited the "Charlotte Gardens" area in 1997, the South Bronx was experiencing a dramatic resurgence, with new residential construction, rising property values, and growing population.

Community organizing, government assistance, economic growth and more generous lending practices all contributed to the revival of the South Bronx and other troubled areas. But much of the rebuilding would have stalled if a dramatic reduction in the crime rate had not made city life safer and more appealing. Until the 1990s, pessimism about urban crime had been so pervasive that neither police nor criminologists were prepared for the astonishing fall in crime rates in that decade.

The numbers began dropping year by year in the early 1990s and then crashed to levels not seen since the early 1960s. Homicide, rape, robbery, and auto theft dropped nationwide by more than a third, with even larger declines in some big cities. Local politicians, particularly Mayor Rudolph Giuliani of New York, tried to claim credit for the shift, but it was a nationwide trend whose causes were complicated. The most powerful influence appears to have been a demographic shift in American society: the percentage of the population in the crime-prone years of 15–29 dropped substantially in the 1980s and 1990s. Unemployment rates and school dropout rates among teenagers also fell; teenagers and young men may have had fewer opportunities to get into trouble than if they were idle. A third common explanation has been the sharp rise in incarceration rates after 1973. By the early twenty-first century, 1.5 million Americans were behind bars, reducing the number of potential criminals—or so the story goes. But the latter two explanations fail to account for a similar drop in Canadian crime at the same time, even though incarceration rates and unemployment rates in Canada had not changed significantly.

Some, such as Giuliani and his sympathizers, have emphasized the effects of new police practices in New York City. According to this argument, the police changed the disorderly culture that had developed in New York by stopping minor annoyances such as homeless men pressuring motorists for handouts by pretending to clean their windshields while the cars were stopped in traffic. It is true that crime in New York dropped twice as much as crime nationwide. The number of homicides, for instance, plummeted from more than 2,200 in 1990 to 629 in 1998 and 523 in 2008. But the cause is debatable. One contributing factor is that the city expanded its police force by 35 percent during the decade, beginning during the term of Giuliani's predecessor. Police Chief William Bratton also changed the way in which the department responded to local crime outbreaks; when data indicated a negative trend developing in a neighborhood, police concentrated their efforts there and "proactively" stopped and searched potential troublemakers. New York City's unusually tough handgun-control laws also may have contributed to its falling crime rate. Whatever the reason, something changed in the culture of the city, to the point where New York is now one of the safest urban centers in the United States.

The decline in crime in New York and other cities made people feel more comfortable moving into neighborhoods that had been notoriously crime-infested in the 1970s and 1980s, and thus it contributed to the success of revitalization and gentrification projects. It is difficult to draw a firm distinction between revitalization and gentrification. The term "revitalization" is almost always used positively, to emphasize physical upgrading and supposed improvements in socioeconomic conditions. The term "gentrification" is more controversial, as it suggests that an influx of affluent people changes the character of the area. However, to the extent that a revitalization project succeeds in physically improving privately owned housing, it will encourage people to stay in the neighborhood by choice. This almost inevitably contributes to higher rents, discouraging the very poorest people from living in the neighborhood.

Cities in the 1990s and 2000s belatedly experienced a surge of affluent people into neighborhoods surrounding the central business districts, as the proponents of urban renewal had hoped 40 years earlier. This process of gentrification had been stimulated in the 1950s and 1960s by some of the urban renewal projects, most notably the Society Hill renovation in Philadelphia. Gentrification after 1980 was on a much greater scale, and was less directly reliant on public investment. It grew so extensive in Chicago, wrote the political commentator Alan Ehrenhalt in 2008, that "A better description would be 'demographic inversion' . . . The poor and the newcomers are living on the outskirts. The people who live near the center—some of them black or Hispanic but most of them white—are those who can afford to do so."[6]

The process of gentrification arose from the deep deterioration of property values in many urban neighborhoods in the 1970s. Property values fell so far that empty lots and abandoned apartment buildings could be purchased for almost nothing either from private landlords or from city governments that had seized them for unpaid taxes. Some of the early gentrification work was pioneered by young adults with a strong desire to live in an urban environment, notably artists, musicians, and gay men and lesbians. As the pioneers renovated older buildings, property values in the neighborhood began to rise, attracting further investment by entrepreneurs sensing new opportunities for profit. Unlike in previous decades, redevelopers did not have to await the formal assistance of government slum clearance and "write-downs." They simply followed the lead of the pioneers in buying land on the open market or from the municipal government. Real estate investors also bought up old factories and other commercial buildings that had been made obsolete by economic change, and converted them to condominiums that could be sold to lawyers, stockbrokers, and other "young, urban professionals," known at the time as "yuppies." Where the process took hold most strongly, the resulting rise in rents, property values, and real estate taxes pushed out many of the poorer residents who had lived there before gentrification, and even the early gentrifiers themselves. One neighborhood exemplifying this process is New York's SoHo, where artists helped pioneer a process of reinvestment that ended up making the area unaffordable to artists. Gay gentrifiers experienced a similar transition in Boston's South End, Brooklyn's Park Slope, and Washington, D.C.'s Dupont Circle. Even the Castro neighborhood in San Francisco has been affected.

The Castro (along with New York's Greenwich Village) had been a cradle of the gay liberation movement in the late 1960s and 1970s. The possibilities for open expression of homosexuality in the bars and the streets drew thousands gays from throughout the United States, transforming what had previously been a working-class, Irish neighborhood. By 1977, an estimated 20 percent of San Franciscans were gay. That was the year in which Harvey Milk, a gay activist from the Castro, was elected to the San Francisco Board of Supervisors. Supported by liberal Mayor George Moscone, Milk won passage of a city ordinance banning discrimination against gays, and helped defeat a state proposition that would have forced the firing of gay teachers. Moscone and Milk were assassinated in City Hall in November of 1978 by a disgruntled former member of the Board of Supervisors, Dan White. White was convicted only of manslaughter, after he persuaded a jury that he had been made temporarily insane by eating too much junk food. Following the verdict, over 5,000 outraged protesters marched on City Hall and caused over $1 million of property damage. The next night, 20,000 held a block party in the Castro to mourn the death of Milk and to reaffirm their strength. The Castro continued to flourish as a gay neighborhood despite the ravages of the AIDS epidemic in the 1990s. By the 2000s, the rising housing values there were forcing some residents to disperse into other neighborhoods. Nevertheless, the area retains a strong gay presence and attracts many gay tourists.

Gentrification has often been blamed for diminishing the supply of affordable housing and displacing low-income people from the city's central neighborhoods. It is debatable whether the effects on affordable housing are as extensive, or as negative, as some critics have suggested. On the one hand, it is true that rents have soared in the gentrified areas of a few prominent cities, notably Chicago, New York, Boston, and Seattle, as well as San Francisco. Yet these cities are not representative of American cities in general. "For every San Francisco or Manhattan where real estate has become uniformly too expensive, there are many more cities like Detroit, Trenton, Syracuse, Milwaukee, Houston and Philadelphia that could use all the gentrification they can get," argues the architect Andres Duany.[7] Gentrification has been most extensive in cities whose economies have thrived to an unusual extent from global finance, corporate management, higher education and high technology; these economic opportunities have drawn disproportionately large numbers of affluent, white-collar workers. San Francisco's gentrification boom has been driven not just by job growth in the city, but also by the thriving computer-related economy of the Silicon Valley, to which many San Franciscans commute. Further, gentrification does bring some significant public benefits: for example, the influx of affluent homeowners slows the outward drift of wealth, consumer purchasing and tax revenues, and thereby helps pay for city services for everyone. Some cities have tried to encourage the trend of revitalization by providing tax breaks and other incentives for first-time homebuyers.

One of the most inflammatory aspects of gentrification is its effect on the racial and ethnic composition of neighborhoods. Affluent whites have displaced poorer Latinos and African-Americans in Chicago's Lincoln Park, New York's Lower East Side, Atlanta's Kirkwood, and San Francisco's Mission district. Sky-rocketing rents significantly diminished the African American population of San Francisco, which fell from 13 percent of the total in 1970 to under 7 percent by 2007. But gentrification does not necessarily mean racial change. Affluent African Americans have been buying and restoring old brownstone town houses in New York's Harlem and dilapidated graystones in Chicago's Bronzeville, bringing new investment to these historic black neighborhoods. The growing affluence in Harlem enticed national retail chains to open stores along the 125th street commercial corridor, and in 2008 the City Council approved a controversial rezoning that would allow the construction of office towers and more than 2,000 market-rate condominiums. Opponents argued that Harlem was in danger of being overwhelmed by an influx of whites.

In Chicago, gentrification in the 2000s spread quickly through Bronzeville and the other south side neighborhoods between the Loop business district and the Hyde Park neighborhood anchored by the University of Chicago. Most of the affluent newcomers were black professionals and businesspeople, whose numbers have grown sharply in Chicago and other major cities in recent decades. The transition in South Side Chicago has been less acrimonious than in some neighborhoods, observes the sociologist Mary Patillo, who bought a house in that area. Still, there have been some tensions between established residents and newcomers. Crime and subsidized housing are touchy subjects in these areas. While rates of violent crime have dropped dramatically, gentrifiers have redirected their attention to minor infractions and non-criminal behavior such as playing loud music, loitering, and barbecuing in public spaces. "Many of the residents are convinced that there is a slippery slope from loitering to assaults, from barbecuing to theft," Patillo writes.[8] Like white gentrifiers, they are also acutely sensitive to anything that might hurt their property values. On the issue of subsidized public housing, the gentrifiers have annoyed some of their neighbors by speaking with disgust about the housing projects nearby. They have welcomed the demolition of the nearby high-rise projects as if the buildings themselves were the cause of crime.

IMMIGRATION AND DIVERSITY

New immigration from Latin America, Eastern Europe, Africa, and Asia added to the diversity of American cities, and contributed to their renewed population growth in the 1990s and 2000s. Immigration had been drastically curtailed in 1921 and 1924 by Congressional acts, in keeping with prevalent beliefs about the racial superiority of people from northwestern Europe. Immigrants from the Americas were exempted from the restrictions, but Asians were almost entirely excluded. Congress finally ended the preferential quota system in 1965, when it passed the Immigration and Nationality Act. The act relaxed restrictions on Asians and Africans and ended the favored status of northwestern Europe. Instead, it established annual limits of 120,000 immigrants from the Western Hemisphere and 170,000 from the Eastern Hemisphere. The law gave preferential treatment to people with relatives already in the United States and to those with needed job skills.

The act's limits on immigration from the Americas proved difficult to enforce. Immigration from Canada, the Caribbean and Latin America had been growing since the 1920s, in the absence of firm restrictions. Immigration from Mexico continued to increase in the final decades of the twentieth century, only now much of it consisted of people crossing the border without permission. Mexicans who were caught wading across the Rio Grande, and forced to return to Mexico, often tried again and again until they succeeded. By the late 1980s, legal immigration had returned to levels not seen since the early 1920s, and the high numbers have since continued without major interruption. By 2003, more than 33 million residents of the United States were foreign-born, of whom 53 percent had been born in Latin America and another 25 percent in Asia. Mexico has remained the largest single source of new immigrants. Because of immigration and rapid natural increase, Latinos doubled in population between 1980 and 2000 and surpassed African Americans as the largest ethnic minority. By and large, the American cities that continue to gain population are doing so because of their growing numbers of Latinos.

Though New York continued to receive newcomers from every part of the world, Asian immigration helped Los Angeles replace New York as the major port of entry. Los Angeles also became the second largest Mexican city in the world. One of every four residents of California is now foreign born, including large numbers of Mexicans, Chinese, Filipinos, Vietnamese, Koreans, and other Asians. By 2000, non-Hispanic whites had become a minority in California. Continuing migration from Cuba and other parts of Latin America had turned Miami into a Caribbean capital, with a majority of its population born outside the United States. Immigrants also settled in areas not previously known as gateways for newcomers, such as Charlotte and Atlanta. The Minneapolis/St. Paul area developed a large community of ethnic Hmong immigrants from Laos. Many newcomers were well educated and upwardly mobile; they opened shops and moved into professions. Half of all Chinese-born residents, for instance, hold managerial and professional jobs. But large numbers of immigrants from Central America and Southeast Asia had fled political repression and war-related violence, and were unskilled by U.S. standards.

Immigrants profoundly reshaped urban demography. By 2002, one-fourth of New York City's black population was from the Caribbean. By 1990, the combined Latino groups outnumbered the native black populations in Miami, San Antonio, Houston, Phoenix, Los Angeles, and San Diego. Asians were a significant nonwhite presence in San Francisco, Seattle, and other West Coast cities.

The quintessential urban cultural form of the late twentieth century, rap and hip hop, was one striking product of the new racial/ethnic mixing. Rap music emerged from Jamaican practices of using DJs, or "toasters," to add street poetry over

Hip Hop Nation in Iowa, 2003. The Puerto-Rican artist Paco, break-dancing in front of a mural which he had painted in Cedar Rapids, Iowa, on the wall of a local youth center, working with high school students as part of a fine arts summer school program featuring DJ performance, slam poetry, dance, and painting.

basic instrumental dance music and using "mixing" and "sampling" sounds from turntables. Hip hop culture's use of language and sampling from a wide range of musical sources revolutionized the music business and provided a hybrid musical form that was easily and enthusiastically adopted by African-American, Puerto Rican, Dominican, Mexican, Cuban, Korean, and white musicians to speak to the urban and migrant condition.

Unlike earlier generations, many of the new immigrants have settled in suburban areas, sometimes without ever passing through the central city. The U.S. Census Bureau estimated that in 2003, slightly more than 50 percent of all foreign-born residents of the United States lived in metropolitan areas outside the central cities. Lebanese and other Arab-Americans have established a large presence in the Detroit suburb of Dearborn, for instance. Metropolitan areas that attracted large numbers of foreign-born people, such as Los Angeles, New York and Chicago, tended to have the most ethnically diverse suburbs. In suburban Los Angeles, people of Mexican descent formed the majority in Santa Ana, while those of Asian ancestry predominated in Monterey Park.

Monterey Park, in the San Gabriel valley, has been called "the first suburban Chinatown." Once a heavily white district of semirural homes and truck farms, it developed rapidly in the 1950s with housing tracts occupied by white veterans; smaller numbers of Latinos, Japanese and Chinese from Los Angeles also settled in the area. Growing numbers of affluent Chinese newcomers transformed Monterey Park in the 1970s and 1980s, many arriving directly from Taiwan, Hong Kong, or mainland China. Asian grocery stores, restaurants, herb shops, and other businesses (including a Chinese-language cinema) replaced older businesses. By 2000, nearly two of every three residents were Asian.

Native-born African Americans have seen their share of the population decline in some cities not only because of white gentrification and the arrival of new immigrants, but also because the migration of blacks from the South has stopped. Experiencing the decline of racial oppression in the South after 1970, and hearing of diminished job opportunities in Northern cities, black Southerners chose to stay in their home region. By the 1990s, many more blacks were moving to the South from the Northeast, Midwest, and West than were leaving the region. Since 1990, both the total numbers and the percentage of blacks have been declining in some of the northern industrial cities that had developed big African American communities in the mid-twentieth century: Boston, Chicago, Pittsburgh, and Washington among them. This trend, though, does not mark a return to white predominance in the urban population. Rather, growing numbers of Latinos and Asians are taking the place of non-Hispanic blacks and whites.

The growing diversity of American cities in recent decades has contributed to a broadening of political representation in local government. The pioneering elections of two African American mayors in 1967 (Richard Hatcher in Gary and Carl Stokes in Cleveland), were followed by the increasingly frequent rise of black mayors across the United States in the 1970s and 1980s. By 2000, African Americans had served as mayors of New York, Los Angeles, Chicago, Houston, Philadelphia, Detroit, and many smaller cities. Latinos have been somewhat slower to gain municipal power (or regain it in southwest) partly because most cities have not had substantial blocs of Latino voters until recent decades. Since the 1981 election of Henry Cisneros in San Antonio, though, Latino mayors have held office in Miami, El Paso, San Jose and Los Angeles, which elected Antonio Villaraigosa in 2005.

Despite their gains in electoral politics, Latinos and African Americans have continued to experience racial and ethnic segregation. School segregation has intensified since 1970, as a result of large increases in African-American, Latino, and Asian enrollments, continued white flight to the suburbs, the persistence of housing patterns that isolate racial and ethnic groups, and the termination of court-ordered desegregation plans. In Charlotte, North Carolina, one school went from being 68 percent black to being nearly 100 percent black within one year after the end of court ordered desegregation. In Boston in 2000, most black residents were likely to live in neighborhoods that were more than 50 percent black; the large numbers of Latinos and Asians who moved to Boston have not altered the reality that most whites and nonwhites still live in separate worlds. As Latino and Asian groups increased in size, they clustered in enclaves of their own. According to the 2000 census, cities growing more segregated included Detroit, Milwaukee, New York, Newark, Chicago, Cleveland, Miami, Cincinnati, Birmingham, and St. Louis. There were some exceptions: proximity to military facilities helped to explain diminishing segregation in cities such as Norfolk, Charleston, Raleigh-Durham, Jacksonville, Sacramento, and San Diego.

CHANGING SUBURBS

Like Asians and Latinos, African Americans are increasingly living in suburbs, often in clusters with other black neighbors with similar levels of wealth. Black suburbs are nothing new, as previous chapters have noted, but the earlier ones formed largely because of racial exclusion, while the newer ones are often formed by choice. By 2000, large black suburban areas had emerged outside Washington, D.C. in Prince George's County, Maryland, and outside Atlanta in DeKalb County. Black suburbs include enclaves of mansions and expansive lawns in places like Lithonia, Georgia, but more commonly middle-class districts of tract housing such as in Bloomfield, Connecticut. Low-income black suburbs have also grown in number since 1980. Some, such as the Chicago suburb of Ford Heights, have evolved into pockets of black poverty more isolated than those in central cities. Moving to suburbs of this sort is hardly a step upward, particularly as job opportunities and public transportation are more limited than in the urban core. Lacking a substantial tax base, impoverished suburban municipalities are hard-pressed to maintain basic services.

By 2005, more poor people lived in suburbs than in central cities. This was one of many ways in which suburbia had evolved away from the postwar pattern in which suburbs were significantly whiter, wealthier and more residential than the central cities. Suburbs in the early twenty-first century showed considerable diversity in every respect. Some were residential, some were industrial, some wealthy and some modest, some white and some black. In the Los Angeles area, racial and ethnic minorities had become as likely as white Anglos to live in suburban districts. Some of the highest crime rates can be found outside the city limits, such as in Compton, a mixed black and Latino suburb of Los Angeles whose gang violence was brought to national attention by the "gangsta rap" groups of the 1980s. Aging housing stock in inner suburban rings around such places as Chicago, New York, Washington, D.C., and St. Louis increasingly made these places indistinguishable from the adjacent urban core. These suburbs had begun to experience problems of crowding, an aging population, and poverty that were haunting inner cities.

Even the most widely recognized feature of suburban life, commuting, underwent changes as companies that moved to urban outskirts brought thousands of both blue-collar and white-collar jobs with them and reversed commuting patterns. Pollsters in 1980 found that over 70 percent of suburban residents worked in their own or another suburb. In the New York area, one-third of suburban workers were employed in a suburb other than their own, and only one-fifth commuted to the city. "Reverse commuters" now clog the outbound lanes of expressways in Chicago and other cities during rush hours.

Outside metropolitan borders, "exurbs," "out-towns," and "mall towns" had grown into major residential and commercial centers, providing residents with amenities of urban life while making it unnecessary to travel to a nearby city except for special occasions. Communities with full services of shopping, entertainment, banks, schools, water, and police and fire protection had grown up around airports such as Chicago's O'Hare and the Dallas–Fort Worth Airport, around sporting complexes such as New Jersey's Meadowlands, around malls such as the Cumberland/Galleria complex outside Atlanta and Tyson's Corner, Virginia, and around high-tech industrial regions such as southern California's Silicon Valley.

Joel Garreau, senior writer for the *Washington Post*, labeled these places as "edge cities" in his 1988 book, *Edge City: Life on the New Frontier*. Garreau argued that American civilization was experiencing a major revolution in how it was building cities. He asserted that the majority of metropolitan Americans now work not in brick factories and downtown skyscrapers but in glass-enclosed, low-rise buildings surrounded by parking lots, trees, and superhighways. These new urban centers, he said, owed their existence to new modes of communication over the airwaves and across the freeways. Garreau predicted that "edge cities" would be the centers of the postindustrial, information- and service-oriented future. Identifying some two hundred such places across the country, he defined an edge city as a place containing at least 5 million square feet of office space (more than in downtown Memphis) and 600,000 square feet of retail space. "Density is back," he proclaimed.[9]

Garreau's edge cities have continued to grow over the past twenty years, but they have done little to slow the sprawl of American metropolitan areas. Rather, these suburbs have generated low-density suburbs of their own, farther and farther from the original urban core. The result has been the expansion of what some observers have called a "post-suburban landscape," a jumble of dissimilar types of development with only a limited connection to the original urban core. An example is Orange County, between Los Angeles and San Diego, where one can see startling juxtapositions of large office parks next to residual farmland, older villages near malls and tract housing. Much of the Northeastern Corridor between New Hampshire and Virginia now follows a similar pattern. Former industrial towns serve as high-density clusters of relatively affordable housing, from which people can commute by car to distant jobs. Most job and population growth is dispersed throughout low-density parts of the metropolitan region, not clustered in the old downtowns or even in the edge cities. In place of the concentric ring pattern of development, identified by Ernest Burgess back in the days of the trolley, expressways now provide a web-like structure to these regions.

"Post-suburban" development emerged as a contentious political issue in the 1990s and 2000s, as a wide range of people criticized what they called "suburban sprawl" or simply "sprawl." State legislative acts and local ballot initiatives aimed to rein in the vaguely described phenomenon by preserving open space or imposing new zoning restrictions. Public opinion polls found broad majority support for somehow bringing sprawl under control. A variety of different criticisms have been made against sprawl, which is most commonly understood to be minimally planned, discontinuous development featuring a hodgepodge of strip malls and low-density housing. Critics have often shied away from attacking sprawl for being ugly and for destroying distinctive local landscapes, perhaps for fear of being called elitist, but these concerns are evident in much of what has been written on the subject. Criticisms have focused more often on environmental concerns, such as sprawl's destruction of farmland and forests and its encouragement of a car-dependent lifestyle that worsen air pollution. Areas of sprawl depend on extravagant use of natural resources to build the roads, drive the cars and water all the lawns, environmentalists assert. Other critics argue that the lack of functioning public spaces like

Edge Cities in the San Francisco Area. Sprinkled around the downtowns of San Francisco and Oakland, and linked by superhighways, a chain of emerging edge cities has come to represent a recent form of urban economic and residential development. According to journalist Joel Garreau, similar networks of edge cities exist around virtually every major American metropolitan area.

sidewalks and parks damages community life, which is also hurt by the profusion of gated subdivisions that overtly exclude outsiders. Others claim that the new development wastes public money by forcing the duplication of basic services such as roads, sewers, schools and emergency services that can be more efficiently provided in higher-density settings. A public health critique has linked the car-centered lifestyle to the problem of obesity. Most of these charges are difficult to prove, and each has been contested.

Conservative and libertarian writers have defended current patterns of development by pointing out that "sprawl" is the product of choices by businesses and individuals operating in a free market. Presumably, according to this argument, people must want to live, work and shop in a low-density, car-friendly landscape, or they would make different choices; the process cannot be stopped without imposing government restrictions on individual freedom. Aspects of sprawl are increasingly evident in Europe, Australia and developing parts of Asia, conservative writers point out, suggesting that there may be a universal human preference for dispersed settlement. The anti-sprawl forces, on the other hand, counter that the particularly vigorous sprawl of American metropolitan areas has been encouraged by numerous government policies: among these are policies of highway construction, limited public transportation, FHA and VA mortgage programs, tax incentives for home buying, tax write-offs that favor new commercial construction, and local zoning, subdivision and building regulations. The enemies of sprawl argue that poor planning, rather than public preference, has allowed the leap-frog development of strip malls and low-density housing. As an alternative, they propose redirecting government incentives and regulations to promote "smart growth." This would involve planned development along the lines of New Urbanism, with higher-density clusters of mixed housing and businesses that would preserve open space for public use and allow more people to walk or use public transportation. Portland, Oregon, is frequently cited as embodying some of the "smart growth" principles.

THE DISASTERS IN NEW YORK AND NEW ORLEANS

By 2000, America's central cities seemed to have moved beyond the crisis they faced in the 1970s. Deindustrialization had faded as a public concern in most of the cities of the Northeast and Midwest, largely because there were so few manufacturing jobs left to lose. In place of manufacturing, urban economies now rested on finance, corporate management, health care, tourism, entertainment, education, and other service-sector jobs. Prosperity had returned, even if it was not as widely shared as it once had been. Population loss had stopped or reversed in most places, and the abandonment of housing had slowed in all but a few cities such as Detroit, where whole city blocks were returning to prairie. Gentrification was bringing affluent people back into big urban centers, while people with modest incomes were buying homes and revitalizing their neighborhoods. Crime rates had fallen back to the levels of the early 1960s. Obviously, many older problems persisted, including poverty and racial discrimination, and newer issues had come to public attention: homelessness, AIDS, suburban sprawl, and the social and cultural tensions that accompanied immigration. Some cities still struggled, but the mood in most places was much more optimistic than it had been in 1975. For every grumpy Anglo who left Los Angeles, a hopeful newcomer arrived from Mexico or the Philippines.

Two terrible disasters in the 2000s interrupted the positive mood. On September 11, 2001, airplanes hijacked by terrorists rammed and destroyed New York City's twin World Trade Center towers, killing several thousand people. Together with an almost simultaneous terrorist attack on the Pentagon, these incidents propelled the United States and its cities into a new era of uncertainty. Death and destruction were not new to American cities; the New York City draft riots of 1863, the Chicago Fire of 1871, the San Francisco earthquake of 1906 all had similar devastating effects. But the 9/11 attacks came at a time when American city dwellers were feeling relatively safe and confident. The economic boom of the 1990s had not yet dissolved, and the new president, George W. Bush, was focusing on sustaining prosperity and improving education. These conditions made the terrorism all the more appalling, and when a widespread electrical blackout rolled across the Northeast on August 14, 2003, plunging 50 million people in cities from New York to Cleveland to Detroit into darkness, the country had more reason to feel vulnerable even in an advanced technological age.

The foremost consequences of the 9/11 attacks were the American invasions first of Afghanistan and then of Iraq. But there were two particular effects on American cities. First, the deaths and terrible infrastructure damage in New York, coupled with the new attention to "homeland security," prompted cities and suburbs to worry more about protecting vital structures and services: airports, water supplies, port facilities, power plants, and the like. Many new security measures were funded in part by the federal government, but states and localities also had to expend funds in this endeavor. Second, the extraordinary attention that President Bush directed toward international terrorism and protecting American interests around the world with heightened defense budgets and military action overwhelmed any sort of urban-oriented domestic policy the Bush administration might have been considering. Though Bush did push Congress to pass a No Child Left Behind Act that aimed to improve education, including in cities, by mandating—but not funding—annual testing of schoolchildren among other measures, most of his actions affecting cities involved withdrawal rather than engagement of federal participation.

New York City suffered additional consequences. The destruction of the enormous World Trade Center complex displaced a significant number of jobs that would never return to the financial district. The displacement contributed to the shift of investment firms to suburban Greenwich, Connecticut, and the adjoining edge city, Stamford. The numerous inconveniences that beset lower Manhattan in the immediate aftermath of the disaster contributed to the decline of the remaining garment manufacturing business. Fortunately, the city's economy recovered more quickly than expected, long before the new Freedom Tower began to rise from the vacant site at "ground zero." Developers converted some of lower Manhattan's aging office buildings into housing, and wealthy young couples with children became common sights on streets that had not been residential for more than a century.

The second disaster was the effect of Hurricane Katrina on New Orleans in August, 2005, combined with incompetent emergency management. This was a natural disaster only in the sense that storms are natural occurences. In the century or so

Urban Resilience. On September 12, 2001, New Yorkers poured into the streets to acknowledge the heroism of the municipal firefighters, police, and rescue workers in the face of the unprecedented devastation caused by the terrorist attack on the World Trade Center buildings. In spite of incalculable losses, from the deaths of over two thousand men and women to destroyed property and jobs, the city's spirit of gratitude and determination emerged powerfully in the aftermath.

before Katrina, New Orleans had expanded into reclaimed swampland, turning the city into a huge, sea-level basin rimmed by artificial levees. When Hurricane Katrina caused a storm surge to breach the levees in several dozen places, water poured into the basin and flooded about 80 percent of the city at depths of up to ten feet. Because poor African Americans disproportionately lived in the most low-lying districts, their homes received some of the worst damage. Nearly two of every three African Americans' homes in metropolitan New Orleans were flooded, but only one of every four whites' and Hispanics' homes.[10] Lacking cars, many low-income blacks had failed to leave before the storm hit or had chosen not to, despite Mayor Ray Nagin's mandatory evacuation order. Some 40,000 people, mostly black, took shelter in the damaged Superdome stadium and the chaotic convention center, where they were confined in sweltering heat for several days before state and federal authorities managed to rescue them. More than 1,500 residents of the New Orleans area died in the disaster, some drowning in their houses. For days after the storm, bodies rotted in the streets or floated on the floodwaters. There was virtually no truth to the rumors of anarchic violence, publicly repeated by the police superintendent and reported as fact on national television. The mayor and the governor both complained that the federal government was slow to respond to the crisis. Evacuees complained of infuriating bureaucratic delays in getting assistance.

Amid continuing controversy about how much of the city should be allowed to rebuild, many of those who left chose to remain in Houston, Baton Rouge and other cities to which they were relocate. By the following summer, less than half of black population had returned to New Orleans, but nearly two-thirds of the whites. The city also attracted many Latino newcomers, who sought construction work. Though the city has retained a black majority, it is clear that blacks no longer outnumber whites two to one. Thousands of ruined houses continue to blight the city, parts of which seem unlikely to ever recover.

The slow federal and state response to the disaster became a political liability for President George W. Bush and Governor Kathleen Blanco. Blanco chose not to seek re-election. The mismanagement of the disaster response contributed to the deep decline in Bush's popularity ratings during his final years in office. Then, in 2008, a third disaster hit the United States: a financial crisis, linked to the collapse of the housing market, that brought down several major investment and financial services firms. The crisis contributed to a global recession that grew deeper in early 2009 despite the efforts of newly elected President Barack Obama.

Obama, the first black president of the United States, was a former U.S. Senator and a professor of constitutional law from Chicago. Like many in his generation of African-American leaders, he had won election without emphasizing issues of race and poverty. He said little on urban issues during his campaign, though by providing assistance to some victims of foreclosures he is addressing a problem that threatens to devastate many city neighborhoods. His efforts to redistribute the tax burden and to reign in high corporate salaries also address the widening class divisions that have emerged in cities since the 1970s.

The outlook for American cities, daunting and foreboding as it may seem, still has hopeful features. Since recovering from the crisis of the 1970s, cities have regained their sense of optimism and their reputation for livability. Better planning, neighborhood activism, and creative leadership have fueled inner-city revival in many cities as diverse as Baltimore, San Antonio, and Seattle. Cities today remain what they have always been—centers of economic, social, and cultural opportunity. As Mr. Dooley, the fictional turn-of-the-century saloon keeper and home-spun philosopher created by humorist Finley Peter Dunne, once observed,

> Ye might say as Hogan does, that we're ladin' an artyficyal life [in cities], but, by Hivins, ye might as well tell me I ought to be paradin' up and down a hillside with a suit iv skins, shootin' the antylope an' the moose, by gory, an' livin' in a cave as to make me believe I ought to get along with sthreet cars an' ilictric lights an' illyvators an' sody wather an' ice. "We ought to live where all the good things iv life comes from," says Hogan. "No," says I. "The place to live is where all the good things iv life goes to."

Bibliography

On the effects of deindustrialization, Howard Gillette, *Camden After the Fall: Decline and Renewal in a Post-Industrial City* (2005); Steven High, *Industrial Sunset: The Making of North America's Rust Belt. 1969–1984* (2003); Sherry Lee Linkon and John Russo,

Steeltown, U.S.A.: Work and Memory in Youngstown (2002); Guian A. McKee, *The Problem of Jobs: Liberalism, Race, and Deindustrialization in Philadelphia* (2008); and William Julius Wilson, When Work Disappears: The World of the New Urban Poor (1996).

Works exploring globalization's impact on cities include Carl Abbott, *Political Terrain: Washington, D.C. from Tidewater Town to Global Metropolis* (1999); Janet L. Abu-Lughod, *New York, Chicago, Los Angeles: America's Global Cities* (1999); Peter Marcuse and Ronald van Kempen, eds. *Globalizing Cities: A New Spatial Order?* (2000); Saskia Sassen, *Globalization and Its Discontents: Essays on the New Mobility of People and Money* (1998); and Sassen, *The Global City: New York, London, Tokyo* (1991).

On race, poverty and social policy since 1975, see Peter Dreier, John Mollenkopf, and Todd Swanstrom, *Place Matters: Metropolitics for the Twenty-First Century* (2001); John Hartigan, Jr., *Racial Situations: Class Predicaments of Whiteness in Detroit* (1999); Christopher Jencks, *The Homeless* (1994); James Jennings, *Understanding the Nature of Poverty in Urban America* (1994); Jennings, *Welfare Reform and the Revitalization of Inner City Neighborhoods* (2003); Michael B. Katz, *The Price of Citizenship: Redefining the American Welfare State* (2001) and Katz, *The Undeserving Poor: From the War on Poverty to the War on Welfare* (1989); George Lipsitz, *The Possessive Investment in Whiteness: How White People Benefit from Identity Politics* (1998); Alice O'Connor, *Poverty Knowledge: Social Science, Social Policy, and the Poor in Twentieth-Century U.S. History* (2001); Stephen Steinberg, *Turning Back: The Retreat from Racial Justice in American Thought and Policy* (1995); and William Julius Wilson, *The Truly Disadvantaged: The Inner City, the Underclass, and Public Policy* (1987).

On public housing, D. Bradford Hunt, *Blueprint for Disaster: The Unraveling of Chicago Public Housing* (2009); Sudhir Venkatesh, *American Project: The Rise and Fall of a Modern American Ghetto* (2000); Rhonda Y. Williams, *The Politics of Public Housing: Black Women's Struggles against Urban Inequality* (2004).

On urban tourist economies, M. Gottdiener, Claudia C. Collins, and David R. Dickens, *Las Vegas: The Social Production of an All-American City* (1999); John Hannigan, *Fantasy City: Pleasure and Profit in the Postwar Metropolis* (1998); Dennis R. Judd and Susan S. Fainstein, eds. *The Tourist City* (1999); Alexander J. Reichl, *Reconstructing Times Square: Politics and Culture in Urban Development* (1999); Lynne B. Sagalyn, *Times Square Roulette: Remaking the City Icon* (2001); Michael Sorkin, *Variations on a Theme Park: The New American City and the End of Public Space* (1992).

On the Los Angeles uprising of 1992, see Nancy Ableman and John Lie, *Blue Dreams: Korean Americans and the Los Angeles Riots* (1995); Mark Baldasarre, ed., *The Los Angeles Riots: Lessons for the Urban Future* (1994); and Robert Gooding Williams, ed., *Reading Rodney King, Reading Urban Uprisings* (1993)

On crime, Alfred Blumstein and Joel Wallman, eds., *The Crime Drop in America* (2000); Bernard E. Harcourt, *Illusion of Order: The False Promise of Broken Windows Policing* (2001); Jonathan Simon, *Governing Through Crime: How the War on Crime Transformed American Democracy and Created a Culture of Fear* (2007); Franklin E. Zimring, *The Great American Crime Decline* (2007)

For works on neighborhood issues, including gentrification, see Janet Abu Lughod, *From Urban Village to East Village: The Battle for New York's Lower East Side* (1994); Elijah Anderson, *Streetwise: Race, Class, and Change in an Urban Community* (1990); Anderson, *Code of the Street: Decency, Violence, and the Moral Life of the Inner City* (1999); Larry Bennett, *Fragments of Cities: The New American Downtowns and Neighborhoods* (1990); Arlene Dávila, *Barrio Dreams: Puerto Ricans, Latinos, and the Neoliberal City* (2004); Lance Freeman, *There Goes the Hood: Gentrification from the Ground Up* (2006); Evelyn Gonzalez, *The Bronx* (2004); Steven Gregory, *Black Corona: Race and the Politics of Place in an Urban Community* (1998); Jason Hackworth, *The Neoliberal City: Governance, Ideology, and Development in American Urbanism* (2006); Derek S. Hyra, *The New Urban Renewal: The Economic Transformation of Harlem and Bronzeville* (2008); Maureen Kennedy and Paul Leonard, "Dealing with Neighborhood Change: A Primer on Gentrification and Policy Choices," Brookings Institution Center on Urban and Metropolitan Policy, April 2001 <http://www.brookings.edu/reports/2001/04metropolitanpolicy.aspx>; David J. Maurrasse, *Listening to Harlem: Gentrification, Community, and Business* (2006); Mary Patillo, *Black on the Block: The Politics of Race and Class in the City,* (2007); Mary Patillo-McCoy, *Black Picket Fences: Privilege and Peril among the Black Middle Class* (1999); Roger Sanjek, *The Future of Us All: Race and Neighborhood Politics in New York City* (1998); Mario Luis Small, *Villa Victoria: The Transformation of Social Capital in a Boston Barrio* (2004); Neil Smith, *The New Urban Frontier: Gentrification and the Revanchist City* (1996); Sharon Zukin, *Loft Living: Culture and Capital in Urban Change* (1992).

On new immigrants and the new racial and ethnic mix in American cities, see Rachel Buff, *Immigration and the Political Economy of Home: West Indian Brooklyn and American Indian Minneapolis, 1945–1992* (2001); Mike Davis, *Magical Urbanism: Latinos Reinvent the U.S. City* (2000); William V. Flores and Rina Benmayor, *Latino Cultural Citizenship: Claiming Identity, Space, and Rights* (1997); Nancy Foner, *From Ellis Island to JFK: New York's Two Great Waves of Immigration* (2000); Guillermo Grenier and Alex Stepick, eds., *Miami Now! Immigration, Ethnicity, and Social Change* (1992); Peggy Levitt, *The Transnational Villagers* (2001); David Reimers, *Still the Golden Door: The Third World Comes to America* (1992); and Roger Waldinger, *Still the Promised City? African-Americans and the New Immigrants in Postindustrial New York* (1996).

On rap, hip hop, and immigrant youth cultures, see Joe Austin, *Taking the Train: How Graffiti Art Became an Urban Crisis in New York City* (2001); and Joe Austin with Michael Nevin Willard, ed., *Generations of Youth: Youth Culture and History in Twentieth Century America* (1998); Murray Forman, *The Hood Comes First: Race, Space, and Place in Rap and Hip Hop* (2002); George Lipsitz, *Dangerous Crossroads: Popular Music, Postmodernism, and the Poetics of Place* (1994); Sunaina Maira, *Desis in the House: Indian American Youth Culture in New York City* (2002); Jeffrey O.G. Ogbar, *Hip-Hop Revolution: The Culture and Politics of Rap* (2008);William Eric Perkins, *Droppin' Science: Critical Essays on Rap Music and Hip Hop Culture* (1996); and Rachel Rubin and Jeff Melnick, *Immigrants and American Popular Culture* (2004).

On recent suburban trends and concerns, Alan Berube and Elizabeth Kneebone, "Two Steps Back: City and Suburban Poverty Trends, 1999–2005," Brookings Institution, Dec. 2006 <http://www.brookings.edu/reports/2006/12poverty_berube.aspx>; Edward J. Blakely and Mary Gail Snyder, *Fortress America: Gated Communities in the U.S.* (1997); Robert Bruegmann, *Sprawl: A Compact History* (2005); Andres Duany, Elizabeth Plater-Zyberk and Jeff Speck, *Suburban Nation: The Rise of Sprawl and the Decline of the American Dream* (2000); Timothy P. Fong, *The First Suburban Chinatown: The Remaking of Monterey Park, California* (1994); Joel Garreau, *Edge City: Life on the New Frontier* (1991); Oliver Gillham and Alex S. MacLean, *The Limitless City: A Primer on the Sprawl Debate* (2002); Rob Kling, Spencer Olin and Mark Poster, eds., *Postsuburban California: The Transformation of Orange County Since World War II* (1991); Michael F. Logan, *Fighting Sprawl and City Hall: Resistance to Urban Growth in the Southwest* (1995); Gregory D. Squires, ed., *Urban Sprawl : Causes, Consequences, & Policy Responses* (2002); Jon C. Teaford, *PostSuburbia: Governments and Politics in the Edge Cities* (1996); Jennifer Wolch, Manuel Pastor Jr. and Peter Dreier, eds., *Up Against the Sprawl: Public Policy and the Making of Southern California* (2004).

Notes

1. Sherry Lee Linkon and John Russo, *Steeltown U.S.A.: Work and Memory in Youngstown* (Lawrence: University of Kansas Press, 2002), quotation at 132.
2. Quoted in John Herbers, "Administration Seeks to Cut Aid to Cities, Charging it Is Harmful," *The New York Times,* June 20, 1982.
3. John Hull Mollenkopf and Manuel Castells, "Introduction," in Mollenkopf and Castells, eds., *Dual City: Restructuring New York* (New York: Russell Sage Foundation, 1991), 16–17.
4. Brookings Institution Center on Urban and Metropolitan Policy, *Los Angeles in Focus: A Profile from Census 2000* (2003), [http://www.brookings.edu]
5. Jo Becker, Sheryl Gay Stolberg, and Stephen Labaton, "The Reckoning: White House Philosophy Stoked Mortgage Bonfire," *The New York Times,* Dec. 21, 2008.
6. Alan Ehrenhalt, "Trading Places: The Demographic Inversion of the American City," *The New Republic* (http://www.tnr.com), Aug. 13, 2008.
7. Andres Duany, "Three Cheers for Gentrification," *The American Enterprise* 12, no. 3 (April/May 2001): 37–38.
8. Mary Patillo, *Black on the Block: The Politics of Race and Class in the City* (Chicago: University of Chicago Press, 2007), 262.
9. Joel Garreau, *Edge City: Life on the New Frontier* (New York: Doubleday, 1991).
10. Richard Campanella, "An Ethnic Geography of New Orleans," *Journal of American History* 94, no. 3 (Dec. 2007): 704–715.

PHOTO CREDITS

Chapter 1: p. 2 Cahokia Mounds State Historic Site, painting by William R. Iseminger. p. 4 Courtesy of the Library of Congress. p. 5 Archives Nationales, Section Outre-Mer, Paris, France. p. 8 I.N. Phelps Stokes Collection, Miriam & Ira D. Wallach Division of Art, Prints and Photographs, The New York Public Library, Astor, Lenox and Tilden Foundations. p. 11 Courtesy of the Library of Congress. p. 21 The Library Company of Philadelphia. p. 27 The Metropolitan Museum of Art, Bequest of Charles Allen Munn, 1924. (24.90.1566a)

Chapter 2: p. 33 Collection of The New-York Historical Society. p. 34 Courtesy of the Library of Congress. p. 37 Miriam and Ira D. Wallach Division of Art, Prints and Photographs, The New York Public Library, Astor, Lenox and Tilden Foundations. p. 43 Gore Place Society, Inc. p. 49 Courtesy, American Antiquarian Society.

Chapter 3: p. 58 "The Beauties of Street Sprinkling, NYC", by Thomas Worth, 1856, watercolor on paper, Collection of The New-York Historical Society, 1924.151. p. 61 Collection of The New-York Historical Society. p. 62 Courtesy of the Library of Congress. p. 65 Courtesy of the Library of Congress. p. 70 Collection of The New-York Historical Society, 73259. p. 73 Courtesy of the Library of Congress.

Chapter 4: p. 77 Courtesy of the Library of Congress. p. 79 "Courtesy of the Rhode Island Historical Society, Negative number RHi (x3) 487." p. 85 Chicago Historical Society. p. 88 Courtesy of the Library of Congress. p. 89 Chicago Historical Society. p. 91 National Archives and Records Administration. p. 92 Chicago Historical Society. p. 93 Courtesy of the Library of Congress. p. 94 Chicago Historical Society. p. 96 Picture Research Consultants & Archives. p. 98 Montana Historical Society, Helena.

Chapter 5: p. 105 Courtesy of the Library of Congress. p. 111 Courtesy of the Library of Congress. p. 114 Slater Mill Historic Site. p. 123 Chicago Historical Society. p. 138 Courtesy of the Library of Congress. p. 126 Courtesy of the Boston Public Library, Print Department.

Chapter 6: p. 138 Courtesy of the Library of Congress. p. 141 Brown Brothers. p. 142 Brown Brothers.

Chapter 7: p. 158 Picture Research Consultants & Archives. p. 160 Courtesy of the Library of Congress. p. 163 Richard J. Daley Library. p. 166 Picture Research Consultants & Archives. p. 167 Courtesy of the Library of Congress. p. 172 Courtesy of the Library of Congress.

Chapter 8: p. 178 Chicago Historical Society. p. 182 National Archives and Records Administration. p. 184 Courtesy of the Library of Congress. p. 187 National Archives and Records Administration. p. 188 Natural History Museum of Los Angeles County/Seaver Center. p. 193 Courtesy of the Library of Congress. p. 197 Special Collections Division, University of Washington Libraries, Photo by Lee, Negative #20102. p. 201 Franklin D. Roosevelt Library. p. 202 Courtesy of the Library of Congress. p. 205 Courtesy of the Library of Congress. p. 206 Courtesy of the Library of Congress. p. 208 Courtesy of the Library of Congress.

Chapter 9: p. 216 Courtesy of the Library of Congress. p. 221 National Archives and Records Administration. p. 222 Courtesy of the Library of Congress. p. 224 Courtesy of the Library of

INDEX